THE
MODERN MILITARY
IN
AMERICAN SOCIETY

THE
MODERN MILITARY
IN
AMERICAN SOCIETY

A Study in the Nature of Military Power

by CHARLES WALTON ACKLEY

THE WESTMINSTER PRESS
Philadelphia

ISBN 0-664-20925-4

LIBRARY OF CONGRESS CATALOG CARD No. 77-172154

BOOK DESIGN BY
DOROTHY ALDEN SMITH

Published by The Westminster Press ®
Philadelphia, Pennsylvania

PRINTED IN THE UNITED STATES OF AMERICA

This book is dedicated to my shipmates: to that silent majority of men and women and their families who, in every time and clime, in every sea and service, have given of themselves cheerfully and unstintingly, even to "the last full measure of devotion," always for country and often for Man.

I cannot rest from travel . . .

. . . .
Much have I seen and known,—cities of men
And manners, climates, councils, governments

. . . .
I am a part of all that I have met;
Yet all experience is an arch wherethrough
Gleams that untravelled world whose margin
    fades
For ever and for ever when I move.

. . . .
        Come, my friends,
'Tis not too late to seek a newer world.

        —"*Ulysses*," *Alfred Lord Tennyson*

Contents

Preface

We need to know more about the *thinking* of military people
if we are to understand the *nature* of military power. And it is
only as we come to understand military power that we can
place and keep it in positive relation to national and human
good, and deal intelligently with the tragic persistence of war.
There is, of course, no dearth of discussion about the military
as an institution apparently coincident with civilization, nor
about war as its natural and enduring province. Quincy Wright,
Walter Millis, Alfred Vagts, Lynn Montross, and others, in-
trigued by the causes of war, have added immeasurably to the
abundant historians who have dealt more descriptively with
the fascinating phenomenon.[1] Janowitz and Huntington have
achieved near-classic status for their sociological studies of the
military as a way of life for millions of men and women from
every part of American society.[2] Bramson and Goethals, among
others, have followed Freud in speculative explorations of the
murky depths of man's seeming commitment to violent force.[3]
Novelists and moralists, of course, from the time of the ancient
Greeks[4] have had a field day in describing and evaluating the
do's and the don'ts of military life and the making of war.
Especially has this been true in the twentieth century which

has brought to us the absoluteness of war and the knowledge that the nuclear sword of Damocles hangs by such a slender hair above our heads.

In recent years this voluminous and searching inquiry into war and the military has focused especially upon the dangers of the burgeoning military-industrial complex to which the hero-President Eisenhower called attention in his farewell address to the nation in early 1961. Since then the Pentagon, as the country's largest employer, has become a large and favorite target for accusations of waste and inefficiency. The Pentagon has also been central to the "System" of Big Government with its increasingly military orientation which many of our citizens, especially the youth, vehemently, and at times militantly, have denounced. The convergence and intensity of such widespread interest in the military have begun to reveal the vast intricacies of the organization. The results have been progressive disillusionment with much of what we have seen and rising suspicion and fear of what we have not seen (as yet).

Despite the volumes of material which flow daily from the presses and are argued without stint in the media, however, remarkably little has dealt in any organized or critical fashion with the *thinking* of military men themselves. They are quoted, unsystematically and often out of context, but what are the patterns of their thought, the scales of their values? What do they consider to be the nature and ultimate intent of their power, and is it seriously modifiable in the direction of a nonviolent future for man? Is there really a "military mind," and more important, is there a truly democratic "military mind"? These questions have to do with the very nature of power as military, and with our rising concern for its meaning in a democratic society and nuclear world. And implicitly, if not explicitly, we continue to guess as to the self-understanding of military people respecting their role and power in the modern world. Why not let them speak for themselves? Recently, Ward Just in *Military Men* (better entitled "Soldiers" in its earlier

Atlantic release),[5] did just that in searching out and listening to American soldiers from West Point to Vietnam. The result was a probing, perceptive, if limited, revelation of the deep inner drives and frustrations of modern American soldiers, particularly of officers. It is hoped that Just will pursue his in-depth interviews with members of the other services.

This book represents a broader and deeper effort than more or less formal interviews can afford. It speaks, rather, from life, from the living give-and-take of more than twenty years that I spent as a career chaplain with other officers, my peers and superiors, and with "the men" and their families who were generally the core of my work and associations. In the wardrooms of ships, which are the homes of officers while at sea, in the mess halls of enlisted men afloat and ashore, in every compartment and on every deck, in hospitals and on air stations, in offices and countless homes, in worship services and on military exercises involving other units and the nationals of other nations, in Marine tents and Navy BOQ's (Bachelor Officer Quarters), in home ports and overseas—the living and the thinking and the trying to understand the meaning of the military in modern life went on. But beyond the informal osmosis of the daily military climate which has left its residue of impressions and convictions to form a background for this book, serious attention has been given to the often carefully thought out position papers of military writers. Such writings are surely important. If they are often mundane and lacking in "serious insights," as Just suggests,[6] still even that says something, perhaps of consequence, about the authors and the climate in which they live and move. But this is far from the truth today.

The quite strenuous competition and continuous, often sophisticated and highly theoretical training which the upper echelons of military personnel especially undergo today equip them at the very least to be knowledgeable and articulate. Many find time despite critically demanding actional schedules

to write clearly, forcefully, and sometimes perceptively about
"the things that matter most" to them, especially their country
and their duties. The modern American military, no longer
isolated on the wild frontier but responding to the enormous
demands of its civilian context, is found in almost every village and city, in factory and office and school, in "think tanks"
and government. The military is everywhere in the body politic, and in its own way and from its own specialized training
and perspective, knows that body politic. Military personnel
are thus a substantial and growing part of the American people. As much as any other profession or class, they *are* the people and deserve to be heard. They believe that they have a
message, or rather messages, for military people do not speak
with one voice any more than do other professions or segments
of our people. At the very least, interservice rivalries prevent
unanimity of opinion, but beyond this lie the concerns of true
patriots (as well as the interests of the usual self-servers—again
true of other professions), who cannot always agree in conscience. An intense and lively debate has characterized each
phase in the tortuous growth of the military establishment in
this country. Certainly since the forceful reservations expressed
by President Eisenhower, the struggles of the American military to understand itself in a free society and modern world
have shown no signs of abatement. Controversial positions respecting the "new military," if not "militarism," have been developed by several of our recent military leaders and authentic
heroes, as well as by a rising number of some rather determined
junior officers and men. Surely a military establishment that
can even think of going "mod" [7] deserves examination on its
own merits, however strong may be the received stereotypes of
its nature.

The concern of this study, therefore, is to marshal the
thoughts of military thinkers and writers, especially American
and modern, respecting the nature of military power, and to
reflect upon the impact of its values in a free society. Because

our roots as a nation and the foundations of the military establishment are embedded deeply in the past, it is important to review elements of that past. Especially does an understanding of military power as an American problem require detailed attention to the "fears of the Fathers," and to the ambiguous checks and balances provided in the Constitution for the use and containment of the military. We must also take into account certain novelties and ambiguities inherent in the situation today which threaten containment of the military by the free society.

From this specifically American and problematic background an analysis of military power in terms of its distinguishable elements as understood and stressed by military thinkers themselves follows in successive chapters. The approach initially is univeralistic, reaching back into the past for those thinkers and doers who have provided the basic traditions that Americans have both honored and modified according to their own needs and democratic lights. The study then focuses on the writings of numerous thinkers in the major services since World War II. These materials include both official and unofficial service directives and publications, but more particularly contemporary writings in professional military journals. These journals, although unofficial, are often more revealing of the pragmatic issues and values that govern the day-to-day operations of the Armed Forces and the lives of our uniformed men and women. More than a decade of these publications have been examined and compared to establish trends, changing attitudes in the military, and differences in point of view of the major services. Just how representative of their respective branches of the military may be the writers in military journals is of course arguable. The fact that their views are selected for publication, and that they are inevitably read and discussed, and oftentimes supported or rebutted in mail and personal columns, indicates their importance. Moreover, the number of senior officers and rising juniors who thus speak to issues beyond the purely technical is impressive and growing. These thoughtful and sustained dialogues on compelling issues may be superior to interviews.[8]

I am not unaware of the possibility of bias and subjectivity in this study in view of my own particular experiences as a career officer and chaplain in the United States Navy. My work and responsibilities provided certain kinds of knowledge and perspectives, while precluding others. In particular I know the Navy far better than the other services, but this has worked to some advantage. I have been fortunate in having somewhat representational experiences of the military as a whole in serving at sea, on shore installations in the United States, Asia, and Europe, with the mobile Marines, and generally being involved with air personnel. Nevertheless, I have attempted to guard against weighting judgments in the Navy's favor.

The nature of this study, however, is not simply descriptive nor even analytical. It is, rather, moral and evaluative. Indeed, I am convinced that the problem of military power, especially in America, cannot be comprehended in less than moral terms. For better or for worse, we have from the beginning treated the military as a necessary evil, morally objectionable, except when we have been constrained by circumstances to use it. Then, of course, it has become morally virtuous. Hence, the function of military power, especially the prospect of its prolonged dominance, is more than a matter of the simple arithmetic (or even higher mathematics) of protection—it is a matter of morality, of what a people understand to be the ultimate good, and the habits or virtues by which that good may be sought and attained. Thus any serious examination of the modern military in American society must attempt to plumb the depths of ourselves as a people. This is the large, perhaps unattainable, objective. But the careful weighing of military thought through the centuries, especially the "American century," should help us to understand better who we are and where we are bound as a people, and doubtless as a world.

I have tried to be careful about unrecognized assumptions and value judgments. Insofar as possible, I have allowed the case to build itself. Then I have drawn those implications and conclusions which seemed justified by the weight of the analysis. In doing so, I have doubtless been influenced far more than I know by the genuine friendships, and the very real frustrations, that I knew as a career officer in the Navy. With a host of others I have shared the felt privilege of serving "both God and country," and with many more than might be supposed in the modern American military, I have known a deepening concern for the awful drift of power toward the nuclear abyss.

These, and more, have contributed to the making of this book. My debts, therefore, are many and of long standing. More specifically and recently, colleagues and friends, as well as a long-suffering family, have helped me in countless ways. Floyd Ross and Otis Starkey early suggested guidelines and changes that affected the whole book, and William Smith and John Esterline proved to be mines of insight into the attitudes of the colonists and modern government respecting the whole problem of standing armies. John Hutchinson and Harvey Seifert, my teachers, never ceased in their encouragement and were highly specific in their critiques of the concluding chapters. Two former senior naval chaplains, Roland Faulk and Glyn Jones, read the whole manuscript and strengthened the argument at several points. David Barnes and Pierce Johnson, pastor friends, were most patient and meticulous in catching errors of grammar and form and generally making the whole as readable as it is. Theodore Weissbuch and librarians Joseph Jerz, Walter Roeder, and Karen Puffer chased a number of elusive sources and footnotes. Many of my students, veterans and nonveterans alike, contributed continuously in prolonged and intensive discussions in and out of the classroom. Doubling as typists, Ellen Joos, Linda Evensen, Cheryl Piatt, and Margery Vinton, with Lois Ingram, often went beyond the requirements of duty because of their interest in the work. I have been especially fortunate in having at every step of the lengthening project the sustained interest and patience of the staff of The Westminster Press. Lastly, to my wife and son, who only partially succeeded in sharing the house when it was not possible to share the writer during the last intensive months, and who with our other children have continuously shared the living experiences and much of the agonized searching to find and to record the meaning of these things—to them I owe debts, and depths, beyond repaying. This book, then, has been a community endeavor which will surely account for its merits. Its faults must remain my own.

C. W. A.

Diamond Bar, California

PART ONE

THE PROBLEM

Chapter 1

The Military and the Crisis of Confidence

I. MY LAI A WATERSHED

In years to come, My Lai may stand out as a kind of watershed in the public thinking about the nature and import of the modern military in American society. Not because it was a totally unexpected "aberration," one of a kind, and we suffered momentarily its sharp and shameful guilt, but rather because it happened to *us,* and the proliferation of like incidents raised to sharp focus our deep and traditional fears that the military is always an uncertain, if unavoidable, stranger in the house of democracy. My Lai is troubling because it happened coincidentally with the military's coming of age as a dominating institution in America. We remember only too well the atrocities ascribed to major enemies of the past when their societies became militarized. The incongruity of superb intelligence and technological expertise issuing in the gross and dark inhumanity of Germany's death camps was frightening. The most confident believer in the rationality of man must pause at this suddenly exposed abyss of irrationality in a great and civilized people. Could it happen to us?

From time to time Americans have agreed, with almost easy

jocularity, that "war is hell," to quote General Sherman, although the bitterness of that truth is still remembered "from Atlanta to the sea" in the Old South. But the "foreign expeditionary forces" which have constituted our efforts in the great and small wars of this century, so confidently launched to "make the world safe for democracy," have failed to keep the "hell" at a distance. The chasm has opened at our feet, in the streets of our cities, even in our very living rooms. For the first time a war has literally been fought in the public eye. Vietnam has engulfed us as truly a "world war" in the most psychological, empathetic sense. Disconcertingly, what we have seen daily on the television screen and thought we had put safely into the hands of our Armed Forces is not unlike the civil strife that swirls and eddies through the nation itself.

We have been surprised and thrown back upon ourselves in a subdued and questioning mood, for we have habitually looked upon ourselves as a peaceable and peace-loving people. We are sure we have opted for war only as a last resort, only to preserve the peace. "Live and let live" has been our simple motto, although the daily communist kill tally required some temporary adjustment in our thinking. For these reasons, we have never considered the military establishment as anything more than a necessary evil, a stopgap measure for emergencies, but certainly not the rule of the day. Yet emergencies have become the rule of the day, almost without abatement since World War II. And the military has stayed on to come of age. as it were, grown to gigantic size and apparent permanence in our midst. The unabated activity of this structure, which from the beginning has had to endure the suspicion of being antithetical to the deepest interests of the nation, has aroused increasing concern. It is as though the stripling who went forth to the wars has come back to take over the homeland. To the unexpected and embarrassing deviations abroad, even when excused as part of war, must now be added the growing and unpredictable violences at home sometimes even perpetrated by duly constituted and therefore similar forces for "law and order," e.g., at Kent State and Jackson, Mississippi. It is not, then, surprising that traditional fears of the military have been underscored and serious questions raised as to the import of military values in a free society.

II. MILITARIZATION OF THE NATION

Do we face the actual and imminent militarization of our nation? And just what might this mean were it to become a fact rather than merely a fear? The crude possibility of an actual governmental take-over by the Armed Forces as dramatized in *Seven Days in May*[1] is probably remote. Still the question will be asked from time to time. Long suspicious of military power in itself, we have rather carefully tried to keep it like a pet cougar on a heavy leash for the sole purpose of protection against outside aggressors. In this we have been remarkably successful. With the exception of the burning of Washington in the War of 1812, we have never suffered invasion, and we take great pride in asserting that "we have never lost a war." But the cougar is now grown to full and powerful adulthood, and having tasted the joys of victory and blood, has earned both the gratitude and fear of its masters. The question now arises in a sense quite new for us as a people: How long can we keep it on a leash? Is its appetite becoming insatiable? And will it always so readily distinguish between friend and foe, especially in these latter days when the fluid fronts have moved into the very streets of our cities? In short, have we really domesticated the beast or only increased our own vulnerability to its immensely sophisticated training and magnified power?

A much more likely, and more somber, possibility than a military coup is that we may indeed "domesticate the beast" and still be vulnerable to its spirit and appetite. That is, the increasingly demanding presence of the military may encourage a further fashioning of the American character in deepening patterns of rationalized violence to which, in time, the term "militaristic" might aptly be applied. This would achieve in subtler, but probably more effective, ways the militarization of the nation. It would be the easiest thing to do because it requires no thought, nor any particular planning, review, or change of direction. Already there appears to be confusion of power with morality at the highest levels of the government in the President's expressed determination to "prove" our "manhood" by the simple expedient of applying more power in Vietnam. Hans Morgenthau, one of the deans of American political science, astutely observes that the very traditions of success for American arms push both the President and the Armed Forces toward the use of tactical nuclear weapons in Vietnam. We need a quick and unquestioned victory in order to preserve our troops "as an effective fighting force," and our image in the world as a nation that never backs down.[2] The question seems to be, not what is right, involving the possibility that we may be in error, but what the neighbors will think. This "politics of 'manhood,'" as the columnist Flora Lewis puts it,

has to do with a demonstration of power, but it seems to be a demonstration of power against secret doubts, power based on a willfulness that does not find justification enough in reason.[3]

Unquestionably, such an image of ourselves as virile and "manly" is encouraged and strengthened by the continued growth and use of a huge military machine in our midst which symbolizes in quite tangible ways the necessary resort to brute power. By indefinitely continuing a larger than desired military establishment we confirm as normal our massive post-World War II emergency dependence upon the military to solve our problems. Thus we may "make a virtue out of the necessity" of a large standing army to which most Amer-

icans have assented during the "cold war" years. To the image
of "manliness" has been joined in our experience the conviction that we are a righteous and peace-loving people. In
the subtle progress to militarism we would likely hold on to
this image which would serve our purposes and in any case
is so deeply ingrained it could not readily be given up. Such
a self-image could act as a shield for our motives and actions
to prevent us from coming to ourselves, to see ourselves as
others, friends as well as enemies, already see us—in ghettos
where the races have clashed hatefully, on college campuses
where students have massively confronted "the establishment,"
on too many city streets where the earnest cries for peace have
incongruously and tragically taken violent and brutal forms.
The pervasive violence has even leaped to cut down popular
and elected leaders in their youth. It has not always been
contained even in those persons and agencies supposedly dedicated to its understanding and proper use, such as government officials and the police. The President's Commission on
the Causes and Prevention of Violence, necessitated by this
tragic rending of the social fabric, has sadly confirmed that
indeed "we have historically been a violence-prone people." [4]
Surprising to some, disappointing to many, it is still not clear
how many Americans are prepared to accept this judgment
and will move to counter its implications.

There is grave danger here. The historical conditioning of
Americans in the easy and often successful use of violence is
daily confirmed by very real and savage events, both abroad
and at home. To these intense pressures from within and
without must now be added the fantastically accelerated input
and appeal of the military as "managers of violence." [5] It
does not seem farfetched to anticipate that if these factors
continue operating in our experience, and especially as they
come to be accepted as normal, we may bring about a "garrison
state" mentality whether or not a formal military restructuring
of the nation occurs. Daniel Berrigan, himself a tragic illustra-

tion of the deep and dangerous confusions of the American conscience with respect to the uses of violence (and whether or not he is guilty), has put the matter well in *They Call Us Dead Men*:

A climate of war creates its own horizons, its own justification and method. Subjected to such an atmosphere for a long period of time, men come to accept it as normal and self-evident; they create a logic that suits their state of soul. They create tools of violence as entirely normal methods of dealing with "the enemy"; once created the tools are used with ever-increasing ease.

Peaceableness, communication with others, discussion, public candor—these are less and less trusted as methods of dealing with human differences. . . . In such an atmosphere, men gradually come to accept a totally different version of human life. . . . Such men live in the dreamworld of the schizoid or the adolescent. . . . The stranger becomes the enemy. The enemy is everywhere. . . . And almost inevitably, as the complexities of human relationships merge into the single image of the enemy, a complementary image of ourselves arises. We become the beleaguered defenders of all that is good and noble in life, the society whose interventions are always governed by superior wisdom, whose military might serves only the good of humanity.[6]

These observations suggest at the least that the means for our survival may overwhelm the ends of national and human good in American culture. The unending and sophisticated fashioning of a methodology of violence may cause a general forgetfulness of the ways of peace. We may become warlike in spite of ourselves, i.e., in spite of the sincerely held view of ourselves as peaceable. Indeed, for much of the world and many of our own people, especially the youth, we have already arrived at a position of militarism. Some even of the military establishment itself have adopted this conclusion.[7] Certainly the danger seems real if we stay, unthinkingly, on our present course. The undergirding of such fears, which makes the danger more persuasive, has to do with the dynamic nature of power, which looms so large on the American scene.

III. THE DRIVE TO BIGNESS

Power, it seems clear, is one, if not *the,* major value we have chosen as a people. It is a commonplace that we revere bigness in all its forms: we have a "heritage of bigness," as Henry Steele Commager has said.[8] Quite early the immensity of the land created for us the ever-receding horizon and beckoned us to that drive and mobility which have expressed themselves magnificently in the dynamism of our technological change and growth. In the Old World the progress of upstart business and industry was slowed by anciently fixed patterns of crown, church, the military, and even sometimes by labor with its restrictive guilds and bondage to a particular soil. In the New World the limitlessness of the land, almost empty of recognizable restrictions, cried to be filled by private venture and private enterprise, by the pioneer and entrepreneur. The task and the joy of it seemed inexhaustible. Public benefaction, the subduing and developing of the land, the building of cities and the making of institutions, the creation of a civilization in what was thought to be a wilderness, flowed from individuals and their combines; and it was *growth* rather than any end of national well-being which came to be the thrilling motivation. "What was wanted," says Commager,

was more of everything: more land under cultivation; more cattle on the High Plains; more production of iron, steel, oil and gas; more domestic and foreign trade; more money in banks, and more investments in stocks and bonds; more airplane travel; more automobiles on the roads; more highways; more telephones; more television sets.[9]

But although we have often been accused of the accumulation of things for things' sake, i.e., materialism (as we generally understand that term), it is rather the *drive* to accumulate, the *power* of creating and having, which has fascinated and enlisted Americans in the making of their great success story. We are not ordinary empire builders: we are *spiritual* empire builders, with a Puritan disdain for attaching ultimate values to things of sense, but nonetheless finding their growth at our hands immensely satisfying evidence that we are "on the side of the angels." God is *our* God, and blesses us. Isn't this evident? And generous-hearted as we know ourselves to be, surely such blessing is meant for all the earth—so the growth must go on, leaping oceans and cultures, seeking in its own pragmatic, businesslike way, a "One World," bearing the unmistakable impress of "Made in America."

An aspect of this dynamism which is not always so obvious because of the broad mask of our proud pluralism of being the "melting pot" of the earth is the decided tendency toward consolidation and concentration.[10] It may be argued that this is characteristic of power and of life itself: the coming into existence of anything at all is always at a point in time and space. But the points themselves are also in motion, coming together in patterns, seeking wholes. At any rate, monopolies and antitrust legislation occupy a significant place in the growth of our country. Now, the marriage of the giant military machine to a technology that has no comprehension of limits is ominous indeed. If, as we have suggested, it is a commonplace that we revere bigness in all its forms, it is equally true that wars greatly accelerate change and growth because they accentuate power in very direct ways. And when that power is both the product and the focal point of speeding technology it cannot help maximizing and thus profoundly affecting the technology itself, almost surely re-creating it in its own image.

Thus American power is expressed most technologically in war and war preparations: three quarters of the federal budget, the best brains and skills of the nation, and the very highest of priorities, which endure year after year—for a generation now with no diminution in sight. It is even frequently argued that the unquestionably high American standard of living is due in large measure to the substantial "spin-offs" of civilian products and conveniences from "crash programs" of the military. Nuclear power itself is, of course, the most prominent example, but also greater speed and safety in transportation, medicine, food concentrates and preservatives, and even procedures that have invaded the business community and are now more or less taken for granted. Former Commandant of the Marine Corps General Shoup sees such

military procedures—including the general staff system, briefings, estimates of the situation, and the organizational and operations techniques of the highly schooled, confident military professionals— spread throughout American culture.[11]

It is not that we should not learn from the military if we can. Let us be grateful for the spin-offs. But the logic which is clearly implied in urging our gratitude is subtle and dangerous: that such progress is due *only* to the military or at least that it comes about a lot quicker via the military than it would otherwise. Such presumptive justifications for the military presence may or may not be true in special instances, but they do ignore what might come from a reallocation of the massively disproportionate expenditures of our national resources to the military for desirable and growingly necessary civilian needs and pursuits. Even more important in the long run is the consideration that our power, expressed most technologically in war-making, may, in view of our massively pivotal position in world affairs, determine that the "One World" of the future will be violence- and military-oriented. Harvey Wheeler, at the Center for the Study of Democratic Institutions, Santa Barbara, has called attention to the "unique condition" of the modern age, which is that the hitherto divergent cultures of man are now rapidly converging into "one story," one culture. In all previous ages, men were separated enough to pursue different life-styles, which became distinctive institutions, ways of life and meaning, cultures, civilizations.

During all this time, no matter what happened to its individual branches, the basic tree of human culture was never threatened with complete extinction. When any one branch had reached out to its limit and fallen victim of its own overextension, there were always others in reserve ready to move into the breach . . . [until] . . . the close of the 19th century. Then, speeded by a series of world wars and revolutions, there began a massive process of world-wide culture homogenization. Human society gradually ceased to show many different faces and came instead to exhibit everywhere the same dominant pattern. . . . A permanent irreversible change was introduced into the condition of mankind. Men came to belong everywhere to the same cultural species.[12]

Now what will happen if catastrophe intervenes and threatens not just a branch (for they are gone, or nearly so), but the trunk itself?

Wheeler asserts that

if industrial man should falter in his headlong dash through cultural time, there is no different cultural system standing by ready to grasp the baton of civilization and carry on the human race.[13]

By reducing man's cultural options to "one story," i.e., Western science and technology as he seems surely to have chosen, the possibility of finalizing that story by a wrong turn is immensely enhanced. This is the burden of world leadership which we as Americans carry today. The turns, in an age of nearly limitless power, cannot help involving all mankind—especially so when called by a nation accustomed to "thinking big," and for whom defeat is not only unacceptable but probably incomprehensible. The question of the militarization of American values, then, is one concerning the very future of mankind.

IV. CAN THE MILITARY BE DEMOCRATIZED?

But, it may be asked, are these old and deepening fears of military power actually realistic in the American context, considering the possibility that the American dream of "a new beginning for man" (a la Jefferson) may in time so democratize the military as to make it truly responsive to our own deepest and best selves? With the rapid overcrowding of the planet and the increasing complexity of human life and endeavor, may we not be forced to turn to the military to provide in some sense a model for order? And might not the American military, nurtured in a democratic, even (nominally at least) Christian environment, possess that potential, despite its currently low profile? Presumptive here, of course, is our deep innocence as a people and the ability of human nature to change in significant ways. After all, the resort to armed force has been with us a very long time, doubtless from our very beginnings as a race. Shall we then presume that we can actually corral and permanently subordinate the explosive power of the military to national and human good? There is no convincing historical parallel or justification for such a hope, although the British and perhaps the Byzantines may be considered to have approached it. But then, with our dream and seeming ability to "refashion history" toward optimistic goals, we hardly feel the need for parallels from the past.[14] In any case, the situation confronting the American military is vastly, even uniquely, different from any possible past parallel. The ultimate threat of nuclear extinction and the self-propelling nature of modern technology at the very least make serious limitation of military growth difficult to sustain.

Perhaps, then, we ought "to roll with the punch," to make the military work for us over the long haul, not simply taking advantage of its spin-offs, but humanizing it. In a "time of troubles" a generally agreed upon first requisite is order, tempered as much as possible by service that is compassionate. The military is rarely characterized by compassion, but it does, of course, count among its number individuals who are compassionate—and loyal and disciplined. The combination of these values, fired and fused in the white heat of a crucible that only the military knows, is important and may be crucial

to the future of man. For a commonplace among military
men is that the conditions for ordered and even compassionate
service are most admirably, if not exclusively, met by themselves. Not unlike the most radical and demanding of religious
orders, the military requires service under a contract of "unlimited liability" [15] (unto death), motivated by a selfless love
of country as the highest value. Other values quickly following

include all the virtues and beliefs used to motivate men of high
principle: . . . honor among fellowmen, courage in the face of
danger, loyalty to organization and leaders, self-sacrifice for comrades, leadership, discipline, and physical fitness.[16]

Taken at face value, such "military virtues," tempered and
refined in the American democratic process, may be justification for the almost lyrical approbation for the American
military with which Samuel P. Huntington closes his important *The Soldier and the State* in describing the merits of
West Point over the nearby village of Highland Falls:

There join together the four great pillars of society: Army, Government, College, and Church. Religion subordinates man to God for
divine purposes; the military life subordinates man to duty for
society's purposes. In the severity, regularity, discipline, the military society shares the characteristics of the religious order. Modern
man may well find his monastery in the Army.

West Point embodies the military ideal at its best; Highland Falls
the American spirit at its most commonplace. West Point is a grey
island in a many colored sea, a bit of Sparta in the midst of Babylon.
Yet is it possible to deny that the military values—loyalty, duty,
restraint, dedication—are the ones America most needs today? That
the disciplined order of West Point has more to offer than the
garish individualism of Main Street? Historically, the virtues of
West Point have been America's vices, and the vices of the military,
America's virtues. Yet today America can learn more from West
Point than West Point from America. Upon the soldiers, the defenders of order, rests a heavy responsibility. The greatest service
they can render is to remain true to themselves, to serve with silence
and courage in the military way. If they abjure the military spirit,

they destroy themselves first and their nation ultimately. If the civilians permit the soldiers to adhere to the military standard, the nations themselves may eventually find redemption and security in making that standard their own.[17]

But the matter is not so simple. How can we know that the ordered gray stone of West Point would be a wise or even acceptable exchange for the cluttered freedom of Highland Falls unless we know more of what goes on within the walls of the fort and beyond to the battlefield? For human history also remembers with mounting anguish the arbitrary, ruthless, often barbaric destructiveness of military power. What is the nature of this ordered, and at times almost incongruously beautiful and attractive, power which encompasses destruction as a central aim and mission? Is military power different in kind from other power? Or is it simply more intensely the same as that which governs all human relations? Can it of itself provide an adequate ethic for man? Or does West Point owe as much or more to Highland Falls for what it is and may or may not become as Highland Falls owes to West Point for its own continued existence?

V. WE NEED TO EXAMINE MILITARY VALUES

These fears and questions and even hopes require a serious examination of the American military experience and values. Perhaps this is already beginning in this country. It was a common saying where I grew up that "everyone complains about the weather but nobody does anything about it." By the tiniest of fractions we have begun to do something about the weather, as we have come to study seriously the elementary forces of nature. In a similar vein it must be admitted that the military has become the object of considerable and growing criticism in recent years but hardly anybody has a very clear idea of what to do about it. I suspect this is because there is so little understanding of what the military really is.

> It's Tommy this an' Tommy that, an' "Chuck him
>   out, the brute!"
> But it's "Saviour of 'is country" when the guns begin
>   to shoot.[18]

It is, of course, not even that simple today, for the guns are shooting and still the criticism mounts. The confusion lies deeper, in the ambiguities of the spirit of man and the nature of military power and the values it generates and honors. We are asking ourselves whether this increasing power can much longer be tolerated, or can its values indeed be used or fused into the civil culture in positive ways? To these questions our forefathers answered, almost to a man, with a resounding negative. We will do well to listen to their arguments, even though we may not take counsel of their fears. Both are examined in the next two chapters. But however well-intentioned and adequate for their day, the conclusions reached in previous generations cannot fully meet the exigencies of our own. Especially must this be true if the Atomic Age we have entered with such trepidation and promise is in any real sense new. We must listen to every voice and not least to those who have found in the American military a way of life and even hope for the nation and world. Consequently, the thrust of this book, after the examination of our historically conditioned attitudes toward the military and its fearsome size in our time, is concerned with the range and meaning of contemporary American military thinking.

Chapter 2

The Evolution of the Military as an American Problem

I. FEARS OF THE FATHERS

BEFORE THE REVOLUTION: THE TYRANNY OF ARMIES

The military is as old as our traditions as a people. Indeed, it is part of those traditions. Born of revolution, we have expressed from our very beginnings a conscious but contradictory relationship to the military as an institution which from time to time has affected the use we have made of and the treatment we have accorded its personnel. Myles Standish, who organized the defense of Plymouthtown, the hardy pioneers and English regulars who wrested a domain from the wilderness during the long, bloody French and Indian War before the Revolution, and the minutemen of Lexington and Concord who fired the shot "heard round the world" are enshrined as national heroes and known to every schoolchild. Nevertheless, our forefathers feared the military as such, and especially when at times it became self-conscious, a proclivity the colonists attached ominously and without exception to all standing armies. Indeed, one cannot read the numerous and varied writings of that era without being struck with what

Bernard Bailyn calls "the almost excessive concern in the colonies with standing armies." [1]

As early as 1697, John Trenchard had published his classic *An Argument, Shewing, that a Standing Army Is Inconsistent with a Free Government*. In the early 1720's Trenchard combined forces with Thomas Gordon, another Englishman, in a striking series of pungent, hard-hitting essays which pleaded for republicanism in government and maintained that standing armies constituted the gravest of threats to the preservation of freedom.[2] "Armies," they said, are "a Remedy almost worse than the Disease. . . . A State sometimes recovers out of a Convulsion and gains new Vigour by it; but much oftener expires in it." [3] These writers and many of their contemporaries on both sides of the Atlantic insisted that the reasons for the high mortality rate of states convulsed by military activity were perfectly obvious: the insistent longevity and unexpected tyranny of the very forces meant to save them.

The fears of the colonists were based not merely upon a puritanical understanding of power and human nature. In their own lifetimes they had seen most of the countries of the world tragically illustrate the surprising ease with which armies abetted a simple or even worse exchange of tyrannies. From Spain to Sweden, from England to Turkey, from the Americas to India, the incessant warfare, involving the rise to nationhood of most of the states of Europe, surged and fell like the waves of a cruelly driven sea. The sea of troubles had dissolved the ancient free states of Italy, especially Venice, so long a republican bastion, and now (in the 1760's) had engulfed Sweden after its auspicious start as a democracy. England was left a parliamentary island, "the freest in . . . [a] world" which shuddered in dread of the aggressive and bloody tyrannies of Turk and Russian, of Spaniard and Frenchman.[4] There seemed no respite from Trenchard and Gordon's bitter observation of a generation before that

power encroaches daily upon Liberty, with a Success too evident; and the Balance between them is almost lost. Tyranny has engrossed almost the whole Earth, and Striking at Mankind Root and Branch, makes the World a Slaughterhouse; and certainly will go on to destroy, till it is either destroyed itself, or, which is most likely, has nothing left to destroy.[5]

Yet, despite the cold wash of fear over their little island which threatened to inundate the colonies as well, for these writers and others in the colonies, the specter of a standing army which might save them only to enslave them was more vivid and ominous still. Destructive and pitiless ambition was typified but not exhausted in Louis XIV (1643–1715), the "Grand Monarch" of France, one of the first rulers to experiment with a standing army. He had turned it most ferociously upon his own loyal Huguenots, to the lasting impoverishment of France. The dragoons he quartered so brutally in Protestant homes to force conversions and the education of the children in an alien faith remained a living and searing memory among thousands of refugees who managed to escape to the colonies.[6] Their English neighbors also suffered the traumas of ancestral memories of military tyrants. Ironically these centered upon their own kingly "protectors" from the excesses of the French kings, upon Charles I and Cromwell. The irony deepens in the bitter spectacle of the aristocratic king and his republican nemesis and destroyer, both of whom it was felt were subverted by the resort to standing armies. The fall of the king was perhaps understandable, if inexcusable, as a classic example of a ruler violating the rights of the people in order to make himself absolute. But with the Parliamentarians themselves in power and undergirded by the religious and moral sanctity of incorruptible men, the revelation of the ease with which even a man of the people could become a tyrant etched itself unforgettably into the soul of the English. Parallels were easily made between London and the fall of ancient Rome to Caesarism, and the increasing role of the Praetorian Guards as a standing army supportive of tyranny. It is instructive to note that Charles's difficulties in paying his armies (especially the Scots!) encouraged their longevity under a desperate agreement that they should not be disbanded until paid.[7] Seven years later the victorious Roundhead armies of Fairfax and Cromwell refused to be disbanded by their own Parliament and indeed enforced successive and widening demands upon the Parliament leading to the Protectorate of Cromwell and a standing army of some thirty thousand.[8] (Washington was to be faced with a similar crisis at the close of the Revolutionary War in the colonies.)[9]

Another momentous step was taken a half century later by the temporarily humbled Grand Monarch of France. Goaded by the revengeful greed of the victorious English and Allied captains whose claims approached the unconditional, Louis XIV appealed to the people themselves and rallied what became a standing army in time of peace and which was turned with great success, as we have seen, against many of his own people.[10] Thus the first tentative gropings toward national armies of citizens came about in a kind of dialectic of economic pressures and the pride of kings and captains.[11] Such armies multiplied the number, and oftentimes the ferocity, of soldiers pitched against one another in bloody battles that recalled the savage excesses of the Thirty Years' War of a century before. And then, on the eve of the Revolutionary War, Frederick II, King of Prussia, brought the scattered, unshapen experiments and trends to a kind of perfection in a war machine of Roman discipline without Roman pride. He inculcated instead a slavish fear of the officer caste which held every enlisted man in utter contempt. Enlisted practically for life, Frederick's soldiers were "held under a surveillance which amounted to captivity." [12] "Prussianism," because of its successes, became the model of the age—but it was loathed in the colonies. Prussian troops, hired out as mercenaries, would shortly become known to the rebellious Americans as "Hessians" and would earn their contempt as unthinking automatons. But the "automatons" earned their king the title of "Great" (as the ruthless dragoons had for Louis XIV), and elsewhere in Europe similar armies loyal to kings made them everywhere absolute over the common man. "What is got by Soldiers, must be maintained by Soldiers," Gordon had written;[13] and the colonists could not help agreeing. England, having expended troops in the New World, itself seemed increasingly determined to rule *its* New World by troops.

It is not surprising, then, that the colonists, faced with the growing arbitrariness of England, reached back to the writings of Trenchard and Gordon, among others, for grist for their tracts of the times. They reached even farther, to the sad case of Denmark of the century before, which had been popularized in a famous treatise. The affair was lifted up as a bitter object lesson of a state that had "dropped its guard and allowed in a standing army which quickly destroyed the constitution and the liberties protected by it."[14] Gordon, writing in 1721, feared the same would come to pass again in England. "Heaven preserve me," he cried, "from ever beholding contending Armies in *England!*" For

they are different Things from what they once were. Our Armies formerly were only a Number of the People armed occasionally; and Armies of the People are the only Armies which are not formidable to the People. Hence it is, that, in the many Revolutions occasioned by the Strife between the two Royal Houses of York and Lancaster, there never was any Danger of Slavery from an armed Force: a single Battle decided the Contention; and the next Day these popular Soldiers went Home, and resumed their ordinary Arms, the Tools of Husbandry. But since that Time Armies have not been so easily parted with; but after the Danger was over for which they were raised, have often been obstinately kept up, and by that Means created Dangers still as great. . . .

Cicero did not dream, when he employed *Octavius* for the Commonwealth, that his young Champion for Liberty would ever be the Tyrant of his Country. Who could foresee that *Cromwel* would enslave those whom he was employed to defend? But there is no trusting of Liberty in the Hands of Men, who are obeyed by great Armies.[15]

There are curious and striking parallels between these early Englishmen and modern Americans in their understanding of the world and the need for a military establishment. The history to which Gordon refers when "these popular Soldiers went Home," before the time when "Armies . . . [were] obstinately kept up," reminds us of our own long-time habit of disbanding our forces after the victory parades—until the cold and peculiar wars of the past quarter century forced our armies to be "obstinately kept up." Moreover, as we have seen, for the colonists as for us, freedom was in retreat. Fifty years after Gordon's impassioned warning, the colonists found unremitting confirmation of his fears not only in the world about them, but on their own soil and in their own homes. The "contending Armies" had arrived in this proud extension of the Motherland, this hopefully planted "New England." To the pervasive and growing oppressions of the world, the colonists now regretfully and almost unbelievingly must add England herself, while coming "to think of themselves as preserving these patterns of freedom in purer form even than the British at home." [16]

It was the Quartering Act, putting a standing army most obviously and brutally into their very homes and reminiscent of the dragonnades of Louis XIV,[17] which ripped away the uneasily accepted excuse for the permanent introduction of British regulars into the colonies following the Seven Years' War, i.e., frontier protection. The fruition of this hated act, the Boston Massacre (March 5, 1770), followed only by weeks a similar fatal confrontation in London between a regiment of Foot Guards and a crowd of citizens sympathetic to John Wilkes, an impassioned and imprisoned democratic Parliamentarian.[18] The parallels between these events, especially the acquittal of the soldiers responsible in both cases, deepened and confirmed the general fear that the very citadel of liberty had yielded to "a kind of fourth power that the [English] constitution knows nothing of." This, it was thought, was a ministerial lobby around the king which used Parliament and favored a standing army to provoke a decisive and crushing quarrel with the colonies. Some went so far as to claim that " 'the MONSTER of a standing ARMY' had sprung directly from 'a *plan . . . systematically* laid, and pursued by the British *ministry*, near twelve years, for enslaving America.' " Even Jefferson, cooler and reasoning more closely, agreed that it could not be accidental that the oppressive policies had survived "every change of ministers." [19] It is especially noteworthy that John Adams and Josiah Quincy, Jr., who successfully defended the Boston soldiers in court, blamed rather the policy that put them there. The Massacre was "the strongest of proofs of the danger of standing armies," and public discussion was urged concerning the "fatal effects of the policy of standing armies . . . and quartering troops in populous cities in time of peace." [20] The American colonists differed on many issues but they seemed universally agreed that "unhappy nations have lost that precious jewel liberty . . . because their necessities or indiscretions have permitted a standing army to be kept amongst them." [21]

Washington Suggests, Congress Rejects, a Standing Army

To these sentiments Washington fully subscribed, although the protracted misery of trying to weld an effective army from short enlistments and jealously guarded controls by the states forced him to write Congress almost bitterly:

I see such a distrust and jealousy of Military power that the Commander in Chief has not an opportunity, even by recommendation, to give [his officers] the least assurance of reward for the most essential Services. [22]

Indeed they did distrust him and his army, especially when he urged the double insistence that the militia, darling of the politicians and philosophical democrats as the virtuous "peo-

ple's army," could not, and should not, be relied upon, and
that partly for this reason, enlistments should be extended
from three years to the duration of the war. This was calling
for a *regular* army, and however persuasive the need in time
of war, who could say it would not become a standing army
in time of peace? Welded together as veterans of long and
hazardous service, self-conscious as a unit set apart from control by the states, and increasingly embittered and resentful
toward a Congress that consistently and blatantly short-
changed them, might not the Army open up the way to a
government of its own making? These very suspicions were
nearly realized in what James Thomas Flexner suggests may
"well have been the most dangerous hour the United States
has ever known," [23] the so-called Newburgh Affair. Only the
commanding nobility and winsome appeal of Washington
himself, "not only grown gray but almost blind in the service
of my country," as he said, saved the Continental Army from
the "dreadful alternative" of itself seizing justice for its dis-
tressed and underpaid soldiers.[24] Washington's success at this
crucial point, at the very brink of disaster, accomplished by
a selfless appeal to the deepest and best in his men and based
upon the unquestioned integrity of his own leadership, perhaps helped to modify his maturing judgment respecting a
standing army and an adequate navy. In after years, allied
with Hamilton, Washington was to plead versus Jefferson and
others for a professional, if small, military service, a standing
army if you will, but accommodated to democratic values and
needs.

It is not surprising, then, to find that six months after the
Revolutionary War, the American Army numbered only seven
hundred men. Even before news of the peace treaty had actually been received, but hearing that the British were leaving
New York, the Continental Congress officially confirmed the
release of nearly all of Washington's army, most of which had
already gone home on furlough. Washington's own cautious

hope for a modest peacetime military establishment of 2,631 officers and men to include the remnant of the Continental Army (an action which would have helped to ease the bitterness of injustice felt by many veterans) was fearfully and carefully put aside. Even though the Commander in Chief urged that the "Bulwark of our Liberties should be a National Militia," sponsored by the individual states and to include local bodies of minutemen (although it would be uniformly organized and equipped), and that the largest expenditure should be on a navy to repel aggressors and assist in ferrying troops, still the overtones of potential tyranny were heard by jittery Congressmen.[25] On June 2, 1784, after much debate and many lost motions, the Continental Congress agreed with Elbridge Gerry that "standing armies in time of peace are inconsistent with the principles of republican governments, dangerous to the liberties of a free people, and generally converted into destructive engines for establishing despotism." They ordered even the remnant of seven hundred reduced to eighty caretakers:

Resolved, That the commanding officer be and he is hereby directed to discharge the troops now in the service of the United States, except 25 privates, to guard the stores at Fort Pitt, and 55 to guard the stores at West Point and other magazines, with a proportionate number of officers; no officer to remain in service above the rank of a captain.[26]

The states were then requested to furnish seven hundred militia to garrison the western frontier. The small, and effective, Continental navy was disbanded and the last vessel sold in 1785.[27]

Thus, notwithstanding the restless Indians on their borders and the dubious English in control of the seas, with the billeting of redcoat regulars still fresh in their minds and contemptuous of the military tyrannies of Europe, Congress contented itself with the simple protection of military stores and left the defense of the frontiers, for the time at least, to the states concerned. In this way the unsure and floundering young nation, despite a climate of insecurity and against the advice of the beloved "Father of his Country," initiated, or rather confirmed, decisive patterns for the use and containment of the military which have governed us almost to this day: the precipitate reduction of our Armed Forces following every war and the seesaw gropings of the Federal Government with the states to define and to exercise the military power of the nation.

CONFEDERATION AND CONSTITUTION:
CONFUSION AND COMPROMISE

The heat of debate generated by an amazing depth of continuing concern during the interim Confederation years is revealed in *The Federalist* papers, one of whose anonymous writers turned out to be a Huguenot (John Jay). Placing safety "first," he pleaded for a "cordial Union" of the states as the best means of dissuading would-be aggressors, and also to provide an incomparably larger pool of leadership in both peace and war.[28] Most of the argument relating to a peacetime army, however, was provided by the major contributors—Alexander Hamilton and James Madison. Hamilton was something of a hawk, as we would say today. Especially sensitive to dangers from any one of a number of possible aggressors whom he saw on every side, he pleaded against the kind of constitutional "interdiction" or restriction on establishing a military force in time of peace which might tie the hands of the young republic in case of a sudden war. "A power equal to every possible contingency must exist somewhere in government," he stoutly maintained. Efficient, orderly, always somewhat enamored of the *regular* military, Hamilton was rather scornful of the idea that a citizens' militia, divided up by states, could meet "every possible contingency." [29] Nevertheless, Hamilton also reflected the general distrust of the military, conceding to some degree with Madison that the liberties of both ancient Rome and contemporary Europe had "been the price of [their] military establishments." [30] In fact, Hamilton displayed a coldly logical understanding of the tendency of armies to make themselves first benefactors, then protectors, and finally irreplaceable tyrants, when the state continually looked to them for help against its neighbors. For this very reason, he opposed a loose confederacy which might break up into several nations and thus repeat the distress of Europe with armies at each other's throats. The new nation, united, had the opportunity, he felt, to benefit from the insularity of great distances from its neighbors, a providence that England shared as an island, and a circumstance that had assisted it greatly in keeping its army subordinate to the civil authority.[31] This geographical fortune, combined with the incomparable advantages of union of all the colonies so as to obviate the need of armies against each other, and ensured by the precaution of building definite regulatory powers over the military into the Constitution, were as much as man, predatory and selfish but rational, could do. In the end the matter would remain a calculated risk that the new nation must take if it were to endure. Madison put it well:

A standing force, therefore, is a dangerous, at the same time that it may be a necessary, provision. On the smallest scale it has its inconveniences. On an extensive scale its consequences may be fatal. On any scale it is an object of laudable circumspection and precaution. A wise nation will combine all these considerations; and, whilst it does not rashly preclude itself from any resource which may become essential to its safety, will exert all its prudence in diminishing both the necessity and the danger of resorting to one which may be inauspicious to its liberties.[32]

"The clearest marks of this prudence," Madison believed, "are stamped on the proposed Constitution." [33] These were the division of powers in levying and using troops, and the legislative command of the purse strings, the ambiguous effects of which will be dealt with in the next chapter.

By 1789, when Washington was inaugurated first President of the new republic, frontier requirements compelled an increase of the Confederation Army to an eight-company regiment of infantry and a four-company battalion of artillery, 595 men in all. The new Constitutional Congress of 1790 raised the infantry regiment to twelve-company strength. After successive defeats at the hands of the Indians, Congress in 1792 authorized five regiments of infantry with appropriate cavalry and artillery support totaling 5,000 men. With this "Legion of the United States," "Mad Anthony" Wayne won the famous battle of Fallen Timbers and broke the back of the last Indian confederacy to face the original colonies in what was then the Northwest Territory.[34]

The same year (1792) saw the passage of the Militia Act, which was to become part of the foundation of the permanent military policy of the United States, proclaiming reliance not on trained regulars as in Europe, but on the armed citizenry between eighteen and forty-five years of age. But leaving the procurement of weapons to individual militiamen and enforcement to the states, and with no federal standards of training and proficiency, the act did little more than affirm the principle of citizen service which would be invoked in times of national peril. The other half of the foundation, the Regulars baptized with fire at Fallen Timbers and welded into the semblance of a standing force under Gen. Anthony Wayne, now faced the erratic rise and fall of public need and favor which has characterized the military as an institution in America to this day. With the subsiding of the Indian threat and with the British relinquishing the nearer posts, the Regular Army was reduced until the next emergency. When war threatened with France after the XYZ Correspondence (1798), Congress authorized 40,000 regulars and 75,000 volunteers; but the John Adams administration never saw fit to create this force. Destruction of the growing U.S. commerce by Barbary pirates, however, caused Congress to authorize six frigates in

1794 and to establish the Navy Department in 1798. Friction grew with Hamilton, who enthusiastically sought a military buildup and actually politicized the Army by ensuring that no Republicans received commissions—especially in the higher ranks. Reputed to favor a permanent force of some size regardless of outward events, his partisan activities within the Army could not help arousing lasting suspicions respecting his motives.[35]

AMERICA'S FIRST CENTURY: GARRISON DUTY TO "MANIFEST DESTINY"

The "quiet revolution" of 1800 brought Jefferson and the Republicans to power, and "Hamilton's army" folded rather abruptly. With it disappeared the precedent nearly set of the Army used as a political weapon, for Jefferson was a militia man who advocated that the regular force should be reduced to the bare minimum and kept in service no longer than necessary. The new President set the Army at tasks not especially military, such as exploring, road-building, treaty-making, etc.,[36] which assisted the nation in pushing westward, and became an important precedent for the future of the Armed Forces. Jefferson also founded West Point, the artillerists and engineers being exceptions to his general view that the duties of soldiers were too easily learned to require the training of regulars.[37] For these reasons, despite continued tensions with France, Jefferson early in his administration allowed attrition to reduce the authorized strength of the Army from 5,438 to 3,794. Pragmatically responding to increasing threats from abroad, however, Jefferson by 1808 permitted the authorized strength to climb to 10,000. On the eve of the War of 1812 the Army had increased nearly fourfold to 35,603 on paper, but only 6,686 were actually under arms.[38] The war itself nearly doubled the paper strength (58,000), but probably only a sixth of this number actually served. Perhaps five times as many militia and local combatants, however, were involved.[39]

The advancing nation had need of the continuity and experience of a professionalized cadre in the long and busy years to the Civil War, and the Regulars in consequence alternated between severe reductions and reluctant expansions to meet Indian alarms and the Mexican War. In the prevailing egalitarianism, Superintendent Sylvanus Thayer of the new Academy at West Point, and Secretary of War Calhoun (1817–1825) educated and organized the tiny and precariously accepted military establishment as though war were indeed a science and the nation's needs might require professional leadership for the sudden expansion of the Armed Forces. The Army was, then, ready for the struggle with Mexico over Texas, though at its beginning it had shrunk to only 5,300 soldiers scattered over more than 100 posts. It acquitted itself surprisingly well. Weigley says that President James Polk was the first under the Constitution actually to balance civil and military power effectively and to outline the boundaries of those powers for future wartime Presidents.[40] A disturbing and perhaps instructive note is found in the excessively brutal behavior of Gen. (later President) Zachary Taylor's troops in this first American conquest of foreign soil. The Regular officers blamed the volunteers who had swollen the ranks by some 20,000 men.[41]

The real expansion came with the Civil War, the first experience of America as a nation in arms. From 12,698 men just before the war, the combined strength for North and South jumped to more than 2,300,000 at the height of the conflict. Casualty percentages jumped, too, surely to one of the highest in history—some regiments losing 50 to 80 percent of their men.[42] Warfare had entered the costly stage of attrition, to last until the coming of the tank and plane. Technology had reared its uglier face. For the first time resort was made to the draft, in the Militia Act of 1862 and more definitely in the Enrollment Act of March 3, 1863. The reluctance to take the step of conscription is evidenced in the loopholes allowed those who could afford to escape military service: the possibility of substitution or commutation whereby a draftee could purchase exemption for $300. Conscientious objectors also were recognized and generally treated rather generously, being assigned to hospital duty or allowed to pay the commutation fee. Despite the low-key enforcement of the draft, dissent and riots occurred and the act proved valuable more as pressure toward volunteering.[43] It is clear that despite initial enthusiasm on both sides for the War, and the continuance of volunteering, both governments and people felt certain reservations about a universal military requirement. Nonetheless, the principles of national conscription and appeal from military service based upon conscience had been set. Of equal importance were the cautious movements of the central government toward direct enlistment of volunteers without formal ties to their states. The United States Colored Troops were such an example, marking their official entry into American military history, since although they had served in previous wars, they had been barred from the Regular Army and the states' militia.[44]

The Reconstruction period is notable in at least two regards: the struggle between President Johnson and the Congress over military control of the occupied South, and later the slow, lingering malaise of the military establishment to the end of the century. The swift rebirth of Southern white power, encouraged by the President, posed problems of both duty and safety for the Army. The duty concerned protection and justice for all persons, including Negroes, under Congressional Reconstruction policy, and safety became both a physical and a court issue when soldiers were made targets of increasing abuse from disgruntled whites.[45] The polarization of the Executive and the Legislative branches which followed the struggle with and impeachment of President Johnson, foreshadowed recurrent, if not always as severe, difficulties at the highest levels of government in managing the military. The recent controversy over Laos and Cambodia is only the latest of such near impasses. The victory of Congress over Johnson also involved the Army in another thorny problem that has arisen to goad us today—what Weigley calls "the limitations of armed force as a means of social transformation." [46] Pacification by force when many or most of the populace are apathetic or hostile poses at the very least the risk of counterproductive reaction. At the same time the spirit of Jefferson is here, seeking socially positive ways to use military power even in times of peace. As we shall see later, the modern American military is vitally concerned at this point.

Between 1866 and 1878 the Army declined from 38,540 men to less than 20,000; and the Navy, "the strongest . . . in the world when the Civil War ended," could count "only a few . . . [vessels] in condition for normal cruising," let alone fit for warfare, by 1881.[47] The military establishment had entered upon a long "twilight" [48] until the close of the century. In 1896, the Army numbered less than 25,000, "the smallest force in proportion to the total population since the Revolutionary War." [49] But that force had won the West even more completely than the South. In isolation on far-flung posts it had forgotten political entanglements and found itself—hard, proud, and disciplined. The thrust to world center stage occurred in the fight with Spain and found volunteers in abundance. In less than a year of war the 25,000-man Army had expanded to more than 273,000 officers and men. All the exuberance of a young nation ready for world adventure was found in the war fever of civilians crowding to join the colors, in the almost hilarious "snafus" in transportation and training and supplies, in the loud cries of waste and disorganization. The giant had awakened with a start, awkward, clumsy, but with frightening potential. The expansionist and interventionist policies that followed in the climactic wake of the conquest of the Spanish colonies did not so readily permit the severe reduction of troop strength as had occurred following the occupation of the South after the Civil War. Congress raised the maximum strength of the Army to 65,000 in 1899 and then to 100,000 in 1901. Contrary to the post-Civil War experience, the military would retain its augmented strength. "Manifest destiny" had its costs.

The Twentieth Century: The Awakened Giant

In this century, the subconsciously remembered "fears of the Fathers" have been most notably effective in the hasty disbanding of the huge military machines we created in two world wars, and in the monumental inability of the experts to persuade the nation to commit itself either to universal military training (UMT) or to a truly professional, even volunteer, standing army as an acknowledged feature of our national policy. The confusions of the Spanish-American War had revealed the need for better organization of the Armed Forces, and the retention of its augmented strength into the new century required it. Moreover, planning must now keep the state of the world in mind, and that world was slithering rapidly toward the dark and seemingly bottomless trenches of the First World War. The establishment of a General Staff Corps in the Army in 1903 provided a policy-making and coordinating group for the specialized branches and liaison between field soldiers and the Secretary of War and his staff. The National Defense Act of 1916 boosted the authorized strength of the forces threefold and reorganized the establishment to include the National Guard, an organized reserve, and a volunteer or emergency army. A year later two million American soldiers were on their way to an exhausted Europe. But they were not all volunteers, as most had been in every previous war. The National Guard mobilization of 1916 failed to recruit the Guard to full strength and it was realized that conscription would be necessary for modern war. The Selective

Service Act of May 18, 1917, was the result. The essential un-preparedness of the United States for this conflict, despite its efforts to modernize after the Spanish War, reveals both the geometric progression of modern arms which put Germany almost incomparably in the lead and the traditional distaste of Americans for the military as such except in a time of jingo-istic or deadly peril. Jingoism could be, and was, induced, but Germany was not Spain or Cuba, and President Wilson was cautious and idealistically devoted to peace. Having entered upon the fray, however, we made it, characteristically, a moral crusade, a "war to end all wars," to "make the world safe for democracy."

Our entrance into World War II seems like a rerun of World War I—with important variations. The swift decline of our forces after World War I, the rejection of any form of UMT, our general unpreparedness, and the attempt at some form of neutrality, reveal the same deep dislike of a standing army of any appreciable size in any period that could con-ceivably be called "peaceful." But the hard-core professional military cadre which survived the interim years now thought seriously and more or less cooperatively in world terms. Wil-son's anger upon discovering in 1916 that the newly created General Staff had contingency plans for war with Germany seems naïve beside the acknowledged and encouraged Rain-bow plans of worldwide contingencies drawn up by the Joint Planning Committee of the Joint Army and Navy Board in 1939.[50] Moreover, reorganization of the National Guard, crea-tion of a reserve pool of manpower, and mobilization during World War I proved invaluable in the much greater expan-sion and mobilization of World War II. Finally, the close co-ordination with industry to make America literally "the arsenal of democracy" identified the American military with business and labor in ways wholly new to the American experience. The Manhattan Project, Hiroshima, and Nagasaki flowed directly and ominously from this partnership to end the war but not bring the peace.

The devils of two global wars were not exorcised, and we entered into and have not yet emerged from the strange half-light of the "cold war" fought in every conceivable way under the dark shadow of the nuclear cloud. For a little while it seemed that the Pax Britannica might yield almost gracefully to a Pax Americana, but the dream has been shattered in Berlin and Korea and Southeast Asia. Meanwhile, unlike any previous time, we cannot disband and disperse the troops at home. To the traditional argument of our favorable geographical position, we had thought to add our overwhelming industrial competence, proved in two great struggles, to discount the need for universal military training or a professional army of significant and lasting size. But geography has yielded to missiles. And ironically, it has been our industrial progress, plus the threatening political climate, which have brought about what the military alone was never able to accomplish in its wildest dreams, "the consolidation of a gargantuan military enclave . . . alongside the traditional legislative, executive, and judicial departments." [51]

II. FEARS OF THE FATHERS REALIZED

THE SIZE OF THE ESTABLISHMENT

A measure of the problems posed by the aberration of such an enclave and the depth of frustration it has generated with respect to the enduring suspicions of the Fathers, may be found in a few simple figures of comparison. The new American nation under Washington, intent only upon "keeping the stores," numbered less than four million citizens. Today, with a population fifty times greater, our "peacetime" military forces have grown to more than five thousand times the size of that post-Revolutionary company—a ratio increase of more than 100! [52] From the few "stores and magazines" of those early days the Pentagon now controls upwards of thirty million acres in the United States alone, comprising 400 or more major bases and perhaps 5,000 lesser ones. In addition, some two million acres abroad support upwards of another 400 major bases and some 1,900 minor ones.[53] Altogether the area is equal to seven of the original colonies plus Vermont.[54] It is worth more than $210 billion, which as long ago as the Cordiner Report made it "by any yardstick . . . the world's largest organization." [55] More than three million men in uniform man these installations, with over a million being deployed outside the United States. The men and women in uniform constitute a segment of American society as large as those who are in construction jobs, or on our farms, or in the combined fields of insurance, finance, and real estate.[56]

Behind the uniformed forces stand another three and a quarter million National Guard and Reserve personnel, nearly a third of whom are in paid training status.[57] In addition, civilian employees of the Pentagon reached 1,348,000 in July, 1969,[58] roughly as many civilians as live in the States of New Hampshire, Vermont, and Maine combined.[59] Together, civilian and military jobs generated by defense spending mushroomed from 5,971,000 to a peak of 8,438,000 (1968), accounting for at least one out of every ten jobs in the United States. Probably, when everything is taken into account, one fifth of all Americans depend upon the military for their livelihood.[60] The present administration's widely publicized efforts to "pull back" and "cut down" on defense spending stress a decline ranging from 16 percent to 33 percent.[61] This means, it is said, that very soon "only 1 in 13 jobs will be related to defense." Moreover, it is pointed out that for all its size,

defense today gets almost exactly the same share of the U.S. output it got a decade ago. The 78 billion dollar arms budget in the year ending June 30 [1969] is 8.8 percent of total U.S. goods and services, and 43 percent of all federal government outlays. In 1960, military costs were 43 billion, or 8.7 percent of output, and 47 percent of all federal spending. Thus, other government spending has increased more than military spending.[62]

A. E. Lieberman, a manager of marketing services, in an article entitled "Updating Impressions of the Military-Industrial Complex," supports this contention, even suggesting that the government may have done "too well" in containing the economic power generated by defense spending.[63] With an estimated drop to $73 billion for the year ending June, 1971, and prospects of going below $70 billion in 1972,[64] coincident with the "winding down" of the Vietnam conflict, optimism might seem warranted.

Yet the trend in military material orders seems to increase (nearly double in the nine-year period 1960–1969),[65] and it may be significant that despite the claims that more than 300 military bases have been closed or cut back since Mr. Nixon came to power, only 27 of these were overseas.[66] More sobering is the lengthening shadow of the ABM defense system, approved by the narrowest of margins as a "thin" barrier which hardly anyone doubts will, if no more than by its own momentum, press on to a "thick" system costing untold billions of dollars. This prospect dilutes any hope that the decline in military expenditures can be anything more than temporary. Like cancer that has metastasized, the institution of defense has spread into the whole body politic so that while it is being cut back in one place it finds new growth elsewhere. The lively satisfaction with which the hope of a new civilian-military job ratio of one in thirteen is proclaimed in itself reveals the frightening ease with which we have accepted defense as the economic way of life. Such satisfaction is not only blandly unconscious of those more hidden dependencies on the military which suggest a ratio closer to one to five, but it seems to assume that one in thirteen is livable and a kind of return to normalcy.

The truth is, even if we could get back to a pre-Vietnam expenditure base, the cost and the threat would still be staggering. Even before that massive buildup, over one half of the federal budget was going direct to the military, with upwards of 30 percent additional being spent for security-related matters such as atomic energy, the space effort, veterans benefits, war debt interest, the CIA, research and development, etc. This means that for this generation some three quarters of our revenue has been going for past wars, the "cold war," the "limited wars" of Korea and Vietnam, and preparations for future wars—with little prospect of significant change in sight.[67]

<h2>THE NOVELTY OF THE ESTABLISHMENT</h2>

The important thing to note is the novelty of the military as a dominant factor in our "peacetime" way of life. Although the military percentage of the dollar has continued to mount as war has succeeded war, still there was no essential disproportion established between the military and civilian sectors in any prolonged fashion until Korea. Today, for the first time in our national experience, we have a standing force of such dimensions that we readily speak of a "permanent war economy." Indeed, in Senator Fulbright's view, "violence has become the nation's leading industry." [68] As the largest single activity in the country, the Defense Department has contracts with 22,000 prime contractors and 100,000 subcontractors. Nearly $50 billion a year pours into more than four fifths of the nation's 435 Congressional districts.[69] Some 5,300 cities and towns have at least one defense plant or company, and many are entirely dependent upon military-industrial activity for their economic life. It is therefore only natural that local leaders and Congressmen find it most difficult if not impossible to entertain the prospect of cutbacks in military spending. The larger issues of peace and national security are buffeted and torn and often overwhelmed in the daily struggle to preserve and even expand contracts and jobs and thus to maintain the politician's image of a "fighter for the folks back home." Power blocs are formed by states and regions to pressure for larger slices of the "defense pie." Each wants his "fair share" as Representative Ken Hechler (Dem., W. Va.) told the House on June 1, 1959; and by "standing up and roaring," he lifted West Virginia from 46th to 26th place in the nation by 1963.[70]

But others "roar" also. It is not surprising that Texas moved from ninth to second place during the Johnson years, that California and New York are now in first and third spots, and that Georgia, home of the late Senator Russell, powerful head of the Senate Armed Services Committee, has thirteen major military installations as well as the giant Lockheed-Georgia plant to keep the state continuously in the top ten on the military-industrial payroll. "One more base would sink the state," one general has commented. In parallel fashion, the home district of the late Chairman of the House Armed Services Committee, L. Mendell Rivers (Dem., S.C.), has been aptly described as a "microcosm of the military-industrial complex," a fact for which Representative Rivers claimed almost total credit.[71] Charleston alone has nine installations with more planned (at least until Rivers' death in late December, 1970), and the Chamber of Commerce claims that more than 35 percent of the total payroll for 1970 was military exclusive of defense contracts. Representative Rivers' funeral was the occasion for "genuine grief" and widespread concern in Charleston even among blacks who could overlook his anti civil rights stance because the jobs he brought benefited them too.[72] Whether the nation gained to the same extent is open to question: "It's anybody's guess how the Pentagon views Charleston from a port and military standpoint," the President of the Chamber of Commerce is quoted as saying. The location of the new Polaris submarine base at Charleston is acknowledged by a high military official "unquestionably" to have been influenced by the fact that it would be easier to get money out of Congress for Rivers' district than for another. Since the new

Chairman is from New Orleans, the expectation now is that military business will go there.[73]

It is, then, understandable that Secretary of Defense Robert McNamara, "the only Defense Secretary ever to wrest complete control of the Pentagon away from the military establishment" [74] (and during whose tenure there were more closings than openings of military installations), after his announcement of November 18, 1964, phasing out 95 bases here and abroad, received 169 phone calls that same afternoon from irate and aggrieved Congressmen.[75]

The emphasis, it must be noted, is upon "defense." The old Department of War, suggestive of "manifest destiny" and perhaps even idealistic concern to remake the world, has yielded to Department of Defense, implying interior concerns and pragmatic solutions. The daily meaning is not the making of war, but the maintenance of prosperity for millions. For this generally silent, but always hard-working segment (if not a majority) of the American people, diffused like leaven through the body politic, security is practically synonymous with prosperity. That the one depends directly upon the other seems not at all incongruous but a quite satisfying and self-justifying expression of what has been labeled the finest flower of twentieth-century man, i.e., "heroic materialism." [76] In the factory as on the battlefield the struggle against the forces of evil goes on and the measure of success is curiously the same, in the "body count" of more and more bombs and ships and systems, in the unlimited expansion of facilities and demonstrations of their power. It is sobering to realize that the more than $70 billion now being spent annually on the military is more than the total profits of all American business.[77]

THE MILITARY INDUSTRIES

The staying qualities of the giant corporations the military has spawned have pressures of their own which may not be best for America's future. Jack Raymond, in plotting the top ten military industries since World War II, observes that with some variation "the cluster at the top is a 'hard core.' . . . Four of the ten have been at the top the past 23 years." [78] In testimony before the House Committee on Banking and Currency, Admiral Rickover confirmed that competition in many areas is practically nonexistent. "The cards," he said, "are stacked against small companies. . . . In 1967 over 85 percent of military procurement was awarded under negotiated contracts; advertised contracts amounted to less than 15 percent." Especially is this true in the designing and building of turbines where only General Electric and Westinghouse have the capability and a prospective rival actually would need ten years to compete! [79] Add to this the constant temptation to declare adequacy for a prospective company in order to avoid the laborious paper work of cost description, as well as the ever-increasing "cronyism" which obtains from the steady influx of military retirees into peer positions in industry, and we have the possibility of "a new economic order . . . characterized by large industrial organizations that maintain a partnership between themselves and government." The Admiral speaks of this as "in effect, a fourth branch of government" without legal or political responsibility. Part of the cost of maintaining such a partnership of giants is the "hoarding of scientists and engineers" which by creating "artificial shortages in trained manpower . . . has hurt small business . . . delayed essential programs, and . . . added to government expenditures." [80]

Expenditures are ever on the rise, despite attempts at safeguards such as the "Truth in Negotiations Act," because contractors have not been required to submit cost data if a contracting officer determines that there is adequate competition. Hence, despite even Defense Department protestation of good faith and "low profit" by contractors, i.e., perhaps as low as 2.5 percent, Rickover, with the reluctant assistance of the General Accounting Office of the Navy, has demonstrated that profits are rather in the 10 to 25 percent bracket. They are often hidden as costs, including such items as advertising, which is clearly unrelated to military contracts, and other expenses usually listed as general overhead.[81] An analysis by Ralph E. Lapp in his *The Weapons Culture* of thirty-eight of the largest military contractors shows how heavily dependent they are upon government business: fifteen derive more than half of all their business from defense, and ten more about a quarter from it.[82] Lieberman, using a broader base of 100 top contractors, finds that in "intensity of interest" 82 companies are not exclusively military, and the greatest number are only "lightly" involved. With some pride he stresses that all but 24 are listed with the *Fortune 500* industrial companies or among the supplemental listing of leading transportation companies or utilities and thus constitute a broad base which "overlaps extensively with the base of the bluest of the blue chip industry." Therefore

it is valid to point out that the industry portion of the military-industrial complex is not some obscure group of companies seeking to benefit from the eternal curse of mankind, but the substantial activities of many of the most preeminent industrial organizations in the field today.[83]

This is, of course, exactly the point, whatever hope we may have concerning the willingness and ability of American industry to convert from war-making to peace products. As Admiral Rickover astutely observes, with "the award of about $180 million in contracts each working day," [84] there is ample and daily reason for both the Department of Defense and the Department of Commerce to "have an industry-oriented philosophy. They think like industry. And that is the problem." [85]

"Thinking like industry" obviates the need for a theory of conspiracy. According to a distinguished group of Congressmen, this vastly intricate and interlocking web of government-military-industrial complex is "not a conspiracy; it is an enormous, self-perpetuating institutional organism" composed of the armed services and related bodies such as the National Security Agency, the Atomic Energy Commission, the CIA, and others provided for in the National Security Act of 1947. Together these bodies are

closely linked to the aerospace and armaments industry, segments of the labor movement, and a new middle class of scientists, engineers, businessmen, and universities with defense research contracts. . . . It receives such a disproportionate amount of Federal funds that there is no effective counterbalance to it.[86]

This may be seen not only in the measurably massive economic dependence suggested above, but even more in "opportunities foregone" as the Congressmen state so eloquently.[87] They suggest that for the funding of the Manned Orbiting Laboratories, six hundred thousand ghetto students with college potential could have been provided Upward Bound summer courses; that unchecked excessive contract costs annually cover more than Head Start education for two and a quarter million additional children, plus a year of school lunches for twenty million more children; that Safeguard missile funds for 1969 could have trained five hundred and ten thousand more hardcore unemployed. In the past decade, $551 billion in direct defense expenditures amounts to twice the amount spent for all new private and public housing, and almost twice as much as all federal, state, and local governments allocated for education. In one year alone (1967) military-related spending of $100 billion equaled more than all the monies spent by all agencies—federal, state, and local—on hospitals, health, old-age benefits, welfare, education, unemployment, and agriculture.

The Congressmen go on to state that

this order of priorities prevails at a time when twenty million Americans live in dilapidated, rat-infested housing while the building industry cannot even keep up with the population increase and is in fact declining in productivity; when there are at least ten million victims of malnutrition and untold thousands of children with permanent brain damage because of insufficient food; when there are close to forty million people living in poverty with little access to medical or welfare care; while millions of children are doomed to lives of misery and poverty because of inadequate or non-existent school facilities.[88]

Contrary to the long-trumpeted "merchants of death" thesis which did not question the economic wisdom but only condemned the exploitative greed of war preparation and making, economists such as Kenneth Boulding now point out that actual "economic damage" due to this "massive allocation of resources . . . into the 'rathole of the competitive weapons systems'" reduces the annual rate of growth by as much as 2 percent.[89] Again, it is said in many localities that the effect of substantial defense installations has been to enervate the very will to innovation and diversification, and often to retard necessary social reform by "reinforcing prevailing patterns of segregation and economic rigidity."[90]

The Military in Education and Research

The effects upon the educational and international arenas have been no less disturbing. Senator Eugene McCarthy has estimated that "defense and space programs since 1960 have amounted to fifty-four percent of total expenditure on research and development in the entire country."[91] The implication, amounting to a conviction for many faculty, students, and civic leaders throughout the country, is that federal funding of academic institutions leads to implicit (at least) political control and direction of studies and projects, especially when they are defense related.[92] Specifically, examples of area imbalance are startling. A student publication at Berkeley claims that that institution receives 70 percent of its research grants in the social services and nearly 90 percent in the physical sciences from the Federal Government. Senator Fulbright sees a relationship between these assertions and the student rebellion that has characterized Berkeley in recent years. More especially must this be true when it is understood that the Naval Biological Laboratory administered by Berkeley's School of Public Health involves faculty members in aerobiology, which has to do with transmitting communicable diseases.[93] Berkeley is only one instance. Most of the top universities of the country are heavily involved in such "pragmatic" defense-related projects, which may turn important energies from the classic disinterested pursuit of truth to functioning as hirelings of the state. According to Walter Adams and Adrian Jaffe in a recent Congressional report, not only student unrest but student neglect is involved, and most ominous of all, distortion, downgrading, and neglect of the humanities in the headlong rush to prestige, profit, and the "opportunities to orbit deans around the world." [94]

In 1968 alone the total research budget of the Defense Department was eight billion dollars, of which 1.6 billion was allocated for basic research. This was about six times the amount the National Science Foundation spent in the same period of time. Donald McDonald finds that in direct comparison with the State Department, the Department of Defense spends $13.3 million annually for foreign area social and behavioral science research and policy-planning studies in foreign politico-military problems as against a mere $125,000 a year set aside for State's research budget.[95] Admiral Rickover has decried the Defense Department as involved in

research having only the remotest relevance to the problems encountered by the armed services—matters at no previous time, nor anywhere else in the world, deemed to lie within the province of the defense function—just because it has the money; . . . more money than any other public agency.[96]

For these monies some very interesting and controversial social science programs have been pursued by several of the top universities in the country. For instance, Project Camelot, an Army-sponsored $6 million operation of the American University Special Operations Research Organization, involved social scientists from the University of California, Princeton

University, University of Michigan, and the Massachusetts Institute of Technology, in an assigned mission to build a model of a developing society with particular reference to its manipulatable and breakdown possibilities. The storm raised by this and other military planning ventures in nation building or unbuilding (described as "insurgency prophylaxis") caused a number of leading universities to sever their connections with the Institute of Defense Analysis, but they have kept in touch with the defense organization in less formal ways.[97]

GLOBAL PRESENCE AND POWER

The upshot of such research and "social science" activity by the American military is to give it a global presence and universal claim not always in keeping with the "open society" it was fashioned to protect. There is rising criticism that we are engaged in wholesale meddling in national and international affairs simply because it is "to our interest to be there." Recently, the Navy was caught in the spotlight of criticism when it became known that some of its carrier admirals had been actively pursuing a policy of intervention in foreign disputes beyond the knowledge and approval of the State Department.[98] This has reduced the State Department for "all intents and purposes, [to] a junior partner," says Admiral Rickover, and despite the Congressional prerogative to make war, "may confront it with situations that make war inevitable." [99] This may mean the propping up of alien regimes, even antidemocratic ones, such as Spain, concerning which a recent disclosure by the Senate Foreign Relations Committee warned that our military presence there had assumed a "quasi-commitment" to support the government, possibly even in a civil war. Our continued support of Batista in Cuba, when we might have encouraged moderate and democratic reform, is too well known now for comfort. Our present relationship to the Greek junta again bears the impress of so-called military realism.

Such executive agreements, Senator Fulbright suggests, may be called the "functional equivalent" of treaties approved by the Senate and indeed may have more weight because they are usually backed up by tangible military strength on the spot. For example, the apparent upgrading of our limited agreement with Spain to a *de facto* defense obligation came about in the following manner. General Earle Wheeler, then Chairman of the Joint Chiefs of Staff, acting in this case under instructions from Secretary of State Rusk, provided Spanish military authorities with a secret memorandum which asserted that the presence of American forces in Spain "constituted a more significant security guarantee than would a written agreement." [100] In the judgment of a number of senators, the same could be said of our forty thousand troops in Thailand, put there by executive order alone. Their presence in implicit promise and expectation "creates a *de facto* commitment going far beyond the SEATO agreement." [101] On another front, a former ambassador, loyal but worried, states that with large Military Assistance Group (MAG) missions comparable in number to embassy staffs, "the very size of our defense establishment in Europe cannot but affect the style of our diplomacy . . . [and] make our diplomatic effort appear to be the handmaiden of our military policies." [102] According to Senator McCarthy, with almost five thousand military agents scattered worldwide under our military assistance programs, men who represent our government without formal Congressional examination or public awareness, it is inevitable that many sensitive missions will be carried on with strong political overtones and incautious if not disastrous implications and results.[103]

The CIA and Clandestine Activities

In this connection, criticism has been directed especially toward the Central Intelligence Agency (CIA). Although not formally a military organization, it operates under the National Security Council and is accused of being arbitrarily venturesome in paramilitary ways. As a special child of Congress, the CIA has been specifically exempted from most restrictions that apply to other government agencies. It operates in secrecy and may expend funds, make contracts, and even admit aliens on its own. Increasingly, the CIA has gone well beyond intelligence-gathering to active manipulation in order to control events politically. Roger Hilsman, a Kennedy official, claims that as early as the end of the Eisenhower administration, the political use of the CIA had become a "fad" of such dimensions as to compare with the ubiquitous activity of communist agents and even to embarrass the government itself.[104] The coup against Iran's Premier Mossedegh, now admittedly a CIA action, has not been forgotten by thousands of Iranian students in this country alone, many of whom have expressed considerable bitterness to me. Miles Copeland, an American management consultant who helped organize the CIA, alleges in a recent book that our clandestine involvement in the Middle East has been serious and often counterproductive. For instance, he claims that the U.S. sponsorship of the 1949 *coup d'état* of Husni Zaim in Syria "began the ceaseless putsches that have since marked that country's political life and produced increasing Soviet control." Nasser is reported to have said to Copeland at one point that

the genius of you Americans is that you never made clear-cut stupid moves, only complicated stupid moves which make us wonder at the possibility that there may be something to them we are missing.[105]

Thus to bungling is added unending suspicion as to the meaning of our moves. The cumulative effect of such incidents has been to corrode "one of our major political assets, the belief in American intentions and integrity." [106] Even when we are not compromised, the emphasis upon secrecy and double-dealing encourages the specter of the conspiratorial theory and attitude which is beginning to wreak its havoc of universal suspicion in our communities and courts at home. It compounds fear in an age of fear. The recent exposure of Army spying on civilians, although dismissed by one judge as a badly bungled "Keystone Kops" affair, did nothing to assuage the growth of such fear at home.[107] And now, with the belated admission that the Defense Central Index of Investigations (DCII) includes information on twenty-five million individuals,[108] the range and depth of the problem of "The Surveillance Society" [109] is only beginning to be understood.

BLANK CHECK FOR THE MILITARY

The exploiting of fear, often honestly believed, combined with the runaway sophistication of modern weaponry, which defies lay understanding and competitive study and purchasing, make congressional control of the purse strings of war almost a farce. The "systems" have a dialectic of their own, invention or improvement calling for a counterweapon, and so on. Moreover, each weapon calls forth its own "allies," other parts of the burgeoning system. The genesis and perfecting of such systems have produced an intricate complex of scientists and "think men," who must project the technological evolution of the arms race and sell the military on the weapons it should have. The pressures are such in the deadly race to excel that a veritable *revolution* takes place every four or five years. This means that planning, to be at all adequate, must look ahead at least five to ten years. In such circumstances of accelerating sophistication, the ever-widening web of contracting and manufacturing, and the necessity of long-term projection, the annual appropriations reviews by Congress are at best only ineffectual delaying tactics in attempting to control "a juggernaut in search of a mission." [110] The result, according to Senator Proxmire, is a "Blank Check for the Military," which allows for unbelievable waste and incompetence: cost overruns of "200 to 300 percent more than the Pentagon estimated . . .

on about 90 percent of the major weapons systems";[111] the practice of "buying in,"[112] which may push costs as high as 700 percent overrun; up to two years or more delay in receipt of purchases; and shocking substandard performances on weapons after delivery.[113] A kind of protectionism exists, or perhaps the torpor of a giant knight unable to move in his own armor, for according to a Budget Bureau specialist,

those firms with the worst records appeared to receive the highest profits. One firm, with failures on five of seven systems, earned 40 percent more than the rest of the aerospace industry, and 50 percent more than industry as a whole. One other company, none of whose seven weapons systems measured up to performance specifications, still had earnings in excess of the industry average.[114]

Senator Proxmire suggests that weapons procurement today is a kind of "welfare system" which guarantees that the great companies can do business with the Government. By making inflated "progress payments," the Pentagon actually provides "free" working capital, underwrites incurred costs, and develops a financial stake in contractors that amounts to a continuous subsidy.[115] The appalling inability of the Comptroller General to estimate with any degree of confidence the extent of our arms gifts and sales is but one reflection that we have no uniform accounting system for defense procurement and that in fact such a system is not desired by too many who benefit from the confusion. The fact that as long ago as 1965 the Comptroller General singled out for a House Committee much the same costly failings of "unmanagement" (as Proxmire puts it, rather than "mismanagement")[116] of military procurement,[117] with little or nothing having been done about it, reveals the depth of Congressional apathy. Contrast this with the speed with which Congress passed the 1970 military authorization bill. After striking down every meaningful attempt to require study of specific requests and greater accountability of contractors, Congress then "included, at Representative Rivers' insistence, four hundred and fifteen million dollars for Navy ships that the Pentagon had not requested." [118] We begin to suspect that we are seeing only the tip of an iceberg that is closer and deadlier than we think. One cannot help agreeing with Prof. Hans Morgenthau that

the real problem with military budgets and military commitments is that the great majority of the American people will buy anything once it is wrapped in the flag and the Joint Chiefs say it is necessary for security.[119]

What, then, the Joint Chiefs say and how they use the flag is of inestimable importance on the home front. There is a battle on the home front, which the military traditionally fears will be lost by the apathy of civilians. But if the battle is lost in America it will hardly be due to a failure of nerve or patriotism. Rather, the matching of public gullibility and selfishness with Pentagon extravagance and inefficiency will simply overload the circuits until the awesome power fails. The military is avowedly fighting on the home front for everything it can get, with dubious cost accountability, as though the only thing that matters is victory abroad. Perhaps, as Morgenthau goes on to say, the greatest need in the restructuring of our values is the realization that "the Pentagon is not oracular." [120] It makes mistakes, and the very nature of its power is such that the mistakes not only may be tragic, but final.

The Public Relations Apparatus

The problem lies in the almost unimaginable size and diversification of the American military establishment, which is global in its concerns and operations. The dynamism of modern technology, obedient to the uninhibited ethic of "free enterprise" and heroic pride in "bigness," undergirded and directed by the zealous "conscience of the military" which sees the nation and world absolutely threatened by evil forces, cannot help encouraging the American military toward every nook and cranny of the world. The bureaucracy is so vast and intricate and self-serving, having identified its own interests with those of the nation, that decisions do not, and perhaps cannot, always wait upon proper ordering and clearance. Often, then, the right hand really does not know what the left hand is up to, as the unproductive raid on Sontay, a North Vietnam prisoner of war camp, clearly demonstrates.[121] But "after the fact" explanations are always forthcoming, for the public relations apparatus of the Defense Department has kept pace with the growth of the institution itself, and with typical Yankee vigor and ingenuity sells the military solution to every problem. The various service publications can be expected, of course, to plug for their own particular brand of military expertise. More ominous, however, as Senator Fulbright points out, is the fact that

the Department of Defense, with more than twice as many people engaged in public relations as the USIA has in all of its posts abroad, operates to distribute its propaganda within this country without control other than that of the Executive Branch, and it floods the domestic scene with its special narrow view of the military establishment and its role in the world.[122]

Of course, the military needs an information program, but it should be one designed to inform, not promote or possibly deceive.

But deceive it appears to be doing, whether intentional or not. Americans, after most of the rest of the world, have come to suspect, among other things, the flood of body count figures from Vietnam which have sought to reassure us that our casualties are only a tenth of the enemy's, and so naturally we are winning the war. Herman Kahn has skeptically suggested that "the NLF and the North Vietnamese can replace their losses at the present rate (1968) for the rest of history." [123] Colonel Donovan in two hard-hitting chapters, "A War for Everybody" and "The Great Bombing Hoax," reveals that pressures from the very top, even if slight, have required "facts and figures to show progress in the war." Each successive link in the chain of command brings cumulative and irresistible weight at the bottom to tell the story not as it is but as it is desired to be.[124] Against mounting skepticism, the armed services have increasingly used all the tricks of the trade of a powerful lobby: self-promotional films and television shows, speakers at community functions, elaborate and expensive exhibits at state and local fairs, pleasant cruises for VIP's to Hawaii aboard aircraft carriers.[125] Senator Fulbright claims that since 1959, Pentagon public relations costs have risen from $2,755,000 to $40,477,000, a 1,500 percent increase in eleven years! (He would like to impose a firm ceiling of $10 million annually, which seems ample enough.)[126] The result, the senator concludes, is that too often other and more properly concerned agencies of government have been "awed as well as outmanned, outmaneuvered, or simply elbowed aside by Executive military decision-making." [127] Cambodia and Laos are certainly cases in point. The premature release of "The Pentagon Papers" confirms this propensity and suggests the calculated use of deception when it is feared that the nation may not readily support certain arbitrary and risk-laden decisions. Senator Fulbright complains that "foreign policy has, in all too many instances, become the creature of decisions made by planners in the Defense Department," [128] an observation already made by concerned voices from within the military establishment itself, as we have seen.

THE TRAFFIC IN ARMS

A grim expression of the posture of military salesmanship is our worldwide traffic in arms. Indeed, Pentagon officials have largely replaced the onetime "merchants of death" in aggressively providing lethal weapons for most of the world.

Just how much is not known, a fact that is both startling and profoundly disturbing. In an article entitled "U.S. Arms Aid: Encouragement to War," [129] George Thayer estimates that in the quarter century since 1945 over $50 billion worth of military hardware has been given or sold to nearly a hundred countries. This is more than three times the total arms exports of the rest of the world ($16 billion). But recent testimony by Congress' Chief Auditor, Comptroller General Elmer Staats, indicates that "nowhere in government is there a complete tabulation" of such expenditures and sales. Indeed, the total figure since 1945 may reach $175 billion! [130] The $50 billion outlay which is more or less accounted for is staggering enough, but that nearly treble this amount is a no-man's-jungle of statistics and fluid accountability can only encourage fear of the runaway propensities of our modern arms bureaucracy. Thayer traces the rapid, overwhelming growth of this organization from a few hundred employees in the early post-World War II years to the more than seven thousand now attached to military missions, advisory groups, and embassies around the world who are acting as arms salesmen. Most of the billions were given away, especially in the first decade after World War II. But with the lessened tensions of the mid-fifties, the new rationale was "that of selling arms in order to offset our unfavorable balance of trade." In 1961 our foreign military sales program was formalized with the establishment of the International Logistics Negotiations Office in the Pentagon, which was headed until early 1969 by Deputy Assistant Secretary for Defense Henry J. Kuss, Jr.—"in effect, America's first supersalesman of arms." Kuss completely reversed the procedures from grant aid to sales, though the poorest nations still receive some arms free.[131]

But a nation must be poor indeed not to pay for the proffered arms, even if it means the use of food money! Comptroller Staats estimates that *Food for Peace* gifts have led to the purchase of nearly a billion dollars in arms over the past six years through the "development" device of demanding that amounts equal to food gifts be set aside for arms! Senator Proxmire termed this arrangement "double think . . . Orwellian" and suggested that the program be renamed "Food for War." [132] Earlier, a reporter for the *San Francisco Chronicle* warned of the " 'Poor Man's' Arms Race Peril." Although rationalized in terms of defense, "the purchases are fueling . . . brushfire conflicts" in notably tense and unsettled regions of the world such as Africa and the Near East.[133]

Periodic attempts by Congress to put ceilings on such sales have had small effect, although the Conte, Symington, and Ruess Amendments have restricted the sale of "sophisticated" weapons to underdeveloped countries and perhaps slowed their abilities to divert their own or U.S. development funds to excessive military expenditures. The Deputy Assistant Secretary of Defense for Military Assistance and Sales in 1969 proudly noted "significant" sales figures and policies, and claimed that the

very high percentage of total sales orders . . . placed by developed countries (74 percent for Europe) shoots down the uninformed, but unhappily persistent, claim that military purchases are jeopardizing economic progress and fomenting arms races among underdeveloped nations (only 3 percent).[134]

This, however, is blithely to overlook man's desperate hunger for bread in the very quarters where the purchase of arms is urged. John Kenneth Galbraith, former Ambassador to India, testifying before a Congressional committee, deliberately assigned the cause of the 1967 Indian–Pakistani War to our arms traffic with those countries, and added: "There is something intrinsically obscene in the combination of ill-fed people and well-fed armies deploying the most modern equipment." [135] The important ratio to note is the ominous imbalance created in rising small nations where military expenditures appear to be outdistancing their gross national product and are higher than the world average. The Stockholm International Peace Research Institute late in 1969 found that in the last fifty years arms spending has multiplied twice as fast as the production of nonmilitary goods and services, and world arms outlays have been doubling every fifteen years. In fact, the acceleration has reached 50 percent in the last three years (5.9 percent for 1959–1965; 8.9 percent since 1965).[136] It is now estimated that in the past seventy years the world has spent more than $4,000 billion on wars and military preparedness, but if the present rate of *increase* continues, another $4,000 billion will be consumed in only ten years.[137] The most spectacular rise has been in America: in 1913 our military expenditures were only 1.5 percent of the gross national product; in the thirties, 2.5 percent; but since World War II the percentage has been 10 percent, representing nearly half of the world's total and twice as much as expended by the USSR.[138] And this imbalance is dwarfed by our *direct* contribution to the arms race by sales and services of war goods to other countries which, as we have seen, is somewhere between three and eleven times the total of the rest of the world.

Arms Accumulation and Military Retirees

It remains to suggest two final aspects of the modern military in America which make its effective control, and certainly its reduction, dubious: arms accumulation and the tremendous and increasing influx of "military graduates" into American society. There is logic in the plurality and near autonomy of our various deadly systems poised against the communist world, but each has now grown so as to provide irrationally large overkill. For instance, each of forty-one nuclear submarines will soon be able to destroy 160 Russian cities. But, in addition, our one thousand-plus land-based ICBM's can take out those same cities six times over! We are actually able to deliver over four thousand nuclear warheads, less than one tenth of which, according to former Secretary of Defense McNamara, could destroy one third of Russia's population and one half of its industry.[139] And there is yet the burgeoning MIRV system which by attaching three to ten thermonuclear warheads to each ICBM will increase their capacity tenfold!

The controversy on biochemical warfare still makes news. President Nixon's moves to renounce the use of germ weapons and the "first use" of chemical weapons has lessened the anxiety following certain "unfortunate" accidents and publicity about the weapons. However, the promised destruction of some stockpiles of these weapons cannot fully dissipate the lingering specter of the years of their costly refinement for expected use, and the well-known ability of bureaucrats to circumvent official decrees. There is, for instance, confusion on definition of "stockpiles" sufficient to enable Army officers to save these weapons, or some of them, as "limited components for biological testing." [140] In any case, the mood of overkill is difficult to diffuse when, given one deadly nerve agent developed by the Army in an amount sufficient to wipe out the present global population thirty times over, the complaint can still be made that we are not doing enough in this field since the Russians have eight times our capacity! [141] Even the Administration does not seem convinced by this kind of logic which accepts as fact that the Soviets are really committed to a first-strike strategy, and that unlimited quantity is the measure of security. President Nixon himself has made it clear that the Russians "have always thought in defensive terms," [142] and he has suggested "sufficiency" rather than "superiority" as the true measure of our defense.[143] It is rather that the military attitude is always to assume the worst possible. This attitude can be invoked by civilians as well as by those in uniform.

Even serious attempts to reduce or to destroy weapons often produce their own counterproposals simply to shift them elsewhere, as part of the huge giveaway and sales programs that we have mentioned. We are naturally more cautious about unconventional and terror weapons, but given the "mad momentum" of which Secretary McNamara once spoke,[144] weapons tend to justify their existence in deployment and then in actual use, and the threat of proliferation is always there. The recent criticism of the Navy for certain interventionist activities referred to earlier has revealed that the apparent motivation was "to justify floating airfields" in a time when the carriers are increasingly judged to be "an outflanked maginot line." [145] The threat is not lessened by the huge number of military officers who have been streaming into the nation's businesses, political establishments, and schools upon retirement from the services. Even ten years ago the startling nature of this trend was commented upon.[146] Today, according to Senator Proxmire, three times as many high-ranking officers are carried on defense payrolls as in 1959.[147] The conflict-of-interest potential is great enough to induce the Congressional Subcommittee on Economy to seek annual disclosure of "officials who have moved from the Pentagon to defense industries or vice versa." [148]

We have become a nation of veterans, nearly twenty-eight million as of June, 1970, comprising at least one fifth of the adult population.[149] These are citizens who, on top of the notably welding experiences which war often brings to its participants, have generally been educated, job-trained, granted degrees, or otherwise prepared for positions of influence and leadership in every community and stratum of life in the land. Not only in the armaments industry, but throughout the business world, in academic careers, and in the highest levels of government, military men and women have been and are making their marks. Not all, unfortunately, possess the candor and objectivity of Dr. Jerome B. Wiesner, President Kennedy's adviser on scientific affairs. He once told a conference of business and professional leaders that he was "an example of what's wrong with the American posture" in the field of disarmament: billed as "an expert on arms control" his entire life had been spent in military technology. "I came to an arms control problem with all the biases and prejudices of someone who has been working very hard on military weapons—and, unfortunately, most of the people who work on arms control come to the problem from this same background." [150] It has been noted that the apparently widespread assumption which governs the choice of the appointed elite of the Administration at home and abroad, i.e., expertise in business management, is apparently the basic criterion for representing democracy at its best,[151] and readily includes high-ranking officers. The old breed of warriors has largely given way to the new "military managers" who move easily from the Pentagon to executive suites and ambassadorships and are known more for their crisp, definite solutions to every problem than for any thoughtful, long-range humanism concerned primarily with persons and peoples. In shattering times such as ours, decisiveness and the instant readiness to employ force can be very attractive. But the question remains as to the nature of the deeper values of such leaders imbued so long and carefully with military training and experience. Do they adequately and appropriately represent American democracy and the best for the future of man? This becomes especially important in the growing controversy respecting the future of the military in our society and whether, for instance, all-volunteer armed forces may be the answer to the mounting problems and criticism.

The depth and pervasiveness of the controversy betray the ambiguities of the thought patterns we have historically entertained toward the military and the difficulties we have had in applying the Constitution to its growth. It will be instructive to examine these contributing factors before attempting to explore the nature of the modern military in the American context.

Chapter 3

The Ambivalence of Civilian-Military Relations

I. TWO SCHOOLS OF THOUGHT

It is apparent that several schools of thought have from the beginning contributed to the continuing debate on the role of the military in American society. A recent book by an English student of the American scene, winnowing materials covering the ninety years between the Revolutionary and Civil Wars, finds three contradictory views held by Americans during this period, and they felt no compulsion to reconcile them. The Quaker expressed a sincere, simple piety, often shrewd, always diligent, sometimes ingenious, in his accommodation to military necessity. The Riflemen and Chevalier embodied heroic individualism in the different levels of enlisted and officer status, the one a skirmisher and rule breaker, the other the authoritarian and mounted heir of a gracious tradition.[1] These models are easily distinguishable in theory but hardly in practice, especially in today's complex world. The rifleman and chevalier are anciently known but in America have been modified by local customs and attitudes (Massachusetts minutemen vs. Virginian aristocratic tradition), and both have often been undergirded by religious convictions and zeal broader than Quaker piety.

More useful in understanding the peculiar tensions and ambiguities involved in the evolution of the American military are two sharply differing approaches which were suggested in the previous chapter as parts of the foundation of American military policy: a regular army of *professional* soldiers, and/or a *citizen army* of various components (militia, national guard, organized reserves, selectees).[2] The convictions and confusions generated by adherents of these differing and often clashing positions are likewise part of our understanding—or misunderstanding—of the nature of military power. They have, for instance, affected the Constitutional provisions for the establishment and use of the Armed Forces. And, clearly, in recognizing and espousing the complexity of the problems of military power they have not contributed to its simple solution. This is doubtless a gain in realism, but it has tended toward confusion. An examination of the roots of this confusion reveals that they are both ideologic and pragmatic, differing ways in which we view the military and seek solutions to the problems it poses for us. Having sketched in somewhat surface fashion the phenomenal fulfillment of the fears of the Fathers, it is important now at a deeper level to examine those attitudes and actions which have acted as guidelines, not always in concert, in the fashioning of the modern military establishment in America.

The Federalist School

The two schools of thought may be called the *Federalist* and the *popularist* emphases, with Washington and Hamilton representing the former and Jefferson and Jackson the latter. The Federalist position is so called because of the prominence given its arguments through *The Federalist* papers edited largely by Hamilton. The plea and plan were simple and direct: a well-trained, if small, professional military force, supplemented in war by militia raised and trained in peace through a form of universal military training (UMT). Washington's long experience had convinced him of the inadequacy of untrained volunteers on the field of battle. Although he is often quoted to the contrary, it is clear that he would have preferred a regular standing army commensurate with the country's growing needs. But knowing that neither the temper of the people nor the resources of the fledgling nation would admit of such a solution, Washington pleaded as we have seen for what may be called the *expansible* army—a strong skeleton of regulars to be fleshed in with a well-trained militia in time of need. Beyond these trained regulars and reserves the citizenry in general were to be tapped as required. Hamilton's plan varied little from Washington's,[3] being governed by his more sensitive view of how to get any plan approved by Congress. Successively, Henry Knox, Secretary of War under Washington, and John C. Calhoun, Monroe's Secretary of War, attempted refinement of this concept and with as little success in having it adopted. But neither was it to die. It provided a living option that eventually would come into its own.

The Popularist School

The popularist view, as might be expected, drew its strength from the people themselves. It had strong champions in Jefferson, "the people's choice," and, perhaps surprisingly, in another hero who became President, Andrew Jackson. Jefferson, with the liberal's distaste for professional militarism, and perhaps even fearful of Federalist "plots" to subvert the state through this very means,[4] reduced the Regulars and called for the "military sovereignty of the people." [5] The militia should be universal in scope—"every citizen a soldier"—well disciplined, organized, equipped, and classified. Jefferson sought the opposite of Hamilton: a militia to deal with emergencies in peace, a regular army for war. He was no more successful than Hamilton: Congress preferred to limit the regular force to inconsequential size and pragmatically, if with risk, meet emergencies as they arose. Jackson, with a like faith in the individual citizen, especially the superior American frontiersman, and doubtless taking himself as an example of the self-made military success story, did not even see the need for peacetime training of militia.[6] In this he was supported by the temper of the times which, aside from the Indians, saw little threat to the nation's security after 1815.

During the thirty years before the Civil War, the militia companies degenerated into almost purely social organizations lacking military discipline and military skill. Jefferson wished to educate all citizens to be soldiers; the Jacksonians assumed that all citizens could be soldiers without training.[7]

One effect of this languishing policy was to harden the small regular contingent and isolate it from public affairs.

THE AMBIVALENT CONSTITUTION

What part has the Constitution itself played in the formation of the American military system? It is ambivalent. With respect to the military, the Constitution is a mirror of the tangled fears and good intentions of the Founding Fathers, and perhaps, as well, of their wisdom. Three strong precautions are urged in the Constitution.[8] The first put the power to raise and support armies into the hands of a civilian Congress with the attached condition that appropriations for the Army must be reviewed biannually.[9] The second precaution provides for a militia under control of the respective states, thus decentralizing military power in peacetime. The third safeguard makes a civilian, the President, Commander in Chief of the Armed Forces, but without power either to declare war or to appropriate money for the military establishment. A fourth principle may be added, one that is more positive in nature and was to have immense relevance to the citizen-soldier concept: "The right of the people to keep and bear arms . . . shall not be infringed." [10] With the organization of a militia in mind, this "right" of the individual citizen to defend his country was to encourage both a sense of duty and confidence in the discharge of that duty—but the spelling out of the means was left to conscience and to time.

The intention of the precautions written into the Constitution was to divide, and thus to rule, the military. But by mixing political and military functions the establishment of direct civilian control was not to be easily achieved. Civilian, as well as military, responsibility was divided and direct access of military authorities to the highest levels of the government was permitted. The resulting vacuums of power have provided tempting arenas for struggles between the military and civilian agencies of the government to the present day.[11] Huntington summarizes the ambivalence of the military clauses of the Constitution as follows:

1. Within the total federal system of government, the militia clauses divide control over the militia between the state and national governments.
2. Within the national government, the separation of powers divides control of the national military forces between Congress and the President.
3. Within the executive branch of the national government, the Commander in Chief clause tends to divide control over the military between the President and departmental secretaries.[12]

II. TWO HISTORICAL CONSTANTS

THE LIBERAL SOCIETY

Two historical constants, reflecting the continued influence of the Fathers, have prevailed in the evolution of the American military system. The first of these is *ideological:* the liberal society has provided a climate in the main antithetical to professional military careerism. The second is *structural:* the conservative Constitution has had the almost paradoxical effect of hampering civilian control of the military.[13] With respect to the first constant, the liberal society, Huntington in *The Soldier and the State* vividly contrasts the liberal traditions of Europe and America:

The universality of liberalism in the United States and its essentially static quality contrast with the variety and dynamism of ideologies in Europe. The Frenchman has had firsthand experience with aristocratic conservatism, revolutionary democracy, Bonapartism, clericalism, monarchism, liberalism, socialism, communism. The American knows only liberalism. The political outlook of the Englishman today, be he socialist or Tory, is fundamentally different from that of the average Englishman at the end of the eighteenth century. The political ideology of Woodrow Wilson was essentially the same as that of Elbridge Gerry. Liberalism in the United States has been unchanging, monotonous, and all-embracing.[14]

The Greek classics and the English philosopher Locke combined to produce a high view of man, subject to natural law and unified by reason.[15] America's very geography, huge and isolated for so long, conspired to keep such an optimistic view of man in the ascendancy. Even the dark threat of Puritan pessimism was still subject to the overruling providence of God who chose to "work all things together for good to them . . . who are called according to his purpose" (Rom. 8:28, KJV). The purpose was abundantly revealed and confirmed from the distinctly religious beginnings of a people separated from the Old World and destined to create a New World, a "new beginning for man." [16] Until our own times the optimism was never seriously challenged because economic pressures and political threats were for so long absent.

Steady economic growth diluted class conflict. There were few struggles over the distribution of the pie because the pie was always growing larger. No nascent group ever developed a radical ideology challenging the established order; it was always too quickly assimilated into that order.[17]

National security was a simple given fact, the starting point of political analysis and not the end of conscious policy. Only two groups in American history ever failed to adhere to the liberal philosophy, and both were amalgamated by the end of the Civil War: the Federalists of New England, who controlled the nation until the unexpectedly quiet "revolution" of Jefferson's common people in 1800, and the antebellum South, an "illiberal island" that lost its autonomy through the Civil War. "After 1865 liberalism reigned unchallenged on the American scene." [18]

The secure society, self-centeredly engaged in expanding westward, could find no place for the military in its scheme of things, except as a frontier police. Its attitude toward the military was actually "hostile, static, and dominant." [19] The awakening would come, of course, but until World War I— and even beyond—priority would be given to domestic issues at the expense of foreign policy. "Magnificently varied and creative when applied to domestic issues, liberalism faltered when applied to foreign policy and defense." It did not seem to "furnish means to think about war, peace and international relations." [20] Essentially, American liberalism was isolationist in international affairs. The application of successful home policies to world conditions, such as free trade, industrialization of backwardness, elimination of poverty, arbitration treaties, the World Court, outlawry of war—all were well-intentioned and helpful gestures but really answers posed on another plane. The search for objective standards and ideal goals in the international jungle of human emotions and motives was doomed to rejection and disillusionment because it came too cheaply. It was not real involvement in the human plight.

Even the temporary popularity of the so-called "Neo-Hamiltonians," [21] who crested into power through the Spanish-American War, and the emergence of Theodore Roosevelt as a popular military figure could not basically alter the prevailing moods of neutrality and pacifism of the American public. This "splendid little war," like the "war to end all wars" that would follow within half a generation, only confirmed the liberal spirit which could produce such slogans. The "hostile image of the military profession" [22] remained and would be deepened. The versatile character of the "Rough Rider" President—politician, military hero, writer, conservationist—and the seeming ease with which the too quickly trained doughboys of Pershing yet saved tottering Europe effectively confirmed once again the lack of need for the military in peacetime and the invincibility of the hastily mobilized citizen army in time of war.

As a constant in American history we may say that the liberal approach to civil-military affairs has been twofold: (1) *extirpation,* i.e., supporting the virtual elimination of all institutions of violence and thus abolition of the problem of civil-military relations entirely; (2) *transmutation,* i.e., when necessary to maintain an armed force, to refashion it along liberal lines so that it loses its autocratic characteristics. Transmutation has been the attitude during war, as extirpation has been the objective during peace. Transmutation may be further seen at work during peace in the use of the Army for public works activities (Army Corps of Engineers).[23] For the military, this double-edged policy has meant to conform or die.

THE CONSERVATIVE CONSTITUTION

The second constant, the conservative but ambiguous Constitution, has provided the structure for ordering the liberal ideal with respect to the military. As earlier suggested, the Constitution has not so much provided for civilian control as for the separation and spreading of powers. The result has been especially noticeable in the development of the militia, which we know today as the National Guard. Civilian control has been hampered in two ways. First, Constitutional sanction is given a semimilitary force which can never be completely subordinated to military discipline nor completely removed from political entanglements. The tragedy at Kent State (1970) is a case in point.

> The consequence at Kent State was that troops in Army uniform, using Army guns and bullets and trained at Army expense, applied deadly force in a manner and under procedures contrary to Army doctrine.[24]

And four students died. The resulting controversy spawned a most dubious Grand Jury action and engulfed the state and nation to the highest levels in political recrimination.

Secondly, to dual control by state and national governments is given Constitutional approval, which necessarily involves the military in politics. A past president of the National Guard Association has freely admitted that

> were it not for these [militia] clauses, the Guard and the National Guard Association would not exist with the influence which they have today. . . . [It is] "an empire within an empire." [25]

The Guard does not forget that it has the longest continuous history of any military organization in America, proudly tracing its lineage back to the Old North Regiment formed in Massachusetts in 1636. Other contingents were formed as need occasioned in the growing colonies, and the outbreak of the Revolution brought many old and new ones under Washington's command. Though often indispensable,[26] the militia units at times received the lash of Washington's bitter contempt for their divided loyalties and undisciplined ways. Despite his earnest insistence that Congress prepare "a uniform and well-digested plan" for the continuance of the militia units in the new nation, they were simply and loosely recognized in the First and Second Amendments to the Bill of Rights, and in the Federal Militia Act of 1792, as the right and privilege of local communities to form protective associations. Although Congress in 1795 gave the President authority to call out the militia in times of emergency, this was subject to veto by the state governors concerned.

From 1872 to 1903 the militia was under state control in time of peace and dual control in time of war. Since 1903 it has been under dual control in peace and federal control in war. The latter development represented a victory over the Army for the citizen-soldier concept. It also symbolized the states vs. the Federal Government issue. All in all the Guard has the best of two worlds. Under the militia clause it is protected against the Federal Government in peacetime. Under a 1933 act which makes it a reserve component of the Army it is assured a prominent role in war.[27] As peculiarly the child of Congress, its lobbying power on Capitol Hill is prodigious.[28] This, plus the always diverse pressures from the states, make the Guard almost impervious to reform, as former Secretary of Defense McNamara discovered in five consecutive years of attempting needed changes in the institution. Called to serve two masters, the Guard has found ways to make the inevitable tensions and anomalies of such an arrangement work to its own advantage.

The separation of powers is also noticeable in the Federal Forces, being

a perpetual invitation, if not an irresistible force, drawing military leaders into political conflicts. Consequently, it has been a major hindrance to the development of military professionalism and civilian control in the United States.[29]

The framers of the Constitution in general reproduced the division of authority over the military which prevailed in England and its colonies in the mid-eighteenth century, with the President inheriting the powers of the English king and Congress the powers of Parliament. But the differences were also significant. Congress was given the power to make war and the President was by office, not by profession, made the "Commander in Chief of the Army and Navy of the United States." [30] The latter provision has been the subject of much debate and continuous reinterpretation. As Commander in Chief his specific powers and functions are left open and may range from the extremely broad power to conduct war to the narrowly restricted power of military command. It has also invited presidential expansion into the legislative domain at the expense of Congress (Lincoln, Roosevelt, Johnson, and now Nixon), which has furthered conflict and indirectly encouraged military involvement in political controversy.

A balanced pattern of executive civil-military relations is not facilitated by our constitutional system. The lines of authority and responsibility are not clear and direct between the President and his Secretaries, the military chiefs and Congress. The historic retention of his powers as Commander in Chief by every President has tended to push the executive structure beyond a simple coordinate or shared exercise of power, toward a definitely vertical pattern. The Secretaries and military chiefs both have interests and precedents in seeking the ear of the President direct and exclusively. And Congress naturally resents the periodic excursions into territory normally reserved to itself. The results are continual tension and varying degrees of inefficiency and ineffectiveness. On the other hand, this may be, as Huntington suggests, a reasonable price to pay for other benefits of our constitutional system. "Foreign countries may have more effective systems of civilian control but no country has as effective a system of restraints upon arbitrary political power or such a unique balance of executive unity and legislative diversity." [31]

The rising fear today, however, is that the swiftly accelerating speed of modern technology and the absolute nature of the threat of nuclear extinction are demanding instant readiness and executive decisiveness to such a degree that it may destroy the historic, if often irritating, balance with Congress.

III. THREE STRANDS OF AMERICAN
MILITARY TRADITION

The indigestibility of the military in American society, and the conflicts which this has engendered in the body politic, have profoundly affected the nature and growth of the military

to its present peak of unrivaled efficiency and power. This
growth, erratic but conclusive, may be traced via three distinct
but interwoven strands of the American military tradition:
technicism, populism, and professionalism.

TECHNICISM

Very early this interest, which owed much to Jefferson and
was already advanced in the culture of early nineteenth-century
America, emphasized the specialized sciences and mechanical
crafts that contributed to the soldier's trade: civil engineering,
ship design, cartography, hydrography. Technicism was essentially a principle of specialization, calling for the mastery of
technical detail and application which paved the way to
modern "technology." Before the Civil War, the good military
officer did not so much share in a separatistic military aptitude
which bound him to all his brethren-in-arms as he was expert
in a technical skill which brought him close to civilians prac-
ticing the same specialty. Thus the military structure was
actually divided into subgroups each of which generally had
more in common with a similar segment of the civilian community than it had with others in the same uniform. In this the
military was following Jefferson whose personal interest in
science supported his dream of a well-trained citizen army that
would abolish the distinction "between the civil and the
military which it is for the happiness of both to abolish." [32]
Enamored of the French, their lead was followed in stressing
fortifications, artillery, and engineering, which helped to produce in the Army and its newly created West Point a high
level of technical and scientific achievement. In fact, West
Point was founded as an engineering school, only one fifth of
the military university urged by Hamilton. It was "a technical
institute designed to serve the entire nation as a practical
scientific school, not a professional academy for the military
vocation." [33] It is said that it has "produced more railroad

presidents than generals";[34] engineering was to dominate the curriculum until after the Civil War.

Technicism was even more pervasive in the Navy and until very recently[35] could be seen in the highly specialized bureaus of that service. The tradition which still lingers in the Navy that "the only place for the education of an officer is on the deck of a ship," and the long willingness of this branch of the service to leave to the Secretary the sticky business of politics, only slightly illustrate the traditional pride of technical competence that has been the naval man's deepest satisfaction.

Two effects of technicism were to be causative in their own right. The military, in relation to itself, was segmented, the services specializing in the excellence of certain functions that would encourage pride and make their eventual unification a difficult task to accomplish. On the other hand, ironically, the natural bonds fostered between specialists within and without the military were to pave the way for the quarreling military and industrial strangers of the nineteenth century to marry one another in the twentieth. Although technicians within and without the military respected one another as experts and tradesmen, the post-Civil War period had little place for the military. The rising industrial nation followed the lead of Spencerian economic philosophy and Puritan moralism in fashioning a "business pacifism" which provided an uncongenial climate for anything more than military stagnation. Social Darwinism redefined the "survival of the fittest" in economic terms and found an outspoken prophet in Andrew Carnegie, industrial tycoon, whose tireless, conscientious, and generous support of organized peace movements forced a dichotomy between militarism and industrialism.[36] Drawing together the Jeffersonian and Jacksonian strands of the past, the new business pacifism opposed the military as an antithetical way of life. The military watchwords of authority, subordination, and violence had nothing in common with a laissez-faire industrial society which "fostered in its citizens a spirit of independence, little faith in governments, hostility to arbitrary power, reliance on individual initiative, and a respect for the individuality of others." [37] For Jefferson, war had been a present reality requiring a nation in arms; for Jackson, it was a thing of the future, to be met when the emergency arose. For the business pacifist, however, war was outmoded, a contemptible, brutish method of the evolutionary past, "ethically wrong, economically ruinous, and incompatible with modern civilization." [38] Americans felt vastly superior to Europeans, still bound by "war ideals," and they pressed for the elimination of armaments and armies.

Yet the seeds of technicism were there, dormant during the long "Dark Ages" [39] and nadir of the American military which, despite the Spanish-American War interlude, lasted until nearly the outbreak of World War I. Such men as Lieutenant William Sowden Sims, United States Navy, by persistent efforts in the face of possible court-martial,[40] encouraged the latent service capacity for technology. His were a struggling interest and a dedication which seem strangely incomprehensible in the light of President Eisenhower's taut warning and our knowledge of today's virtual marriage of industry to the military. The extent of this interdependence has been suggested, but the emotional involvement may be even more surprising. This can be readily found in not a few shipyards and other installations where cutbacks from time to time have forced civilians out of long-tenured jobs. It is not simply a matter of economics, although this is very important, but of the partnership which for many has become a way of life as surely as though they were career military or professional people. It may even have international repercussions, and can certainly affect the stock market. When the much-heralded summit meeting between Eisenhower and Khrushchev collapsed in 1960, *The New York Times* reported a stock market gain!

Traders decided that the "cold war" was due to heat up considerably in the coming months . . . and that this would mean a step-up in the nation's defense program. . . . The upshot was the most exciting week for the stock market in many months.[41]

Deeper than the economic and emotional involvement, and far more subtle, is the threat of technology itself to the spirit of men surrounded by ever more complex machinery which insists upon being used while heralding greater machines to come. This is in the nature of a contract; industry more and more reserves her favors for the military; and the military, in the dizzy spiraling of power, must use them and beg for more. The nostalgia of many old-timers for the quieter days of yore is more than the regret of having to relinquish the reins of power. It is an uneasiness with the perpetual acceleration of technicism, a warning signal which can hardly be noted by those who, like the Air Force, and growingly all the services, have known nothing else. As found by President Eisenhower, an old-timer who could hear the warning, we have here one of the most radical and potentially ominous changes in American society. The alliance, even merger in large degree, of the military with history's greatest industrial potential is new to the nation and even to the world, but despite occasional misgivings both parties give every sign of wanting to make the union permanent.

POPULARISM

If early technicism built bridges to the civilian community, which in modern technology have become a superhighway, the political popularism of Jackson sought no less than the amalgamation of the military with the body politic which in our day has become a near reality. Where Jefferson wished to educate all citizens to be soldiers, and failing that, to train well the regulars, the Jacksonians assumed that all citizens could be soldiers when needed, without training. Militant enthusiasm replaced technical competence as the requirement of the good officer. This was the anti-intellectual drive to conformity remarked upon by de Tocqueville.[42] The abolition of West Point was recommended because as an "aristocratic institution" and caste maker, it contravened the principles of the Founding Fathers and monopolized commissions in the Regular Army.[43] One long-range effect of the popular sentiment was the spreading of academy appointments throughout the nation as a matter of Congressional prerogative. But entry direct from civilian life into the higher ranks of the officer corps became so common prior to the Civil War that West Pointers were almost completely submerged.[44] This disproportion, together with lack of experience and training, had its effect on the progress of the Civil War, especially seen in "Lincoln's search for a general."

A further influence of popularism that has plagued us from time to time has been the encouragement of officers to enter politics. The Fathers were recalled as examples.[45] Prior to the Civil War an actual pattern was set by Commanding Generals of the Army,[46] one actually campaigning for the Presidency while still commanding troops.[47] The difficulties earlier touched upon concerning the separation of the powers of the President, his Secretaries, and the Armed Forces in time congealed into a type of coordinate pattern that made the Commanding General independent of the Secretary of War and directly responsible to the President.[48] The bitter quarrels of General McClellan and Secretary Stanton under Lincoln, and of General Sherman and Secretary Belknap under President Grant, foreshadowed the Truman-MacArthur dispute, the McCarthy-Army hearings, and the rough debate over reorganization of the Defense Department and unification of the Armed Forces in our own times. We have had yet another general elected President, and many military men are involved in politics, but almost without exception after leaving or retiring from the service. In general, the trend has been toward reaffirmation of the Sherman doctrine of strict neutrality in politics while in service[49] as being in closest accord with professional military standards and the security of the nation.

This has, in turn, led to rather ambiguous and differing attitudes of passivity and responsibility with respect to national policy and defense. The Army early became the handyman of the government, "the country's general servant, well-disciplined, obedient, performing civil functions . . . merely a machine, and . . . as irresponsible." [50] It was not for soldiers to question the legality of their orders. On the other hand, the Navy, limited to enforcing the national will in foreign affairs, became self-consciously "the nation's first line of defense," and proud bearer of its culture in opening up the trade lanes of the world, a favored position it would not readily yield to the later (and upstart) Air Force. Awareness of immediate responsibility for the nation's security in situations beyond easy referral and possible assistance encouraged a sense of duty beyond unquestioning obedience "to make its professional opinions known." [51] Naval officers gained experience in international diplomacy in situations that allowed greater latitude for private judgment (such as Commodore Perry's "opening" of Japan, etc.). Thus the Navy's relation to civilian control assumed a more positive, tensional role, which has been evident to the present time. The "knightly" character of the Air Force, in the beginning at least, largely preempted the romantic areas of popularism and encouraged a sense of finality in having *the* answer to the problems of security, i.e., airpower. However, all branches of the profession have agreed upon the subordination of strategy to the national policy as set by civilians.

It was the function of the civilian policy-maker to determine the ends of national policy and to allocate the resources which the military might use to achieve those ends. It was then the job of the military to apply the resources to the achievement of the goal.[52]

In the growing necessity for coordination between civilian policy makers and military achievers, the attractiveness of the power concept, once held in lonely isolation by the military, came to the fore. The writings of Hans J. Morgenthau, among others, are typical in stressing that the statesman must think of the national interest as a power among powers.[53] The treatises on peace and the polemics against war that characterized the early part of the century, gave way in our times to denunciation of "the moralism, legalism, utopianism, Wilsonianism, and sentimentalism of the American diplomatic past," by "realists" of one kind or another, if not pessimists, such as George Kennan, Reinhold Niebuhr, and John Bennett. Herman Kahn, Thomas C. Schelling, and Bernard Brodie, as specialists in nuclear theory and deterrence, added an entirely new dimension to the discussion of power. By 1955 it was apparent that the increasing attention given by colleges and universities to military affairs was largely motivated, like the military itself, by the common search for security.

This added up to a new conservatism for the nation as a whole. In 1964 Huntington was able to distinguish

in virtually all the strands of the new conservatism . . . a stress on the limitations of man, an acceptance of institutions as they were, a critique of utopianism and "solutionism," and a new respect for history and society as against progress and the individual.[54]

The years following have woven the strands more tightly into the social fabric of the nation. Disillusionment with the experienced nature of man in two world wars and two "limited" wars, our assumption of world leadership with its frustrating and despairing problems, the continuing pressures of cynical and morally relativistic Communism, the frightening experience of extremism on both sides in the civil rights and campus revolutions—these events and movements have severely shaken the old optimism of "live and let live." For a while it even seemed that because of these disruptive experiences, the civilian community was being brought much closer to the traditionally conservative military services as standard-bearers for "law and order." But the extremism has also been counterproductive for the conservative trend. The growth of the radical right with its militant ideologies and techniques and even armed groups, and now the Armed Forces with their tarnished image, have stirred up old fears and new anxieties with respect to the management of violence. To some degree we have been shocked into a radical reexamination of our very foundations as a nation. Reluctantly we are relinquishing our long-cherished illusion of peaceableness as a people and we are taking a wary second look at our well-camouflaged capacity for violence. In this process the military occupies an ambiguous position. Until the current disillusionment with our presence in Vietnam (and for many, despite that experience), the military was being discovered as less pessimistic than realistic, and often less radical than their civilian counterparts and superiors. But who can judge now?

The situation is that the image of the military officer, or regular, has undergone significant changes. Huntington made an interesting comparison of three best-selling postwar novels to illustrate this fact.[55] In 1948 appeared Norman Mailer's *The Naked and the Dead*, presenting the stereotyped regular Army officer as a fascist at heart, operating by the twin ethic of power and fear. But three years later came *From Here to Eternity*, by James Jones, whose ideals are definitely military ideals, whose heroes are true soldiers. The same year came Herman Wouk's famous *Caine Mutiny*, which after getting all possible mileage from the hated Captain Queeg, in the end defers to him in principle as basically right, while Maryk, the simple fisherman representing the Rousseauian natural goodness of man, and Keefer, the liberal intellectual, are represented as wrong. Queeg, too, is repudiated by court-martial because he failed to live up to the military ideal. The United States Navy actually emerges as the real hero! In just a few years the regular officer and the liberal intellectual had neatly changed roles. As late as 1964, on *The Defender* television program, a dramatization of the Marine Corps attempted to reverse the roles again, casting the drill instructor in the old brutal role against the nice young recruit, only to meet with instant criticism from the press.[56] Even more recently, *In Harm's Way*, by James Bassett, is admittedly a tribute to the dedication and integrity of high-ranking officers of the Navy, written from the perspective of the many who felt privileged to serve under the redoubtable Captain Rockwell ("The Rock") Torry and enthusiastically shared in his well-earned selection for admiral and command of a victorious task force against the Japanese.[57] *The Admiral*, by Martin Dibner, pleads a similar case for Captain "Hardtack Harry" Paige, who fought the "clean war" of the Pacific, "in which the only goal was victory," and became a hero back home.[58]

But the Vietnam war has slowed and soured the emerging popular face of the military. For a while, the mounting suspicion and criticism were bitterly, but discriminately, directed against the civilian policy makers (President Johnson and Secretary McNamara, in particular), and the Joint Chiefs of Staff, as engineers of a heinous system that must be changed, rather than against the soldiers in the field.[59] This might point to a growing realization that the dilemma of war and violence is rooted much deeper than simply in the man in uniform, that it rather has to do with "the system" of extreme competitiveness which engulfs his civilian brother as well. But the crescendo of hatred for "the system" has now spilled over once again to lash and to isolate military men and women themselves as though they were responsible for the evil time. The uproar on campuses across the nation against recruitment for the Armed Forces, the disestablishment of ROTC at prestige schools, the increased tempo of pillorying and buffooning everything military, perhaps most seriously the coldly inhuman treatment too often accorded individual men in uniform by their peers on campuses and city streets—these reactions have reached that pitch of violence which makes believable a recent writer's accusation that "anti-militarism has become the anti-Semitism of the intellectual community." [60]

Perhaps My Lai has been too much. The whole bitter experience of this strangest and longest of our wars has for many come to focus in this tragedy and the rash of like incidents now coming to light. Such "inhuman" revelations are frighteningly disappointing and unacceptable to liberals who may earlier have moralized our position in Vietnam, perhaps unconsciously counting upon the unspoiled and boyish goodness of the raw recruit. (After all, did not Gomer Pyle *always* win out and remain unspoiled while doing so?) Perhaps such relations are unabsorbable even by the growing communities of conservatives and "realists" who not long ago held out hope of bridging the distance between the traditionally liberal society and the conservative military. Perhaps it is war weariness and deepening disgust with the whole venture, a deep and still camouflaged disappointment with ourselves. Gomer Pyle doesn't stand a chance against the daily fare of Vietnam in our very living rooms, which tells it like it is. The screen venture of *Patton* labors to pursue the old heroic image and rather succeeds in discovering a very fallible man for whom one can feel some compassion as not really knowing the demoniac nature of the furies he so proudly unleashed. So much closer to the truth, as Sherman ("War is hell") tried long ago to tell us, is the arrogant, brutal, obscene personal reporting and appeal, "Don't judge me, be me" of Guy Sajer's European best seller, *The Forgotten Soldier*.[61] Perhaps now we are beginning to suspect the truth: the intolerably expensive cheapness of war itself. But we are not yet ready for it. One cannot help suspecting that the strongest of moves from the highest of quarters to form a volunteer service is more than economic and professional "realism." It suggests the old, perhaps still unconsciously guilty, desire to divorce the left hand from the right, indeed from the whole body, to guarantee a place for the military and its continuing activities outside the province of our conscience to confront us daily with ourselves. At the very least such a radical change could have the effect of making permanent the chasm once again opening between the military and its parent society.

PROFESSIONALISM

The protracted struggles of our generation have finally emancipated the American military from foreign models and made it "an ascendent influence in the military affairs of the world." [62] American military professionalism has given birth to flowers that have faded, but the roots are strong. After losing its great apologists, Washington and Hamilton, it came to be nurtured in the South.[63] The more static Indian frontier in the South, combined with the antebellum romantic cult of "gentleman" and the always martial ideal, encouraged early interest in the military as a vocation. In the absence of commercial and industrial opportunities the military offered a road to gentlemanly fulfillment and service. From this Southern leadership came what has been called the "Military Enlightenment," extending from Jackson to the Mexican War (1832–1846). This period saw an "outpouring of military thought and writing which was . . . unique in American history." [64] Military societies were founded, books and magazines printed, the idea of a military profession was expounded and defended. The two outstanding figures, both Virginians, Matthew Fontaine Maury and Dennis Hart Mahan, effected no lasting institutional reforms but their ideas of the science and "art of war" were to mold professionalism in the latter half of the century.

For, as was indicated earlier, the post-Civil War period was the "Dark Ages" of the American military, and it is perhaps ironical that it was just this time of bitter rejection which shaped the American professional military mind. With the sympathetic support of the South gone and industry rejecting it as illegitimate, the Navy stagnated while the Army was spread thinly along the advancing frontier against the illusive Indian. It was not only rejected and reduced,[65] but it was isolated. Like "military monks . . . they lived apart in their tiny, secluded garrisons . . . and rarely came into contact with the mass of our citizens." [66] When they did, as in performing their new strikebreaking role in the labor disputes of the latter quarter of the century, it was to increase bitterly their psychological distance from the common people.[67] Once so influential in education, West Point went its own way.[68] Assuming responsibilities abroad after the Spanish-American war, Navy men as well as Army personnel found themselves scattered and often divorced from one another and the nation which was rapidly becoming urbanized. Compelled to operate on a shoestring, technicism lagged.

But professionalism did not.

The very isolation and rejection which reduced the size of the services and hampered technological advance made these same years the most fertile, creative, and formative in the history of the American armed forces. Sacrificing power and influence, withdrawing into its own hard shell, the officer corps was able and permitted to develop a distinctive military character. The American military profession, its institutions and its ideals, is fundamentally a product of these years. No other period has had such a decisive influence in shaping . . . the American military mind. . . . The military officer who, at the end of the period of isolation, rejoined civilian society in World War I and . . . II, was a fundamentally different creature from his ancestor who had withdrawn in the 1860's.[69]

He was different because his values and outlook were basically at odds with those of the mass of his countrymen. The harsh times "had injected steel into his soul which was missing from that of the community." [70] It was this steel which would be in high demand in two world wars and a strange "cold war" to follow.

In the positive, creative role thus posed for the military in isolation, several names stand forth, who, unlike their Enlightenment counterparts, were to revolutionize the structure and intent of the military. The most famous of these is General William T. Sherman, a Civil War hero who dramatically and firmly eschewed politics. Commanding General of the Army for fifteen years, he sparked the professional reform movement. Being particularly aware of the need of military education, he fathered Fort Leavenworth as an infantry and cavalry school, and espoused a complete system of military education at West Point to combine both liberal and professional military subjects, with advanced schools to give specialized knowledge and preparation for higher posts. More significantly, perhaps, was the high tone of professional dedication absolutely divorced from politics which he exampled and encouraged throughout the armed services. This political neutrality was to last until after World War II.

General Emory Upton contributed heavily through his writings to renewed interest in European professionalism, especially Prussianism. Endorsed by Sherman, his *Military Policy of the United States* (1904) became "the Bible of the Regular Army in its disputes with the militia advocates." [71] The "Uptonians" were to be reckoned with down to the present time. Enamored of the logic and efficiency of the autonomous German war machine, they believed that democracy was ill-equipped by comparison and probably unable to maintain an effective army without definite strictures on civilian control.

National characteristics, which become governmental ones in a democracy like ours, make it impossible to organize and discipline an effective army from the point of view of military experts.[72]

But American professionalism could not rest in such despair. A way must be found within the content of a democracy which insisted upon civilian control for an effective military force. General John M. Schofield, a former Secretary of War, discovered the solution in his voluntary subordination to the Secretary and President as only the Chief of Staff. He thus rejected the Clausewitz-Upton absolutist concept of war

because in a democracy only the responsible representatives of the people could determine the purposes of a war, and such determination was involved in the way the war was to be fought. Differing choices of military means could alter the scope and the nature and intent of a war, and therefore the ultimate choice even of military means must reside with the civilians.[73]

It remained for Elihu Root, Secretary of War after the Spanish-American War, to incorporate the general staff concept into extensive reforms to bring the military establishment up to date in the twentieth century as a professional but democratically oriented body.[74]

The making of the American military mind was peculiarly the product of the years between the Civil War and World War I. The long period of isolation, only briefly interrupted by the Spanish-American War and the Neo-Hamiltonian honeymoon, had welded the military forces into an integrated, though small, whole, "with a stable pattern of belief and a fixed way of looking at the world." [75] The elements of this military way of looking at things, the military ethic, may be summarized under the following four headings:

1. War became a science, a distinct field of study, and the practice of that science was the only purpose of the Armed Forces. They existed to fight. In this they were uniquely different from civilian professionals but they were professional nonetheless in the exact sense in which Huntington defines the concept "as a special type of vocation" whose "distinguishing characteristics . . . are its expertise, responsibility, and corporateness." [76] The importance of the genius, such as Napoleon, gave way to the German model of the machine, the "triumph of organized mediocrity." [77]

2. In hardening and distinct contrast to the early and prolonged liberal, pacifistic society, the military emphasized a pessimistic or "realistic" view of man. Man's pride, acquisitiveness and avarice made war inevitable. Individualism was scorned and unquestioning obedience to the group was emphasized as the only alternative to anarchy.

In contrast to early military thinking, history came to be stressed and the military virtues glorified: loyalty, duty, discipline, and hierarchy.

3. In sharp contrast to the officer corps attitude of the 1830's, politics, from the Civil War on, were renounced. "The concept of an impartial, nonpartisan, objective career service, loyally serving whatever administration or party was in power, became the ideal for the military profession." [78] In the main this has obtained to the present, although the post-World War II reorganization debate encouraged some departure from complete silence, and at a deeper level fears as to the incompatibility of democracy with professional integrity have been felt and occasionally voiced. Moreover, a significant number of Reserve military officers have openly pushed their own military responsibilities and advancement while pursuing political careers. Senator Barry Goldwater, a Reserve Major General in the Air Force, is a ready example.

4. The Armed Forces were convinced of the moral superiority of the power ethic over the self-serving commercialism of the general public. Unconsciously harking back as far as Plato, they despised the frenetic rush of civilians for material gain and rejoiced that they were free "from the sordidness and misery of the money-getting trade." [79] The losing appeals for universal military training after each of the great wars have only confirmed the military in its conscientious certainty that the country needs the virtues of the military ethic as much as the Armed Forces need trained men. If anything, this attitude has been strengthened by the welter of events in recent years which have seemed to indicate that our values have evaporated and we have lost our way in a confusion of voices shouting contradictory directions.

For brief moments following World Wars I and II it seemed possible to identify the military with their civilian world, but it did not last. Despite intensive efforts on the part of the professionals after World War I to prove the values of the military establishment for all kinds of civilian needs and projects, the public was not listening. By 1927 the Cadet Yearbook could complain that "there is still prejudice in civil life against the West Pointer." [80] All the varied military oppositions came to the fore: the rugged individualism of pioneer stock, the bitter experiences of Old World immigrants with military aristocracy, the lingering pacifistic business community.

The triumphs of antimilitarism were not due to Bolshevism, but to the natural apathy of the American people, their inherent dislike for war, their linking of the military with war, and their faith in a future of peaceful progress. The Neo-Hamiltonian compromise was impossible in the postwar world. The opposition was not a few pacifists and radicals. It was America itself.[81]

IV. THE AMBIVALENCE DEEPENS

Rejected as in the previous century, the military retreated again into isolation. But the insulation this time was far less complete, and the tumbling events called the military to center stage more quickly than anyone, except perhaps the military itself, dreamed possible, and their stay was to be longer than even they could have predicted. What the American military could not do, with either naturalness or impunity, the military pressures of other nations could and did do most effectively: force the radical reorientation of our total outlook and with it the reorganization of our entire economy in terms of national defense upon a permanently indefinite scale. The once optimistic, liberal society found itself the island in an illiberal, irrational world. This time the problems were not "solved" overnight and the sometimes prophetic, realistic quality of the military would finally gain a hearing. This time the differences between the American military and its host society were far less pronounced, and perhaps weightiest of all, industry found the military much more profitable as an ally than as a whipping boy. Yet even a turn to the Right by the American society in these latter and troubled years has not really made the modern military seem "as American as apple pie." The Armed Forces are again in disfavor. Is this the same deep, inner, traditional American suspicion of the military reasserting itself? But this time the Armed Forces cannot so easily, probably cannot at all, be pushed aside and forgotten, for their entanglement goes very deep, into the subsoil of the economy itself. It is significant that in this new situation of emotional but hardly economic rejection, the military faces renewed isolation, but under the deliberately appealing guise of greater professionalism and higher pay, i.e., the volunteer concept. It is also significant that military leaders and thinkers are not nearly so enamored of this prospect as their civilian leaders.

What, now, is the inner nature of this soaring power which the American military holds and exercises, and which has become so intertwined and synchronized with the very functions of the body politic as to affect daily the nature of American man and the future of democracy?

PART TWO

THE ELEMENTS

Chapter 4

The Priority of Reason

I. DEFINITIONS

THE NATURE OF POWER

If we are to understand the inner nature of military power, we must begin with the nature of power itself, of which military power is a certain species. But the word "power" is so common to our language and experience that it is not easy to track it to its lair. This very fact, however, provides a clue—its commonality. In one way or another everything seems involved with the notion of power. This is true. And before the separate elements of military power are exposed to view we need to see that power, even as coercive, is always present. Paul Tillich put it simply—and profoundly: "Being is the power of being. . . . It is being actualizing itself over against the threat of non-being."[1] This is philosophical language to say that power is the most basic description or quality of reality. It may be useful to pursue this definition of power to some depth to find that ground from which military power also springs.

It seems redundant to say that power is being, being is power, but the terms describe by their implications. If being as such cannot be defined (because in every definition being is presupposed), yet certain terms that we habitually use can point to being in a metaphorical way. And, conversely, such "pointers" are themselves illumined in the process. Power implies "something over which it proves its power," [2] and being, by the very fact that it *is*, establishes itself over nonbeing, which is logically and existentially possible only as the negation of being. Being, then, does not struggle with nonbeing as with something foreign altogether, but in actualizing itself in the particular expressions of finiteness includes and at the same time points beyond its own limitations. Power is the promise and the process of being actualized, "the possibility of self-affirmation in spite of internal and external negation. It is the possibility of overcoming non-being. Human power is the possibility of man to overcome non-being infinitely." [3]

In this neutral, all-pervading sense, power, then, is the persuasion of reality—the convincing that this particular exists—from the most infinitesimal of neutrons or the flicker of an eyelash on a ballroom floor, to the incomprehensible energy of star-suns or the complex, intricate social relationships of human love, business, and politics. Power, then, as the expression of being, can never be avoided. It can only be recognized, accepted, countered, adapted, used. As the self-actualizing expression of being, always in particular and thus finite forms, power is both dynamic and hierarchical. A stone is not a mountain, although in certain circumstances, thrown or catapulted, it might bring immensely more and deadly power to bear upon the head of an unfortunate person. Realities are unequal and the inequities themselves are vastly unstable. Power expresses the infinite encounter of being with being and "the ever-changing balance which is the result of those encounters." Life, and especially human life, because it transcends itself, is the most fascinating arena for the expression of being as power.

It pushes forward, it runs ahead, and it encounters life in another human individual which also pushes forward, or . . . withdraws or

. . . stands and resists. In each case another constellation of powers
is the result. . . . One transforms the resisting powers or one adapts
oneself to them. . . . These processes are going on in every moment
of life, in all relations of all beings. They go on between . . . man
and nature . . . man and man . . . individuals and groups, between
groups and groups.[4]

In the human community, power, as might be expected, is
often defined in terms of intention and purpose, especially to
control other men. Thus Harvey Seifert defines power as "the
ability to achieve purpose," [5] and John Bennett, seeking as he
says to come "closer to the ordinary observation of power," and
modeling upon Bertrand Russell, defines it "as the capacity to
produce intended effects." [6] This definition allows a broad
spectrum to cover what Russell calls "naked power," i.e., sheer
coercion as well as forms of persuasion.[7] Hans Morgenthau
expands upon this conception: "Power may comprise anything
that establishes and maintains the control of man over man"
and thus

covers all social relationships which serve that end, from physical
violence to the most subtle psychological ties by which one mind
controls another. Power covers the domination of man by man, both
when it is disciplined by moral ends and controlled by constitutional
safeguards . . . and when it is that untamed and barbaric force
which finds its laws in nothing but its own strength and its sole
justification in its aggrandizement.[8]

Bennett, rightly I think, finds Morgenthau "missing" something in limiting power, as it appears, to the control or attempted control of man over man. However, I think that
Bennett, too, does not do full justice to the complexity and
totality of power as the expression of being in all its diversity
in the human community. This is of especial consequence in
understanding military power, which is considerably more than
"naked power" to which "persuasion" may be added. Power,
military or otherwise, is never "naked"; it is the expression of
being in its complexity and profundity and is revealed in some
kind of form. The inanimate and concrete—weapons and

geography, for instance—are important as loci of military power, and the unconscious and irrational in motivation and behavior, as well as the conscious and purposive in strategy and execution, are expressions of power. All power, as Walter Millis has observed,[9] expresses coercion (in the minimal claim for recognition as reality), and thus has a legitimate or at least expedient "right" to affirm itself, to become what it already is.

This ontological analysis of the nature of power provides a kind of headquarters from which patrols must now be sent out into the wilderness of the vagaries and misconceptions of the nature of power as military. They will return with the report that the many and the different forms of power are at bottom one and often the same, that military power is an expression of being, although particularized in ways which justify its claim to uniqueness.

THE NATURE OF MILITARY POWER

Military power, certainly, is a special use of and perhaps a special kind of power. It has generally been distinguished from simple police power, and it can hardly be equated with mob violence. Let us consider the directions in which it may now be defined.

John Bennett was probably not attempting a strict definition of military power in equating it with Bertrand Russell's "naked power," for he quickly allows for its combination with "persuasion." [10] Rather similarly, Rear Admiral Henry E. Eccles speaks of "military force [as] the ultimate form of pressure." [11] But he distinguishes "pressure" from "attraction" (which seems close to Bennett's "persuasion") as also exerted by power. The recognition of "naked power," "ultimate pressure," or what might be called "raw force," the untempered expression of being, is better expressed by Walter Millis in defining war— the historic business of the military—as *organized* violence involving armed forces with a command." [12] Samuel Huntington, in like vein, refers to military personnel as "managers of violence." [13] In all these approaches to definition it is to be noted that expressions such as "raw," "naked," "ultimate," and "violent" are not permitted to stand alone. Military power is "*organized* violence involving armed forces with a command, with weapons, and all the rest of it." [14] So particular is Millis at this point that he finds it difficult to "accommodate the other types of aggression such as subversion, stealth, pulling down governments that you don't like, without resorting to military violence"; these are "perhaps the kind of substitute for war that we will ultimately come to." [15] Presumably those involved in such pressures are hardly expressing military power, which requires a more formalized organization and structure. I think Millis has confused the traditional accretions and evidences of military organization with the factor of organization itself as fundamentally expressive of military power. But the intent is clear: military power is not mob violence.

In the spirit of Millis' cautious restrictiveness, I think a third factor, implicit in both Millis and Huntington and probably in Bennett, needs to be spelled out: the sense of social responsibility. It is significant that it is a military leader and thinker who clearly sets this forth, Lieutenant General Sir John Winthrop Hackett, British Army: "The function of the profession of arms is the ordered application of force in the resolution of a social problem." [16] Somewhat earlier, in the Lees Knowles Lectures of 1962, General Hackett had stressed that "the *ordered* application of force [is] under an *unlimited liability*. It is the unlimited liability which sets the man at arms apart." [17] In gathering up these distinguishing aspects of military power we may say that *military power is violence organized in an ultimate fashion on behalf of a state or society.* This, it seems to me, differentiates military power from police power, which is considerably less ultimate in organization, objectives, and weaponry, and it leaves open the question of forms and techniques. These may include so-called irregular, even guerrilla-type movements which seek to apply "ultimate pressure" in an organized, if unrecognized, fashion, but still on behalf of an existing state or society *or one which they seek to create.*

II. THE RATIONAL EXPRESSED IN WESTERN MILITARY HISTORY

With this general definition of military power as it appears to us in institutionalized and even noninstitutionalized forms, we can proceed to a more analytical identification of those elements which historically have distinguished the military as a clearly recognized form of power in human society. Contrary to the persistent image of the military as nonintellectual, the first insistence of those whose lives are identified with its use, traditionally and more profoundly so today, is that it is *rational.* The claim is ancient, persistent, and universal. Indeed, the *intelligent* use of naked power or violence clearly lies at the heart of the modifier "organized." But the cruel reasons for wars and the harsh excesses in war have often occupied the attention of man so as to create a stereotype of irrationality for the military that is not far from the blood lust of the mob. Long ago Aristophanes gave agonizing attention to the phenomenon of war in his derisive comedy *Peace.* He echoed the groans of Athenians still bearing the endless burdens of war some sixty years after Marathon and Salamis. In disgust the gods themselves have moved away, and when Trygaeus asks why, Hermes replies:

> Because they got so angry with you Greeks.
> Rented the whole establishment to War,
> And gave him a free hand to deal with you.
> They moved upcountry—far as they could go—
> To where they couldn't see you fellows fight,
> And couldn't hear your prayers, you hypocrites!
> . . . you never failed to vote for war,
> Whenever we put peace within your grasp.[18]

Freud tried to equate war with a "death instinct" in man,[19] and Toynbee has sorrowfully and angrily denounced war as indeed the decimator of civilizations.[20] William James was sickened by "the irrationality of it all" and especially disappointed that it should overwhelm the rational Greeks.[21] The general ruin of war as due to irrationalism and naked violence has received much specific support from numerous psychoanalytic and personality studies in our own day, from Maslow's theory that man craves the "optimum stimulation" of war as "a peak experience,"[22] through the projection-displacement mechanisms favored by Durbin and Bowlby,[23] to Levinson's "authoritarian personality,"[24] and Gordon Allport's "role of expectancy."[25] Important as these possibilities and insights are, they have had the effect of beclouding the primary role of intelligence and the exercise of the rational in military power. In his monumental *A Study of War,* Quincy Wright notes that war seems to be equated with civilization, and the more complex the society, the greater the warlikeness.[26] In *Men in Arms: A History of Warfare and Its Interrelations with Western Society,* the authors contrast primitive conflict with war in civilized societies at the very point of the rational. Primitive warfare is static, highly individualistic, and nonrational in the sense that it involves little or no planning, makes little or no advance in weapons or strategy, and is generally undertaken for glory or revenge rather than for economic or material gain.[27] Thus it is suggested that war arises to meet the requirement of civilization for organization and material progress. Indeed, Walter Bagehot goes so far as to claim that "civilization begins, because the beginning of civilization is a military advantage."[28] There is no need to claim so much, and Montross in his *War Through the Ages* is content to assert that "anthropologists are fairly well agreed that war is one of the youngest of human institutions, an outgrowth of civilization rather than savagery."[29] This is not to claim that any specific military action is "reasonable" or that war is not often irrational. But the military as an institution organizes and uses its power according to a certain logic and rational intention. Wars are generally premeditated and certainly those who fight them select goals and follow plans which involve to the highest degree the capacity for the abstract. This is abundantly evident early in the history of Western thought.

THE BRILLIANT GREEKS

The Greeks tried to "understand war" and laid claim to the priority of the rational in military power. One of the first historians, Thucydides, was propelled into his self-assigned task from his vantage point as a general of the Athenian forces and admiral of the Greek fleet. He once defined military success as a combination of "good judgment and money." [30] But, then, his own seamen, coming in and out of the harbors of Athens, were reminded by the last rays of the sun glancing like golden spears from the magnificent golden statue of Athena, standing thirty feet high on the Acropolis, panoplied in full armor, her shield bearing the head of the Medusa, that the protector of their beloved city was the renowned goddess of wisdom, sprung full grown and armed from the very head of Zeus, father of the gods. Indeed, it is significant that "the germ[s] of all future European military development" are to be found among the free Greeks, citizens bound by laws of their own making to almost lifelong military service.[31] The phalanx was perhaps the first "civilized" fighting body, well suited to the molecular structure of Greek society, allowing for the individual hoplite's pride of equipment as well as skillful cooperation with his neighbors in presenting an impenetrable and awesomely moving wall against the enemy. The elements of tactics, i.e., line, column, and square, were employed and refined, for a while at the expense of generalship which was not encouraged by punishment for honest failure.[32] Epaminondas, in his famous victory over the Spartans at Leuctra (371 B.C.), helped to correct this by unexpectedly weighting his left wing and rolling up the right of the enemy in a surprise departure from the Hellenic past.[33] By this time, Sparta, earliest of the Hellenic democracies, was already evidencing the brittle failure of a fixed military state which had begun as a highly rational attempt to organize minutely and timelessly the whole structure of its society. Refined to perfection, the army became "so precious an instrument that one aim of Spartan diplomacy was to avoid using it." [34] Hence, at the critical juncture, having removed the rising threat of Athens, Sparta turned its back upon peace by empire and gave itself wholly to law, affirming the priority of the rational in military power but in terms of structure rather than dynamism.[35]

Meanwhile, to the north, in the fastnesses of Macedonia, a new military machine was being created which in innovation, strategy, and generalship would become a model on the earth, the genius of the Greek mind applied to power. Philip's war machine was the first national standing army, employing selective service for set periods, and the first artillery arm in the ancient world.[36] Inherited by Alexander, it was perfected as a truly professional army in every sense of the word, being the first balanced force of historic times.[37] It included a staff, engineering corps, and baggage train, in addition to the three cooperative arms of infantry, cavalry, and artillery. Alexander, more than any previous commander, exhibited the genius of generalship. Still studied for their masterful strategy[38] are his unerring campaigns, fantastic sieges, total victories, the use of the knockout blow by employment of cavalry at the decisive moment, and the patience of relentless pursuit. Alexander learned well from Aristotle, that master of the logical, the inductive, and the meticulous. It is probable that he also had before him a military classic by a countryman, the *Anabasis* of Xenophon, which is the account of the retreat of the Ten Thousand from the very heart of the Persian Empire—a brilliantly detailed triumph of cool reason against incredible odds.[39] Alexander accepted the risk of clearly unacceptable odds against the Persian hosts at Issus and Arbela, and against the wily Indians on the Hydaspes with their amazing elephants. He turned these adverse odds to magnificent advantage by the deliberate use of reason as audacious as it was careful and cunning. Alexander sought always the moral surprise. He confused and convinced the vastly superior enemy to yield to panic, and to this end he enlisted every stratagem of reason backed by meticulous observation and scientific planning, all executed with the creative verve of an artist.

THE PRAGMATIC ROMANS

The Romans, pragmatic and methodical, always barbarian by Greek standards, had small interest in the abstract and did not single out the rational very specifically as a quality of military power. Vegetius is perhaps typical when he says that the Romans conquered the world through "no other cause than continual training, exact observance of discipline, . . . and unwearied cultivation of the other arts of war." [40] But the oblique reference to "the other arts of war" is at least suggestive that military power could not be bound to the mundane and predictable. The penchant for statesmanship and the development of law characterize the priority of policy in the Roman building and use of military power. "Policy" may be said to be the reasoned course of action of the polis. It is generally prudential and advantageous. The long succession of leaders of the growing republic, and the ease with which they often exchanged the toga for the sword, sometimes in tandem leading their men to battle,[41] emphasized the civil and political nature of the military and the usually cool subordination of tactics and passions to policies and reason. The thirteen-year struggle with Hannibal, especially the "masterly inactivity" of Fabius, and the brilliant Ilerda campaign of Caesar in

Spain by which he gained the surrender of an army of seventy thousand without the loss of a single life,[42] illustrate the Romans' understanding of military power as the rational extension of national policies, unheralded but vitally necessary at the point of prudence, patience, and practicality.

It is in the Byzantines, inheritors of the Eastern Roman Empire, that the implicitly rational is made explicit and crowned with recognition. This remarkable society[43] devised a defensive technique of survival for a thousand years, against perhaps the greatest succession of implacable enemies any people have ever faced, and in doing so provided a bulwark behind which a nearly defenseless Europe was permitted six centuries to develop its civilization along Western lines. "Cool skill and intellect, . . . less . . . muscular than cerebral audacity" [44] characterized its power. The "valor of the mind," essentially Greek, had only disdain for the erratic and brutish chivalry of the West and with great professional pride the Byzantines tailored their tactics to their different foes, made a science of the strategy of trickery, and almost always subordinated power to the humane in treatment of the wounded and the moderation of objectives.[45] The noble families, politically responsive, were well educated and heavily committed to the armed forces. They made their contribution not only in shrewd and superb generalship but in the creation of military textbooks, such as Leo's *Tactica* and Maurice's *Strategicon,* which virtually became Byzantine weapons of war in the Dark Ages and models for the rational conduct of field operations for centuries to come.

CHARLEMAGNE AND THE CHURCH

With the exception of the East Romans, the Middle Ages show us sustained military power only briefly in Charlemagne whose "intelligent military reforms" changed the Frankish dependence upon bulk to something approaching reasoned organization and strategy, and thereby "put an end to the chaos of three centuries and built up the first adequate system of defense the West had known since the fall of Rome." [46] The church also applied reason in a restraining role with her concept of the just war and the Truce of God, and through the development of substitutes for fratricidal conflict such as the lethal tournament and the Crusades. Near the end of the era, in the rise of the Swiss, we have a revival of infantry[47] under a democratic conciliar command which has been compared with that of the West Romans early in the Republic.[48] Unfortunately, "the army looked upon itself as a democracy entitled to direct proceedings of its ministry." [49] This excessive emphasis upon the value of everybody's ideas undermined discipline and finally froze the Swiss, like the ancient Spartans, into a single stereotyped method with similar disastrous results in a more rapidly changing world.

MODERN EUROPEAN MODELS:
MACHIAVELLI, NAPOLEON, CLAUSEWITZ

In Machiavelli (1469–1527), the "first man to write about the significance of modern warfare and to portray it accurately," [50] politics is divorced from morality, and success is reduced to stark and nearly naked force. But reason is all the more in the ascendancy as the expedient and sole guide. The unlimited justification of force is matched by the unlimited use of reason for its efficient and total application. Goaded by religious or racial fanaticism, which was ideological in structure, military power became brutal enough in the Thirty Years' War to rival the inhumanity of this century's Hitlerian death camps. The terror illustrates what Kahn has significantly called "the rationality of the irrational." [51] Between these two events military power in the Western world has oscillated from restraint induced by revulsion for the Thirty Years' and Napoleonic Wars to the mass armies and professionalism that are also legacies of Napoleon. Grotius and Vattel present a classic argument based upon the law of nations and the concept of the just war for limitation in the use of military power.[52] For a time tactics succumbed to drill, and battles became so stilted and infrequent that Marshal Saxe could claim that it is not only possible, but reasonable, that "a general can wage war all his life without being compelled to do" battle.[53] About this time the drillmaster Jean Martinet, by his insistence upon at least five years of practice for the marching, wheeling soldier, made him again too precious to kill.[54] Vauban, the siegecraft master, organized the first engineering corps of uniformed soldiers. Their operations, combined with other arms, followed such intricate and accepted rules of etiquette as to make surrender as rational as checkmate in a game of chess if one were convinced by superior fortifications and dispositions of troops.[55] Henri Jomini, following Napoleon, but not a little indebted to Vauban, sees war not as a state of confusion for personal genius, but a field of human activity subject to rules, such as initiative, maneuver, concentration, mobility, surprise, and rapid pursuit.[56]

Napoleon, who rightly claimed for himself "profound genius," credits unity of command and resolution for his victories. But his "resolution" is informed by his "intelligence [which] should be clear as the lens of a telescope. . . . A general should never paint pictures [of a situation]." [57] Again he says: "In war nothing is gained except by calculation. Whatever has not been profoundly meditated is totally ineffectual." Indeed, this is what military science is all about: "First calculating all the possibilities and then . . . making an almost mathematically exact allowance for accident." And

this apportioning of knowledge and accident can take place only in the head of a genius, for without it there can be no creation— and surely the greatest improvization of the human mind is that which gives existence to the non-existent[58]. . . . It is not a spirit which suddenly reveals to me what I have to say or do . . . —it is reflection, meditation.[59]

Analysts of his campaigns credit his decline to deviation from this very principle. This is seen especially in the futile Russian adventure, "since history punishes stupidity even more swiftly than evil." [60]

Napoleon was a child of the Enlightenment. There was also plenty of antimilitary thought floating about during the period in persons such as Voltaire, Fichte, Rousseau, Kant, and others who opposed standing armies as "caste ridden, . . . composed of automatons, the bulwark of the absolute monarchy, . . . [and] contrary to nature, rights of man, and Reason." Nevertheless, it was the degenerate particular form and not the universal possibility of military power to which they objected. Rousseau called upon the Swiss as a model, and all were encouraged by the American revolutionaries. A "natural" army, on call and disbanding after a war, was seen as "composed of all able-bodied citizens, equal in arms," under the control of reason.[61]

It is in Karl von Clausewitz (1780–1831) that the absolutes of force and reason meet with that decisiveness and yet ambiguity which made this Prussian general perhaps the most quoted and misunderstood military theorist of all time. War, he wrote in his masterwork *Vom Kriege* ("On War"), is

a wonderful trinity, composed of the original violence of its elements, hatred and animosity, which may be looked upon as blind instinct; of the play of probabilities and chance, which make it a free activity of the soul; and of the subordinate nature of a political instrument, by which it belongs purely to reason.[62]

Along the lines of Kant's *Ding an sich* ("Thing-in-itself"), Clausewitz assumed "the existence of an archetypal or absolute form of war, toward which all military operations should be directed." [63] He thus used an absolute abstract yardstick to measure the highly concrete operations of military power in war. It is for this reason that "violence must be pushed to its utmost bounds" (in the initial, primary terms of the abstract), and "moderation would be an absurdity." [64] Yet reason is not only pure but practical and recognizes that "war is not made with an abstraction but with a reality. . . . The Art of War . . . has to deal with living and moral forces, the consequence of which is that it can never attain the absolute and positive." [65] Military power serves always as an instrument of policy, "not to be regarded as an independent thing but as a political instrument. . . . This is the only means of unlocking the great book and making it intelligible." [66]

But the seedbed which is Clausewitz in rank and luxuriant growth has pitted reason against reason. Montross, acknowledging this dark side of the great theorist, says:

And if Clausewitz fathered the most bloody and wasteful era of warfare in modern times, it is because lesser minds accepted his philosophy rather than his tactics, his flashing phrases rather than his sober modifications.[67]

The *Kriegsakademie* of Clausewitz, in which the first modern, systematic studies of war eventuated in his classic, became the model for French and American schools.[68] At West Point, Dennis Hart Mahan, a young cadet who studied military history a la Clausewitz, offered a rationale for the academic type of training, and insisted that officers needed to know principles over techniques. With the exception of Robert E. Lee, who graduated earlier than Mahan, his students numbered the top commanders in the Civil War which followed shortly.[69] In that war and two world wars yet to come, curiously, tragically, reason was carried to rationalization, a kind of reasoning after the fact which can apply and then justify power in its most radical forms. As E. H. Carr has said in another and parallel connection,[70] "now human reason, having challenged and destroyed all other values, ends in turning the same weapons against itself."

The use and misuse of reason often go hand in hand and are hardly distinguishable at times. *Ideology,* which is the systematizing of ideas whether or not they are true or valid, has been a heady factor in American war-making from Revolutionary times, and shows clearly as the springboard to action. "If you want war," said William Graham Sumner, "nourish a doctrine . . . because doctrines get inside a man's own reason and betray him against himself. Civilized men have done their fiercest fighting for doctrines." [71] Witness the Civil War: Grant and Sherman, identified with brute power and mass tactics, are yet its great originals. Sherman was a college president who brought to his harsh task a "well-stocked mind" and achieved a position closer to Mahan's professional image than did his superior. Yet he was probably more ruthless, while providing a rationale for the unlimited nature of war, defining it a la Clausewitz, estimating carefully the psychology of the enemy, stressing "the rightful law and authority" of the government in Washington.[72] "Above all he understood that he was engaged in a people's war," [73] something new, although preshadowed in both the American Revolution and the Napoleonic wars. Similarly, Grant's greatness as a commander may be attributed to the fact that "he was the first federal general 'to see that it was the mind of the south we had to conquer, not alone fortifications and territory.' " [74] Grant paid the same tribute to his troops at Shiloh: "Men who knew what they were fighting for . . . must have been more than equal to men who fought merely because they were brave." [75]

AMERICAN FORMULAS

The search for a truly American formula for the maintenance and use of military power continued through the late nineteenth and early twentieth centuries. Major General John Pope and John M. Schofield, Secretary of War after Stanton's resignation in 1868, and later Commanding General of the national forces, both stressed the need for understanding between Army and people, and reason over passion in planning and operations. Schofield had held a chair of natural philosophy at Washington University in St. Louis. He practiced his own teaching by voluntarily subordinating himself while Commanding General to act in effect as chief of staff to the Secretary of War and the President.[76] Elihu Root, and Generals Leonard Wood, John Palmer, and George Marshall carried forward reforms that bore the strong imprint of the rational. In "Marshall: The Tempering Years" and "Marshall at Benning," we see a rare teacher who possessed a revolutionary willingness to experiment and innovate, thus vastly influencing the American military leaders in World War II.[77] Marshall's attitude is reflected in the words of a near namesake, also an interpreter of military power and events:

Active intelligent response vitalizes all human relationships. To trust another's leading when there is no respect for his mind is impossible—impossible, I say. When we cannot feel in someone placed above us an intellectual . . . bond, we feel uncomfortable and on our guard. In a familiar phrase, ideas rule the world, and where ideas are lacking, there is no reason to follow.[78]

And Major General Fuller, an English theorist in wide repute among Americans, scorns the "mystery" of war, "for it is the most commonsense of all the sciences." [79] Admiral Eccles claims that war is closer to art than to science, since it is not so bound by the principles and rules it acknowledges, but rather it is creative, living, "having its spring in the mind of man." [80] Even Tristram Coffin, bitingly skeptical of the military in *The Passion of the Hawks,* admits that there are "some fine, humorously skeptical minds in contemporary American military," and he closes his bitter account by quoting approvingly from General Omar Bradley, a former chairman of the Joint Chiefs of Staff:

The central problem for our time—as I view it—is how to employ human intelligence for the salvation of mankind. It is a problem we have put upon ourselves. For we have defiled our intellect by the creation of such scientific weapons of destruction that we are now in desperate danger of destroying ourselves. . . . I am sometimes discouraged. It is not by the magnitude of the problem, but by our colossal indifference to it. I am unable to understand why— if we are willing to trust in reason as a restraint on the use of a ready-made, ready-to-fire bomb—we do not make greater, . . . more imaginative use of reason and human intelligence in seeking an accord and compromise which will make it possible to control the atom and banish it as an instrument of war.[81]

III. THE RATIONAL EXPRESSED IN CONTEMPORARY MILITARY THOUGHT

THE CREATIVE ROLE OF REASON

The fact is that the modern military in America are extremely conscious of the necessity of the rational as a basic factor in the definition and use of military power. There is almost unanimous agreement in the services concerning this aspect, judged by an analysis of their own official and semi-official publications and magazines over the past decade. All are committed to the educational race, each branch seeking to better its own schools academically and to provide not only more sophisticated technological training but exposure as well to the social sciences for a growing proportion of officers and men.[82] As a consequence, both West Point and Annapolis have undergone extensive, if painful, revision of curricula and teaching methods,[83] and the new Air Force Academy was almost ostentatiously modeled upon leading civilian institutions.[84] West Point proudly points to its Rhodes Scholars, exceeded only by Harvard, Princeton, and Yale.[85] The Navy points to its traditionally strong emphasis upon formal education over experience in its initial selection of officers such as chaplains and others, and the Air Force now happily claims more Ph.D.'s than its sister services.[86] Let us now examine representative writings of the major services.

Army: Qualitative Competition

Articles have blossomed in Army publications which often in their very titles stress the creative role of reason: "Soldiers Who Are Scholars," "Encourage the Thinkers!" "Creative Thinking in the Military Profession," "Thinking About Military Thinking," "Military Innovation and Creative Thinking." [87] In "Rembrandts of the Military Art" two types of creative reason— deductive ("frontal" research) and dynamic (artistic and intuitional)—are distinguished, with the claim that " 'unexplainable' victories are the end product of creative intelligence in action." [88] A report on "Liddell Hart and Warfare of the Future" emphasizes that tomorrow's leaders must be concerned with *truth* over dogmatism: "For now—and it would appear increasingly in the future—competition in arms (and hence the validity of a strategy of deterrence) is mainly qualitative, not quantitative." [89] A favorite model, Napoleon, admittedly had less combat experience than many of his subordinates and older generals, but he proved his genius for command "by the sheer intellectual power of his own experience and by his capacity to reflect upon the universality of the human experience." [90] Such reflection, to arrive at "the principles of war," is absolutely essential to a "renaissance of generalship," according to Colonel Mark M. Boatner, III, who fears default as *thinkers* to civilians.[91]

In this context, "Our Embattled ROTC" [92] pinpoints an area of increasing concern for the academic soundness of military education on and off campus, before and after actual induction into active duty. The heady jump in the educational level of Army enlisted men[93] has forced many to take "A New Look at the Military Profession" [94] as necessitating, and justifying, intellectual prowess second to none. In "A Profession Comes of Age," Major General John H. Hay puts this "wave of the future" on the line in calling for a new Master of Military Art and Science degree which "holds promise that the soldier's calling will soon take its place as one of the learned professions." [95] Ward Just, from the point of view of an outsider, cannot hold out much hope that this could be a reality very soon if gauged by the sluggish response of the hard-shell conservatism that grips most departments at West Point. Still, as he himself admits, "most of the action at the Point is now in the social sciences." [96] And it may be of interest that the Duty-Honor-Country series in the *Army's Character Guidance Discussion Topics* has emphasized the *intellectual* nature of courage (Socrates' "knowing what to be afraid of"), as the prime soldierly virtue, as well as "practical wisdom." [97]

Navy: To Command Is to Think

The Navy puts the concern for the rational perhaps more consciously philosophically in "A Philosophy for Naval Atomic Warfare," and "A New U.S. Military Philosophy." In these approaches reason is treated as the most basic principle, "the product of hard thought," writing, and testing, and altogether essential to methodology.[98] In "Ideological Responsibility" [99] we are told that if we are to survive, understanding both ourselves and the Communists is required. And in "Should Politics Be Taboo?" President Kennedy's advice is affirmed that "today requires sophisticated understanding of politics." Stressing the Navy's politico-military program, he went on to say that "the pens of naval and military officers provide advice and counsel to the civilians who fashion and direct the use of the sword." [100] There is need to sharpen the pens for the best use of the sword. "The Restless Mind" suggests that we need more restless rather than satisfied minds,[101] a theme that is picked up in "Professionalism—a Wardroom Debate," "The Pentagon's Whiz Kids," and "The Ph.D. in Uniform." [102] The call is for scholars in the military lest it default to technology and the civilians.

Indeed, a new breed has arisen. These "defense intellectuals" are scholars whose attention has been directed full time to matters of warfare once jealously guarded as the exclusive province of professional military men.[103] Admiral Joseph C. Wylie in his recent book *Military Strategy* seems almost to abdicate the traditional claim of the military to the study of strategy by contending that it is properly the province of the social scientist and scholar.[104] The dialogue thus encouraged soon found the Naval War College calling for "free discussion, free thinking . . . particularly an enquiring mind." [105] And because the increasing fluidity of events must inevitably modify objectives, especially subsidiary ones, "the need for highly developed mental power on the part of high executives and senior commanders" likewise grows: the commander is not only one who wills but also one who thinks.[106] Even the Marine Corps, hardly the image of academia, has recently called for substantial changes in military education in view of the "revolution in educational methods, teaching techniques and concepts" which has taken place in the last fifteen years.[107] The completeness of the "revolution" may be seen, at least in embryo and thrust, in two recent developments. In a long and carefully detailed letter, Secretary Ignatius of the Navy advised the president of the board convened to select new admirals for fiscal 1969 that "the ability to think analytically" and to teach others to do the same assumes first importance.[108] And the announced basis for the "mod" changes being rapidly introduced by Admiral Elmo Zumwalt, the new Chief of Naval Operations, is that "these kids are different, smarter, tougher-minded. Some of them have college degrees and you don't push them around too easily." [109] Like the Army, the Moral Leadership Training Program has for some years emphasized the selection of leaders on the basis of what they know and are, stressing that "knowledge is a defensive weapon." [110]

Air Force: Analytical Ability

The Air Force, lacking an earlier tradition, is supremely conscious of technology and the increasing need for expertise in handling sophisticated weapons. Hence analytical ability rates high,[111] and strategy seems an overriding concern.[112] "The Liberal Challenge in the Military Profession" reveals the vigorous debate which has been going on for some years in the armed services with reference to the "new military mind." [113] With Army General Maxwell Taylor, Air Force men proudly assert that there is indeed a military mind, not in the mythical stereotype of rigid authoritarianism, but as there is a "lawyer mind" or a "business mind." "The military service requires as much intellectual talent as any other profession." [114] Nay, more. SAC Is PRIDE reads a giant sign as one enters and leaves a great California air base, part of the tremendous Strategic Air Command chain of facilities. And not least is there pride in the command of computerized reason. As the decade has replaced the century, whole ages are spanned now in a single lifetime, and the cascading effect of this forward rush to science and technology has been to thrust the Air Force elite into the front ranks of those thinkers and planners who must bring the new world to birth. The possibilities seem limitless:

In our focus on the future, we recognize no limits to the quickening march of human accomplishment and scientific adventurism. . . . Knowledge is power. . . . No one in the Systems Command who is engaged in managing military technology can accept the concept of an intellectual or creative stalemate. There will always be a crying need for new ideas, for creativity, for intellectual breakthroughs and quantum jumps. . . . We see . . . a limitlessness of man's intellectual capacity to grow.[115]

This is not done—is not desired to be done—in a corner. The pride is also in teamwork with the best in the civilian world, "the science-industry-military-civilian team." [116] In evidently satisfying detail the long-term, intimate, and extensive relationship between the Air Force and the scholarly research of the university is recounted again and again. Despite rising criticism which has forced some cutbacks, "most major graduate departments in science or engineering receive some Air Force support," and the continuing relationship is still "cru-

cial . . . for both the DOD and the universities." [117] Recently,
the Aerospace Educational Foundation, in cooperation with
the U.S. Office of Education, sponsored the first National Laboratory for the Advancement of Education, in Washington,
D.C., "to demonstrate outstanding innovations in education."
It was a three-day gathering of educators, government officials,
civic leaders, and industrial executives, who apparently were
anxious to learn from the Air Force educational techniques
that might cut learning time by as much as 50 percent.[118]

In this hopefully reciprocal role, Air Force apologists are
increasingly quick to correct the image of *their* military education as being solely technological, a matter of training robot
technicians who can with the utmost efficiency push the atomic
buttons. A recent issue of the *Air University Review* (November–December, 1968) contains four articles on the increasing
role of the humanities in the Air Force Academy. The fact that
thirteen graduates of the Academy have been Rhodes Scholars
and that with two selectees it was the only service academy to
be represented in 1970[119] understandably encourages considerable pride in their product. The Air Force service magazines
continually "plug" the rising merits of Air Force education
and the rising expectations and demands for such education as
absolutely necessary to success in today's world, tomorrow's Air
Force.[120] The Moral Leadership Program keeps in quick step
with the general alacrity, stressing liberal arts values, as though
it were (as indeed it is)[121] more easily identified with the civilian
world.[122] The Air Force seems quite preoccupied with "image"
and "professionalism" as embodying the *thinker,* and as the
youngest of the services, it is sure that it has found the key to
the future—"by the power of his knowledge." [123]

DISCOVERY OF THE SOCIAL SCIENCES

In the light of all this emphasis upon the rational and
academic (even humanistic), Martin Blumenson has raised the

question why the military have not been accorded full respect in an America which has had its full share of military heroes. He finds in World War II the watershed in improvement of civilian-military relations.[124] Thousands of officers and enlisted men came into the mainstream of a society convinced at last of their continuing if painful need, and the military on their part were encouraged to foster this deepening relationship by serious reading, especially in history and government, and by greater professionalism. Deeper than this lay the need for new doctrine, i.e., rational alternatives to the actual use of the bomb. President Kennedy deliberately encouraged an enlarged vision and a more aggressive political stance on the part of military personnel because they simply ought to know what is going on in the world, a world increasingly sensitive to psychological and political pressures as well as to brute force.[125] Social science professors at West Point, themselves reflecting the perturbation and uneasiness that has seized the services with the decline of fixed doctrine, speak of the new catalyst as "a political component" which every military officer must now have.[126] Military officers have noted with envy and some apprehension the loss of leadership and power to civilian strategists while they have devoted themselves to the refinement of tactics.[127] Thus with the shrinking of the world and the enlarging of the bomb, and reacting to quite pragmatic internal pressures for their own future, the armed services have in varying but significant degrees discovered the social sciences.[128] It is at this point that some of the most interesting and significant differences appear between the services in their redefinition and use of military power as rational.

Army: Civic Action

The Army is especially conscious of its historic role in civic action,[129] and sees this as an increasing trend toward actual nation-building in the international sphere.[130] In 1963, Gen-

eral Westmoreland, then Commandant of West Point, drew
attention to the social achievements of the Army, reminding
the nation that the school was thirty years ahead of civilian
Rensselaer Polytechnic Institute in developing a school of
engineering.[131] That same year *Army* featured several articles
detailing military civic action in ten countries around the
world under a byline from President Kennedy: "The new
generation of military leaders has shown an increasing awareness that armies cannot only defend their countries—they can
help build them." [132] In "The Social Scientist and the Soldier"
increasing awareness of new missions and roles has inspired
the search for new knowledge and for the skills of the social
scientist. Whereas the classic role of the Army has been
"therapeutic," i.e., to win an open conflict situation, the current emphasis is rather "prophylactic," the prevention of conflict. No longer can dependence be put upon "pure military
skill or naked power . . . [but] upon the geopolitician and
educator concurrently. . . . America's leadership must be
guided by the lights of learning and reason," requiring increasingly the training of military personnel, especially its
leaders, in the humanities.[133] The Secretary of the Army has
emphasized the same theme in "Prepared to Deter, to Fight,
to Build," stressing the Army's role in preventing war and
noting the number of rising young nations under military
aegis.[134] The poverty of emerging nations in leadership, administration, and technical skills often leads to the "discovery" of the Army as having those "peculiar features of a
centralized command, a hierarchical structure of control, the
persuasive use of discipline, a self-contained communications
system, and a corporate *esprit de corps*" made to order for
the chaotic strivings of national power.[135]

Again in "Land Power Missions Unlimited" the stereotyped
dual purpose of the Army to fight conventional or nuclear
wars is scrapped in favor of a "multipurpose" role, for "anything, anytime, anywhere." [136] "The attack [is] to build," to

engage in a wide variety of civil affairs and civic action operations.
. . . [The Army] may have to help train local police forces, institute
land reforms, establish public health services, organize labor unions,
develop agriculture extension programs.[137]

Admittedly these are tasks which go beyond traditional war
and war-making, but they are justified as the national extension of the modern military mission:

Taking all of the published doctrine together, civil affairs adds up
to being that branch of the military art aimed at the intelligent
handling of our relations with civilians to best assist the commander
in the accomplishment of his mission.[138]

The seeming incongruity is defended even against reporters
who often "do not seem to sense that the function of the
Armed Forces has greatly expanded . . . to include a non-
fighting responsibility of perhaps even greater significance." [139]
General Train, saddened by the death of his own son in Vietnam, finds comfort especially in the fact that "he exemplified
civic-mindedness." [140] The increasing employment of the military, especially the Army, in civic action in Vietnam is too
well known, and controversial, to detail here. Suffice to say
here that this is the trend. The Army especially is aware of
its possibilities in this direction, and because of the nuclear
stalemate on the edge of the abyss of total (and destructive)
power, a significant shift appears in the making toward a
redefinition of military power as limited and constructive.

Navy: The Changing Nature of Power

Eccles has sensed and put this rather well as "today's paradox of power," quoting Sir Stephen King-Hall:

"First, the astonishing novelty of the notion that something which
has been true since the beginning of history; i.e., that the principal
component of Power was a capacity for physical violence is no
longer true when violence is nuclear. Second, that the old rule still
holds good in situations where for the time being . . . non-nuclear

violence is in question. . . . But even where non-nuclear violence is an element of Power there are signs that other factors of Power are becoming important." [141]

But it is Captain Carl H. Amme, U.S. Navy (Ret.), now at Stanford University, in "The Changing Nature of Power," who has most clearly fixed the shift and analyzed its meaning.[142] MacArthur, "last of the classicists," plaintively "objecting to the political considerations which hampered his destruction of the enemy's power," is contrasted with our landing in Lebanon in 1956 wherein "the significant point is that it was not the use of military force which made the operation a success; it was the restraint on its use by both sides." The greater, and graver, illustration of nuclear deterrence as threat suggests that self-ordered military power convinces by its greater power, and military persons as well as their political superiors are beginning to see this. Thus Amme is led to the conclusion that "the most effective use of military power as a technique of action will be found at the very threshold of violence, where insurgency develops and insurrection threatens." [143] War as such has become less useful because it has become less rational. That discovery having been made, the military is free to and indeed must research other forms of conflict short of war, at least major war in the nuclear age.

As early as 1955, in an address given at the Naval War College,[144] Prof. James A. Field suggested that the roots of the new emphasis can be found, as West Point found them in civil engineering, in the very early "missionary" use of "the old Navy." This was not for seizures of territory, but to open and keep open the trade lanes, to add to the sum of knowledge as a scientific institution,[145] and for the encouragement of liberty and self-determination of peoples. To these is now added, according to Rear Admiral John D. Chase, the ninth "function of the Navy, . . . a means to implement social reforms." Specific reference is made to "the Navy's role in equal opportunity and fair housing." [146] Field had suggested that a middle isolationist period followed the Civil War, which found the Navy inflexibly identified with war as its sole function. But the ensuing third period, since the defeat of Japan, reveals tremendous growth in naval power adapted to a revived governmental policy supporting freedom of the seas and of backward nations. There has been added of late a pricking of the conscience with reference to social problems at home.

There is an aura of the brotherhood of man in these social gropings. In the view of Professor Field, more is at stake here than hard-nosed economic motivation and containment of the "broiling powers" which reflects the usual concern for order.[147] One article, drawing upon the laudable experience of the floating hospital ship *Hope,* comes closer to the Army insight in stressing that thinking is needed with respect to "our humanitarian regard for other societies." It suggests new fleets, operable "on the rivers, lakes and coasts of Eurasia, Africa, and Latin America," and specially oriented toward "nation building so that Western technology can help nurture a permanent revolution in the underdeveloped nations of the world."[148] Professor Bader, U.S. Coast Guard Reserve and widely traveled in South America, indeed finds that the Latin American military have already set this concept in motion:

It has been transformed by an influx of young and reform-minded officers from a rigid defender of the social and economic status quo to a significant vehicle of social progress and national feeling.[149]

As such "it plays a far more significant domestic role than it does on the stage of international relations."[150]

To this end, moreover, the Navy has not been lacking in pleas and programs for increased psychological and cultural understanding of peoples. Increasingly, discussions of Communism seem concerned to understand the theory and the peoples back of their frontal behavior as enemies.[151] Indeed, one is impressed with restraint as characteristic of much naval writing both concerning total war and total invective against an unregenerate enemy. In dealing with Marxism, the Moral Leadership Training Program proposed to lay bare the historical roots and real accomplishments of Communism in an effort to evaluate its power. The degree of objectivity, of course, has depended greatly upon the administration and teaching at the local level. And it must be admitted that condemnation of Communism has been the usual objective both by rational and by other means.

Aboard many ships, "schools" came to be held during the long sea voyages to acquaint personnel with the cultures and religions of peoples whose ports we might be entering. This was a more or less positive attempt to understand aliens, friendly as well as enemy. An extension and refinement of these approaches has now been formalized for personnel in Asiatic waters in the "Personal Response Project" initiated in 1965 by the Commanding General, Fleet Marine Force Pacific, as the "Southeast Asia Religious Project" and to which a naval chaplain was assigned for an "in-country study of the beliefs, customs, religious practices and value systems of Vietnam." [152] The program has its defenders in print. Major J. R. Lewis, U.S. Marine Corps, claims that "it is vital to tactical success in Vietnam that SNCO's and officers learn all they can about that country and its people so that honest personal response will prevail." [153] Another enthusiast would even add "friendship" to the principles of war! [154] Of more immediate weight is the closely reasoned and historically grounded statement of a senior Marine officer given at the Naval War College in defense of "the non-military use of the military." [155] It is noteworthy that some of the strongest and most frequent civil action statements come from the Marine Corps whose function relates them, like the Army, more closely to the people than either the Navy or the Air Force.

It is clear that at least in the higher echelons the concern is still basically prudential, and short-range utilitarian, i.e., to obviate the alienation often thoughtlessly induced by the mis-understanding and misbehavior of Americans. It seeks to "profoundly influence . . . behavior . . . which . . . cannot help but result in greater safety to our personnel, less anxiety for the Vietnamese, and earlier resolution of discord between the two groups." [156] Moreover, "this approach offers the best possibility of winning the hearts and minds of the Vietnamese people to the desire for and defense of their own self-determination as a nation." [157] An officer friend of mine of many years frankly admits that the Navy's concern "is not moral but rather prudential." Yet, as one of the natural virtues, prudence is a kind of wisdom, especially in restraint of power in the nuclear age, and is moral, even if minimal and self-serving. The concern here can be much deeper than mere prudence. It can encourage the maximizing of values between peoples and in the world. The project thus is sponsored by the Chief of Chaplains, U.S. Navy, who considers it "to be secondary only to primary religious and counseling duties" and which evidently looks beyond simple prudence to brotherly concern for the dignity and faith of all men:

It is only when we get into the realm of ideas, values, emotional responses, and aesthetic judgments that we are really participating in the lives of the people. The Vietnamese do not regard themselves as merely biological machines, for each individual is a distinct, self-conscious entity. If he is to be profoundly influenced it must be on the level of behavior which is far more personal and less material.

As the individual American meets the individual Asian, the goal of the PERSONAL RESPONSE PROJECT is to assure that the American, overtly, takes the initiative to support, respect and value the basic worth and dignity of the Asian as a person while the American maintains his own values, proper role and identity.[158]

Air Force: Time to Get Involved

The Air Force has produced considerably fewer published articles and ideas with respect to the changing nature of power and military civic action, but as though determined to catch up has of late increasingly directed attention to this area of concern. As the youngest of the services, popular but lacking the warnings of long experience that popularity is a fragile thing, self-conscious of its major role in today's world, and of all the Armed Forces the most committed to speed, mechanical change, and technological expertise, the Air Force has probably had all it could do to keep abreast of present and daily demands. Less diversified than either the Army or Navy, committed essentially to a one-weapon system, there is less natural conflict of priorities and ideas, less questioning of the one idea of its own privileged mission which in success may seem the total answer to national security and international peace. Pride in its own superior rationality cannot balance the tremendous organizational and emotional stake which the Air Force has in the delivery of decisive power. This applies to the military as a whole but especially to the youngest service which is limited essentially to a highly sophisticated and more or less uniform delivery system.

In the nature of the case the "man in blue" is highly individualistic, usually moving in neither the large masses of the Army, nor even in the smaller, more compact, and time-spanning groups who man the ships of the Navy. Imbued with an idea that has indeed revolutionized the world, but fragmentized into crews and individuals serving the marvel of a machine which rarely allows for the meeting of persons except on its own terms, it is perhaps not to be wondered at that Air Force personnel have given less thought to the constructive use of power except as pure deterrence, and only recently with respect to civic action. It is true that in 1963 General Curtis E. LeMay, then Commander of the Strategic Air Command, spoke of "Civic Action by the Air Force—The Air Commandos," in which he stressed that SAC's mission is actually to create an environment where humanitarianism can flourish. But this appears ulterior and narrowly utilitarian, a deliberate means to assure the success of our own counterinsurgency which is "dependent upon a world environment free of major conflict." Seemingly of even greater concern was the hope that "an Air Force which identified itself with the progress and well being of the populace will be accorded public good will, respect and support." [159] This attitude, clearly defensive at times, suggests an ethic of egoism. Air Power, it is believed, is very nearly the only power. And its mission is destruction of the enemy, not his rehabilitation. Not long ago Senator Barry Goldwater, a Major General in the Air Force Reserves, took Secretary McNamara bitterly to task for the growing use of U.S. fighting forces for "social rehabilitation" in Vietnam.[160]

But this attitude is less typical than it was. A striking, if lonely, voice for a time was that of R. H. Anthis, who appealed for "Twentieth Century Centurions" who would be concerned with "the third face of war . . . the face of human need . . . the untended sick, the hungry family, . . . the illiterate child," and he went on to quote a young American major returning by choice to Vietnam:

"We need a new type of Centurion, a man who is imbued with a zeal to help these people facing Communist terror while they are trying to progress. We must have military people who are willing to understand them and stay with them until the job is done." [161]

Anthis went on to say:

Unknown to many of our citizenry, we are developing a new breed of military with far greater sophistication, understanding, and empathy. . . . We need more of them. We need soldiers, sailors, marines, and airmen who are not only trained in the use of conventional weapons and tactics but who are wise and judicious in the application of thought and action in a world that has neither war nor peace.[162]

A year later (1968) two new books were cautiously reviewed in the *Air University Review* under the caption "Civic Action —A Weapon for Peace." [163] The motivation again was strictly utilitarian and self-serving: civic action was "one method of counter subversion," and

one is impressed . . . [with] the military as having the most natural and widely applicable systems of training, education, and career development to provide for the needs of developing as well as developed nations.[164]

But earlier that same year "Operation Haylift" had excited considerable attention as Air Force Reservists assisted in a gigantic haydrop to isolated and snowbound Hopi and Navaho Indian reservations.[165] The publicity exceeded expectations and was gratefully received in a year not altogether kind to the American military. In 1969, in the wake of our deteriorating image in Vietnam, the momentum for social concern found expression in strong and even enthusiastic articles. Lieutenant Colonel Bounds, stressing that "Air Force civic action has progressed from nothing two years ago to a very influential factor in Vietnam today," justified the growing effect on the hard basis of economics: it costs $55,000 to *kill* each Viet Cong, but only $125 is expended "for each defector through psychological operations/civic action. . . . Any way you look at it the price is cheap." [166]

One notes the twin relationship of psychological warfare and civic action, and the subordination of all things to victory. Indeed, the very first principle which this writer deduced "could apply anywhere" respecting this new use of military power is that "civic action cannot be motivated by humanitarian principles alone." [167] Which leads one to wonder as to the motivation for military civic action when, with considerable spirit, it is focused upon conditions at home. In April, 1969, Secretary Laird established the Domestic Action Council by means of which "DOD takes aim at the ills in our society." Under the title of "Domestic Action—What It Is and How It Works," appearing in *The Airman* (July, 1970), the subheading informs us that "today the Air Force, as part of DOD-wide effort, is helping wage a vigorous campaign against the social and economic ills of the nation." [168] Former Air Force Chief of Staff General McConnell, complimented for his attention to the "special role of airpower" in civic action programs, explains that in the spirit of freely offered services characteristic of the military in frontier days, the modern Air Force can do so much more in providing better communication and transportation, etc.[169] In "Time to Get Involved," we find that this *can* mean Airman Habegger taking on some troublesome overage sixth-graders who didn't like school.[170] But General McConnell is thinking rather of the unrivaled expertise of the Air Force "to promote internal stability" in needy nations.[171] One is left with the deep suspicion that the belated, sudden surge of interest in civic action in the Air Force is on the part of many, and especially the hierarchy, a grasping at any straw for victory. Civic action appeals as a rational alternative to the pure power approach, which has been disappointing at best, and is expressive of the romantic, youthful claim for affection that seems to dominate the Air Force's preoccupation with "image." That it is rational, there is little question; that it is genuinely humanitarian remains in doubt.

In this connection, the Moral Leadership Program of the Air Force has for some time reflected something of the dialectical tension by which the concept of civic responsibility may be gradually evolving to include the world community before and after war, and in terms of persons beyond restoration or maintenance of stability. The chaplains often see such responsibility as a missionary dimension of their work and directed toward individual needs. But even here the responsibility is not simply religious; it is prudential and pragmatic and as such involves the whole structure of officers and men.[172] In 1963 a quarter was devoted to group discussions on "The Air Force Family in the Community," but the next year the theme had moved toward "Overseasmanship," "As Others See Us," "The Art of Being Believed" (by foreign na-

tionals).[173] The emphasis has been small in ratio to other
themes but it appears to be growing.

We have attempted to trace military power from its known
beginnings in our cultural heritage as insisting upon the
rational as a primary aspect. The modern American military
is profoundly aware of this dimension, encouraged today by
considerable soul-searching because of the specter of irrationality at the nuclear abyss. The headlong pursuit of the ultimate in "naked" power by the "managers of violence" has
been thrown back upon itself within sight of that objective,
to rediscover and refurbish uses and portents of military
power in our past in order to redefine and make creditable
its use in the nuclear era. The Army and the Navy especially,
doubtless because of their long, traditional, multifunctional
and flexible roles, and people-involved stratico-tactics, are
giving serious thought to positive and constructive possibilities. The youngest service, in its sudden eagerness to exploit
the new "weapon" of civic action, in itself expressive of a
high degree of rationality, also reveals that rationality is not
necessarily humanitarian and may readily become the prey
of the emotions. But military power is first of all rational,
carefully subordinate to its legitimate authority, which is the
"responsible use" of extreme and perhaps ultimate physical
force for social ends, "the good of all" (though the "all" bears
further definition). As rational, military power carries with it
the possibility of the positive, which is altogether important
in an age that has finally identified the military with the ultimate in negation, i.e., nuclear war.

Chapter 5

The Risk
of
the Irrational

If reason is a primary element in military power, it is a factor that must be accepted in an age which too easily equates war with the irrational and thus too often evades responsibility by simply protesting against its managers. Still, it remains only a third of Clausewitz' celebrated definition, "a wonderful trinity," of violence, chance, and reason.[1] It is in the matrix of violence and freedom that irrationality is born. Irrationality is not a quality which can be established ontologically but is rather the subversion of the rational which becomes evident as a consequence of choice at the juncture of reason and violence. It is "emotion without rational structure," as Tillich has put it, and has "all the qualities of the demonic," either as mere subjective feeling, empty of content, a vacuum "into which distorted reason can break without a rational check," or as carrying some rational control, it attacks formalized reason and becomes blind and fanatical.[2]

Clausewitz defines the violence of war as raw, elemental power composed of the original violence of its elements—hatred and animosity—which may be looked upon as blind instinct.[3] As such it is undetermined, "the play of probabilities and chance, which make it a free activity of the soul."[4]

But freedom is more than the random play of chance—it is the centered self selecting among options.[5] Reason suggests but cannot determine and the "soul," or the self, acting, chooses or wills not according to an absolute abstraction but "with a reality," with "living and moral forces"—the variant circumstances of finite and concrete existence. "War," then, Clausewitz says, is "in all branches of human activity most like a gambling game." "Everywhere [there is] a margin for the accidental." [6] "War is the province of danger . . . uncertainty, . . . chance." [7] But the gamble and danger are ultimate, involving the life or death not only of individuals but of societies and civilization, and perhaps now of a world. The existential impact of this consciousness of "unlimited liability" [8] in the handling of military power is that of decision and will, for which reason is only the preparation. This reality—this numbing reality at times[9] of the "unlimited liability" which the military man must assume for his choice, especially in war —lies at the heart of the constant insistence upon leadership, responsibility, and obedience. Military power is essentially *voluntaristic,* and as such may open the door to the irrational.

I. VOLUNTARISM EXPRESSED IN WESTERN MILITARY HISTORY

CLASSICAL DECISIVENESS

Before Clausewitz the factor of will in military power is not as clearly spelled out as that of reason, but it is abundantly illustrated and everywhere implicit in ancient and medieval warfare. The *Anabasis* classically demonstrates the dependence of the free-wheeling Greeks upon the repeated decisiveness and strength of will of Xenophon, heretofore hardly more than a nobody in the ranks.[10] It took disaster and the almost daily possibility of annihilation by Persians and hill tribesmen thousands of miles from the security of their Grecian homes to reveal the mainspring of one man's will to which reason itself had at times to be subordinated in order to prevail. About a century later the first modern army was fashioned as the daily creation of the scarred and limping Philip from the unlikely rough material of Macedonian hillsmen. Its success "to the farther Ind" has long been credited to the flashing but determined genius of his son, the imposition and interpretation of whose will on a score of battlefields snatched victory from the jaws of reasonably certain defeat. Hannibal, crossing the Alps with his elephants to harry the Romans in their own backyard, is known to all of us. "But there was nothing at all miraculous about Hannibal and the force he led," says Montross. "Both were the products of one man's will. That man was Hamilcar Barca," who, with hate as a motive, carved a personal empire out of a third of Spain, conquered the tough Iberian tribesmen, and fashioned them into a tool of destruction against Rome. Like Alexander, Hannibal received a superb instrument and made it his own, the force of his own will giving unique cohesion to his oddly assorted, multinational, multilingual army, always in the minority, but never really defeated in fifteen years in enemy country.[11]

Indeed, Montross credits this very quality of the will for the final, crushing triumph of Caesar over Vercingetorix and his Gaulic allies:

That relentless will to victory, which distinguishes the warfare of civilization from the strife of primitives. . . . Method, organization, discipline are contributing factors; but in the end the physical courage of the defenders is unequal to the moral ferocity of men fighting for power and property.[12]

The Saracens under Muhammad especially, and the Byzantines under numerous generals, exemplify the same stubborn, decisive quality extended to whole peoples. The Byzantines, as we have seen, exploiting the rational in military power more assiduously and successfully than any other people in

history, combined with reason the equally necessary will to
survive as a people and as an empire, although surrounded by
some of the hitherto successful scourges of the Western world.

FRATRICIDE FROM THE DEPTHS

The irrational, however, as Senator Fulbright has said,[13]
lurks close below the surface, as "emotion without rational
structure," the blind impulsion of the restless energy of being. Or as carrying some rational control it reasons against
reason and is overwhelmed by decisions that open up the
depths of being as fanatical power. The fratricidal self-destruction of the Greeks, willing excellence in the parts but unwilling to cooperate on the whole,[14] the moral frightfulness
of the Mongols who, except for a sword, came and returned
empty-handed; Timur the Lame, who conquered the wrong
"enemies," his own brethren and fighting allies, and with
"exhaustive cruelty . . . dealt the stricken Iranic Society its
death blow," [15] a demise that included himself and all his
conquests; the French "horde" that perished in the Russian
snows; the terrible enthusiasm of the peoples of Europe running like lemmings to destruction in 1914; the sickening gas
chambers of Buchenwald and Auschwitz; perhaps our own
ironic "thinking the unthinkable" in the nuclear age—these
all illustrate the rise of the irrational from the depths as the
power of being which breaks the bonds of reason in the very
act of will that reaches beyond the bounds of reason. This is
what has come to be called the "demonic" in personal and
social relations, the assumption of divine and absolute pre-
rogatives which do not integrate but split men and nations.[16]

BETRAYAL BY THE "GENERAL WILL"

The importance of will and the risk of the irrational is
perhaps most clearly seen in the rise of the nation-in-arms

concept under Napoleon and its exploitation by the modern democracies. Like Plato distinguishing justice more easily on the larger canvass of the state, so we find the concept of the *levée en masse* before Napoleon in the enthusiastic enaction of Article I of the French Convention meeting August 23, 1793. It was really expressive of a kind of "general will" of the people:

All Frenchmen are permanently requisitioned for service in the armies.

The young men shall fight; the married men shall forge weapons and transport supplies; the women will make tents and clothes and will serve in the hospitals; the children will make up old linen into lint; the old men will . . . rouse the courage of the fighting men, to preach the unity of the Republic.[17]

The wild acclaim with which this total conscription of a nation was received [18] is matched only by the incalculable influence of this law, beyond any "law in the statute books of any nation." [19] Machiavelli perhaps first suggested the idea.[20] Francis Bacon, in his "Of Unity in Religion," condemned as "a thing monstrous" putting the temporal sword into the hands of the common people. But it was Rousseau with his doctrine of the "general will" who induced the coming of total conscription:

Thus the jinni of popular absolutism was released from the monarchial brass bottle, to oust the absolutism of kings, to rebuild the tower of Babel, and to transform the auction-room of war into a slaughterhouse.[21]

Concorcet, and others, have connected "the rise of infantry with the rise of democracy":[22] the hoplites of Greece, the legionnaires of Rome, the Swiss democrats, the French "horde," the GI's of two world wars. Fuller even claims "the infantry-man made the democrat: the power to kill and therefore to force equality at the bayonet point." [23] But if he "made the democrat," he began with himself, his weapon representing his vote in the polis, the senate, the council chamber. He had a stake in the social order which made it altogether reasonable that he defend it. The transition to offensive action in order to preserve and even to share the benefits of their cultures has seemed surprisingly easy for democracies, but the imperialism of the common man has been too often overlooked as a major cause in the growth of military establishments and the outbreak of wars. Indeed, we cannot speak very correctly of war "breaking out," as though it were mysteriously "one of those explosions of human energy which transcend ordinary considerations, . . . mysterious, dreadful . . . [a] cosmic enigma." [24] War involves some very ordinary wills which, swollen in the immense context of the human situation, provide fertile ground for the rise of more than ordinary wills who are yet basically reflective of the energy, values, and decisiveness of their peoples. Fuller chides Toynbee for his hurt puzzlement as to how democracy can act as an antisocial force, since democracy (according to Toynbee) "breathes the spirit of the Gospels . . . and its motive-force is Love." Fuller suggests that Spencer and Hobbes are closer to the truth in distinguishing ingroup from outgroup morals and the virtues of peace from those of war.

The motive force of democracy is not love of others, it is the hate of all outside the tribe, faction, party or nation. The "general will" predicates total war, and hate is the most puissant of recruiters.[25]

I cannot agree that it is hate—any more than that it is love —but the possibility exists and arises in the multiplicity of individual concerns and willed actions which tend to push beyond reason in conflict. In times of peculiar stress and strain, which can involve boredom as well, decision may be forced to the top and channeled via the military as the one institution that openly acknowledges and values the will and its action. So the Comte de Guibert, ten years before the storming of the Bastille:

A man will arise, perhaps one who hitherto was lost in the obscurity of the crowd; . . . a man who in silence has meditated; . . . who perhaps did not know his own talents, who can only become aware of them when called upon to exercise them; one who has studied little. That man will seize hold of opinions, of fortune, and will say to the great man of theories, . . . "All that my rival tells you, I will carry out." [26]

So came a Corsican engineer with his "whiff of grapeshot" to force decision on October 5, 1795. Carlyle exclaimed: "There was, . . . in this man, a soul to dare and do. He rose naturally to be King. All men saw that he *was* such." [27]

Even in the absence of such a man, and sometimes against their own leaders and the military itself, the "moods of the people" may require the use of the military. So Vagts explains the Crimean War:

The sting of the epithet "nation of shopkeepers," was only *now* being felt, after nearly forty years of peace . . . as they began to yearn for a more romantic action, to revive the knightly qualities. . . . Submerged in commercialization, the public was delighted when its statesmen challenged foreign nations, or their diplomacies. . . . In this mental state of Englishmen, the Crimean war was a relief. . . . Least of all was it desired by the British Army.[28]

Montross says that if one basic cause of World War I may be isolated it must be

consent of the various peoples. . . . This indictment applies as much to the masses of Russia as to the more privileged citizens of France and Great Britain. No country of Europe, however autocratic, could afford to make general war without the support of the public approval. . . . In every capital the order for mobilization was applauded with an excitement bordering upon frenzy. . . . If the price came high, no murmur was pitched loud enough to alarm the various capitals. Nor could it truthfully be said that the people had been deceived or betrayed by their rulers. More often the statesmen and generals had to brace themselves against a popular clamor for war.[29]

THE SUICIDAL DOCTRINE OF "ATTACK!"

The pathetically suicidal doctrine of *Attack!*, pushed with such relentless vigor by Foch and Haig in World War I, was the monstrous child of Rousseau's "general will" and the

Schopenhauerian-Nietzschean doctrines of the "will to live" and the "will to power." After the disaster of 1870–1871, the French turned to the antimaterialistic German model, and following Ardant du Picq, spiritualized war as the will to conquer, i.e., to be sure of victory *is* victory.[30] Belatedly, Clausewitz, who had defined war as "an act of violence intended to compel our opponent to fulfill our will," was discovered. He bequeathed the so-called "annihilation principle" to posterity: "The *military power* must be destroyed. . . . The *country* must be conquered" so that it cannot produce a new military power, and certainly "the *will* of the enemy" must be "subdued."[31] A young professor of military science at the famous École Supérieure de la Guerre, Major Ferdinand Foch, electrified his students by refashioning this "principle" into the doctrine of the "universal offensive" (*"Attaquez! Attaquez!"*) as the solution for all war problems. Foch, trained as a Jesuit, added *faith* as justifying any sacrifices. "The moral factor," he liked to say, "is the most important element in war; the will to conquer sweeps all before it."[32] Almost every page of his highly intellectualized lectures and books on the science of war stress the *will:* "Victory = *Will.* . . . A battle won is a battle in which one *will* not acknowledge oneself beaten."[33] Admittedly this was a matter of faith, but the later Marshal of France persuaded his subordinates to believe that belief itself "is acquired through will power, like muscles, like instruction."[34] Montross sees here the influence of Bergson and French mysticism, encouraging the intuitive and the instinctual over "cold reason," and thus opening up the prospect of irrationalism at the point of decision.[35] The paradox is that only a man of Foch's superior intelligence and unquestioned integrity and confidence could provide, in his message to General Joffre, the key to the great victory of the First Battle of the Marne (September 5–12, 1914): "My center is yielding, my right recoils, situation excellent. I am attacking!"[36]

But also, only such a doctrine, pursued fanatically, could provoke the awful slough of Flanders, the horrible, beaten stench of waist-deep mud literally engulfing three hundred thousand men in an Allied offensive that gained an average of only five miles. It is no wonder that General Haig's Chief of Staff burst into tears on his tardy visit to the wilderness of the front: "Good God, did we really send men to fight in that?" [37] And why? General Bullard of the American Expeditionary Force (AEF), speaking of his own Army but applicable to Flanders, touched the truth: it was "the product of many brains but one will. Its like could be provided only where one will governed." [38] General John J. Pershing, the "one will" for the Americans, has been accused of responsibility for "probably 25,000 deaths" because he insisted on the identity of American troops as fighting units. He fought right up to the very hour of the Armistice and still wanted to continue the war.[39]

Mid-twentieth-century warfare illustrates again the crucial factor of will in military power. Hitler's dominance over reluctant generals; the defense of Stalingrad; Dunkirk; the London blitz and Churchill ("At moments of crisis he crystallized the national will");[40] the decisive victory of Midway, turning, it is said, upon the lone decision of an American squadron leader to fly his planes past the point of no return;[41] the Inchon landing, MacArthur alone insisting upon the feasibility of the proposed action—a thousand known, tens of thousands of forever unknown actions flowed from the wills of warriors and their leaders who applied reason to the uses of violence but not always enough to save it from the terrible excesses of emotionalism and fanaticism.

II. VOLUNTARISM EXPRESSED IN CONTEMPORARY MILITARY THOUGHT

ARMY

The Mainspring of the Will

The soldiers themselves, especially the soldiers, stress the moral factor of the will. If the number of expressions in articles and books is any clue, it would appear that in the mid-sixties, the Army became particularly concerned about the strength of their own and the nation's will against the ominous backdrop of the uncertain nuclear threat. In 1964, *Military Review* published several articles to stress the concern: "The Nature of Future Wars: An Italian View," claimed that nuclear war is credible only through a "combination of power, the will to use it, and the recognition of these two elements . . . by a potential aggressor." [42] "Men, Motivation and Material," going back to du Picq, argued that will is fundamental to moral force and gave historical examples to illustrate the like thesis of *The Young Lions,* one of the best of the postwar novels, that war is a conflict of will, a symbolic duel.[43] However good our weapons, we need moral force and the willingness to sacrifice. Like an Athenian son obedient to his mother, one must come back from battle bearing his shield or be borne upon it. "The will of the American people is neither remote nor abstract. . . . Our Army is not a caste apart. . . . In men, motivation, and material it expresses the moral determination of all of us. Our Army is US." [44] In June, 1964, "War and Morality," [45] affirming the *will to live* as the highest value, set in motion a controversy that extended well into the 1966 issues of *Military Review.* Major General Edmund B. Sebree, U.S. Army (Ret.), reminded his readers that Maurice de Saxe's famous characteristics of the successful military men included "health," which is more than stamina. It is energy also, the "energy of greatness" as the Germans put it, i.e., the *will to power.*[46] In an interesting analysis of "What Do We Mean by Win?" Lieutenant Colonel W. I. Gordon the next month stressed that "the will to win is an inherent element in the American character and is fundamental, in the absolute or classical sense, to military operations in the field." [47] A review of *The Liddell Hart Memoirs* (perhaps "the most formidable military writer of the age")[48] quotes approvingly his early appraisal that "in the human will lies the source and mainspring of all conflict" and hence "our goal in war can only be attained by the subjugation of the opposing will." [49] And the reviewer goes on to say that modern warfare has become just this—"more and more . . . a battle of the spirit, of ideas, and of the human will." [50]

The Threat of the Irrational

Army writers, and a number of chaplains interviewed on a large Army installation, seem, for the most part, very aware of the threat of the irrational in the emphasis upon the will, especially with the possibility of nuclear warfare. But the risk may have to be taken and attitudes vary greatly as to how catastrophic that would be. Escalation is accepted as "inherent" in war because war deals with the largely uninhibited and therefore its growth is always more probable than its limitation.[51] Impatience, fears of enemy growth, and even victories that stimulate hope, encourage escalation in times of war. And there is a natural progression in the use of weapons. Rear Admiral C. H. Coggins, writing on "Weapons of Mass Destruction" in *Military Review,* contends that such weapons are really *not* cruel, at least by comparison with past weapons and considering the fact that "we use against the enemy the same substance with which we put our beloved pets to sleep" (gas?).[52]

The Senior Chaplain of the above-mentioned Army post felt the same way. The nuclear bomb, he said briskly, was only "a bigger stick—like gas; and you know we've never used *that.* But it's READY . . . *any*time." Someday we may have to use such a weapon (we'll never be the first, of course), but we should realize that all great advances are at first startling and unacceptable. A colleague, a former line officer turned chaplain, agreed. He had just officiated at the funeral of his own son, and his pride allowed not a trace of bitterness. "Military people are about as much threat as farmers," he said with infinite patience.

They never corrupt. . . . They are both *dirt* people—they can't get away from problems. Horseshit can't become icing. Nuclear weapons are no different *tactically* from other weapons. So, we will use them if we have to.

Another chaplain spelled this out: "If we face defeat, we'll use them," and Vietnam was clearly implied. But others were far from sure. One emphasized prudence, fearing that Hiroshima and the saturation fire bombings of the last war constituted precedents that could be turned against us. Therefore, "I see no justification for nuclear war," he said. Another chaplain, recently inducted and still obviously feeling ties with the civilian community, kept returning to the analogy of an "internationalized police force" to explain the military as necessary but found himself hung up on the apprehension that the military "almost creates violence." Troubled, this young minister in uniform could envisage the possibility that if it actually came to a showdown, it might be better to "surrender and bore from within." A friend, also torn within, tried desperately to balance the certain irrationality of resort to nuclear war against the no less believed-in certainty of the integrity of our leaders. He would "eschew unlimited force as tragic"—but then, are not our leaders moral and should they not be followed? Still, "what we would save must be more than we would destroy: hence nuclear war is irrational. It is simply unthinkable to allow total nuclear war." [53]

But "War and Morality," mentioned earlier, cautions against paralysis of our will by oversensitivity to ethics:

> The West should not hesitate to use, in measured response, all its weapons. . . . The weapon choice should be made on the grounds of efficiency and enemy capabilities to retaliate. Weapons are simply a function of the will to live. If this will is morally correct, then the means of implementing it should not be restricted unless suicide is to be given a higher value than survival. The will to live, applicable to men and nations, is the motive force of all existence.[54]

Prudence and an ethic of the right must temper compassion, and the author seems almost to welcome the return of "unlimited enmity" as evidence of a dynamic society: "The only non-warring societies are those that are static." [55] This Darwinian survivalism is given dramatic and gory form in an imaginative tale, "The Teton Men," which purports to recount how in the wake of a suicidal Russian-American holocaust, the Chinese move into America unopposed and are only finally routed by the mystic fury of the near-primitive defenders, reduced, it would seem, to their very essence, the will to survive, the last but enduring Americans.[56]

The Will to Restraint

But by far the greater emphasis in Army publications is in the reasoned direction of restraint, the willed patience to endure the stalemate by insisting upon redefining our objectives as limited. "To win" means a wooing of the wills of peoples, beyond the sometimes necessary but always measured application of force, to shared order and reforms. At least since the appearance of "The Relevancy of Ethics" in June, 1962 [57] —pleading that war is not inevitable but is determined by our heads and our hearts, and citing in detail the "hoary history of restraint" against the easy contention that man always uses the ultimate which he creates—the steady drumbeats of common sense and caution have been heard in Army publications. In January and February, 1963, two articles lashed out at air power extremism, especially as propounded by Douhet, the Italian flyer. The articles claimed that air power is the "new absolute" which in elevating destruction over control, and assuming that man has abandoned reason, approaches the irrational.[58] In pleading for "one more generation," the author calls to mind "another blind, courageous charge" at the wrong target, the Light Brigade at Balaklava: *"C'est Magnifique, mais ce n'est pas la guerre!"* [59] Rather, the call is to "Rational Victory," admittedly a problem that extends to the mood of the people and their education for lessened expectations in a nuclear world.[60] In "Clausewitz: A Reappraisal" the subordination of war to politics is reemphasized with the conclusion that nuclear war has changed the very nature of conflict:

No statesman who is sane can tolerate the idea of nuclear war as a progression of policy. In these conditions war can no longer be a continuation of policy but rather a negation of policy.[61]

The difficulty of absorbing tactical use of nuclear weapons without escalation is pointed out in numerous articles in Army publications.[62] The U.S. and the U.S.S.R. are likened to two mountain climbers roped together and thus forced to co-operate at the chasm. Captain Amme, in his usual careful way, writing in *Army*, calls for an explicit doctrine of possible tactical use of nuclear weapons, but anticipates the end result as a "tremendously destructive stalemate," from which extrication would come only by hard bargaining.[63] A quite different Italian guest writer, Major General Ottavio de Casola, warns of the paradoxical fact that "the operation of a deterrent could diminish precisely in proportion to the increase of its destructiveness, since it would give rise to a reduced credibility of the threat of reply." [64] In "Disarmament: Hope or Hoax?" the military admits to skepticism but suggests that we must entertain the possibility of disarmament because "the other choice [is] just as precarious" and although "we know that we cannot trust the Soviets, . . . perhaps this is not as important as it once was." [65] At the least, a nonproliferation treaty is in the right direction, although the controversy still goes on respecting "adequate safeguards." [66]

Biological warfare is seen as requiring considerable restraint, being akin to nuclear warfare.[67] At the same time it is clear that the Army has been resistive to cutbacks in the biochemical research operations. In "Military Objectives in the Nuclear Age," Korea is cited as the rational model, the first truly limited war in the twentieth century.[68] It is significant that nearly a dozen members of the U.S. Army College class of 1964–1965, writing their theses on some aspects of the problem of defining what it means to "win" in the era of the "cold war," agreed upon the national need to identify limited objectives in future wars as "a step toward 'winning' so long

as these steps lead ultimately toward the attainment of the
nation's overall objective formulated from our national purposes." [69] This formula has been applied repeatedly, if guard-
edly, to the Vietnam situation by ranking Army personnel.
One of the more surprising statements—as early as 1966—was
an article entitled "Peace in Vietnam—An Acceptable Solution," which called for revival of the Geneva accords, recognition of the Viet Cong as a legal party with a voice in the
government, and withdrawal of American troops after disarmament of the Viet Cong.[70] About the same time Lieutenant
General Gavin, a vocal critic of escalation, very thoughtfully
claimed, in "Military Power: The Limits of Persuasion," that
military power yields to economic power today, and that the
bomb "was the beginning of the end, if not indeed the very
end, of man's search for energy to be used as military force.
. . . And it marked a beginning of a new quest—the search
to find new ways and means of influencing the behavior of
other humans." [71]

This, Gavin says, explodes the myth of "Clausewitzian orthodoxy [that] holds that wars will be fought and won." [72]
Indeed, Clausewitz has become the subject of considerable reappraisal because "his own strategic ideas were simplified and
distorted almost beyond recognition . . . with devastating results." His *On War* was rashly treated as an "operation man-
ual," with modern armies trying to outdo one another in the
unlimited application of force when his own quite cautious
prescription was always the subjection of military force to
political reality.[73] Brian Bond continues by saying that today,
given the realities of the nuclear peril, this must include acceptance of "the undecisiveness of modern war." The next
year (1968), French General André Beaufré suggested that we
are being forced to employ "an indirect strategy" which "seeks
to obtain a winning result by methods primarily other than
military: and thus definitely limiting the sphere of conflict." [74]
Even the word "winning" has become obsolete as belonging

on the playing field and on the tactical battlefield, not at the strategic planning table. . . . The concept of total military defeat belongs to another era; it is as archaic as the halberd and has no constructive place in national policy circles. . . . There may be no need to destroy the enemy's forces, much less his non-combatants. It is not even necessary to break the enemy's will to resist. In fact, the only thing that must be defeated is will to *continue* the conflict.[75]

The truth is that

there has always been something illogical about war . . . [for] what could be more irrational than rich nations squandering their resources on weapons whose destructive power renders them almost unusable while two-thirds of the world's peoples live in abject poverty for want of the very capital used for bombs? Surely, we should be able to isolate the catalyst . . . which makes this unhappy reaction possible and, having done so, find the antidote.[76]

The catalyst, it is clear, is the *will,* the self acting in relative freedom and not always "listening" to reason but making up its own reasons and thus opening the door to the irrational "emotions without rational structure." The truth is, we can will restraint as well as escalation and today it is necessary to do so. The power of the military is simply too big, too effective, too destructive to be credible, as such and alone, any longer. It "cannot overcome an enemy's will to resist," ample evidence of which we have found in Vietnam, and should have known from the Battle of Britain and many other examples. Some are from our own history, and often reveal the counterproductivity of direct pressures. These again emphasize the centrality of the will rather than the determination of the instrument, however brutal, however refined.

The Success of Restraint

Finally, it is noted that the more recent articles lack the intensely somber overtones of the nuclear threat which characterized the 1950's and even the early 1960's. The ABM question has been controversial but it has hardly generated cold

fear; it has had more the character of a snappy game of ana-
grams. For instance, "The Must Case for the ABM—Truly, a
Weapon for All Seasons," [77] is cast in quite academic terms,
almost as a dispute in semantics involving the integrity of
our own Government, and the overriding necessity of trusting
our own leaders. There is mild concern that "recent changes
in deterrent power threaten to upset The Delicate Balance."
But actually the mood reflects the success of the nuclear deterrent which now "has resulted in a paralysis of will and
imagination in Western leaders who may believe that the
status quo based upon nuclear stalemate can last indefinitely." [78] We have, in other words, been too successful! There
is even time in a detached, armchair sort of way for wistful
reflection upon those unexpected successes in battle for which
"The Victorious Will" seems still the only key.[79] More than
Russia, perhaps, an "Orwellian, computerized world" is feared
and must not be allowed to sit in judgment on the chances—
the judgment and the will—of an underdog to pull the decisive upset sometime in the future.[80]

NAVY

The Mood of Fatalism

The Navy and the Air Force have not been, it seems, so
explicit in emphasizing *will* as the Army, but the specter of
the bomb is there with its demand for control. As early as
1955 a speaker at the Naval War College seeking "The Cause
of War" found that however useful war had been in the past,
it was no longer so for "the obviously cataclysmic nature of
its end product may have made it virtually impossible . . .
to function in international society." He quotes approvingly
from Sir John Slessor that "war—in the sense of total war—
has abolished itself as a practical instrument of policy." [81]
Yet in "Background to Disarmament" war, however senseless
and irrational, is seen as almost certain if not inevitable; "un-

planned it breaks out": Clausewitz is too rational; disarmament is probably hopeless. Still, the effort to control human passions must go on.[82] This mood of the inevitable, almost fatalistic, is perhaps more characteristic of men of the sea, threatened for long periods of time by the overwhelming, dwarfing forces of nature, harsher, more decisive, and impossible to avoid, subject only to limited control (even with modern equipment), the powerful, mysterious, tragic world of Moby Dick. Naval theorists are caught in the tension between a profound awareness and deep distrust of the bomb as irrational, and the equally profound awareness of the limits of man and his propensity, as Kahn puts it, to subscribe to the "rationality of the irrational," to ride Moby Dick to his own death. Hence, they can castigate the almost inevitable nuclear war and call, like the Army, for maximum restraint, raising the plaintive question, "How have we gotten ourselves into the mood for all-out war? Perhaps in keeping with our natural character of doing things in a big way." [83] They can argue that since nuclear warfare, even limited, would tend to maximation, therefore both nuclear war and limited nuclear war are alike unacceptable;[84] that nuclear war is not the "sensible way," but "Patience: [is the] Bedrock Strategy in the 1960's"—the alternative being suicide.[85] They can assert that the "destruction complex" of the Air Force must be resisted, since winning at the end and not maximum damage must be the objective, and while unconditional surrender may be necessary "limited" victory is just as likely.[86] Indeed, "winning" is hardly likely but losing still is; hence MacArthur was wrong in divorcing victory from political control.[87]

With this tensional attitude toward pessimistic alternatives, "balanced force" is rated superior to "counterforce" as allowing a more flexible, restrained response;[88] and both disarmament and the United Nations deserve support even if they are not the full answer.[89] Power is eternal and must be used, but war is becoming useless as such and we must begin to

think, and to will, in the direction of "The Changing Nature
of Power" to allow for socially acceptable and racially secure
expressions of military thought.[90] These expressions may well
include, in a turn reminiscent of the sophisticated, often bloodless maneuverings of Vauban, a strict avoidance of battles as
no longer "the payoff." Vietnam has taught us, surely, that
battles can be won—and the war prolonged, and possibly
even lost. Dr. Stefan T. Possony, long associated with military
intelligence and psychological warfare and now Senior Fellow
at the Hoover Institution on War, Revolution, and Peace at
Stanford, California, urges that

given superior, stronger, and more secure forces-in-being, fast operational reaction times, as well as combat readiness and eagerness to
fight expedient battles—and only those—many modern wars should
be conducted with a minimum of tactical contact and a maximum
of military detachment. In the main, they should be contests between political parties . . . [who must] compete for legitimacy and
acceptance by the mass of people. For it is the people who render
the ultimate verdict of defeat or victory.[91]

On the other hand, in a 1969 Prize Essay in *Naval Institute
Proceedings,* Lieutenant Charles L. Parnell argues that "there
must be a limit to our self-imposed limitations. . . . We
should not over-emphasize our willingness to negotiate, for
. . . limited wars are ideally suited for the Communist delaying tactics." [92] The seemingly unlimited capacity of the enemy
for patience, and even restraint, is clearly frustrating for activist Americans and, if the truth were known, doubtless unnerving, especially when it is so unexpectedly (if not illogi-
cally) combined with aggressive and hardened tendencies elsewhere in the global struggle.[93] Russia's recent dramatic turn
to the sea, interpreted (naturally) as "a search for supremacy"
in that medium, is viewed with increasing alarm when measured against vociferous demands at home for our retrenchment from foreign waters.[94] Hence the concerns of the late
1960's for the ABM and for China, both of which occupied

naval thinking pro and con,[95] have of late yielded to more personal and pragmatic fears for the future of the American Navy as unquestioned mistress of the seven seas.

The nuclear threat continues to recede, but it never disappears. Rather, it acts as a large and gloomy backdrop to every serious discussion. It is the conditioner of ultimacy, making the streets of the world "without joy," granting to every gesture and word and act something of enormity and uncertainty and eternity, the possibility, small and remote perhaps but *nonetheless there,* that this one event may be the spark of doomsday. Naval personnel are convinced that the stakes are not only high but ultimate: the very salvation of Western and Christian civilization—"Their way of life or ours." Hence, the Marines—and others—can demand "The Right to Fight" [96] even though Former Commandant Shoup and others have called for a sweeping reappraisal of the whole military establishment and its attitudes. Lieutenant General Krulak speaks for many when he cries that the whole issue must be reduced from the head to

the midsection—we are suffering a shortage of that four-letter commodity called "guts." There is a passive unwillingness on the part of the vast bulk of our people to stand up and be counted; to fight what is wrong. . . .

If the American people will show the guts to face the issues as they really are and to make themselves heard over the din of those who would destroy our society, the future has to be bright. This particularly has to do with military, with the preservation of its image, with the damping of the downward tilt of the curve of our popularity with the protection of our strength, of our right to fight, of our opportunity to defend our land.[97]

This attitude is perhaps more bitterly illustrated by Captain Hanks in "Against All Enemies," which was directed especially at General Shoup for his "distinct disservice" in casting doubt on the military establishment from within which was eagerly supported by "the most widely known dissenter in the United States . . . Senator J. William Fulbright." [98] Hanks's sense of urgency is in the mood of earlier declarations that we ought not to let ethics get in the way of waging "final" war. President Truman was not the only statistician to see the new nuclear weapon as a shortcut, and that strategically the end *may* justify any means:

Democracy may not be right, but it is the only faith we have. . . . Let us accept the test of greatness . . . to sacrifice deliberately the little moralities for the large without fear of breaking our faith.[99]

Even preventive war, under certain circumstances and when it is carefully distinguished from aggressive war (its morality being dependent upon its rationality), "might" be acceptable.[100]

A Plurality of Options

These are strong and even harsh statements of positions deeply, worriedly felt. But in general, they are older kinds of thought and, as always, naval writers feel impelled to distinguish their stance from what is considered to be the "absolutist" attitude of the Air Force, while not allowing it to slip into the "conventional" position of the Army.[101] Even the Marines, for all their vaunted image of "The King of Kill," [102] perhaps following the lead of Shoup while listening to the rhetoric of Krulak, have been seriously reexamining the nature of modern warfare. This is clear in articles such as "The New Conflict," which requires "Political Restraints" and "The Fusion of Military and Political Considerations." [103] The prime virtue of loyalty still operates,[104] but the sodden tragedy of Vietnam comes through increasingly in their writings as provocative questionings and innovative suggestions respecting the future management of conflict.

On the whole, the Navy seeks to keep a plurality of options open before the reason and the will. This may be seen in Commander Keener's "revision" of the "principles of war" to include specifically "initiative" and the employment of "the unorthodox as almost immutable laws." [105] It is clear here that reason, although not mentioned, is presumed as basic to the use of these and other principles which Keener elucidates. But "Unreason," as another young officer puts it,[106] or irrationality, may be and often is as readily involved. For this reason, I have used the term "will," with its correlatives "choice" and "decision," as more basically descriptive of the nature of military power, after the rational. For reason perceives options among which choices must be made and today's options are multiplying with electrifying rapidity and frightening pressure for decisions. In "South of Thirty," Captain Chase sees the interests of the great powers drawn like a magnet for decades to come to an area "South of Thirty degrees of North Latitude" where the trivial, the irritating, the unexpected, but the consequential, in the uneven aspirations and actions of small but rising peoples may indeed preclude the use of nuclear weapons. But they will surely cry for alert and novel responses subject to proper rational analysis.[107]

For there is less and less time for the "analog thinking" of the past, of seeing and evaluating the parts in sequence, i.e., "linear." There is, rather, necessity for "digital," "computer," "systems" thinking which insists upon "looking upon the whole earth . . . simultaneously" for instant decisions.[108] The thinking, indeed, is *for decisions,* and attention to this primary aspect of both government and military is increasingly precise and pronounced. The trouble is, the "wholes" which form the bases of computer decisions keep enlarging in geometric fashion, and coupled with another significantly novel aspect of the modern age—the radical uncertainty introduced into warfare by the atomic question—it is understandable that confusion reigns over the nature and applicability of "rules" and "laws" for modern warfare. Recently the Judge Advocate General of the Navy called for "new laws" to meet "new conditions" which no longer recognize nice and easy distinctions between peace and war but which instead exploit a whole and blurred spectrum of good and evil.[109] The Navy is not without pride that its own long tradition, which has been both pluralistic and diplomatic, gives it an important edge in the battle of service rivalries to benefit the nation. The development of the Marines as "soldiers of the sea" and the long, bitter struggle to retain an air arm are remembered and give substance to what often seems a conflicting welter of analyses and conclusions. The hawks and the doves are all seagulls in these cases, and they are of course delighted that civilian hawks and doves are joining them in pushing the protection of the nation out to sea.[110] Implicitly, respect for the will to give force to reason faced with alternatives perhaps lies deeper in the thinking of men of the sea who are profoundly appreciative of the obstreperous nature of man and the uncertain dynamics of his societies. Nature herself forces decisions upon puny men which go beyond rational analysis and certainty. The immense, inscrutable, and lowering threat of the bomb has put all men to sea in a struggle with the elements which requires decision-making of the utmost consequence as the daily fact of life. Therefore, naval theorists see themselves on the tensional, somewhat pessimistic ("realistic") plane of common sense, holding a median position between the too trusting Army and the trigger-happy Air Force.

AIR FORCE

The Objective Is Victory!

The Air Force, of course, does not so regard itself, but is itself "realistic." Perhaps the admitted fallibility of man is replaced to some degree by the wonderful dependability of the machine, that amazingly sensitive robot which seems to free man from the burdens of time and the constricting powers of nature. The very youthfulness of the Air Force and its popularity may also affect its estimate of the size of the problems and the degree of optimism for their solution. At any rate, Air Force writings seem almost blythe by comparison with the somber intent of the older services. They are less foreboding about the nature of man and his inventions, and almost eager at times to get on with the show.

In late 1959, there appeared in *Air Power Historian* a well-received major article by a rural Alabama high school teacher entitled "Thesis on Decline." The article decried the world "humanitarianism" ("crystallized morality") that has weakened the fiber of our rugged frontiersman individuality and sent us into two world wars from which we have emerged victorious but strained and confused. Now "the 'ivory tower' will have to be abandoned, at least for awhile, since the existing problem is essentially one of practical survival."

We should understand the fact that the same basic principles prevail in warfare today that have always prevailed. . . . The greater one's power, the greater the assurance of victory. . . . Both the idea that war is "immoral" and that war would destroy "mankind" are methods employed by Humanitarians to insure the continuation of "peaceful" methods no matter how disastrous these policies prove to be to the West.[111]

The direct, uncompromising spirit of victory *at whatever cost* emphasized by this article has been reflected in many Air Force publications since that date. In 1960, escalation was not simply inevitable but *necessary* ("The Fallacy of Minimum Deterrence"), since less power may attract aggression and in the end conventional weapons and crash programs prove more expensive.[112] In "Limited War for Unlimited Goals," Colonel A. P. Sights, Jr., was very sensitive to the dizzying magnitude of the millionfold-plus expansion of military power in the atomic era, but still reasoned that "parity" in nuclear deterrence is a factor of instability. Hence, he concluded, there is a clear need for the United States to push to and maintain unquestioned superiority in air power and nuclear retaliatory capability.[113] In 1964, "Overkill and Underthought" arguments against further manufacture of bombs as "overkill" seemed "unconvincing," since he who is ahead is not encouraging an arms race simply by staying ahead.[114] Even "saber rattling" has its place in "The Battle for Men's Minds," since it is proper to use new weapons against tyranny, and the encouragement of fear as wholesome respect for one's power to punish is "an ethical weapon for our use." [115] Lieutenant General Ira Eaker, now retired, would apparently have escalated considerably more than this in Vietnam, being unalterably opposed (1966) to our "graduated response" and calling for the striking of "Ho's factories, harbors," etc., clearly with all we had.[116]

The Bomb Can Be Lived With

The objective has been "to win," and since the struggle is either/or, a general war must always be presumed.[117] The Air Force *knows* who the central enemy is and this clarity, as well as the decisive character of its weapon, makes it the one force best able to plan war to its finality.[118] In "From Cain to Zeus" the call is for "victory" against stalemate, disarmament, and the UN.[119] "We Can Win a Nuclear War" via dispersal of aircraft on every country lane.[120] But if the enemy does the same? Then a war of attrition would develop—all the more reason for a "quick victory through overwhelming air power." [121] The cherished "flexible response" of the Army and the Navy yields here to "determined retaliation," a compromise with the admittedly outmoded "massive retaliation" of the Dulles era.[122] Indeed, in order to maintain "American Security and the Balance of Power in the Nuclear Age" preventive war might be required, limited of course to restoration of the balance.[123] In "Learning to Live with the Nuclear Spread" we are told (1966) that better relations with our allies will follow the sharing rather than the denying of nuclear weapons.[124]

In all of this there is little fear of the catastrophic power of the bomb. It is considered a rational development, the present end of a continuum of the new weapons man has always insisted upon making *and using*. In "History, Ethics and the Bomb," a serious review of two new books dealing with Hiroshima and its implications, a certain fate, like a Greek tragedy, attends the event. "The decision to make was probably also the decision to use [the bomb]," and probably the decision was the best that could be made under the circumstances. The authors see a transformation of ethical standards during World War II which, through the argument of "the lesser evil," condoned obliteration bombings of German cities and thus led straight to Hiroshima and the open question of today.[125]

The Newer Voices of Restraint

Yet the question is open—in the Air Force as elsewhere—and voices are raised against the rush to absolutism. A warning was sounded early (1962) in a Moral Leadership article authored by Toynbee which documents vividly how the nation-in-arms concept has at the point of required military service expressed totalitarianism far in excess of all earlier so-called military regimes.[126] About the same time a writer to an "In My Opinion" column felt that loose talk itself encourages a "momentum" toward nuclear expression and that airmen need to help the administration to find alternatives.[127] In 1966 a review of Nevelle Brown's *Nuclear War: The Impending Strategic Deadlock* favored a measured response, i.e., limited war as "right" instead of "unconditional surrender"; there should be a constant willingness to negotiate.[128] By 1969 it was being suggested, prudentially, that limited wars, if seriously committed to limited objectives, should be *shorter* wars and hence less destructive of the military image which is hard put to wear a halo through a long, difficult period. (Ironically this has been an increasing problem in Vietnam, a supposedly "limited war.")[129] The same caution and acceptance of limited objectives was voiced in "The New American Military," tracing the transformation of the military from its World War II role of "total prosecution" to subordination to civilian control and limited aims.[130] Taking issue with columnist Joseph Kraft's accusation that the military attempted to take over McNamara, Herman Wolk, who for nearly a decade was associated with the U.S. Air Force Historical Division, points out that the reverse is closer to the truth when one notes the extreme limitations under which the military have actually been operating in Vietnam. He intimates that Lasswell's either/or garrison state thesis of total peace or total war is erroneous.[131]

A very capable analysis of "American Strategic Thinking," comparing the positions of Herman Kahn, Thomas C. Schelling, Bernard Brodie, and others, has developed the thesis of the fruitfulness of a plurality of styles of strategic thought in America.[132] A certain progress may be noted in the idea of "strategic stability," an evolving concept which, while too easily dismissing disarmament as unworkable, rejects both massive retaliation and strategic offensive forces as constituting an "offense-only . . . posture." Such a posture is inherently weak in flexibility and encourages the very tensions that induce instability and lead to war.[133] Moreover, considerably less attention has been directed by Air Force writers toward civic action and the "changing nature of power" to allow for a more positive role for the military professionals to broaden their training and tasks to encompass planning the prevention of war.[134] This might well include the later and rather lonely attempt to redefine and redirect chemical warfare (which has such "a bad reputation") to tranquilize rather than kill the enemy.[135]

The depth of this almost about-face in attitude among some Air Force thinkers is rather startlingly revealed in Lieutenant Colonel Bower's "The Twentieth Century Penchant for the Offensive," a hard-hitting exposé of the fact that

twentieth century land, sea, and air warfare has repeatedly demonstrated the strength of the non-rational appeal of the offensive. Indeed, the allure of the offensive has become a dangerous penchant for modern military minds. . . . We seek perspective toward the treachery of the unthinking approach and toward one of its most insidious forms—the irrational offensive.[136]

Perhaps the most interesting thing about this article is the appeal to Clausewitz—to the generally overlooked and troubling preference of the Master for the defensive! Others have called attention to the same preference[137] which appears to follow from Clausewitz' considerable appreciation and even apprehension of those "dark unknowns" of the inner psyches of men. "There is no human affair," Clausewitz wrote, "which stands so constantly and so generally in close connection with chance as War," for it is largely an act of primitive emotion.[138] But, suggests Dr. Miewald,

Clausewitz was too much of a soldier to admit that his profession was fit only for the provision of presiding officers over meaningless chaos. He found hope in the form of a special type of decision-maker, namely, the commander with genius. . . . [One] who was unfettered by predetermined rules and who possessed the gift of the *coup d'oeil,* combined with a sense of resolution, could cut through the fog of uncertainty that envelops the scene of combat. . . . The decisive element in war could be provided by that sphere of the mind outside the purely rational domain of science, by that "field of genius, which *raises itself above rules.*" [139]

The Air Force, it is hoped, is beginning to close the gap of extremism in its understanding of military power and its uses which has rather sharply distinguished it from the older services in the past.

In this section it has become evident that although military theorists are self-consciously insistent upon the importance of the rational, primacy of the will is always assured, opening the way to irrational and demonic excesses, but also encouraging the hope of conscious restraint. For the will can be misused, responding to the erratic pressures of the emotions and subverting reason in the rationalizations of fanaticism. We are

too self-consciously sophisticated to see ourselves yielding
overmuch to these forms of irrationalism. It is rather sophistication itself which is the graver because vastly more subtle
danger. This was the context of that "wise" and salable wordi-
ness against which Socrates struggled long ago in the honest
attempt to recognize and preserve that which is truly human.
The biases of self-interest and pride of service, supported by
the marvelous minutiae of science, have created, especially in
the Air Force, a new military-scientific scholasticism which can
justify even the "rationality of the irrational" in nuclear war.
The danger becomes especially pronounced in a serving institution that places a premium upon the will to power and
action, and in a time when the cry is being heard to turn war
over to the military. The problem thus drives deeper than the
intellectual and the emotional, and beyond leaders to the will
of peoples, especially in a totalitarian age which has hallowed
the mass army concept. Armed with unlimited power, a Frank-
enstein has been created which increasing numbers in the military itself distrust, though less those without a tradition, the
eager children of technology.

Chapter 6

The Fascination
for
the Concrete

Military power may become, as we have seen, highly abstract and voluntaristic, but as military power it cannot be divorced from the concretely particular and coercive. Walter Millis has defined power as "the ability to coerce," [1] and Admiral Eccles has distinguished between its exertion as *attraction* or *pressure*.[2] But the former depends upon the latter. Like paper money, military power must have its hard reserve, payable upon demand.[3] That reserve is unformed energy, raw, "naked" force, the power of being, what Clausewitz calls *violence,* the "original violence of its elements," expressed in physical coercion, battle, and blood. Thus Clausewitz scoffs at "bloodless war," and misunderstood, I think, says that violence must be pushed "to its utmost bounds," and "to introduce into the philosophy of war . . . a principle of moderation would be an absurdity." [4] *The battle* is the decisive element: "the overruling importance of this destructive principle and nothing else." [5] It is interesting that Engels, commenting on *On War* to Marx, understands Clausewitz not as advocating unlimited war but recognizing the fact of the ultimate willingness of power as military to use ultimate force for specific and finite ends.[6] The military as rational is general and qualitative in organizing "raw force" or violence, but it decisively wills its power in particular and quantitative ways. As finite creatures we all will particulars, but military power, concerned with ultimacy, pushes always to the extreme. This swift and often total descent from general principles to particular acts is what I have called the "fascination for the concrete," i.e., for *this* Plan, *this* Order, *this* Enemy—rather than none or another. Military power is rational, but it cannot remain there: it is not academia, though it is often academic. In willing, it specifies the concrete. So principles easily become dogmas, and "contingency plans" actually promote action. The military is fundamentally earthy, and reveals in sudden and molten fissures the violence that is ever seeking to erupt.

I. THE CONCRETE EXPRESSED IN WESTERN MILITARY HISTORY

WEAPONRY

Iron Swords and Phalanxes

There have been those who attempted to evade this final resort to the concrete, but they were brushed aside by history. Genghis Khan found the Chinese inhibited by "grave and elaborate tactics" which satisfied their propensity for making war an art but which did nothing to unnerve a foe who recognized ingenious noisemakers and paper dragons for exactly what they were.[7] Centuries later in Europe, Jean Martinet and Sebastian Vauban nearly duplicated the Chinese toying with war-making, and with like effect.[8] On the other hand, the influence of weapons, as well as topography, weather, and economic considerations, have often been decisive. Toynbee says that the victory of the iron-sworded Dorians over the bronze-sworded Minoans must be attributed in part, at least, to the strength of the new weapon.[9] Later, the hoplites, standing shield to shoulder in solid phalanx before the even, fertile

ground of their own homes, held out for a time and even re-
pulsed the Asian invaders. But limited, conservative, the "very
character [of their fighting] tended to limit the advance of the
art of war," and the barbarian Philip, adding cavalry and
lightly armed peltasts, cut the Greek freemen to pieces on the
uneven ground at Chaeronea.[10] With this highly mobile and responsive "human fortress," Alexander quite unmysteriously cut
the Gordian knot of Asia. The Roman legion developed also
from the republican phalanx, and suffered nearly fatal setbacks
against the Samnites in hill warfare until, lacking a Philip
but given generations of experimentation, a formation was developed "so marvelously supple that it has been compared to
the human hand." [11] Able to feel out an enemy's weakness like
exploring fingers or to close up at once like a fist, it found
and held a world in its grasp for half a millennium.

The Rise and Fall of Cavalry

The demise of the Romans came with the rise of cavalry, to
which they never really adjusted. C. W. Oman, in his classic,
The Art of War in the Middle Ages, says that indeed feudalism
may be viewed as "the rise, supremacy, and decline of heavy
cavalry as the chief power in war." [12] In A.D. 378, in the decisive battle of Adrianople, Gothic horse completely routed
Roman infantry and killed the emperor Valens. For almost a
thousand years—until 1315 when Swiss infantrymen with fearful pike and halberd overwhelmed the mounted knights of
Duke Leopold at Morgarten to win their independence—the
horse and his rider, variously armed and armored, held sway
from the steppes and deserts of Asia and the Near East to the
isles of the Normans and Saxons. The ability of the East
Romans to survive the fall of Rome can be traced in significant
part to their quick adoption of the Gothic horse as *foederati,*
or mercenaries, attached first to generals and later incorpo-
rated into a truly national army serving the empire. Thus the
"Byzantine horse-archer" became the distinguishing key to

the long endurance struggle of the Eastern Empire. To cavalry may be added the more spectacular, but less frequently used, "Greek fire," which measurably helped in saving Constantinople from the Saracens.[13] But even cavalry could and would meet its match. Montross suggests that Genghis Khan and his generals turned back from central and western Europe, "a terrain of forests and mountains, of miserable roads and massive stone fortifications," because they realized they were beyond their tactical depth.[14] The Swiss, the Flemish (Courtrai, 1302), and the Scots (Bannockburn, 1314) challenged the knights successfully. A curious weapon called the "godendag" was first used at Courtrai in clublike fashion to dismount and pin a man in heavy armor. The English longbow, however, is perhaps most acclaimed as a national weapon—in popular opinion, at least—responsible for the long dominance of France by a nation of half its resources.[15]

Gunpowder and the Modern Age

Gunpowder, especially, ushered in the modern age. At Lepanto (1571), Don John beat the Turks with ships to which "guns had been married." [16] The importance of gunpowder to the easy conquests of the rich and highly civilized empires of the New World can hardly be exaggerated. When this weapon, in turn, became the instrument of the *levée en masse* in modern times and was given fantastic respectability in the machine gun, along with fortress armor and mobility in the tank, and a third dimension in the airplane, we have both the liberator and the terror of the modern world. Fuller says that

the musket made the infantryman, and the infantryman made the democrat: power to kill and, therefore, to enforce equality . . . was the essence of the question.[17]

Politics thus can be said to flow from the weapon and the nature of society from the kind of weapons it uses. Ancient and modern democracies have depended upon the "unmounted arm," [18] and it may be an encouraging sign that the infantry-man cannot be dispensed within a push-button age which has its own aristocracy of missiles and computerized strategies. Long-range weapons, manned by fewer skilled crews and backed by "nonkilling" support troops of various kinds, have threatened to depersonalize killing and make it almost abstract by greatly restricting human contact. But guerrilla warfare has again insisted upon the concrete in radical and terribly personal ways.

Instant Armageddon

Despite the exploitation of the common man for aggression at times, it would seem that basically he and his weapons are defensive in nature. The ancient phalanx, the "trinity of bullet, spade, and wire" of World War I, perhaps even the highly mobile operations of World War II and the basic "sweep" tactics in today's Vietnam, despite all their sophistication depend upon the common man and appeal to the conservation of his values anchored at home. But what of the impact of nuclear energy on warfare? In tactics it has provoked guerrilla warfare as the safer substitute for larger actions that would tempt the use of nuclear weapons. As a weapon or weapons system, nuclear energy is "more revolutionary than gunpowder" [19] because now the means can seriously threaten to engulf the end in a way literally and concretely absolute. That is, we can actually destroy civilization—and perhaps the earth itself as habitable—in a few minutes. A weapon that can end the human race is radically new to man's experience. The abstract and impersonal pushing of buttons is at last combined with the finality of unthinkable destruction. The possibility of "instant Armageddon" is real even if improbable. For the wheel of life, *by our own choice, can* and therefore *may* come full circle: "From dust . . . to dust." So far we have actually and completely committed our lives and the planet itself, perhaps, to the impersonal concrete.

THE ECONOMIC AS CONCRETE

In all this the economic, implicitly if not explicitly, underlies the ability to produce and utilize mass and velocity, the factors of weaponry. Ancient sieges are too numerous to mention, with their often horrible starvation and even cannibalism. The Punic wars were trade wars, as were most of the Byzantine struggles. Indeed, gold, as a ransom or tribute or used as the moral weapon of betrayal, was admittedly a vital element in East Roman strategy.[20] The rise of banking and the relation of finance to military power and the development of modern states is an intriguing story in itself. The naval blockades employed on an exceptionally wide scale in the world wars (and seen earlier used against Napoleon)[21] were powerful and effective, and however inhumane were justified by the Allies as the logical and necessary extension of military force well supported by history. Marx had already made this all quite philosophical in economic determinism. Class war, for instance, is a "profound military problem, because the social health of a nation is the moral foundation of its military power." [22] And Engels significantly rephrases the Clausewitzian trinity of "violence, chance and reason" to emphasize also the economic.[23] Despite our denunciation of Communism, we seem uncomfortably close to the Marxian priority on the economic with our finalizing of the marriage of industry to the military, a union that had visitational and common law privileges long before its open recognition in our day. It is perhaps significant that it was a military hero President who warned the nation that in the new "military-industrial complex" more than liaison had come into being. A new structure, a new institution, a new *concreteness* expressive of military power had arisen as a threat to democracy.

THE ONTOLOGY OF THE CONCRETE

Raw Power as Seductive

But beyond the weapons, and deeper than the economic, lies the very ontology of the concrete, the attractiveness of raw power and brute force to man's nature. From personal experience on the brutal battlefields of Europe, Glenn Gray, in *The Warriors,* reminisces on the mysteriously "enduring appeals of battle" as driving deep to the lust of the eye for the spectacle, the "powerful fascination" for the brilliant and ugly, the awe of power as power—and one's subordination to an identification with nature itself on the battlefield.[24] Man becomes "only a center of force, a wielder of weapons. . . . He is lost in their majesty. His ego temporarily deserts him, and he is absorbed into what he sees." [25] This is an escape different from sex or alcohol.

This raptness is a joining and not a losing, a deprivation of self in exchange for a union with objects that were hitherto foreign . . . [a] feeling of the sublime, to which we, children of nature, are directed whether we desire it or not. Astonishment and wonder and awe appear to be part of our deepest being, and war offers them an exercise par excellence.[26]

Ernst Juenger, a German soldier and writer, speaks of

the fire . . . so violent that no one gave any thought to the dead. One had, literally, the dead at his heels. It was only then that I observed the existence of a strange horror, as of a virgin country. . . . I felt no fear but a supreme, almost demoniacal easiness of mind, and . . . surprising excesses of insane laughter.[27]

Thus veterans have sought to understand the peculiar ecstasy observed on many a field of battle, the human spirit lifted above blood and destruction in a strange delirium at the very moment of the utmost personal identification with uninhibited natural power. In lesser degree all of us have experienced something of this awful recognition of power as power, in different guises: mountains and seas and deserts have always impressed and overwhelmed and drawn men to their bosoms "because they were there." Is this not the basis of hero worship, the charismatic quality of leaders, a factor still of vital importance in "power politics" and not unlike the "mana" of primitives? And what about our love affair with violence on television, not to mention the age-old sports of wrestling, boxing, and perhaps especially football?[28] Gray speaks of this as a "recognition of power and grandeur to which we are subject. There is not so much a separation of the self from the world as a subordination of the self to it. . . . [It] satisfies because we are conscious of a power outside us with which we can merge in relation of parts to the whole."[29]

The Ecstasy of Destruction

This aesthetic ecstasy is condemned in the Bible because it is not morally sensitive and pushes all too readily beyond the morally permissive. As "spectatoritis" it is a fugitive from action and becomes transsocial, delighting simply in the spectacle of destruction. But beyond this there is undoubted enjoyment in actively participating in destroying. In Gray's words, a battlefield evidences a "radical evil" which "appears to surpass mere human malice and to demand explanation in cosmological and religious terms."[30] Contrary to what we would like to believe about the human species, and more especially about ourselves, "a walk across any battlefield shortly after the guns have fallen silent is convincing enough . . . that there is a delight in destruction."[31] Again, Juenger with pitiless clarity remembers his part in the last German offensive in the West:[32]

The great moment had come. The curtain of fire lifted from the trenches. We stood up.

With a mixture of feelings, evoked by bloodthirstiness, rage, and intoxication, we moved in step, ponderously but irresistibly toward the enemy lines. . . . My right hand embraced the shaft of my pistol, my left a riding stick of bamboo cane. I was boiling with rage, which had taken hold of me and all the others in an incomprehensible fashion. The overwhelming wish to kill gave wings to my feet. Rage pressed bitter tears from my eyes.

The monstrous desire for annihilation, which hovered over the battlefield, thickened the brains of the men and submerged them in a red fog. We called to each other in sobs and stammered disconnected sentences. A neutral observer might have perhaps believed that we were seized by an excess of happiness.[33]

This the generals call "the will to close with the enemy," an

innocent-sounding phrase [which] conceals the very substance of the delight in destruction slumbering in most of us. When soldiers step over the line that separates self-defense from fighting for its own sake, as it is so easy for them to do, they experience something that stirs deep chords in their being. The soldier-killer is learning to serve a different deity, and his concern is with death and not life, destruction and not construction.[34]

Shades of Shiva! Here may lie something of the truth which has made that mysterious, imperious, complex, and "auspicious" (*shiva*) god one of the great gods of Asia, representing "Life itself, as pure energy or force," and yet at once and from of old the Destroyer.[35] Like the god, men in ecstasy dance the dance of destruction, enraptured, captured by the primeval power passing through them, using them, exalting them. "Burn, Baby, Burn!" is a distinctly human cry of exultation in destruction, not to be reduced in some Darwinian or Freudian sense to the animalic and primitive within us, but rather "peculiarly human, or more exactly . . . devilish in a way animals can never be." It is essentially rushing beyond a recognition of the concrete to a worship of that which informs it, i.e., power unstructured. It is, then, "ecstasy without a union," [36] and drives to the absolute, swallowing up all other pleasures, sacrificing all to its own consuming fire. So

a surgeon, a man of great worth, who was dressing one of the officers [British, fallen at the Battle of Saratoga, Revolutionary War], raised his blood-smeared hands in a frenzy of patriotism, exclaimed, "Wilkinson, I have dipped my hands in British blood!" He received a sharp rebuke for his brutality.[37]

And Hitler, with devilish intuition, could passionately observe:

"Brutality is respected. Brutality and physical strength! The plain man in the streets respects nothing but brutal strength and restlessness—women, too, for that matter, women and children."

And again:

"The people need wholesome fear. They *want* to fear something. They want someone to frighten them and make them shudderingly submissive. . . . Why babble and be indignant about torturing? The masses need something that will give them a thrill of horror." [38]

Hitler seemed to have read quite accurately the minds of his own "nation of shopkeepers" who twice in a generation tragically expressed their preference for blood instead of boredom. Long before Hitler the terrible fascination of physical atrocity was used as a moral weapon by the Great Khan and Tamerlane, to name only two efficient conquerors. Vagts speaks of a French light colonel in World War I who openly advocated: "Terrify . . . until there is nothing left to kill." A lieutenant general in cold sorrow could agree with Sherman's estimate that "War is hell": "To carry on war, disguise it as we may, is to be cruel; it is to kill and burn, burn and kill, and again kill and burn." [39] Our experience in Southeast Asia has surprised us only at the breadth and depth of such fascination for the kill.

The psychologists have had their say: E. F. M. Durbin and John Bowlby in their "Personal Aggressiveness and War" have even suggested as a "common-sense theory of war" that we carry with us an *underlying willingness to kill*—discontent drives people to new adventures which are not enough without blood:

It is not the excitement of change, but the excitement of blood, that fills the streets with cheering crowds and sends the first—though not the last—regiments into war with trumpets. People are less sensible and more savage than . . . rational theories of the willingness to fight seem to suppose.[40]

Gray remarks on the "lightning rapidity" with which

war compresses the greatest opposites into the smallest space and shortest time. . . . In the delirium of liberation, many individuals were constantly going from a group that was hugging and kissing returned FFI comrades to join another that was torturing isolated collaborators. . . . Love and hatred, tenderness and brutality, succeed each other in many a person within moments. . . . Inhuman cruelty can give way to superhuman kindness . . . both qualities in the same person. . . . Inhibitions vanish, and people are reduced to their essence.[41]

And as though this reduction to what I have called the concrete were of the nature of nature, it has been suggested that destroying seems at times to be "a cleansing force. It frees the native from his inferiority complex," said the late Frantz Fanon, an anticolonial revolutionist, and so may even be "the cutting edge of justice." [42] I doubt that this is either psychologically or ethically sound, but it does suggest that destruction is often the herald of justice, and more than an abstract principle. It is insistent upon the concrete as sometimes necessary to sweep away the antiquated forms of power, but in so doing may yield to fascination and idolatry of its own concreteness in descending to destruction. In *The Beardless Warriors* a green young soldier in the horribly exploding battle "realized that he'd just killed two Germans. Something hot expanded in his chest and stomach. He couldn't seem to breathe. He'd killed them. They were dead. It was miraculous." A third, a sniper, is with more difficulty added to the kill. And now

there was a tingling lightness in his body as though he'd been drinking. He seemed to float across the ground in effortless strides, moving as in a dream. Nothing could stop him. Nothing.[43]

The fire storms of Dresden and Hiroshima, and the difficulty of controls in Vietnam, continue to illustrate the fascination which the violent concrete has for us, not only as an element of military power, but as a means that so easily becomes the end. Indeed, the all-consuming tragedy of Vietnam, with its brutal and declared policy of attrition, illustrates this sometimes utter absorption with the violent concrete to the exclusion of alternatives that do not so readily lend themselves to dramatic and measurable results. It is odd, if not irrational, that attrition should be our declared policy, given the tremendously greater manpower of Asia and assuming that our concern for the worth of the individual is as high and genuine as we say it is. It is far from reassuring that a great metropolitan museum should reject a modest Army proposal for "a balanced historical survey from the Revolutionary War to present" for "something livelier," "the utmost in realism," for its viewers, especially children. This was achieved in a diorama of the Vietnam countryside complete with grass shacks which provided simulated live targets for children who fired at them electronically from an Army UH-ID ("Huey") helicopter. Despite protests, especially by the local and state Congress of Parents and Teachers, the show was such a success that the Air Force planned to provide a similar experience via a similarly rigged B-52 bomber.[44]

American Fascination for the Violent Concrete

This is to suggest that fascination for the violent concrete is strongly evident in American history and character. De Tocqueville long ago remarked upon the particular struggle of Americans as a struggle with nature, in contrast to that of the Russians as one with men.[45] That is to say, the ever-beckoning frontier of an untamed wilderness has challenged our attention and doubtless has had more than a little to do with our "love affair with the machine," with inanimate nature as an object to be admired, manipulated, used, copied, and yielding most readily to physical force. This absorption with nature as object and not subject has perhaps made it easy to understand military power as the logical, efficient, ultimate extension of power, concrete and coercive. We are perhaps the most materialistic of peoples, and our pragmatic approach to reality, coupled with a traditional ethic of work and a sense of destiny which have made us secular missionaries of the most materialistic of religions,[46] reinforce and can harden to terrible and unfeeling efficiency "a job to be done." It is a job that despite concern for peaceful means, slips with surprising ease into all-out use of violence.[47] The frontiersman, ready to take the law (i.e., the gun) into his own hand, both because he is enamored with violence irrationally for its own sake and because he has become supremely convinced of its natural utility,[48] seems close to the surface in the average American. This attitude, rooted in the giant land and history of America, and now married to an industrial complex which is the world's marvel, fulfills quite adequately the test of visibility in order to be credible.[49] Quite understandably, "Uncle Sam has become a world-renowned soldier in spite of himself." [50] Without conscious intent he has become a soldier but with every intent impatient to "get the job done."

II. THE CONCRETE EXPRESSED IN CONTEMPORARY MILITARY THOUGHT

ARMY

Bring Back the Tomahawk!

In the nature of the case, the attitude of the services is one in appreciating the role of the concrete in military power; they differ on what this means.

The Army stresses the value of new weapons and carefully notes that they are sometimes decisive. But weapons of the past should not be forgotten: "Why Don't We Bring Back the Tomahawk?" is asked in all seriousness for some of the nastiest antipersonnel work on Vietnamese jungle trails.[51] This seeming anomaly is matched by today's headlines. Not long ago a few ragged guerrilla hijackers held the combined might of the world's great powers at bay by the simple but wholly concrete act of jeopardizing the lives of several hundred innocent travelers. What is at stake—whether airline hijackers or world statesmen—is the credibility of ultimate intent, the utter willingness to redeem the threat to concretize the word whether it is in blowing up an airliner or a world. The illustrations are all around us. The machine gun, we know, has radically shifted the advantage to the defense, and technology and increased firepower surprisingly have encouraged the small army concept and guerrilla warfare as quite effective counters to tanks and planes, as Vietnam clearly shows. The "dream weapons" of the future—hydrogen bombs, laser rays, biochemical warfare, etc.—are seen as nightmarish and chillingly necessary deterrents, perhaps even tactically useful in limited ways.[52] But their effectiveness is measured by the yardstick of whether they are "for real." A recent minor controversy swirled about "The Bayonet: To Toy or to Terrorize?" Strangely, it might seem, its advocates claim that this simple, short piece of steel fixed to the (real?) weapon has the effect of instant, solid commitment:

"It starts the adrenalin flowing, makes a man alert, gives him the feeling that used to be expressed during World War II—you know the cliché—'This is it!' . . . We didn't have to use the bayonet, as it turned out. But we were better soldiers because we had that old bayonet on the end of the rifle. Fixing the bayonet was an act of commitment."

In oddly expressive statement of the impersonality of modern war, other soldiers claim:

"It symbolizes the soldier's basic mission: to close with and kill the enemy."

"The rifle is an impersonal weapon. The bayonet is real personal." [53]

The Resort to "Body Count"

The gruesome ritual of "body count" is doubtless some such longing for, and insistence upon, the concrete in a war of confusing fluidity, but, ironically, it is having the opposite effect of creating vagaries and incredulity. As two writers quoted with strong approval in *Army* put it:

"To think that in the midst of last week's chaos and breakdown of communications, a careful tabulation of such an enormous number of bodies was actually made defies logic and contributes further to the credibility gap." . . .

"Who in the name of God and decency can remember anyone posting daily 'body count' scores during the battles for Salerno . . . Omaha Beach . . . Stalingrad or even Berlin? Someone decided that there must be a way to keep score in a war where there are no victories." [54]

The fixation of world memory upon Hiroshima and Nagasaki, the knowledge that it *did* happen, and the increasingly easier acceptance of "incredible" technological advances as well as lessened respect for distinctions of "innocence" and "noncombatants," have ironically made the nuclear arms race "tend to produce 'stability' " *vice* the old conventional arms race.[55] That is, the very horror of general war has encouraged a stalemate at this level, though opening up the greater possibility of smaller wars.

Identification with the Machine

However, there is significant appreciation in Army writings for the overwhelming growth of the concrete as identified with the machine itself. Liddell Hart can credit the development of mechanization for the "diminished . . . importance of mere numbers," and the rise of "the qualitative aspects of warfare," [56] but the vast complexity and ingenuity of new weapons and the science of cybernetics called in to control them must not be allowed to replace the man.[57] Communication is both necessary and shaped by the decisive and hierarchical structure of the military; hence paper itself can be an ally or become an enemy.[58] Immensely multiplied in tank, airplane, and nuclear weapons, the probability of the necessary materiel's becoming destructive in its own right is the legacy of Italian air prophet Douhet:

The purpose of war [wrote Douhet] is to harm the enemy as much as possible; and all means to this end will be employed, no matter

what they are. Thus it appeared that the purpose of war was being
perverted to serve the capabilities of a machine, not vice versa; and
this danger was magnified as the nuclear warhead appeared.[59]

Now strangely enough, it is a diminutive enemy in the swamps
and forests of Vietnam who has assumed the task of teaching
us the weakness of the machine[60] and the indispensability of
the man. In the final analysis, says General Westmoreland,
the vast institution we know as the Army exists to support
the individual soldier.[61]

NAVY

"This Mystical Nonsense About Ships"
    The Naval War College Review of January, 1955, carried
two reprints of addresses by noted Harvard economists, reflecting the traditional interest of the Navy in establishing and
maintaining trade routes over the world and bespeaking a
deep awareness beyond weaponry to the broader realm of the
economic in the total life of the nation.[62] The naval blockade
as a near substitution in modern times for the ancient land
siege has transferred with it a deeper sensitivity to this form
of concreteness as an element in military power. Ship life, self-
contained and often isolated from normal economic support
for long periods, doubtless also encourages appreciation of
this factor and perhaps explains the periodic concern for waste-
fulness and the generally more conservative posture of the
naval service. The true sailor's adoration of his ship is well
known, a thing apart and not diluted by apparently similar
sentimentality sometimes expressed by the artilleryman for
his guns and the pilot for his plane. The radical and persistent dependence upon a "bark of steel" dwarfed by nature itself cannot help directing continuous attention to the utter
importance for one's life or death of the material, the concrete,
this precise concrete—one's ship, which is one's home. Perhaps,
as Professor Ambrose of the Naval War College suggests, this

mood underlay the "astonishing" fact that England's Grand Fleet in World War II twice nearly lost the Empire through the Admiralty's extreme reluctance to hazard the "Pride of the Empire," the wonderful dreadnoughts, bought (at least in Germany) by the pennies of schoolchildren. No such thought was given a soldier's rifle nor the uncounted thousands dying unheralded in the bitter trenches while the nation mourned the loss of a dreadnought. The navies on both sides in World War I, says Professor Ambrose, "can with some justice be accused of sentimentally valuing things more than lives or even causes." Fortunately, "in World War II there was relatively little of this mystical nonsense about ships." [63] They were seen as tools of war and therefore expendable, but respect for the hard, concrete fact remains.

The Crushing Weight of Technology

Carlton Ward sees this pragmatic recognition and insistence as the real meaning of technology which has given to four or five great empires the crushing edge: the Romans who "worked with their hands," building bridges, aqueducts, roads, and arches as "the underlying basis" of their power; the British industrial revolution and mercantile expansion which created its ships and control of the seas; Germany and Japan who, ingeniously developing ersatz substitutes, nearly won the war; the "leap ahead" of Russia and now China; and, of course, America, the marvel of all, which "with $\frac{1}{16}$ of the people . . . has $\frac{1}{3}$ of the power." [64]

Yet, like the ships and the weapons it now spawns, technology accepted as an end in itself produces a sophisticated wilderness in which the danger of becoming lost or bogged down by the quicksand of concrete detail can be stifling and perhaps fatal. In "The Paper War—Quo Vadis?" (a theme to which many of us can relate!) a slashing attack is made against so-called laborsaving devices and the mounting, endless paper forms which seem in league to swamp time and the very inclination to think.[65] Eccles blames both the modern proliferation of weapons and the unthinkable potentiality of the H-bomb, for

a nation writhing in a semantic labyrinth of its own making. . . . Modern technology has made mincemeat out of the distinction between . . . words. . . . The most dangerous aspect of this careless use of words can be seen in . . . H-bomb technology. How relatively harmless "one megaton" sounds! Preemptive war recalls a Goren bid! Minimization of casualties (to *only* 50,000,000) is regarded as an act of Christian charity.[66]

Here the actual horror of the violent concrete, as in Hiroshima, escapes into the stratosphere of the abstract which in insisting upon a term, such as "megadeath" (a million deaths: who can imagine or feel this?), affirms again the insistence upon the concrete or particular, if only in a word. But the word is meaningless without Hiroshima.

Fascination for the concrete and the worship of things until we are drowned by the sheer, dead weight of the albatross is the threshold of "future shock." [67] The necessity of freeing ourselves from this increasing weight has encouraged Professor Stoessinger at the Naval War College to distinguish between "the uses of force" and "the uses of power":

Force is the physical hardware; power is a much more psychological relationship . . . [which] may include physical hardware. . . . I submit that the more the atomic age advances . . . the less important force, per se, will become and the more important will power including force, but also including other psychological elements, become in the uses of national strategy.[68]

Insistence Upon the Quantitative

The definition, thus, of power is changing, broadening; but the kernel of the concrete—the insistence upon the quantitative, fascination for the material basically, but also fixed abstraction—is never relinquished. This we see in the nuclear deterrent: the bombs are real and really placed in position. Then it is that in a strange irony of each system negating the other because it, too, possesses the same force, "other psychological elements" are employed, or a new concrete, or an old one revived, is found. Such a case can be made for the lowly mine as a Navy tool of limited war,[69] as the Army has made a case for the tomahawk. So small and old-fashioned as to be several leagues below the great "weapon systems," yet the mine's very "mindlessness" and "deployable permanency" may run the unexpected, tactical end in the increasingly abstract, precise, and sophisticated game of war.[70] Without question, being finite creatures in a finite world, our medium is space-time: Just how large can we build a ship or plane or military machine? How small can we make the computer or the effective human unit? And how quickly and for how long? These are expressions of the indispensable but always limiting concrete, and they make crucial differences in the practice of war.[71]

AIR FORCE

The Children of Technology

The Air Force seems most enamored with technology and the validity and utility of the concrete, especially in machines and weapons. Lacking the long and sobering traditions of the Army and the Navy, it is itself a product of the age of technology and manifestly feels quite at home in it. Moreover, as an essentially one-weapon system, it is tied to a particular expression of military power. As we have quoted earlier, Air Force education is especially oriented toward expertise with machines. A typical article, "The Ordering of Technological Warfare," defines it as "the strategic and tactical employment of scientific and engineering discovery to influence adversely the enemy's economic, political, and military posture." [72] The point is that victory in technological warfare is essentially different in that an advantage gained is extremely difficult to match—a nation ahead on the "trend curve" is difficult to catch.[73] Hence, new concepts, ahead of the times, must be sought. This is costly, and one general ten years ago saw an actual "Stalemate in Concepts" due to the economic factor of soaring costs militating against the necessity of experimentation in an age when there is no time between wars for such development. We must, then, live by "anticipation": No longer can we afford the luxury of living the truism that "the military starts each war with the concepts and doctrines that won the last war." [74] But Air Force writers have consistently seen this necessary experimentation as benefiting the economy itself:

In fact, technology now receives its main support from the military establishment to a point where the services have moved into the advanced guard of inventors, and have become the chief employers of the most forward-looking technologists, and where private corporations, in disregard of their assigned function in life, rely on military initiative.[75]

"Future shock," then, holds no terrors for the Air Force. The latest jewel in the royal diadem of technology that fascinates Air Force planners is "technological forecasting," which has developed a number of highly sophisticated methods and models which bring it, so it is claimed, to "the point where it is beginning to look like a science." [76] From this it can easily be argued that the new "terror" weapons represent only the usual shocking advance upon the times, and will inevitably be used. They must be continually refined to permit their flexible and controlled utility:

It is generally admitted that the current definition of roles and missions bears little relevance to the actualities of war. The roles and missions were drafted before the technological revolution in weaponry was recognized. The result is that new weapons are being placed in a strait jacket of obsolescent missions instead of being given missions that conform to an evolving technology and current and future military problems.[77]

The First Stirrings of Doubt

This wholehearted acceptance of technology by the Air Force as a "pure attitude" has been in marked contrast to the frequently hesitant, even dubious, acknowledgments of the value of science from the older services. Yet, as we have seen, the first stirrings of doubt are beginning to be felt and heard in Air Force circles. Dr. Miewald, appealing to Clausewitz for limited war, also details the Master's warning of the incalculable "friction" which "distinguishes real War from War on paper." [78] On paper the organization of men in pursuit of stated objectives is simple enough, especially when no holds are barred, i.e., when ultimacy in power and its application is the key word. But though "everything is very simple in War, . . . the simplest thing is difficult." [79] Friction is the inevitable tension that develops between more or less free individuals compelled more or less to order. It is chance, the unexpected happening, the insignificant—"for want of a nail the horse was lost, . . . the rider was lost, . . . the kingdom was lost." Friction is the possible and intangible become the particular and existent—the appearance in unexpected ways of the concrete. The concrete cannot be avoided; it must be used, and it threatens always to take over and command as the Pure Plan, the Marvelous Machine, the Supreme System. The very insistence of military power on pushing "to its utmost bounds" forces stillbirths in weaponry and strategy, and oftentimes a possessiveness for the particular which effectively militates against the new births that need to be. The eagerness with which air power has presumed to win the war in Vietnam is highlighted by the laconic admission of failure by a former Rand Corporation (the Air Force think tank) specialist. Our fantastic aerial reconnaissance in Vietnam had been simply "too sophisticated," too much:

They [North Vietnamese] have consistently underflown our capacity. . . . We are set for trucks and they use bicycles. They operate just below our threshold.[80]

It is encouraging that some younger officers are drawing back from "too much," having discovered our idolatry of the offen-

sive.[81] Lieutenant Colonel Celick has even opted for a kind
of radical "bicycle approach": a technology that has produced
the atom terror can surely, he believes, and as quickly, "furnish a means of enforcing covenants without killing," i.e., via
effective nonlethal weapons.[82] Warfare for Clausewitz, warns
Miewald, was "an interconnected mass of individual events"
which cannot be reduced wholly to the quantitative, and the
lesson today is that computers notwithstanding, war even in
the nuclear age cannot be reduced to science and the routine,
nor won by superior technology alone.[83] There is still the spirit
of man, the dogged hopes and aspirations of peoples which,
whether right or wrong, are nonetheless real and must be
taken into account.

We see, then, that reason wills the concrete, or the threat of
it, in the resolution of conflict. There is no escaping the ultimate appeal to force, which expresses itself legitimately in
weapons to coerce and even sometimes to destroy in the
supposed larger interests of man, according to military theorists. But complicated as man's motives are by his fascination
for the violent concrete, the slippage from deterrence and limited use of force as a means to destruction for its own sake is a
study in terror. Not only so, but our historical and daily preoccupation with the material may gain us a world at the loss
of our soul; and the military, the spearpoint of our material
thrust, is at times aware of this in the vastly changed dimension
of the concrete as an absolute aspect of its power with the advent of nuclear weapons. This is true except for the Air Force,
at least until recently. For that service still stubbornly pro-
pounds the belief that technology needs only freedom from
fear to solve the problems it creates.

Fascination for the concrete, the dust from which man has
sprung and to which as body he must indeed return, is the
most ancient and persistent of idolatries and dead ends. This
was the struggle of the Hebrews with the ancient Baals which

guaranteed crops and success while God called them to the higher and riskier dimensions of the spirit. "Man does not live by bread alone" even if he can turn the very stones into all the bread he needs. It is perhaps significant that this initial temptation of Christ (which is to say of every man) is immediately followed by the vision of martial order and glory.[84] The age of technology in its promise of miraculous plentitude does not so much satisfy man as tempt him to the expression of power as military because of the military's natural inclination to the use of power as concrete.

Chapter 7

The Tendency
to
Structure

It must be evident by now that the elements of military power are separated with much difficulty, thus reflecting their interaction, a process so constant and pronounced that the whole can be said to be *dynamic*. Power, as the power of being, is itself dynamic, seeking expression, and the attempt to control it directly as "naked" power for rational use is somewhat like attempting to exploit the explosive energy of a volcano by capping and uncapping it at will. Just as the streaming, molten rock, engulfing all life and vegetation before it, seems to have nothing in common with the jagged, black beds of encrusted lava from which the fire tree blooms and from which later arise the gardens and cities of men, so the military combines, or gives rise to, the most intense opposites—aggressive movement and hardened structure.

As rationally controlled violence, military power tends toward structure, the shaping and the capping of the volcano. This is done by reducing life to order, to discipline, to rules and fixed routines. They often result in the stereotypes of "ramrod stiffness," "military bearing," "authoritarian discipline," "unthinking obedience," etc., based upon the need of military pressure to conform to its own. The overall result is a certain distinguishable organized continuity, or *structure*, the habitual ways in which the institution works. Structure, of course, is necessary. Otto Heilbrunn, in his *Partisan Warfare*,[1] credits the victory of Tito over Mihajlović to the contribution which structure made to the greater efficiency of Tito's movement. Two millennia earlier Vegetius singled out not a single Roman hero, nor even the fabled Roman legion itself, as the cause of Rome's mastery of the world, but "continual military training, exact observance of discipline . . . and unwearied cultivation of the other arts of war." [2] Lacking an Alexander or a Hannibal and often tasting defeat, the Romans nevertheless forged a *system* of military power without equal in the ancient world. Likewise, the East Romans survived through an ingenious military structure based quite differently upon defensive and self-sustaining themes, but uniformly evidencing order.[3] The Swiss have been likened to the Romans in the tenacity and machinelike brilliance of their military organization which built for them a ferocious reputation for centuries in the heart of Europe and made them the most wanted of mercenaries. Like the Romans, they deemphasized generalship. Rather, they insisted that "a good military organization and sound system of national tactics are the surest bases for a sustained career of conquest." [4] Again, the Anglo-Saxons, as well as the Germans, in modern times typify the same, giving rise to the military manager as taking precedence over the heroic leader.[5]

All military power as organized power of course evidences structure, but these instances emphasize its importance beyond generalship to the rank and file and over long periods of time. Given the context of technology and attraction to the concrete, the propensity of Anglo-Saxons for organization rather than heroic generalship provides the stimulus to structure as an end in itself. This may be seen broadly in what General de Gaulle has called the "inherent traditionalism in [the] very nature of the military." [6] *Traditionalism* provides a core of values and customs which, preserved against innovation and change, encourage an attitude of what may be called *conservatism*. Traditionalism and conservatism are hallmarks of the historic tendency of the military to structure. And, in assuring both content and context or climate for the military person, they go far toward defining his role and locking him into his particular function as a cog in the military machine.

I. TRADITIONALISM AND CONSERVATISM EXPRESSED IN WESTERN MILITARY HISTORY

TRADITIONALISM

Aristocratic Roots of the Military

From ancient times the military has emphasized its roots in the past, generally as the order to be preserved. The Spartans are a good case in point, and the aggressive army of Alexander still considered itself defensive or at the most the bearers of a superior culture. Moreover, the freeman armies of Greece and Rome for a long while were actually aristocratic, the hoplites and patricians being the voters in the narrow democracies of these states. Only gradually, under pressure of unceasing wars and the depletion of the upper social ranks did war become the concerned business of the lower classes who demanded, and got, the right to vote (and intermarry) as rewards for their increasing defense of the nation.[7] They received even more: land and status, and the very real possibility of a continuing careership for their sons. So the "proud legionnaires" kept for long generations the Pax Romana, for they

had a personal share in its maintenance. The legionary of Britain may never have set eyes upon Rome, but he was nevertheless a proud citizen. His father may have been a legionary before him, stationed at the same border camp. Soldiers of this type were serving neither a patriotic abstraction nor yet a leader's personality. They were serving power and property in which they had a tangible stake.[8]

The rise of cavalry once again ensured the aristocratic mode of warfare and life, the feudal structure of the Middle Ages, by which the privileges of the few were preserved from change by the knight's monopoly to bear arms. Thus the warrior (as a class) was permanent, but not the army. The division of labor was simple: the knights did battle, the clergy prayed, and the people worked, including "war work," i.e., the burden-bearing and the provision of bulk where dangerously needed in battle. The concept of "honor" gradually developed, peculiar to the nobleman as

the prerogative of a highborn estate, which could not be shared with inferiors. . . .

This honor was essentially that of a caste, not of the individual. It was distinct from that idea of inner honor, springing from soul and mind, guided by individual conscience. . . . Such "personal honor" might well clash with the demands of group honor, based on lineage and tradition, and so prove prejudicial to military hierarchy.

Thus, Vagts concludes,

it was this jealous group solidarity of the noblemen which helped make the officer castes of European armies into self-governing bodies, divorced from civilian control and even impatient of royal meddling, ruling themselves by their members' own traditions or corporate whims.[9]

Rise of the Gentleman Tradition

The dikes of chivalry were broken, of course, by gunpowder and the *levée en masse* of the French Revolution and the minutemen of the New World. Yet, the need for tradition continued, Napoleon "noble-izing" the Army by elevating its soldiers above the bourgeoisie, recognizing that "armies are essentially monarchist." [10] A new flag, the tricolor, "gratified emotions previously enjoyed only by the nobility. In short, the whole nation became the nobility, considering its foes outside the pale." Meanwhile, across the Channel, the English saved themselves another Cromwell by diffusing the military below the highest class, while being "most reluctant in granting mass honor." [11] Even after the great victory of 1815 against Napoleon, soldiers were excluded from public parks and gardens in London by a regulation of Charles II. Yet there was a strong tendency to reserve military functions to a class, the *theyn,* built upon the old tribal levy, or *fyrd,* owing service direct to the king, and thus ranking above ordinary freemen but below aristocrats.[12] Wellington, typically as time went on, used the army to preserve the privileges of gentlemen:

He believed in the England that produced such gentlemen, and was resolved to save her by them. He took over his army as an instrument to that end, just as an engineer might take over a gang of laborers to dig a canal, having no love for the gang itself, but determined to make the best of it as a matter of duty. . . . When his purpose was fulfilled, he threw the instrument aside without compunction.[13]

Relative peace lasted nearly a century after Wellington and the gentleman tradition became ingrained. At least until Grant and Moltke, the military officer was a "sheer romanticist in the industrial age," aloof from its technological and economic transformation, socially remote from its rising bourgeoisie. As a class they were largely agrarian and strove mightily to keep even the ranks that way. In England, for instance, they wanted "respectable, docile country lads, brought up by careful, thrifty parents in a decent cottage home." [14] They wanted no part of "poor" urban workers. In America, Tocqueville found something of the same, "some loose notions of the old aristocratic honor"—especially in the South.[15] Vagts goes so far as to say that

the armies were the mainstay of large scale agriculture which, without the chance to provide grain and mounts to them and to place the younger sons in the army and other government employs, would in many places have crumbled under the impact of industrialism.[16]

And in the North,

> the West Point of Thayer and Mahan was divorced from the main intellectual currents of Jacksonian America. Its isolation enabled it to give the regular Army high standards of excellence. . . . [But] . . . American leaders failed to address themselves to the discovery of military programs in accord with . . . life.[17]

As a consequence they were quite unprepared for the mass army warfare that quickly developed in the brutal Civil War, except for those serving under Sherman and Grant, who never fitted into a "West Point mold" even though they had graduated from it. As we have seen, the long ambivalence of Americans toward the military discouraged professionalism modeled upon Europe's standing armies but it did allow for, and indeed drove toward, a small, hard-core career group of officers and men who drew their sustenance from their cherished traditions and awaited the possible call to glory. The call, as we know, was long in coming. Indeed, the Army was called repeatedly by Presidential fiat in the waning years of the century but hardly to glory. Strikebreaking, although it made the troopers visible, only added personal hostility to an already latent suspicion on the part of many of the people. Hence

> the Army officer corps sought justification of its existence in a professional ethic which combined disinterested expertise with conservative values. Unable to be a fully integrated part of American society, the Army was to become the efficient tool of that society.[18]

They stood squarely for the *status quo,* buttressed by the constant reminder of lineage with the saviors of the past, with Washington and Hamilton, Grant and Sherman themselves. Thus, under differing conditions, the American military were hardly less tradition-oriented than their European cousins.

The Backward Look of Professionals

With new confidence gained in the "splendid little war" with Spain, the American military entered the twentieth century and was almost immediately subjected to a "subtle and

pervasive aspect of military behavior which continued to reinforce traditionalism," i.e., insecurity abroad and the necessity to prepare for war and to make war fraught with the
gravest of consequences. The immense risk of modern war
cannot be reduced significantly by the most elaborate planning and the most realistic exercises. In such case, as Janowitz
observes, "what has happened in the past . . . becomes a
powerful precedent for future engagements." [19] Hence, military leaders experienced in combat can and do readily checkmate the advice of scientist and technologist. It has ever been
so:

In the beginning, at least, war is always fought with the means and
thoughts of an earlier time; its character is fixed at the outbreak by
the repressions and brakefrictions imposed by the socio-economic
frame of the previous peace.[20]

Recent history confirms the ease of the backward look of
the military, from the court-martial of Billy Mitchell to the
tears of Colonel George S. Patton who, in 1938, experienced
the "saddest" day of his life as his old cavalry unit stacked
their sabers.[21] And this was on the eve of the war which would
lift Patton to fame through forced adoption of the tank he
hated, a weapon that nearly a generation before had proved
its decisive character in the only significant occasions allowed
it on the Western front.[22] In fact, despite the early nineteenth-
century development of technicism, by which West Point began as an engineering school and the Navy developed its
highly specialized bureaus of technological competence, the
American military shared a general distrust of science and the
specter of monster, rather than professional, armies. They preferred "to study men and animals rather than explosives and
armor." [23] So tradition prone is the military, says Janowitz,
that when they are not defending traditions, they often are
seeking to establish new ones. This is demonstrably true. Not
only in large but in many small matters the love affair with
tradition goes on: Patton and his pearl-handled six-guns,

Eisenhower and his famous jacket, the Special Forces and their green berets. Each service and unit and many commanders seek forms of identification, of singularity, around which the deeds of valor ancient and new can cling like the streamers of over three hundred and sixty campaigns anchored to the mast of the colors of the U.S. Marines. On shore stations, where many men in specialized ratings will never transit to sea, terminology meaningful only at sea is held tenaciously: quarterdeck, bulkheads, deck, starboard and port, etc.[24] The Army is less tradition bound than the Navy, but much of the nostalgia for the "old Army," closely knit and gentlemanly, remains. It is especially striking that the Air Force, very sensitive to its lack of a long tradition, has actively sought to build one.

CONSERVATISM

The upshot of traditionalism is, of course, conservatism. It is hardly to be wondered at that having generally been created by the societies they are called to serve, and conscious of standing under their authority, military men are, on the whole, conservative. Vagts puts it clearly:

As it takes many years to organize and equip an army, a long time stability is necessary in the structure and functions of the society in which the preparation of the army is made. Hence the army by the very nature of things depends for its existence, honor, emoluments, and privileges, upon the order in which it takes form, and in self-defense if nothing more, it is conservative in relation to the order in which it thrives, whether that order be agrarian, capitalistic, or communistic.[25]

Thus armies have "always been closely associated with suppressions, reactions and counter revolutions," [26] and doubtless for this reason, at least, find it difficult to accept guerrilla warfare as having status because it seems like a betrayal of the primary commitment to order. Again, Vagts has vividly and accurately described the sensitive consciousness of the military person, the "specialist in violence," to the ever-present threat of the eruption of violence in chaos:

Masses of men, ideas, machinery, appear to be breaking loose in such an eruption, and this can only be distressing to the soldier's order aspiring mind. So Bonaparte, watching the Paris riots, longed to fire cannister shot among the milling people to bring them back to order. Clinging to tradition, which in itself is a means for him to maintain authority, the soldier is averse to acknowledging and embracing changes forced upon him, particularly if they do not appear to favor his immediate interests.[27]

The Soldier Not a Revolutionary

The soldier, then, is not really a revolutionary, for he sees order only in the established arrangements and lacks perhaps the imagination, and certainly the motivation, to see a new order amid popular turmoil. But the revolutionary may become a soldier, as in our own Revolution. Yet it needs to be remembered, as Weigley has said, that "the American Revolution was probably the most conservative of the great revolutions of the modern world. Many of the American revolutionists fought to preserve the values of a cherished past rather than to force the coming of an uncertain future." [28] Washington's expressed preference for "regulars" and a professional army is well known, as well as his aristocratic bearing in general: "In things strictly military, Washington was scarcely a revolutionary. . . . He accepted military orthodoxy and worked with it." [29] It is, however, important to say that Washington's Continental Army though Regular was yet different. It was the product, largely, of a middle-class society, its officers usually came from the same social strata as the men, and Washington, though skeptical of the militia, yet of necessity depended upon them and "regularized" them. As a result, the United States drew from the Revolution two different military traditions, a revolutionary tradition and a conservative one. The struggle of these traditions, as we have seen, has given us a shaky and ambiguous compromise between the minuteman–mass army concept and specialized, hard-core professionalism—and the search for a better, more equitable solution beyond internal conflict and accommodation continues. The former doctrine (more experience than doctrine) has had the great virtue of impregnating the whole with new ideas and keeping the military structure open-ended. Yet Sherman's "new kind of war" had "deep roots in the conservative tradition." [30] Not the least of these is the religious and moral grounding of generations in the conviction that the struggle with evil is absolute and no quarter is expected nor can any be given—the "Battle of Armageddon" syndrome.[31] Janowitz notes that the military elite is still more conservative than any other, "dominated by a single class—provincial, middle class, white, Protestant (of the traditional, knee-bending variety), small town." [32]

Religion and the Martial Spirit

The new generation is becoming more and more ethnically and religiously cosmopolitan, but it is a slow job. In 1954, of 576 officers in the Pentagon only 5 percent admitted to "liberal" convictions.[33] Vagts observes that "generally speaking, parliaments have been far more 'leftist' than armies, and armies have been more royalist and imperialist than parliaments." He then goes on to claim that nearly all military members are rightist in sympathies.[34] Janowitz in his studies found that more than 75 percent of Army leaders and nearly that number of Navy officers in 1950 came from traditionalist and pietistic backgrounds.[35] The preponderance of Episcopalians, with their strong emphasis upon authority, ceremony, mission, and politics, has long been noted, although in this generation the swing toward pluralism, especially the growth of Baptists, Methodists, and the more evangelical groups, has been marked.

It is important to note, however, that pietism, if anything, has been encouraged by this swing toward greater pluralism. Aggressive Southern Baptists, fundamentalist groups, and other self-conscious and dedicated faiths which often take seriously, and perhaps quite literally, Biblical imagery respecting our warfare against "the sons of darkness" are represented now by officers and chaplains of their own. Marked as the differences may be between religious traditionalists and the many kinds of pietism, especially as seen in the strong political identification of the former and the frequent subordination of politics by the latter, they are yet much in agreement in emphasizing the martial spirit.[36] Moreover, "the Protestantism of the military reflects the social structure of the rural South, from which the military elite has been so heavily recruited." [37]

Finally, it may be noted that Catholics, too, have increased, reducing the majority position of Protestants, but bringing with them only a deepened appreciation of tradition, authority, and a certain vulnerability to moralistic right-wing positions and groups.[38] Often less sophisticated, many being immigrants to whom the appeal of patriotism is deeply meaningful, Catholics also know the discipline of obedience and acknowledge sacrifice as central to faith and life. Thus by circumstance, "on the job training," and the most vivid and deeply ingrained images of personal faith, the insidious and insistent claims of tradition create a kind of "prevailing atmosphere" of militant conservatism for the average military person. It may not, then, be surprising that General Fuller, from whom we have quoted extensively and who himself has pleaded for an open mind, in the mounting chaos leading up to World War II joined the Nazi Blackshirts in England. With a vice admiral he stood at the head of Oswald Moseley's list of candidates for Parliament.[39] We should not be surprised, for we, too, have had our General Walker.[40] Facing Russia across the ugly and threatening Berlin Wall, he not only trained but indoctrinated his troops, being utterly convinced that no accommodation ("compromise") was possible and only the very few ("the remnant")[41] could handle the truth.

But we have also had an Eisenhower, a Gavin,[42] and now General Shoup and Admiral Zumwalt—"innovators," Janowitz dubs them, "unconventional rule breakers" who do not fit the general pattern but are necessary as "prime movers," the "nucleus of the elite" that keeps the machine open to the future.[43] They do not change the machine so much as they keep it well oiled.

II. TRADITIONALISM AND CONSERVATISM EXPRESSED IN CONTEMPORARY MILITARY THOUGHT

The traditional, conservative image of which we have been speaking is readily found in contemporary military writings. It is there, bedrock of the institution, visible in countless pronouncements and analyses of what's wrong with the military or with the nation, often acknowledged with stubborn pride, sometimes with apology. It is clear that the call to creativity, buttressed by continued and higher education, is running squarely into received patterns and attitudes.

ARMY

Tradition vs. "Wave of the Future"

Not long ago an open-forum debate was staged in a small Pennsylvania military college which in mood and clash of unreconcilable positions seemed to mirror the rising controversy in Army ranks today.[44] It is significant that the opposing positions were taken by two career military officers, General Bruce C. Clarke, well-known World War II combat leader who in forty-four years has held every major command post in the Army except the Pentagon, and Dr. Roger W. Little, a retired Army officer, teacher of sociology and with Morris Janowitz coauthor of *Sociology of the Military Establishment*.[45] Dr. Little's "wave of the future" remarks about the utter necessity of drastic changes in military leadership and management styles "to meet changes that are already apparent in American society," such as toleration of "some form of collective protest," correction of many remaining social inequities, and the probable abolition of Saturday-morning inspections ("a massive invasion of privacy"),[46] left the old general in a state of considerable agitation. What does one make of Dr. Weigley, a civilian and noted military historian, tending to agree with General Clarke? His quotes and support came largely from another civilian enamored with the military, Samuel Huntington.[47] The real standoff was between the two military careerists and reflects the intense soul-searching going on in the military establishment today which cannot be identified with any particular age or group.

The cleft is clearly not a "generation gap" in the usual sense. The article quoted above, in describing the ferment in military colleges, vividly contrasts "seven hippie-looking students" who briefly brush shoulders on a narrow lane with cadets going to close-order drill, and has the senior cadet leader say: "For us the past is meaningful. We try to hold onto tradition. With the civilians everything is 'image.' They're always searching for new things." [48] Ironically, the rather obvious sympathy of the article's unknown author for the cadets and General Clarke is overmatched by the far more detailed attention given Dr. Little and his "wave of the future," as though to a magnet which draws even the unwilling and the bitterly hostile. This unevenness is further revealed in the reception given a report instigated by the Army Chief of Staff in 1954 on "How the Army should be organized for combat in the period 1965–1970." The report stressed that by 1965 the Army would have guided missiles capable of carrying atomic warheads 200 miles! The ensuing skepticism was largely confined to the generals, except for the Chief of Staff who found himself in concert with the junior officers who almost alone had read the report and saw the mounting signs.[49]

The System Goes On

Ward Just has made it abundantly clear that the schism appears in all ranks, but that it hardly affects "the System" [50] (although it obviously feels threatened). The System seems capable of running by itself, receiving support at times more from military oriented civilians. For instance, Herman Kahn, Hudson Institute think-tank expert, has suggested flooding the Mekong Delta, a measure that at least one of his senior officer students could not stomach.[51] The Army is changing, as a growing, and sometimes glowing, number of news reports indicate.[52] But it is problematical whether the "changes" reach much below the surface of haircuts, rock music, and even rock gin in the barracks to the "rigid authoritarianism" and the "highly stratified social system" which still look to traditional ways of doing things. These are aspects of military life which Dr. Stouffer and his team found distinguished our World War II armies from civilian institutions. The Army writer citing this study concludes on a rather discouraging note that however brave and knowledgeable the effort, the much-heralded changes in the Army are only

evolutionary and the structure is essentially unaltered, so that the contrast will still be very apparent to those in the lower ranks where the demands of the hierarchical system and the impersonal lines of authority converge.[53]

In the magazine *Army* is found an article almost wistfully entitled "The Dangerous Words Captain Eisenhower Wrote in 'Infantry Journal' and Earned the Displeasure of the Chief of Infantry." [54] Young Ike's "dangerous words," written in 1920, favored tanks as a new method of warfare. This irked his own Chief of Infantry who threatened him with court-martial if he published "anything incompatible with solid infantry doctrine." Now the tank itself has become part of the sacred doctrine and it is, like the cavalry it replaced, subject to the same conserving attitudes, as Ward Just vividly describes with reference to Army reluctance to accept the failure of the Sherman tank in Vietnam.[55] A matter of some interest is the curious attention paid to the Israeli and Red Chinese experiments in "rankless" armies, but always the swift conclusion is reached that the conditions do not parallel America and besides Russia tried it and failed.[56] Rather, with lurking ease there is "found a natural caste spirit born of pride of arms, experience, and the mystical bond of comradeship" which still adulates Bonaparte and Frederick the Great.[57] With astonishing ease, General Koster, former Superintendent of West Point (and once indicted for the My Lai massacre), can say: "I'm not sure all youth wants to be completely free." [58] A brave attempt is made by some military officers to welcome the new, more sophisticated and vocal recruit, but it appears that it is a rationalization of the inevitable, a deliberate straining for some small hope in the uneasy certainty that little comfort will be its accompaniment. Certainly the Army is not going out of its way to appeal to "creative types":

In fact, the deliberate recruiting into a military organization of creative types—a difficult thing, indeed—could easily backfire and at the very least create more difficulties than it would solve.[59]

NAVY

The Navy is proud of its recently completed overhaul of its century-old bureau system.[60] Not that it did not take considerable pressure from the intensely disliked "King McNamara," cold, calculating enthusiast for systems analysis. But having made the plunge into the latter half of the twentieth century, only a little reflection convinced the Navy that it "was [still] decades ahead of the Army in recognizing the need for reform along modern business-like lines." The conviction is attributed to the Navy's early and continued exposure to innovations and progress in foreign waters.[61]

Severe Racial Imbalance

The Navy here, of course, is speaking technologically, of *methods* rather than of men and social progress. (One notes that the favorable comparison is drawn with the Army, not with the Air Force, the most recent and favored child of technology.) A single and very recent article ruefully admits that with regard to civil rights and the whole rate-rank structure "the Navy still has the most severe racial imbalance among its officer corps of all branches of the Armed Forces." [62] We had a grand total of just three black captains in the Navy in 1970, and only one of these was a line officer. In 1971, the first black admiral was selected.[63] Even though the number of black officers has tripled in the Navy in the past eight years, these, together with other minority representatives, still amount to less than one half of 1 percent of the total officer cadre.[64] Minorities have fared considerably better in the enlisted ranks to which they have always been admitted, although from the Spanish-American War until 1946 they were limited to the messmen's branch. On February 27 of that year the Navy officially ended segregation.[65]

The Natural Inequality of Men

The inexcusable slowness to implement fully this order which is now a quarter of a century old is probably due less to intentional stalling than to the peculiarly binding qualities of relationships which so readily become fixed as traditions among men who go to sea. The present Superintendent of the Naval Academy, setting forth with pride and hope the present thrust toward significant change in that hoary institution, sees this movement as cyclic. The push for change, he observes, occurs in times of outward decline and civilian rebuff which encourage a turning of the institution in upon itself. Always "the conservatism which so often becomes a part of the character of men who deal with the sea" [66] is evident as "the albatross" we have "hung . . . around our own neck" (in the case of civil rights),[67] or as anchors too heavy for the windlass in the maintenance of those artificial barriers between officers and enlisted men which are accepted as indicative of *essential* differences in nature between them. Unfortunately, our democratic and equalitarian expectations do not make it easy for Navy people to be fully honest at this point. Obliquely the attitude may best be acknowledged by an English theorist who can bluntly assert that "universal equality is an impossibility," and rank justifiably has its privileges. "The leaders of the Armed Forces, and the governing elite . . . are the brains of the nation," we are told, and the most natural thing in the world is that the serviceman "unreservedly realizes the value of, and fully subscribes to, a rank structure which confers superiority on his seniors." There is a *natural inequality* among men; "equality," indeed, is a "fetish" and should only describe one's concern for "being equal to his job." [68]

In retrospect, it is still surprising to this writer how convincing was "the great gulf fixed" between enlisted rates and officer ranks in the Navy,[69] and the number of enlisted men who accepted it as every bit as natural as the ebb and flow of the tides. I knew many men who simply refused promotion to officer status because it was "not my place." Of those who did, he was a rare one indeed who did not feel that he was "in limbo," being "neither fish nor fowl." Such men were "mustangs," not thoroughbreds (as Academy men are thought to be), but tamed and trained as it were from the wilds because of specific aptitudes and skills. This was particularly true of warrant officers, a minirank created just below the lowest officer rank of ensign.

Sparta Always Wins

The emphasis upon expertise and specific skills involves "professionalism," the tailoring of a man to his job as a sailor. The necessity for such primary training, whether on the job and up through the rates or in the Academy for the essential jump to officerhood, is unquestioned. It is, indeed, significant that the recent reforms in the Academy doubled the professional courses, although by eliminating the highly specified "core curriculum" a larger degree of freedom is accorded students whose interests lie toward "the humanities." But in the continuing contest "between Athens and Sparta," and granting that a "balance . . . must be maintained" between the two, it is clear that Sparta always wins: "I would point out," says Admiral Calvert, Superintendent of the Academy, "that Annapolis became world famous as a training institution that produced effective leaders, not as an educational institution that produced renowned scholars." [70] A comparison between the "reforms" instituted at Annapolis and Colorado Springs, home of the Air Force Academy, rather quickly reveals the greater conservative lag of the Navy's institution.[71]

The combination of "conservative lag" and technological aptitude and concern makes for severe strains in the naval community. It is against this background that what happened to the Navy's Material Bureau System seems like "the stunningly swift demise" of that system.[72] And now comes the "Mod Admiral" Zumwalt! This sort of thing happens so infrequently as to startle and to confound. In an incisive, almost bitter, article Lieutenant Commander Duff, in charge of the Hydrofoil Special Trials Unit at Bremerton, Washington, presented (1969) the truly amazing capabilities of "two small, unconventional naval craft," which as prototypes have "proved to be more reliable than any vessels of their size to join the Fleet to date." But "in all probability . . . there will never be another hydrofoil craft . . . built for the Navy" because "Navy planners are unable to fit this vessel and her capabilities into the requirements." Duff said that the boats "represent revolutionary capabilities that . . . place severe demands upon a Navy primarily accustomed to evolutionary changes." [73]

There is quick remembrance of the long struggle of pilots

to make a place for themselves in the modern Navy. This was the "invasion of the brown shoes" (air) into the traditional "black shoe" (ship) Navy which I remember very well. Then there was Admiral Rickover, "Father of the atomic submarine," whose promotion literally required an act of Congress. It is sobering to recall again that the Allies in World War II nearly lost the war to the Germans because of the intransigence of British naval leaders to the novel idea of convoys to blunt the submarine threat. The great ships and patterns of the past became ends in themselves beyond the preservation of which "the brass" simply could not think.[74]

Iron Ships, Wooden Men, and the Paper War

Ironically, an institution which, in giving necessary attention to the technological, treasures its every invention by firmly putting the stamp of tradition upon it, bids fare to lose out in the technological race itself. For race it has become, and concerned voices are raised with respect to "our Navy [which] is not able to come to grips with, nor to control, the technological revolution which in the past decade has mounted like a giant wave." In concrete terms this is partly due to the sad fact that "our ships are surfeited with marvelous equipments which are inoperative and, in many instances, unmaintainable." [75] The obvious need is for more and better men, especially in the officer ranks, but individual responsibility and command authority are no longer as clearly attractive as they once were. Paper work, conflicting directives, and "ponderous documentation" to substantiate every move reduce the actual effectiveness of the mightiest Navy afloat to something like the frustrating, day-to-day struggle of a flotilla of sailing vessels trying to negotiate the Sargasso Sea.

Our fetish for sending in reports done exactly in the proper format, instead of putting emphasis upon substance . . . [has] resulted in a monolithic empire that often stifles opportunities of command initiative. We check, recheck, summarize, report, consolidate, validate, and again report status and progress until command loses its true individual character, and the excitement, the contest, the challenge is lost, becomes reactive in nature and therefore is ineffective.[76]

What *is* effective in this growth and adulation of structure in the Navy is the resulting diminution of rank status or what may be called "rank inflation," i.e., rank is worth progressively less in terms of the authority, power, and prestige it has traditionally carried and it takes higher and higher rank to accomplish anything at all. In part, of course, the shrinkage of the world and the growth of the bomb have certainly forced the capacity and responsibility to make decisions upward to ever higher levels. But the effect is what Admiral Strauss calls the operation of "Gresham's Law" among the "stars and stripes" of rank, i.e., the tendency for the less valuable and mediocre to become standardized and frozen in positions.[77] The very dynamism of military power creates a "fallout" of static structures, readily seen in the easy growth of traditions. In the nuclear age the process is vastly accelerated and ironically the very necessity for change may be overwhelmed by the longing for structure as evidence of stability.

AIR FORCE

The Claim to Freedom

Air Force writings illustrate the tendency toward traditionalism and conservatism as a study in irony and ambiguity. Almost gleefully uninhibited by the nagging pasts which slow the sister services and pridefully "slipping the surly bonds of earth," eager for every "new view," the Air Force nevertheless tends to create mounting structures, and traditions become set in unwanted ways.[78] Perhaps because the "men in blue" have not really known a time of rejection after coming into their own but have ridden the crest of something akin to popularity (though muted since Vietnam), they seem more readily identifiable with the civilian world. Quoting revised studies by Janowitz which show increasing liberalism in the Armed Forces,[79] a determined plea is made by one author for the acceptance of military professionals as policy advisers in defense matters, since they are indeed a responsible segment of the democracy.[80] Conservatism attaches naturally to the business of security as it does to banking or any other important and responsibly directed human enterprise. Moreover, a new, even younger generation is coming on, imbued with existentialist principles of inward freedom and responsibility, and respect for persons over organization. In effect these younger persons constitute a "cultural value gap" with the older, tradition-oriented leaders.[81]

Schizophrenia: Education vs. Duty

Yet there may be a "military mind," a singular blend of intelligence and expertise, "a perhaps oversimplified but idealistic view of the traditional 'soldierly' virtues, and a pessimism and mistrust concerning the more complex liberal-intellectual values." [82] No apology is required but frustration is inescapable because the higher "generalist" levels in the military hierarchy require ever broader educational, management, and policy-making capabilities. In the view of Major Donald Sandler, the vastly accelerated pace of change is increasingly "at odds with the traditional view of the military role, responsibilities, and organization." The result is a kind of schizophrenia, "an unhealthy combination of both traditional and contemporary concepts of discipline," which encourages both confusion and disrespect for the System. Academically, says Sandler, officer training follows modern and considerably freer concepts based upon mutual respect for personality,

while the military portion . . . bears the full imprint of those who advocate the more rigid traditional views. . . . Whereas permissive, psychologically oriented leadership is stressed in seminar rooms, authoritarian leadership gets the nod in the barracks and hallways.[83]

"Just why," asks the young cadet, "must clothes be equally spaced on hangers, the soap dish placed so many centimeters from the razor blades, socks rolled only in a certain way?" The insult to the intelligence lies in its unreality:

To the reasoning student, this sounds like establishing a program which is designed to perpetuate itself. He suspects that the USAF creates rules only to see if they are being followed.[84]

Tendencies Toward Routinization

It would be fortunate indeed if the problem were confined to the academic phase of the military man's life. Organization breeds organization and structure tends to freeze as ever harder structure throughout the System. The impact of war (and no less of its preparation, especially over long periods), is found in the warning of Clausewitz:

Activity in War is movement in a resistant medium. Just as a man immersed in water is unable to perform with ease and regularity the most natural and simplest movement, that of walking, so in War, with ordinary powers, one cannot keep even the line of mediocrity.[85]

This built-in resistance, or "friction," to which we have earlier called attention as an expression of the concrete, may be seen here as the dynamic "tendencies toward routinization, the bureaucratization of the application of force" which Clausewitz dreaded as creating "the fog of uncertainty." Against this "fog" he appealed in hope of the heroic leader, the decision maker.[86] In the judgment of some, the trend toward "management by committee," democratic as it may seem, may also involve altogether too often an "aversion to decision making." The upshot is that

military management in general and the middle grades in particular have become imbedded in a system which discourages creative thinking and puts a premium on conformity.

The result is a "slow strangulation in the quicksands of complacency and conservative mediocrity." [87]

There is an advantage in committee management of course: greater information input. There is genuine concern respecting "The Information Explosion—Can the Air Force Handle It?"

and the utter necessity of "Megamanagement for the Space Age." [88] Ironically, the Air Force's insistence upon uninhibited freedom in future-oriented experimentation and development in itself makes for an "information glut." The hope, growing somewhat desperate in tone, is still largely fixed upon ever bigger computers.[89] But it also includes a growing insistence upon a built-in capacity for change and adaptiveness. Colonel Fleek, examining the so-called "military mind," sees that "the great question facing the military establishment today may well be how much creative anarchy can be permitted and how can it be encouraged and still limited?" [90] The best minds are worried. Still, there is great confidence that solutions will be found to any problems technology creates. The implicit assumption which seems never to be really questioned is that progress is automatic, at least if we can stay on top of the Russians. We need only intelligence and dedication, reserves of which, especially in the Air Force, may be found in abundance. "We see a limitlessness of man's intellectual capacity to grow," concludes one general.[91]

III. THE MILITARY VIEW OF MAN: PESSIMISTIC

Although the Armed Forces, each in its own way, evidence the tendency toward structure in traditionalism and conservatism, this does not mean that the American military is fascistic, even unconsciously. But as a dynamic, illiberal island in a historically liberal society, and grown to the size and pressure of a continent, the military's basically pessimistic view of man and society may effectively, perhaps tragically, dampen the hopes for optimistic change. A generation ago, Walter Lippmann called attention to the lack of a "public philosophy" and only a few years ago Henry Kariel warned of "The Ideological Vacuum" in American society. In this vacuum, power rather than ideology was thought to be the key to action and the future.[92] But now the country is developing at least an implicit ideology, or perhaps a growing recognition that it has always had one: the Hobbesian view of human nature, predatory at its roots, but combined with a curiously ideal and potentially savage Biblically inspired concern to stamp out evil wherever it raises its ugly head. With God and natural law no longer universal deterrents, and nature itself brought under utilitarian control, the province and possibility of selfish human nature on the loose have been dramatically increased. In this qualified vacuum, however, the American military has an *explicit* ideology, combining a strong, traditional respect for natural law[93] with Hobbesian cynicism, and so readily conceives of itself as the inheritor and preserver of the nation's and the Western world's cultural values.[94] Vagts, concluding his massive survey of militarism, does not find the American military guilty, as yet, of that basic perversion of its power.[95] He does, however, note that the military operates under the strict and self-righteous code of the knight:

The influence of post-feudal nobility as a complex of ideas, sentiments, and "belonging" membership being acquired by conforming to the code of chivalry, diluted and altered but basically still knightly.[96]

This "officer and gentleman" code no longer opposes technology, especially in the Air Force, which is most open to social change. But by the same token, war as competition may not be kept as easily within bounds. Until the latest cessation of bombing over North Vietnam, the list of taboo targets grew ever narrower and the motivation for unrestricted bombing found increasing justification from the military establishment, basically conservative, even pessimistic. An ethic of the right, of duty and obedience, gathers momentum from our history as a favored people, and pietism, strong in the American military, may find not so much horror as a kind of comfort in fulfilled prophecy respecting the apocalyptic terror of the H-bomb. Since it is the nature of military power as rationally controlled violence to harden into structure, and given the failure of the liberal context and the immensity of the danger without, the danger within is an altering of the national consciousness—and conscience—to use any means to the end of securing our traditional, God-given values. The popularity of Generals LeMay and Goldwater, the rise of Ronald Reagan and George Wallace and others who advocate hard and hawkish positions, as well as the proliferation of paramilitary groups—all indicate that this process is already under way. It seems ominous that even those of stated liberal persuasions appear more and more willing to adopt the methodology of the military, the easy resort to force, as well as its ethic, the identification of the moral Good with the political Right.

IV. FUNCTIONALISM AND REIFICATION EXPRESSED IN WESTERN MILITARY HISTORY

THE SYSTEM AS MACHINE

As every serviceman knows, the hardening of controls into structure expresses itself in seemingly immeasurable and irreducible rules, regulations, and fixed routines. The system emerges as some huge, impersonal beast that exists and grows to be served. Rather, it has more often been likened to a vast machine, and indeed it is the intent that it should so behave— efficiently, inexorably, and as unperturbably in the face of the terrible rigors and personal tragedies of war. Despite the determined, continuing, and significant attempts to humanize the structure, it remains in the nature of the case a vast, impersonal organization that must not hesitate to submerge the private wants and necessities of the individual, even to the requiring of life itself. It is, then, strictly functional, and exists to do a nasty, and often fatal, job. Its members also exist primarily for their function, for the part they must play. An invisible bond, without parallel in strength or sacredness ex-

cept in religious orders, binds brothers-in-arms, but their identification with the machine is even greater: the captain goes
down with his ship.

Even a casual glance at the history of war establishes man's
machines as models for his warfare. This marvelous extension
of himself, multiplied in power manyfold and entirely subject
to his will, is one of the distinguishing characteristics of the
human animal and his open-ended freedom to grow. To weld
other living beings—horses, camels, elephants, but especially
other men—into such a device was, of course, immensely more
complex and difficult because of the inherent and rational
resistance of other wills which, as Clausewitz observed, makes
predictability at best problematical.[97] But the rewards were
immensely greater too. It was soon learned that the whole
family or tribe, and then city and country, acting together
accomplished more than each individual's action added up
separately. The Leader appeared, the "one fixed link" in the
chain, predetermining, assigning, and controlling the human
parts to transmit force geometrically rather than simply additionally.[98] Thus the military appeared, coincident with civilization itself.

Ancient Armies as Machines

In this rise of the military as the forceful extension of the
governing class, the ideal became the instant and total re-
sponsiveness of the inanimate marvel which asked no questions
and was always dispensable—if that served the purposes of the
master. The machine existed solely for its owner or user. All
the great empires of the ancient Near East were thus built
upon the absolute authoritarianism of the godlike rulers and
their huge, insensitive, machinelike armies. Two in particular
stand out, the Assyrians and the Persians. The military state
of Assyria, fashioned through a millennium of constant warfare, began with militia for home defense and ended in a

standing army which was probably without peer in its brutally mechanical and massive crushing of all opposition from the Euphrates to the Upper Nile. The Assyrians were the first to equip their large armies completely with weapons of iron and to employ the battering ram and formidable siege machinery. Breasted, in his *Ancient Times,* says that "to maintain the Army was the chief work of the state. The state was a vast military machine, more terrible than any mankind had ever yet seen." [99] The fall, when it came, was devastating and final, with not even a breath of resuscitation, as though the heart had long ago died, but leaving for a time an iron lung.[100]

The Persians, who took over eventually, in Darius and Xerxes especially, were supremely confident that the unquestioning loyalty of the immense masses of men they levied from their vast Empire could not help overwhelming the free but divided Greeks. Xerxes angrily rejected the request of his satrap Pythius that he be allowed to keep the youngest of his five sons at home from the campaign against the Greeks. He had the boy split in two for the army to march through, a vivid lesson to all that, as he informed Pythius, "you and all that pertain to you are my slaves, and are bound to do my bidding without a murmur." Later, Xerxes had the stubborn sea itself lashed with an iron chain when a storm wrecked his first bridge across the Hellespont! The huge size of his army, perhaps a million men, emphasized the inexhaustibility of that which was utterly dispensable, the individual soldier.[101]

Darius and Xerxes lost—to smaller but better machines. The heavily armed Greek phalanx, like a human tank, proved superior to Persian archers, and the huge and unwieldy Persian-Phoenician fleet succumbed to the lightning-like thrusts of the Greeks in the narrow Bay of Salamis. Like Assyria centuries before, the fall from world glory in the total and blind obedience to one will was not long in coming. A century and a half later another and better human machine, created by Philip of Macedon and superbly managed by his brilliant son Alexander, drove from the Aegean to the Ganges, devouring the Persian Empire enroute. The key to its fall, as Alexander knew, lay in the person of Darius III himself, to whom the wills of all his soldiers were absolutely subject. With his demise, and the symbolic burning of his capital at Persepolis, the great Empire, now mindless, ceased.[102]

THE REDUCTION OF PERSONS TO THINGS (REIFICATION)

Western military history is the legacy of Rome. That early republic's dependence upon the pride of freeholders to build its conquering legions provided at least a basis for humanism and the "Roman virtues" of courage, honor, discipline, and service which have become embedded in Western military institutions. The later dilution of Roman patriotism by mercenaries and strangers signals the decline of the Empire as military concerns are narrowed strictly to functionalism. Citizens abrogated the once proud privilege of admittedly unpleasant duty and hired what rapidly became a foreign machine made up largely of provincials who had never seen Rome or cared about it. They took over, for pay alone, the boring and dirty work of maintaining the frontiers and order within the state. Then they took over the state. In some sixty years (A.D. 235–297), forty-six emperors or pretenders were slain as the swollen and imperious "household troops" of the Praetorian Guard auctioned off the purple to the highest bidder.[103] This severance by the citizens of personal ties with the military and its reduction then to an instrument valued only for its use reveals that process of reification or "thingification" [104] which we know as the "decay" of the Roman Empire. The unfeeling military machine, attached only to itself, became the crude and destructive arbiter of the destinies of the shattered Roman world.

Enough has been written about the fanatical loyalty of Napoleon's armies, and enough remembered about Hitler's early invincible, mechanized divisions rolling over Europe, both totally obedient to one will and utterly insensitive to the wastage of human material, to illustrate *reification* for modern man. This reduction of *persons* to *things*—or what Martin Buber, Paul Tillich, and others have spoken of more philosophically as the making of "subjects" into "objects," a "thou" into an "it," [105]—follows in the most direct and immediate fashion from the use of men solely for their function. The utter disposability of human life in and by the armies of the ancient Near East and the deterioration of the once proud and disciplined Roman legions provide a consistent thread of ugly relationship, of continual threat and temptation, to the armies of modern times. If Vietnam is to be taken seriously, even our own army is no exception. More like the early Roman and later Byzantine military institutions, the Anglo-Saxon tradition has offered a more humanistic understanding of the military function than did Imperial Rome and the ancient Near East. But it, too, has had its degenerative episodes and is undergoing considerable soul-searching today, as may be seen in the abundant contemporary writings.

V. FUNCTIONALISM AND REIFICATION EXPRESSED IN CONTEMPORARY MILITARY THOUGHT

Army

Functionary vs. Human Being

Glenn Gray reminds us that "becoming a functionary is not entirely foreign to the nature of the majority of us." [106] In the military the atmosphere, the command, and the necessity are such that men more readily become functionaries. Gray, recalling a French officer who sent a girl collaborationist to her death while joking with her as he might have with a sister,

remonstrated with him about such callousness, [but] he made clear to me that he regarded himself as an army officer in quite a different way from himself as a human being. The two personalities could succeed each other with lightning rapidity. . . . As a human being, he was capable of kindness, even gentleness, and within limits he was just and honest. In his capacity of functionary, he could be brutal beyond measure without ever losing his outward amiability and poise.[107]

Even the great passions—love and hate—become impersonal. The same soldiers who "kill and burn, burn and kill" also pick up stray dogs and orphans and sometimes give their lives for them. Gray speaks of this as "the impersonal passion for protecting and conserving life itself" against the general threat of annihilation.[108] Hatred, except for momentary instances of attempted revenge for the loss of a buddy, is not individual but abstract. As a professional and a technologist the military man regards himself as an instrument of the state and can, too easily, adopt a hostile attitude toward any other state or people "on orders." [109] Indeed, he may do so, almost as readily, toward his own kin in the suppression of internal disorders. In the federal policing of labor disputes around the turn of the century it was found that "the basic attitude of the Regular Army" was that "they viewed themselves as part of a machine . . . simply performing as it was ordered to do." To the surprise of many, the state troops (i.e., National Guard), used during the same period with some trepidation, "proved to be loyal." [110] This fact has been reaffirmed repeatedly since those troubled days, and not the least in the events of the recent past. Viewing himself as nonpolitical and not the source of his orders, the soldier can feel nonresponsible, not guilty, even when ties of blood and class are threatened. One Army officer put it quite bluntly: "When called into action . . . [the Army] is merely a machine, and is as irresponsible." [111]

As such, the military man is recognizably at the lowest rung of David Riesman's famous ladder of moral types. He is almost always "tradition-directed," or at the most "other-directed," which constitutes an "escape from freedom," from the autonomy of self-responsibility. "All is fair . . . in war," especially for machines, which make no moral distinctions and have only "a job to perform." This is the appallingly frequent rationalization of men at war. In "Douhet Revisited," the great Italian prophet of air power is seen in the broader context of viewing "the essential character of war as being formed by the tremendous use of mechanical means," because of which "there are no weapons divisible into noble and ignoble" kinds.[112] From this amoral understanding of the means by which war may be waged, it is easy to see public antipathy to gas warfare as the much overrated "Ghost of Ypres": an emotional, irrational jag that needs correction by "an enlightened program of public information" which will convince the public that "development of war gasses is not immoral but essential to national security." [113] The extension to nuclear weapons has, of course, frequently been made, at least to tactical ones, as well as to germ warfare. The great question concerns the controllability of such near-ultimate means, i.e., What would be left after their use? But the question is not always asked. When it is, it is to suggest that although Douhet would probably recognize that nuclear annihilation exceeds his own call for absolute "elimination of the enemy," yet his dictum to "inflict the greatest possible damage in the shortest possible time" remains the basic principle of war even in the limited engagements of today. For war is reduced to the great machines which can be judged only by their effectiveness. Douhet later modified his views on preemptive war, which had been objected to on moral grounds. But he did so, not on the basis of morality but in the simple recognition that deference to public opinion may be a need of nations at times.[114]

All of this seems eminently reasonable to men accustomed to the "unlimited liability" of their trade and profession. The tragic ease with which men may see themselves as parts of the machine, and even delight in the smooth functioning of its parts in following orders, may simply black out all moral considerations, as in My Lai and elsewhere. We know, of course, that the Nuremberg trials a quarter of a century ago made it abundantly clear that more is required of a man than simply to respond to orders and the prevailing atmosphere. The order must be "lawful," i.e., at least in the direction of the humanitarian principle of preserving life where possible, which, impossible to spell out precisely in every instance, devolves, finally, upon the individual conscience. Yet much of the defense of the men indicted for atrocities in Vietnam, and certainly much of the sympathy generated in their home-towns, rests squarely upon their supposed "obedience to orders" and "the prevailing atmosphere."

The Unhuman Enemy

The atmosphere, of course, can be resisted, but not with ease, for the problems it generates are often confusingly subtle and probably beyond the range of understanding of most of those who have not had combat experience. Sometimes there is respect and even admiration for the enemy and a strange camaraderie may develop between opposing commanders,[115] even a kind of need for "the necessary enemy." ("The next best thing to a good friend is a good enemy.") But this does not necessarily call for any quarter to be given. Gray speaks for Vietnam as well as World War II when he observes that

morally, [the enemy] has no human status whatever. . . . The degree of abstraction in his hatred is immense. He is capable of disregarding all other considerations except the single one of destroying everything that stands in the way of successfully accomplishing his mission. He would be the last to grant . . . that the enemy is a human being. . . . Yet he is ready to grant it when the enemy is subdued and at his mercy. *Generosity and humanity are only possible where there is no equality. . . . In this the predemocratic nature of the military ideal is apparent.*[116]

Under conditions of combat, even in its more relaxed moments, the enemy may not be accorded human status at all, even when he "is subdued and at [one's] mercy." This is the horror of so many Vietnam "incidents." One, involving the Green Berets, made headlines before being eclipsed by My Lai. But they are not peculiar to this war. A veteran of the Pacific War (World War II) remembers having participated well behind the combat lines in a clearing "hunt" of a frightened and running Japanese prisoner and laughing as they made sport and gunned him down as they would have a rabbit back home. Touched later with remorse, he found it incomprehensible that at the time "he had no conscience about it whatever." [117] The dichotomy in conscience is not unusual as many servicemen know, who only afterward experience the horror of guiltlessness at the time for inhuman deeds. The present rash of such remembrances by returning veterans is clear evidence that the problem is a continuing one.

The Subspecies: Homo Furens

This, says Gray from the experience of nearly three years in combat in Europe, "is the abiding curse of the military profession. The total human being has no chance to break through to consciousness because there is no official interest in the whole human being." [118] This may be exaggeration, but the threat and the fear and the bitterness are real for those who have taken up the sword and found it two-edged, wounding the wielder as well as the "enemy." Gray is surely right that the reason for the dichotomy is that the military man becomes an instrument while he makes everything into an instrument. "He is a trigger finger, a tank driver, a bombardier, a scout, and he can take delight in being an instrument. So everything conspires to prevent his coming to himself." [119] It is not that as finite beings we can really avoid playing certain roles and performing certain functions, but that the aspect of "unlimited liability" of military service inevitably places more weight upon the performance of a function than upon the maintenance of a life. Men have been known to weep over the loss of a machine, a tank, an airplane, with buddies falling all around them. "It's a job to be done" covers a multitude of tuggings at the conscience for napalm bombing and the obliteration of villages suspected of hiding Viet Cong—pride and one's instrumentality to the machine. For the love of the machine itself —and I've seen many a pilot caress the sleek body of his aircraft with an affection obviously in a class with that which he had for his wife—is characteristic of the age itself in the West and of necessity is multiplied almost infinitely where life itself is identified with one's weapon. Man becomes "only a center of force, a wielder of weapons, a means of security and survival." Even against his will

he becomes a fighting man, a *Homo furens* . . . a subspecies of the genus *Homo sapiens*. . . . Man as a warrior is only partly a man, yet, fatefully enough, this aspect of him is capable of transforming the whole . . . able to subordinate other aspects of the personality, repress civilian habits of mind, and make the soldier as fighter a different kind of creature from the former worker, farmer, or clerk.[120]

Tocqueville once said that it is "especially dangerous to enslave men to the minor details of life." [121] Robert Nisbet in *The Quest for Community* says that modern man is fascinated by his own disintegration.[122] The irony is that man's belief in himself is weakest when his control of his environment is greatest.[123] He is helpless before alien forces of the spirit, "not the hero who does things, but . . . the hero to whom things are done." Rationalism has taken refuge in impersonality, the state has emerged as the great leveler, the "pulverizing and macadamizing tendency of modern history." [124] The dichotomy in conscience on the battlefield did not begin with Descartes but the legacy of his dualism has created a world in which it is infinitely more possible. *"Cogito, ergo sum"* established not simply self-consciousness but *individual* self-consciousness as the irreducible certainty, the primary reality. Nature itself was bifurcated into "thought," i.e., self-consciousness, *man;* and

"extension," which is matter, or *things*.[125] But self-consciousness is individual, and so man is atomized: "*I* think, therefore
I am." The rugged individual appears who knows himself to
be the center of all that is; even other selves are derivative,
coming after the initial experience of the *I*, and hence readily
understood to be inferior and meaningful only as they can be
used to support the selfish self. The results are self-enclosed
entities, individuals and sovereign states, which regard every-
thing else, including other selves, as objects to be controlled.

That this process has been going on for some time in all
sorts of human and human-nature relationships, from marriage
to nation-state power politics and the despoiling of natural resources, is hardly news. That it has made men lonely and
afraid, imprisoned in their little "yellow submarines"[126] with
only periscopes upon reality, has come with something of a
shock, which is reflected in the modern literature of existentialism, anxiety, and despair. The deepening meaninglessness
oozes from the prefabricated walls of our alienation from man
and nature, which we insist upon treating as objects of control. If the psychologists are right that no self can be—or
become—a self without other selves, we are, literally, commit-
ting suicide in substituting objects at will for subjects who only
can make and keep us human. The deep danger of the over-
grown military today is that it incalculably hastens the process.

The Process of Dehumanization

Among thinkers in uniform today, there is deepening awareness of this dehumanizing process in which the military figures
so largely. The Polish war novel, *The 1000 Hour Day*, finds
the hero of modern war in *the Activity* itself, "the terrible,
frantic activity, the futility and glory of fighting, the mass
enthusiasm and despair."[127] The characters stalk and charge
and die through the book but fail to dominate it; they are
differentiated but colorless. Eugene M. Emme, writing on
"Technical Change and Western Thought, 1914–1945," lists as

the first great influence of modern technology the dehumanization of combat stemming from the accelerated mobility and magnified firepower. He adds the great rise in noncombat civilian casualties, destruction of underemployed military forces and economic resources, and the extremely complex ties of mobilization, finance, organization, commitment of trained personnel, superior weapons, etc., all of which become an immeasurable dead weight upon the individual.[128] The Army continues in its publications to sound the worry of the System. In outspoken criticism of Secretary of Defense McNamara while he was in office, it is asserted that he didn't "understand people" and hence too much attention was given to the System.[129] In a later tribute to the fallen President, it is averred that Mr. Kennedy "did understand people, that men were not machines and that pride, courage, passion and the fog of battle simply can't be computerized." [130] In "Tomorrow's Leaders" the theme is found in a little verse:

> We are all blind until we see
> That in the human plan
> Nothing is worth the making if
> It does not include the man.[131]

As we have seen, Douhet is criticized for his absolute encouragement of subservience to the machine, and in "Technology's Challenge to Leadership" the warning is sounded that in the environment of today's mechanized world "military men may attempt to transform their reasoning to a mechanical process." [132] Some even blame the scholars for having invaded and elevated themselves to positions of unwarranted influence in the modern military establishment. Bringing with them, it is thought, an emphasis upon behaviorism and avalueism, the "eggheads" are often seen as effectively undercutting morality and humanism in the armed services. A reprint of "The American Army: A French Estimate in 1777" dwells upon the essential humanness and freedom of the American colonial fighter compared to the European regular of the time whose "will,

. . . personality, in fact his very instinct for self-preservation have been stifled or destroyed. In battle he is a mere machine, . . . without personal feelings, controlled only by hidden springs." [133] But, as we have noted, a hundred years later it is the American Army, regularized and breaking strikes, which views itself as a machine, "simply performing as it was ordered to do." [134] Nearly a century after that observation was made, it is expressed again to call attention once more to the same phenomenon: the machinelikeness of the military which reduces persons to parts to be manipulated beyond appeal to individual morality and judgment. It is complained that Americans are overemphasizing tactics and technology at the expense of strategy and judgment, both of which are left to civilians.[135] Doubtless this, too, has the effect of easing twinges of guilt, since the military man does not have "the Big Picture," which is available only at the highest civilian levels.

In a particularly insightful study of "Fear and Courage" a French officer experiences in combat the "strange horror, as of a virgin country" and a "supreme, almost demoniacal easiness of mind and . . . laughter," but afterward comes depression, "the dark feeling of guilt which clings to the legal military murder. . . . The dead float before their inner vision." He quotes from Ernst Juenger's diary:

"There exists a responsibility which the State cannot take off our hands; it is an account to be settled with ourselves. It penetrates into the deepest of our dreams." [136]

Again drawing upon the French, we are told that "man is not only a wheel in the military machine, he is equally a citizen concerned in the issue of the conflict." [137] But especially clear and detailed, "Attitudes Toward People" calls for a recognition of the individual as absolutely necessary to the *esprit de corps* of any group:

Deal with people as individuals, not as machines, or work units. . . . Find ways to utilize the unique capabilities of each individual while preserving his human dignity. . . . Self-fulfillment depends largely on . . . providing an environment that will enhance the dignity of man and allow him a high degree of self-expression.[138]

The Concern for Persons

The high tribute paid in *Army* to retiring General Harold K. Johnson as Chief of Staff (1964–1968) centers above all upon his central concern for people. "Put the personal in personnel," was more than a catchy motto with him, it is said. The easy words represented an intense and religiously grounded conviction at odds with an almost global image of the insensitivity of American military power: "the U.S. Army consists, basically, not of weapons and machines, but of people." [139] Shortly afterward, General Westmoreland, sworn in as his successor, echoed the same humanism.[140] The anomaly of the unquestioned Christian character and integrity of such leadership at the top, which knows its Green Beret executions and My Lai "incidents," is the tragic irony of modern war, perhaps of all war. Ward Just notes that the higher the command, the farther removed it is from the actual "dirty dozen" who do the bloody work on a thousand trails in Vietnam. And no less than the grubbiest private, though far more sophisticated and given to rationalization, the generals are obedient to the Machine, the System, the Plan.

From the time of Napoleon a general officer has acted more or less in isolation. Westmoreland's written testimony on the Vietnam War does not differ markedly from the words of General Omar Bradley, which do not differ from those of Marshal Ferdinand Foch. In the memoirs of Foch and Bradley the face of war is almost never seen. There are no mangled bodies, no stink, no blood, just generalship and logistics, command control.[141]

The almost desperate, somewhat frenzied attempts to implement a prevailing attitude of humanism in today's Army is frequent newscopy. How sustained it will be, or can be, lies beyond the crystal ball of anyone in the services who dares speak. For it is very much in the nature of experimentation, and although it has the blessing of Chief of Staff General Westmoreland and a number of senior officers, it also has its powerful doubters, ranging from Bill Mauldin's "Willie and Joe" to the new Chairman of the House Armed Services Committee, Congressman Hébert, who, frankly, is "scared to death." [142] They, too, are parts of the Machine.

NAVY

"Treat Sailors like Spare Parts?"

The Navy, too, expresses concern lest the technology of war overwhelm its art which traditionally concerns the need for personal judgment under conditions of separation and isolation. In "The Changing Nature of Power" the burgeoning of technology has confused our priorities and goals and caused an "erosion of the will." [143] So great is the change that it can be predicted that "WW II was probably the last truly personal war we will ever fight as free-wheeling individuals." [144] Major Carl M. Guelzo won a prize essay with his insistence that

in the last decade, the integration of the military effort into the warp and woof of civilian society and the marked growth of the military segment of the economy further demand a wider vision than is possible from the standpoint of more technical expertness.[145]

The "Crisis in Leadership," "The Ivy-clad Man on Horseback," "Treat Sailors like Spare Parts?"—all warn that we are creating specialists at the expense of leaders, that the danger of subversion is big business invading everything, even on the high seas, that sailors ask only to be treated as well as the ever more expensive but surely replaceable spare parts of a ship or plane.[146] The proliferating jungle of technology is reflected in the increasing problem of semantics. Eccles complains:

If the language of weapons has become difficult, it is nothing compared with the jargon with which the defense officialdom explains its priorities and programming. Even the best informed committee member often has reason to suspect that language is being used deliberately to deceive him. . . . Words don't mean what they say . . . [but] conceal both cause and effect. . . . In effect the military has lost control of their own language. . . . Argument has overwhelmed analysis.[147]

The System Has Gone Mad

But deeper than deliberate deception may be the unconscious resistance to "thinking the unthinkable," the incomprehensibility, i.e., the inhumanity, of the machine grown to stifling, suicidal proportions. Eccles speaks of the "logistical snowball," the natural tendency of

all logistical activities . . . to grow to inordinate size with the immediate effect of lowering the quality of major decisions. Command itself, that distinctive and decisive aspect of military power which assumes life and death responsibility for men and nations, is "institutionalized," . . . the terrible personal responsibility . . . frequently assumed by the authority given to comptrollers, budget officers, special assistants, and systems managers.[148]

War gaming, bewildering complex analyses and models of subversive insurgency,[149] decision making,[150] and the excited call for fully "Automated Control of Logistics—the Next Step," [151] are but a few of the myriad expressions of the rapidly computerized Navy swept along by what one enthusiastic engineer proudly declaims to be "one of the essential characteristics of technology, namely, that it is dynamic and progressive." [152] The difficulty is that the dynamism becomes its own end, and this knows no limits. Near the top the unnerving dimensions of this problem can be sensed as the Honorable Robert A. Frosh, Assistant Secretary of the Navy for Research and Development, warned in 1968 that the

systems idea, which I earlier classified as one of the great inventions, has now gone mad in the sense that we have optimized and systematized and tied everything together so well that if the system is not quite right for the operational situation, we are faced with serious trouble. We cannot change it because it is all tied together so well we cannot pull one piece out without disrupting the whole thing.[153]

This pursuit of perfection, the refinement of every part, the drive to unify all parts into the superbly functioning whole which covers every option and is designed to meet every possibility is the machine mentality which in the end is self-defeating. It gets in its own way and grinds to a halt because it ignores the realities of time and man's finiteness and the necessity of daily choice and action based upon risk and the imponderables of the continuous quest for the Good. The Good is foreshortened to the means, the smooth functioning of the system, delight in the absolutely calculated, always encouraged efficiency of a creation become autonomous, able, we proudly say, "to run by itself." Long before the always surprising weaknesses appear, the machine's very amorality has already eroded the humanity of its caretakers, its supposed charioteers. A visitor to Vietnam reports in the *Marine Corps Gazette* a certain amazement that in joining an air strike against the Viet Cong, "I felt not a twinge of guilt." Yet he had, upon arrival, been shocked at the briefing: " 'You gotta work over the area good and proper.' . . . The man talked as if it were a question of ploughing a field rather than dropping napalm." But afterward, as he watched for hours how "with clockwork precision, an endless stream of fighting machines roared into the shimmering air on missions of death and destruction," it was not of what was happening to human beings in the rice paddies below that he thought.

No such pictures came to mind; I saw only a superbly organized death factor at work. Just forty-eight hours after my arrival, the identification with "one's own side" had become so complete that everyone on the receiving end of the factory had become fair game.[154]

A student of mine, a former Marine pilot, may well have led one of the squadrons that day, and had his painful and shaming insight into his own motivation for a second, and needless, devastating pass over a suspected VC village: the exhilaration of pride in "a job well done." He suddenly realized that he had become captive to his own plane to the inhuman degree that joy in its efficient functioning completely obliterated the tragic, human suffering far below.

Captain Longino, on a different tack, fears for the stopping of the machine itself by the atrophy of human intuition and direction which, whatever our enthusiasm for technology, it can never replace.[155] Eccles strikes deeper, expressing alarm for the quality of our nationhood and its very survival:

For one, I am not prepared to believe that atomic power has made all men alike pigmies. . . . A nation will get what it trains for. . . . When it overrates the products of science and undervalues that of the human heart, it is asking for death.[156]

Others, too, have read the signs and have opened up some avenues of response. The Moral Leadership Program through chaplains and, increasingly, line officers has lifted up the danger. Heroes such as Baron von Steuben, legendary drillmaster of the Revolutionary Army at Valley Forge, who knew and loved his men above the routine of teaching and fighting, are given their due.[157] Admiral Arleigh Burke, former Chief of Naval Operations (1955–1961), underscored his conviction that "tactical advantages notwithstanding, men are essential." [158] The present Chief of Naval Operations appears to be making this believable, if it can last. The difficulty is that it takes more than pronouncements from the top.

AIR FORCE

Positive Values from the Machine

The Air Force, consonant with its own birth in the age of technology, seems less worried and more sophisticated respecting the positive values to be drawn from the machine. The vanishing heroic leader and the emerging military manager have caused a split personality with a developing tension and dialogue which should be fruitful for the future. Instead of being the object of fear and blame, "The New American Military" ought to be complimented, for it has remarkably "accommodated itself to the precise political aims of war in a radically new era." [159] And this, it is claimed, has actually meant a decline in military influence, from initiation to execution of policy. There is, indeed, rising complaint shared with the other services that strategy has been preempted by brainy civilians, leaving the narrower, and not fully satisfying, role of executing tactics to the military forces. This has encouraged the quite legitimate concern lest "professionalism" be simply "equated with technological skill—with functional competence." [160] The introduction of a broader humanities base of studies at the Air Force Academy reflects the same fear of the unthinking machine. But whatever internal sense of frustration is felt by some, the ability and willingness of the military to tailor its overwhelming power to the precise and limited packaging of Vietnam shows that it is an "obviously dynamic" and conscientious profession. There is an awareness of structure as important in its own right, and influential in the relations of adversaries.[161] There is an acceptance of "The Liberal Challenge in the Military Profession" as a healthy impetus to dialogue with tradition to keep the whole open-ended. The formalized rationales of the services, as doctrine, carry with them the danger of inflexibility:

The technical sophistication of weapons and the complexities of strategies require productive criticism and receptivity to new ideas. As in no other period of its history, the American military profession today faces responsibilities that demand officers with open minds, with a point of view reflective of liberal values.[162]

Situation Ethics

But the "liberal values" are less tied to and defined by the past. The willingness here is to allow the age itself to speak to values. The rising younger set who must inherit the Air Force are heavily conditioned by the more inward and personal commitment of existentialism. Colonel Drumm sees this widening "cultural value gap" in the Air Force as pressing the ego-satisfying needs of its younger members ever upward toward self and social fulfillment and away from simplistic and physiological and security concerns. This cannot help meaning increased tension within the ranks and between the generations, and it calls for considerable understanding and personal, creative guidance from the top down.[163] Ethical decisions likely will be conditioned more and more by "the situation" and reflect both the historical context and inward values. Thus it is felt that the decision to drop the bomb at Hiroshima was probably the only one which could have been made *at the time*,[164] but just as surely would command far less support among the rank and file today. The vital distinction is made between the machine that "can run by itself," and persons who are constantly changing, and hopefully growing toward that which is fundamentally human. Such growth dictates that their machines must at all times be controlled for humanistic purposes.

Straitjacketing by the past can no longer, then, be tolerated, and it is perhaps significant that much of the official literature employed in the Moral Leadership Program emphasizes freedom. To be sure this is stressed as a traditional value, but it is one which by implication and mood tends to leave weaponry and the science of warfare open-ended. Some of the same program material, however, does warn that technology is not enough. Almost alone in these writings, largely initiated and still motivated by chaplains, there is a concern somewhat like that of the Army and Navy respecting the alienation and reification of man.[165] Perhaps a straw in the wind, the "In My Opinion" column in the *Air University Quarterly Review* has carried at least one nostalgic note, observing that the Air Force is no longer made up of personal warriors, but they have become deprofessionalized by management and thereby lost something, the image of knightliness. "We are feared now, not admired." [166] Certainly events in Southeast Asia have deepened and confirmed the truth of this remark some years ago. The great dilemma that the Air Force now faces, saddled as it has been with massive responsibilities for ending the ghastly conflict in Laos and Cambodia and Vietnam, is how to "control for humanistic purposes" their devastating power. Growing revulsion may bring to the youngest of the military arms a deeper rejection than the sister services have experienced in the past.

The intent of this section has been to emphasize the dynamic process of military power as tending toward structure, which as a necessary vehicle or means always threatens to become the end, to exist for itself and its own propagation, and thus to subvert, and eventually to diminish military power by static forms and processes. The tragic result is the reduction of men to the amoral character of the machines they operate. In *The Strange Land,* Corporal Selig can't wash the stains of human blood from his hands, but still it is the machines that get

the worst of it. These machines so beautifully built and powerful, and the wonderful things they can do. Smashing them is the real crime and the sin. . . . It's easy to see some of the other things gone. Nobody gives a damn for a million beat-up buildings between here and the Atlantic Ocean. The churches can go too, as far as I care. But not motors. These are the cleverest things a man ever made, and the best to watch, and the best to own. If it's worth living at all.[167]

It is ironic that the youngest military service, escaping by virtue of its youth some of the conservatism of long traditions, yet even more surely yields to reification through its wholehearted and, until recently at least, virtually uncritical attachment to the machine.

Chapter 8

The Tendency
to
Excess

We have seen that since it is rationally controlled, military power tends toward structure. On the other hand, as violence, and therefore as unstructured power of being seeking expression, military power tends toward infinity, the uncapping and even the dissolution of the volcano. Max Lerner says that this is the key corollary to overkill, i.e., *overreach*, that "all power tends to overstep its limits." [1] This sobering conviction is the meaning of *hubris*, the suicidal pride of the Greek tragic hero, and Paul Tillich recognizes it in modern man's anxiety which reflects and causes man's tendency to excess.[2] In the Biblical "fall," of Satan as well as of man, we are close to an ontological understanding of this tendency of power to exceed moral and ethical limits. With the denuding of Western culture of such limits, or shall we say, witnessing the breaking through of almost all restraints in the modern world, we have yet more reason to believe in the *daemon,* the inherent dynamic of power. Marxists speak of the "locomotive of history"; and evolution, automatic progress, the Judeo-Christian understanding of history as linear and apocalyptic, our own Westward push as a nation, the development of progressivism in education, and "galloping technology"—have all contributed a context for the acceptance of violence unfettered as more or less inevitable. For this reason, Lerner distinguishes the present age from earlier ones, by its having, and using, a surplus of power:

There is a sado-masochistic element here which goes deep into the neuroses of our time, a wild satisfaction in the abandonment of personal choice and in the imposition of authority over others. . . . But also an element of appeal that goes beyond the neurotic. At the core of it is the heady sense of an irresistible movement which gathers up men and ideas in its course, and sweeps toward a victory of purpose in an otherwise purposeless world.[3]

I. OVERREACH EXPRESSED IN WESTERN MILITARY HISTORY

THE "ABSURDITY" OF MODERATION

One aspect of this tendency to excess of military power is an overemphasis upon the rational. It is not so dramatic, perhaps, as the physical to which we shall come, but it is tremendously important and basic to the theoretical structuralism we have earlier discussed. Clausewitz claimed that war could be thought better than taught and when viewed abstractly tends to the absolute. Hence, "to introduce . . . a principle of moderation would be an absurdity. . . . War is an act of violence pushed to its utmost bounds." [4] That is, it is limitless in thought, to keep clean the neat packaging of the pure and practical reasoning of Kantian metaphysics. Clausewitz admits that war, dealing also with the concrete, can never approximate such purity of conception.[5] Unfortunately, there were those of his disciples for "whom no historical sense warned that writing on the philosophy of war is, even more than theology, time conditioned." [6] The influence of Clausewitz' abstract absolutism is everywhere found in the modern concrete totalitarianism of war. There are echoes of Clausewitz in the long past, in Sparta, Alexander, Genghis Khan, Tamerlane;

and Clausewitz absorbed much from Napoleon. Sparta's great Lycurgus is said to have "made it preferable . . . to die a noble death rather than remain alive in disgrace." This was according to a System, the dread "master in the shape of Law," which became a " 'categorical imperative' in the soul of every true Spartiate 'Peer' . . . the ultimate driving force which . . . in sheer defiance of human nature" worked for more than two centuries.[7] The godlike weeping of Alexander with no more worlds to conquer, the "moral weapon of frightfulness" deliberately employed by the Great Khan, the almost insane insistence of the lame Timur in fixing absolutely the loyalty of his own kindred peoples, the grandiose ambitions of Napoleon and Hitler which in sophisticated planning left nothing to be desired except humility—all illustrate the ease with which those who deal with ultimate force tend to drive to pure abstraction untempered by other "living and moral forces." Gray speaks of the growth of "abstract hatred" as part of the drive toward moral absolutism, i.e., restraints, restrictions, modifications tend to fall away leaving perhaps only one quality, often out of context, to be hated. Distance increases the credibility of "abstract hatred," the enemy becoming faceless, nonindividual, a hostile power.[8] And hence arise vendetta war, war as vocation, and the moral crusade against total evil.

"THINKING THE UNTHINKABLE"

Less dramatic but still illustrative, one may add the ancient Chinese "science" of warfare which Genghis Khan recognized for what it was, and the rather similar formalistic approaches in the West, such as Henri Jomini's geometric rationalism, Ardant du Picq's spiritualization of war, and Foch's mystical doctrine of attack. The tendency is clearly to be seen in the modern penchant for strategic studies and "thinking the unthinkable," which today are significantly the province of the academic community, the "think tanks" and the "whiz kids."

One has only to attempt to wade through the seemingly endless mass of literature on nuclear strategies and effects to be
convinced of how utterly detached it all becomes from the
tragic realities of war, even conventional war. The problem
of semantics alone, for all our striving for precision and clarity,
has increasingly arisen to anesthetize and keep us from actually
coming to the truth. Eric Larrabee observes in "The Pursuit
of Peace":

The conduct of hypothetical conflicts presents the baffling spectacle
of intelligence at work in an arena from which some essential
element of sanity has been removed; it is, quite literally, thinking
about the unthinkable.[9]

The cool casualness with which Herman Kahn can describe
the effects of nuclear radiation and social disruption on a
scale to retard future generations for a thousand years and
make the present one "envy the dead" [10] may be irony. Perhaps that is the one means left to enable us to break through
the smoke screen of words, the abstract defense with which we
confront the peril of the new age coming to birth or death.
Probably the matter is really unthinkable, for our whole
notion of history and of power is of their ongoingness. But
with our radical surplus of power today—enough now we are
told actually to liquidate all life on the planet—we stand at
the abyss of knowledge itself, the possibility of the end of the
ongoingness, which is an unacceptable denial of the nature
of power and the meaning of history. Some kind of refuge is
found in a dichotomy of mind in the classroom which parallels
that of conscience on the battlefield, by which the unthinkable
millions of deaths by nuclear holocaust can be tolerated, and
even worked with, as "megadeaths," abstractly symbolized on a
blackboard.

It is at least ominous, it seems to me, that those in the vanguard of such thinking about war are largely civilian. The
military itself seems torn between disgust for the naïveté of the
professor or whiz kid approach, and a certain fascination for

their evident success and sometimes popularity. The Air Force, perhaps more than the other services, respects the civilian expert and seeks to emulate him, but spokesmen for all the services seek to return strategy to its claimed proper fold, i.e., to the military where it can be anchored in experience.[11] That experience has at least taught military men in every generation that "war is hell," and if it has bred a certain resignation as to its character and inevitability, it has also induced considerable caution as to its initiation and use.[12] Hitler found his generals reluctant, and the Manhattan Project was the dream child of scientists who later were appalled at their own invention. Civilians also made the decision to use the bomb and much of the demand for its tactical use by military leaders since then is rather a reflection of their distrust of civilian strategies which to them seem unrelated to the concrete realities.

THE "ROLE OF EXPECTANCY"

Not the least of the dangers of the drive to abstractness is the possibility of self-fulfilling prophecy, what Gordon Allport calls the "role of expectancy." [13] If the thought is indeed father to the deed, the strength and persistence of the thought may force an earlier and more certain consummation of the deed. Thus preparation for war is also conditioning for war and its brutalities, and the dynamic drive of being toward self-expression, in thought as in weaponry, cries for demonstration and use. "Thinking the unthinkable" makes it not only thinkable but acceptable by removing its sting of surprise and shock. The escalatory steps of the Vietnam conflict clearly show the importance of expectancy in the actual realization of initially problematic goals. If, finally, the wish is father to the thought and the thought is so powerful in making the deed, self-criticism of what one wants the world to be, against what it is or may be or can become, is an ethical responsibility of the highest order. The pragmatic and prudential dimensions of this factor have long been clearly recognized in the use of censorship against rumor and "leaks" in war. Responsibility for the good of the larger whole of humanity needs to be accepted and sensitivity practiced in an age when there are many and itching fingers on the nuclear triggers.

II. OVERKILL EXPRESSED IN WESTERN MILITARY HISTORY

EXCESSES ON THE BATTLEFIELD

If the threat of escalation is a common awareness of our time, the excesses of the battlefield are as old as history itself. Some excesses, as premeditated weapons of terror, illustrate abstraction. Doubtless most of them represent the dissolving of the volcano itself in uncontrolled force, the countless and often in the aggregate titanic explosions of hostility, savage lust, and even a mysteriously insane joy in destruction itself. "Overkill," a term of our own time which simply (?) means that we have enough power to disrupt, kill, and destroy a given enemy several times over, rather dramatically illustrates the abiding nature of military power to create more than it can use and to use more than it needs. Perhaps the nearest approximation of resources and restraint to needs was the Byzantine system which also in the end failed by way of overreach and overkill. The sweeping and monumental cruelty of a Genghis Khan or Tamerlane finds monotonous, if lesser, parallels since the beginnings of recorded history. James was not the first, nor Montross the last, to be sickened by the "horrible reading . . . the irrationality of it all." And as surprise must attend the anomaly of "the utter ruin [through fratricidal war] of a civilization in intellectual respects perhaps the highest the world has ever seen," [14] so the age of reason and modern times ushered in the bloodiest of all wars.

The roots are deep. The classical doctrines of battle from the Persians and Alexander, the Romans and the Franks, the Muslims, the Tatars and the Huns, the Golden Horde and "the French hordes," the sheer masses of World War I, the overwhelming firepower of World War II and Vietnam—all were concerned with establishing a preponderance of force at a given point, preferably small but vital, the "centre of gravity" as Fuller puts it.[15] Hence, maneuverability, speed, and surprise simply have the effect of "mass multiplied by velocity" to bear upon the objective.[16] So universal is this in the thought and practice of war that there are those who dispute "economy of effort" as in any real sense a principle. Rather, as Coffin observes,

the unit Commanders . . . tend to over-insure a victory and use more firepower than they reasonably need. If one company can be destroyed by a Davy Crockett, why not use two to make sure? Tactical weapons of a low bang tend to be rapidly replaced by more powerful weapons, or what is known . . . as escalation.[17]

THE "SNOWBALL" OF WASTE

The same escalatory problem can be seen in the "logistical snowball" and in the problem of waste. "There is something about preparing for destruction that causes men to be more careless." [18] Gray's insistence upon delight in destruction is classical even if the campaigns of Alexander and Caesar are taken as more representative of the conduct of war than extremists who might be mentioned, for even they were hardly squeamish in obliterating entire enemy forces and whole cities in Catonian strategy at times. Napoleon, watching Smolensk burn (August 17, 1812), exclaimed:

It's like Vesuvius erupting! Don't you think this is a beautiful sight, Mr. Grand Equerry?
Caulaincourt:
Horrible, Sire.
Napoleon:

> Bah! Remember, gentlemen, what a Roman emperor said: "The corpse of an enemy always smells sweet." [19]

Translated into "Americanese," this parallels the remark attributed to Brigadier General George Patton, III (son of Patton of World War II fame), in a pep talk to his men in Vietnam urging them on to the kill: "I sure do like to see the arms and legs fly." [20] Carried to an extreme of fixed policy, the unremitting offensives of Tiglath-pileser III and Tamerlane, with their wholesale slaughter, depopulation tactics, and constant strain of war, illustrate a negative dynamic more cleverly concealed but nonetheless real in imperialism.

THE "PRINCIPLE OF ANNIHILATION"

From like observations Clausewitz logically developed his principle of annihilation, a piece of his abstract reasoning with historical illustration taken over seriously by his disciples. The battle becomes the focal point, the decisive element, and evidences "the overruling importance of the destructive element and nothing else." [21] That Clausewitz thus "fathered the most bloody and wasteful era of warfare in modern times" is less an indictment of him than of the nature of war itself and the times that so willingly chose to ignore his "sober modifications" and provided a context for the fullest realization of his negative ideas.[22] To the strains of Machiavellian amoral force and ideological warfare fathered by the Reformation, both of which claimed unlimited jurisdiction and had evidenced their hideously destructive capacity in the Thirty Years' War, must be added the *levée en masse* of total peoples in arms loosed by the French Revolution. "Hate governed France, hence warfare became interminable." [23] One French royalist spoke bitterly of the

> "hellish tactic . . . worthy of the monsters who had invented it. . . . Fifty thousand savage beasts, foaming at the mouth with rage and yelling like cannibals, hurl themselves at top speed upon soldiers whose courage has been excited by no passion." [24]

Clausewitz called this "virtually a new power, rather than a manifestation of increased cooperation . . . by the people." [25]

It changed the whole basis of warfare. No longer could Shakespeare's satire or Dryden's ridicule dismiss soldiery as

> Mouths without hands; maintained at vast expense,
> In peace a charge, in war a weak defense;
> Stout once a month they march, a blust'ring band,
> And ever, but in times of need, at hand.[26]

It was the people themselves who were the warriors imbued with a zeal that would not quit at the frontier. This has raised the specter of materialism of the masses, of aggression by democracies. Nor would they longer be vulnerable to Frederick the Great's contemptuous "If my soldiers began to think, not one would remain in the ranks." [27] Though less disciplined, they were yet more intelligent for having been recruited from all classes, a factor that was to revolutionize efficiency and morale. It also made soldiers cheap. Napoleon's boast that he could expend 30,000 soldiers monthly[28] is only multiplied by Haig's willingness to throw 300,000 into the ooze of Flanders, by Grant in the battle of the Wilderness, by ourselves in Vietnam. In the machine age the nation-states were organized as machines armed and aimed at one another. With the tremendous advance of weaponry and firepower, motivated by the machine and subordinate to "controlling reason," organized totally as nation-states and operating in the no-man's-land of Machiavellian amorality of force—the results could hardly be less than catastrophic. As early as 1898 Ivan S. Bloch had seen the signs of Armageddon and foretold World War I.[29] We have already seen how the role of expectancy, even desire, encouraged Europe's peoples to plunge into the abyss, and how the tragic and stupid doctrine of attack kept them there for four long bloody years. Although World War II began as limited, several signs, all too early, showed the unlimited nature of its objectives: "the total eclipse of historic nations," the first full-time partnership of scientists with the military in the conduct of the war, the saturation bombing of enemy cities, and the Allies' insistence upon unconditional surrender.[30] A final sign, of course, must be added: the decision to drop the bomb. The latter signaled the opening up of a new age of limitless power for destruction. The classical age of the scarcity of power yielded suddenly, but not joyously, to the age of power surplus, and "balance of power" as the basis of politics and war was replaced by the "balance of terror." With new "weapons generations" now reduced to three- to five-year periods, Walter Millis could advance as a "simple observation" the fact that

since 1900 the mighty factors in modern life . . . have been developing in a steeply rising growth curve . . . now mounting toward an infinity alike of destructiveness and of human uselessness.[31]

THE VIOLENCE OF AMERICANS

It is all the more poignant, and yet I think a hopeful sign, that there seems a growing awareness among Americans that we are by history and nature a violent people, and potentially dangerous to ourselves as well as to others, given the circumstances of modern limitless power. It is not alone Senator Fulbright who shortly after President Kennedy's death warned that we must "revise and strengthen" the American character. Our national life, he said, "both past and present has always been marked by a baleful and incongruous strand of intolerance and violence. . . . Irrationality lies just beneath the surface." [32] Puritan moral absolutism, self-righteousness, crusading intolerance, and our national experience of the frontier —individualistic, initiatory, and self-reliant—have created for us the image of the modern knight, the soft-spoken gunman reluctantly but devastatingly on the side of law and order. "Is Violence Un-American?" asks an editorial in *The Nation:* "If so, so is Old Glory. No nation of modern times is more addicted to violence, legal and illegal. . . . But it cannot take its violence straight. It prefers violence mixed with moral hypocrisy." [33] A recent *Time* editorial, while hopeful that "the country as a whole is growing less violent" (compared to its past and noting public concern for law and order), must admit that "in the industrialized world, the United States undeniably ranks high in violence." [34] The culprit is probably less our frontier history than "the swift pace of social change, which can be deeply disturbing to the less stable personalities in a society." [35] The uneven and competitive pace of social change is doubtless a stimulus to war, and given the cultural acceleration of America, from frontier to frontier, it may rightly be said that "we are the kind of people who fight wars every fifteen or twenty years" [36]—not because we normally delight in destruction (we have too great an appreciation of the sacredness of property for that in itself), but because we grasp for order, and

the people who definitely do not want to fight any more wars must promise annihilation to any nation which starts to fight and must be prepared immediately and ruthlessly to carry out that promise without parley or negotiation.[37]

This involves keeping "ahead of any possible competition" in the maintenance of atomic rocket stations and the development of "ever more efficient methods of killing." [38] But more than one nation now has this power, and so the logic of escalation goes on:

In the absence of anything better, the political dialogue over strategy is still conducted in the Clausewitzian rhetoric, as though any aim which might be implemented by force can be doubly implemented by twice as much force.[39]

It is therefore with reason that W. H. Ferry cries out, "What Price Peace?" We have institutionalized the arms race, he says, and have "grown used to it, and devoted to it, and devoted to its multiplier effects. . . . You have an institution on your hands when you can't imagine getting along without it." [40] Ours is the sin of *hubris,* of overweening pride, the weakness of the vainglorious, who decline to consider the full consequences of their actions, but only the current effects. . . . The vice of the mighty, of a people grown too big for their britches. . . . Perhaps the most staggering of *hubris* assumptions is that we have the right, if we wish to avail ourselves of it, to plunge the world into atomic war . . . to inflict the final violence, to wipe out civilizations . . . to smirch the earth, its innocents and its fruits for untold generations.[41]

It is not that our leaders are potential Tamerlanes or even Caesars,

although the softening effects of their upbringings in Sunday School is often hard to discern. Our leaders are only men caught in an accelerating machinery of violence that they do not know how to shut off though both reason and moral teaching show the absolute necessity of doing so. We are potentially history's most violent nation and violence is always a moral question.[42]

III. OVERREACH AND OVERKILL EXPRESSED IN CONTEMPORARY MILITARY THOUGHT

In considering the attitude of the modern military toward this question, Coffin rather accurately observes that

they share a common discontent, the world has moved too rapidly for them. . . . The machine and forces too complex for [the serviceman] . . . are ruining his good humor. Modern weapons are unique and the soldier has no hand in their invention or management and very little in their use. The scientist and the diplomat have taken over.[43]

What is the probability of escalation? The success of the scientists in creating the long-dreamed-of ultimate weapon has ironically resulted in confusion, frustration, and discontent in military circles. Nuclear weaponry has not assured security but in strange ways its opposite. Its greatest value seems to reside in its nonuse. Yet in the actional environment of the military the weapon yearns to be used and its continual refinement expresses this dynamic toward its eventual tactical employment at least. For "escalation is inherent in warfare, because armed conflict is largely an uninhibited struggle. Victory is the aim, violence the means, and survival sometimes the stake." [44] As an axiom, then, "escalation is more probable than limitation." With the means and the stake characterized as ultimate today, the rush to doom seems gravely enhanced to many, even in the military. In 1968 an editorial by a former deputy director of intelligence of the Canadian Navy, now a systems analyst in California, warned us that our very success in warding off the holocaust for nearly a generation has bred an apathy that overlooks the increasing pressures to use nuclear weapons in lesser wars. As a consequence, "the probability of nuclear war in this decade is at the highest point since the dawn of the atomic age." [45]

The services have not hesitated to take positions highly critical of each other on this crucial question, so the debate goes on apace. Sometimes it is muffled, but it is nonetheless real in individuals and units torn by the confusing claims of reason and security, of service and country, of man and God. General nuclear war is so patently irrational if not suicidal for most theorists that even when contemplated it becomes in effect tactical and limited, hedged about with just war, counterforce, and other restrictive ideas. In other words, everyone is for restraint and limitations to some degree in modern war. The differences arise in the various meanings attached to restraint and limitation, and especially the understanding of the relevance of escalation in general to the possibility or probability of general war. We have earlier outlined to some degree the variant positions of the major services respecting escalation and restraint as reflecting the importance attached to the exercise of the reason and will in military power. It remains to enlarge upon the military as dynamic at this point, i.e., as evidencing the ebb and flow of being itself, the tug and pull of every situation in a world of fearful and fulsome change, and especially in an America enamored with the utility of raw power.

ARMY

The Plea for Limits

General Fuller and Rear Admiral Eccles in the main represent an early and growing body of Army and Navy opinion recognizing the dangers of escalation inherent in military force, and in the nuclear age the necessity for restraint and limited operational responsibilities and objectives. Fuller is even caustic in advising:

Never in war shackle yourself to the absolute. Never bind yourself with irrevocable compacts or decisions. . . . Action should always be adopted to circumstances, and circumstances are always fluid.[46]

Wars, he goes on to say, are either limited or unlimited, "and it is the first and not the second which have been profitable to the victor." [47] He castigates brutality as seldom paying and notes that friends and enemies so frequently change sides that it is a matter of prudence not to drive the enemy to despair. Our tragedy is that with innumerable examples in history to draw upon we have committed the same "unconditional surrender" mistake twice in a generation and the resultant Carthaginian peace has raised its own dragon-teeth armies. It is not that we "can make war well enough, but [we have] forgotten how to make peace";[48] rather, it is that we are "unable to make peace because [we have] forgotten how to make war." [49] War has lost its significance for the simple, tragic reason that as a means it has monopolized its end, and we get only a periodic armistice, not a resolution of conflict.

The momentum of limitless objectives and means to that end carries war inevitably to nonrational inhumanity, which is self-defeating. Churchill, who initiated what he had previously called "the hideous process of bombing open cities from the air," lived to regret that

the human tragedy reaches its climax in the fact that after all the exertions of hundreds of millions of people and of the victories of the Righteous Cause, we have still not found Peace and Security, and that we live in the grip of even worse perils than those we have surmounted.[50]

Fuller sees the culprit in American misunderstanding of war as apolitical, having looked upon it as a "lethal game in which the trophy was victory." The military-industrial marriage is a natural one, since "an army is a body of pure consumers" and both tend to accelerate the other toward totality.[51] The impact of nuclear energy upon war is more revolutionary than gunpowder because it threatens as a means to engulf the end. Common sense is the quality needed in our desperate straits to apportion means to ends, "but, unfortunately, common sense is the rarest of senses in war." [52]

The Success of Restraint

We have earlier listed the articles calling for restraint in Army publications. Just because "escalation is inherent in warfare," and given the unlimited means at our disposal, we can say that a "truly limited war is . . . a decisively won war." [53] Escalation is encouraged by both the passage of time and the prospect of victory, but underlying these and other causes is the basic one of competition for military-technological superiority, "a simple product of the desire to win coupled with the related desire not to be defeated." [54] Traditionally this has involved a certain "gamesmanship," but with the stakes so high today the immoral readiness of the aggressor to escalate is matched by the moral temptation of the victim to chance its use in the possibility, even if slight, of saving his very culture and future. The circumstances in both cases encourage escalation. On the whole, however, the advent of nuclear power, according to Colonel Robert B. Rigg, perhaps has reduced the probability of escalation from a traditional two to one ratio to about seven to five, and limitation has more than the even chance of yesterday.[55] This was suggested in 1963, and four years later it could be said with even greater conviction that "it has been fairly well established that a conventional arms race results in instability, while a nuclear armaments race tends to produce stability." For, it is argued, "the more destructive the weapons, the less chance of their being used militarily." [56] Even the prospect of proliferation of such arms among other nations is not necessarily as risky as first thought because the possession of such weapons by others restricts the options available to major powers in limited war. One of the powers whose options would be restricted if its neighbors possessed the bomb is China, and this could be important.[57] Anyway,

capability is one thing, but a militarily effective force is quite another. The idea that one weapon would ignite massive retaliation now seems to be far fetched. Simple, general war is highly unlikely in today's context.[58]

These expressions in a year that saw a profusion of military articles on the subject were not advocacies of general nuclear weaponry necessarily, much less its actual use, but reflected a growing, even surprised degree of confidence that the "first generation" nuclear stalemate might with intelligence and care be prolonged indefinitely. But not without constant vigilance and review of "The Delicate Balance" between "the elephant and the whale" (as Churchill once described the deadlock of the Soviets' inner continental bloc with the U.S. and its maritime allies).[59] It was to the razor sharpness of this "balance" that a former Canadian intelligence officer called attention the following year.[60] No year since has been without its saber rattling. Born and nurtured upon fear, the mutual deterrence needs a firmer and more rational *raison d'être,* for it threatens always to explode in irrationality. Under such constant pressure limited war has been rediscovered and blessed both by examples from our history and the writings of such men as Clausewitz.[61] The "winding down" of the war in Vietnam in the opinion of some expresses "the limited nature of the war and the desire to keep it limited" even before the announced efforts of the present administration.[62] "Victory," "defeat," even the almost sacred "domino theory," pale in significance and undergo considerable redefinition in the bright heat of the continuing nuclear threat.[63]

Opening Pandora's Box

There is a sense of inevitability in the development of tactical nuclear weapons, but also a sober awareness that they exist as a deterrent and cannot guarantee victory if used. The tribute paid to President Kennedy was that "he was always rational. . . . He faced up to the truth that ultimate use of nuclear weapons is self-destruction." [64] The possibility of pinpointed and therefore limited nuclear casualties is "misplaced optimism." One may recognize the probability of nuclear war beginning as limited, but "perhaps the critically mutual reinforcing set of expectations" would encourage escalation because of the need to justify even larger losses.[65] Thus their use might very well break the dam of general deterrence and "produce possibilities for escalation to an unprecedentedly high level of intensity." [66] The best that then could be expected would be a "destructive stalemate." [67]

If, then, limited war is necessary in the nuclear age, and we dare not risk even the limited use of nuclear weapons, ought this to be announced in the hope of fixing the stalemate, of obviating such tragic guesses on the part of the enemy as apparently occurred with the Communist invasion of South Korea? No, it is not so simple. To know the limits may well invite aggression at least *to* the limits.[68] Ironically, nuclear stability may well depend upon the threat of nuclear probability. We are back again with the element of the concrete, if only in the wings. President Eisenhower employed this tactic in raising the possibility of using nuclear arms to get the Panmunjom talks off dead center, and recently President Nixon deliberately allowed a leak to the Russians that his own responses could not be calculated absolutely. Hence, the newer policy, "flexible response," is "an extremely sophisticated strategy," which operates deliberately upon different levels, not barring in theory or practice massive retaliation, but pragmatically committed to "lower spectrum war." [69]

The Need for National Goals

The inherent fluidity and tensions of such diversified tactics create daily risks that emphasize particularly the need of rational, long-range goals. There is considerable doubt that the nation has such goals.[70] We are far better at analysis than conceptualization, at tactics than strategy, as some of our more thoughtful soldiers are finding out who have been exposed to duty in Eastern lands.[71] Although bowing continuously at the altar of Clausewitz, we still have great difficulty accepting, or even understanding, his subordination of military power to political policy. Thus "The Indecisiveness of Modern War," "this yawning gulf between overwhelming military might and the almost total absence of strategies for employing it short of general war." [72] General Matthew Ridgway, former Supreme Commander of our forces in both the Far East and Europe, has put it most soberly in words that are immediately applicable to Vietnam:

Civilian authorities . . . need to work closely with military authorities in setting attainable goals and selecting means to attain them. A war without goals would be most dangerous of all, and nearly as dangerous would be a war with only some vaguely stated aim, such as "victory," or "freedom from aggression" or "the right of the people to choose their own government." Generalities like these make admirable slogans, but authorities today must be hard headed and specific in naming exactly what goal we are trying to reach and exactly what price we are willing to pay for it.[73]

NAVY

A Heritage of Civility

The Navy is proud of the fact that for nearly two hundred years it "has used its power for the accomplishing of national aims in accordance with international law and in a civil manner." [74] Historically it has been opposed to area destruction which only "impedes . . . progress" and "except for a nuclear holocaust naval atomic warfare in the jet-nuclear age can and must be conducted in a manner consistent with this historical legacy" of accurate gunfire, pinpoint bombing, and specific military targets.[75] It is not the weapons but their use that determines immorality and thus we must distinguish between precise and massive retaliation. "The question is no longer *whether* but in what manner nuclear weapons will henceforth be used." [76] Hence, "it is reasonable and prudent to assume that any local or large-scale war involving the United States will, indeed must, see the use of tactical atomic weapons." [77]

The Guessing Game of Deterrence

The above quotation was written in 1957. Since then the controversy has swirled back and forth with a clear edge to be found with those who advocate limited war and dread even the tactical use of nuclear weapons. A quarter century of absolute restraint in the use of such weapons has helped fix their nonuse as both possible and positive. But the brash and the headstrong must be reckoned with and if to them are added those who are simplistically fearful of Russia and China—those who seem capable of opting, if it comes to that, for a civilization which is "dead rather than Red"—the strength and persuasiveness of the hawkish position is apparent. The issue, however, is not that clearly and honestly joined. "The Case for Anti-Ballistic Missiles," [78] for instance, is simply and surely a matter of "The High Cost of Living," not dying.[79] That is, everything is based upon the conviction that the use of nuclear weapons will be contained in their nonuse (i.e., threat), and if the bluff is called, then in their limited use. If this leads to escalation, it will be selective and not total, etc.[80] Thus the life or death of civilization itself, which is so easily reduced to "our way of life," becomes a guessing game in deterrence. Admittedly, this requires the coolest of heads, the longest of views, and the priority of strategy over tactics.

Hawks and Doves

It is, then, not reassuring to find a heavy proportion of Prize Essays in the *Naval Institute Proceedings* emotionally charged and fundamentally hawkish with regard to stopping the cleverly advancing Russians. We are told that, tied as we are by present circumstances to limited warfare, this is nevertheless "ideally suited for Communist delaying tactics." We must not be trapped by our naturally compassionate, compromising nature into substituting the long and imprecise "winning the people" objective for the clear-cut and immediately rewarding tactic of "annihilation," at least of guerrillas.[81] And guerrilla warfare is essentially "in" today, for the enemy is everywhere. The "Distant Rampart" of Vietnam, it is suggested, is not so distant when we honestly yield the high-sounding but fuzzy ideals of freedom, honor, and humanity for plain, simple "natural survival." [82] In "Against All Enemies" (Prize Essay, 1970), the author leaves no doubt as to the object of his wrath by italicizing the important words in calling upon military men to remember that "we solemnly swore to support and defend the Constitution of the United States against all enemies, foreign *and domestic.*"

In frustrating the aims of those who would turn the American eagle into a lamb, we must continue to single out and eliminate those among us who, by their avarice and indiscretion, despoil our integrity and destroy our credibility.[83]

The virulence of this answer to, and attack upon, a whole array of public figures including a number of senators but especially General Shoup, who had dared to denounce the "hunger for glory" of "The New American Militarism," [84] reveals the depth and arbitrariness of the passion of some

whose fear of the "enemy within," as well as without, out-
weighs the risk even of nuclear war.

But the call to caution, to lowercase military activity, even
to what might be called "retrenchment," is broad and deep.
Significantly, the passionate rhetoric is largely absent and
there is a sense of feeling one's way among uncharted reefs, in
dangerous straits, seeking passage to the more comfortable
freedom of the open seas. As early as 1949, Rear Admiral
Ralph Optie in testimony before a Congressional Commitee
categorically denied both the utility and the morality of
"strategic air warfare as practiced in the past and as proposed
in the future." Although he found an inevitable place for
tactically refined atomic bombs, he could not extend this to
hydrogen warfare:

By no stretch of the imagination can a global thermonuclear war
be militarily sound, effective, morally right, or helpful to postwar
security. It is none of these.

Victory is simply not the end, but "a prosperous United States
and a stable, peaceful world." [85]

A cacophony of voices since then have agreed. Captain
Schratz in "The Caesars, the Sieges, and the Anti-Ballistic
Missile" concludes that "with or without the best possible
defense, nobody can win a nuclear war in any meaningful
sense. . . . Currently, the only real defense in a nuclear war
is not to fight one." [86] Two years later he is again saying:

Defense strategy within the alliance remains too tightly tied to traditional concepts assuming early use of nuclear weapons in situations
of increasing non-utility of such weapons in any but the most im-
plausible of circumstances. . . . A defense tied inextricably to nuclear weapons is less and less plausible for either side on any front.[87]

He agrees with a fellow naval officer in foreseeing ("it seems
only a question of time") that nuclear installations must be
moved away from the land and the cities to the seas, a position now being favored by some in Congress.[88]

The simplest identification of "the enemy," whether without or within, here yields to the agonizing necessity of choosing "from a spectrum along varying gradations of unsatisfactory possibilities what you hope will be less unsatisfactory." [89] Faced with the fact that we cannot escape commitment to a "balance of power" policy short of the formation of a world state,[90] it becomes necessary to exercise critical judgment and restraint upon our own rising expectations as upon the aspirations of all others who seek their places in the sun. The very concept of "balance" involves a certain dynamism of equality, the pairing of weights in some sort of tensional equilibrium. "Coexistence" must be taken literally and given meaning through the constant review upon which life always insists for those who try to walk in concert rather than in tandem.

"The Quest for Common Ground"

In "The Quest for Common Ground," therefore, the suggestion is perhaps less startling than it first appears that we might be willing "to sacrifice a certain degree of national sovereignty in exchange for greater security." [91] In this light, *parity* with Russia is probably a wisely chosen necessity which is less war-inducing than our insistence upon clear superiority. "The name of the game is Sufficiency, not Superiority, as President Nixon wisely observed." [92] Earlier, one noted analyst, carefully examining the possible reactions to such a real *détente,* including the possibility that ruling out nuclear weapons might actually encourage lesser wars, observes that

so far, the Soviet leaders have given little indication that the advent of strategic parity might "make the world safe for aggression." . . . Whatever their alleged dynamism, the Soviets have been exceedingly cautious in the conduct of their foreign policy—as distinct from declarations of supposed intent.[93]

Dr. Joseph I. Coffey (who wrote the above) does not rule out the possibility that with increasing parity may come increasing confidence on the part of Russia to take risks in foreign policy. But the greater danger actually lies with us, "in that the Soviets may overreach themselves and precipitate a disproportionate U.S. response." [94] We are back, then, on our own doorstep, required to examine critically the images and pressures of our own actions and goals, and just how these are interpreted and thus affect the general balance of power. For instance, Captain Ralph E. Williams perceptively points out that following the Cuban *détente* we built both a land-based missile force as well as the Polaris system for submarines, and the unintended duplication of assured destruction capability must have seemed aggressive. "The explanation, of course," he says,

is rather simple and straightforward. At the time . . . no one could have foreseen the incredible success of the Polaris system. . . . Once underway, the Atlas, Titan, and Minuteman programs all acquired a momentum of their own, as large defense programs always do, and even though Polaris had proved its capabilities as early as 1961, it was by then impossible to foreshorten the land-based programs, which proceeded to their completion. Just how much effect, if any, the existence of this overwhelming strike force had upon the Soviet decision to expand its own missile force may never be known.[95]

It may be too strong to say that it was "impossible to foreshorten the land-based programs," but no one can doubt that it would have been extremely difficult from an economic point of view alone, to say nothing of the vested interests of both civilian and military people and given the inherent rivalries of the military services. Moreover, to begin with, we cannot wisely put all our eggs in one basket. Yet we probably sent an unintended wrong signal in this case. We ought to be able to "foreshorten" duplicatory or inadvisable projects. But a more humble awareness that our "best intentions" may, with reason, be misread is probably even more important.

In "The Meaning of Limited War," [96] Robert McClintock argues persuasively that there will be no nuclear exchanges between the Communists and the Free World but paradoxically small wars will be generated, a possibility that Dr. Coffey foresaw. Commander Beavers sees this possibility already being realized as the "subgeneral war level of the balance of power equation [which] is now the scene of intense competition between the superpowers." [97] Had it not been for United States–Russian competition in Indochina long before 1965 "it might have been possible for the U.S. to ignore what was happening in South Vietnam." [98] This raises the interesting question as to what extent we should, or can, justify our presence in the quarrels of the world simply because the rival is there. Commander Beavers suggests as a first principle in his "Doctrine for Limited War" that

not all limited war situations merit U.S. involvement. . . . Risk . . . as a criterion for engaging in limited war, must always be related to what is at stake. In this turbulent world of unstable, modernizing young nations, we do need to understand that not all revolutions or civil wars inspired by idealists, demagogues, or patriotic colonels will importantly affect that balance of power equation that is vital to the United States.[99]

Dr. Frederick J. Honigan, lecturing at the Naval War College in 1968, concluded his remarks with a verse of Scripture (Prov. 26:17) and suggested that we continually ask: "What strife belongeth to us? At what cost? And for what purpose?" [100]

The Call for Limited Goals

The call, then, in the Navy, increasingly seems to be for honest, and perhaps humble, goal definition, and long-range strategy to achieve more unhurriedly those few goals we select. In his usual careful way, Eccles lays it on the line:

What must we control? Why? What is the nature and degree of control? When initiate control? How long maintain control? How, in general, exercise this control? What opposition to expect?[101]

In part, at least, Commander Beavers answers by suggesting that a definition of "limited war" should start with a limitation of objectives which, if applied in our own case, would undoubtedly result in not a little revision of our overseas posture and actual, physical retrenchment from far-flung areas where the people themselves are increasingly less interested in preserving our presence.[102] Stefan Possony, in "Battle: No Longer the Payoff?" suggests that "the time has come to grasp the essential difference between *bitva* ("battle") and *borba* ("struggle") in Russian thinking. He goes on to assert that

many modern wars should be conducted with a minimum of tactical contact and a maximum of military detachment. In the main, they should be contests between political parties which, through persuasion, example, compulsion, and organizational efficiency, should compete for legitimacy and acceptance by the mass of the people.[103]

The turn has been made here to Clausewitz and our own stubborn confusion of war, morality, and politics. Captain Schratz in successive writings has seen the matter most clearly. We have rejected Clausewitz where he matters most, i.e., in always subordinating war to politics, but we have given moral benediction to his seeming absolutes. Schratz puts it this way:

In the American view, war interrupted political processes and did not, as Clausewitz claimed, continue those processes by other means. Morality forbade the use of power to coerce except for total ends, that is, for moral or ideological goals. War was not a tool of the politician nor was politics adaptable to military skills. Wars were avoided vigorously until they were inevitable, then pursued just as vigorously toward total ends such as "to make the world safe for democracy" or "unconditional surrender." [104]

Naval thinkers have for some time feared that this historic penchant of Americans for absolutist ideas of national security, and our naïveté and bluntness in politics, may yield to Air Force pressure for quick and devastating solutions.[105] As early as 1964, Captain Schratz was claiming that there had been a shift in the national consciousness with the advent of nuclear weapons: "Americans are nearly unanimous in the belief that total war in virtually all cases is both irrational and immoral." [106] To keep the "means of irrational power . . . within the bounds of the rational" requires that

> we must make every effort to shape our strategy in the direction of increased "moralization" of the use of force and away from the *Grenzmoral*.[107] America has little to gain by support for a morality of circumstance in which only circumstances, not principles, control moral decisions. . . . The foremost question is . . . the direction in which the whole structure of policy is moving.[108]

The direction in which it has been moving appears to be "toward increasing control . . . by technology," i.e., allowing the availability of weapons, and the zeal of their invention and use, to dominate strategy, which is clearly fallacious. "The ability to develop a hundred-megaton, or a hundred-million-megaton bomb, is not in itself justification for its use," [109] and perhaps not even if it is manufactured by another. This is the essence, the meaning of the courting of tragedy in the arms "race": that we may actually lose in winning, that the great goals of peace and security may be sacrificed to the heady excitement of proving ourselves superior to the Russians.

The "increased moralization" of which Schratz speaks would, apparently, assure responsibility for the fuller life of men and states, before and beyond the harsh means of war which must always be held subordinate to long-range policy objections. Absolutist conceptions and uses of war in the nuclear age are not only counterproductive but threaten suicide for the race itself. Thus the plea for moralization is "not made solely on the basis of Christian morality," but from the necessity of man to be rational. Yet force must be employed in the affairs of men, "ready force, usable force," [110] and so the agonizing dialogue continues. There are grave reasons for rejecting the extremists at both ends, the pacifists and the power enthusiasts. It is some measure of our impotence that despite push-button control of more and awful power than the world has ever known, its use must remain ambiguous and uncertain. The concern has broadened and the conscience has deepened in the Navy during the years of the nuclear debate, but as a whole it probably has not advanced much beyond the position of a spokesman in 1966: Despite

the stigma on the physical employment of nuclear weapons . . . [they] have utility at least, for deterrence, and the possibility of their use in deliberate, controlled warfare should not be rejected off-hand.[111]

AIR FORCE

The Willingness to Escalate

The Air Force, as we have noted, is less frightened by either technology or escalation, is more insistent that we must live with the nuclear spread, and is hopeful of positive gains from the technology so many fear. Chafing under political restrictions in Vietnam has been especially noticeable in the Air Force. The moderate, but scarcely concealed, regrets of former Secretary of the Air Force Brown respecting the blunted role of this service[112] find more popular and vocal expression in attacks upon "gradualism" in the application of force. Such a policy, it is claimed, "promoted and sold to civilian authorities by responsible military men" (particularly Army's General Maxwell Taylor) is "self-defeating," for the "willingness to escalate" is the very key to deterrence.[113] "Flexible response" may indeed make sense in the light of history but not as an *announced* policy which robs the government of the *threat* of massive retaliation, of unpredictability. Coupled with this intended value of instability to lend credence to the balance of terror is the strong, natural drive of weapon technology and its proponents (such as General Bernard Schriever [Ret.], formerly Commander, Air Force Systems Command), who honestly believe that the dynamism of technology should not be resisted.[114]

Growing Doubt and Measured Response

On the other hand, there seems growing awareness and even advocacy of the merits of limited war, assisted by some sobering second thoughts concerning the cost of attrition in a nuclear war between evenly matched opponents, and a long war of any kind.[115] Moreover, to what extent is the public with us in what begins almost innocently as a clear call to the colors? The undeclared wars of Korea and Vietnam somehow refuse to fit easily into the accustomed American mold of "crusade." They are "primarily political," following the dictum of Clausewitz, and thus "alien to [our] traditional way of thinking," [116] which is closer to the "just war" concept of Augustine. Democracies place great weight on public opinion and that opinion reflects confusion and a troubled conscience with the new kind of warfare and its seeming endlessness. Major Philip D. Caine does us a service in his "Study in Public Opinion" respecting Korea and Vietnam as limited wars for the United States in tracing the distinct ebb and flow of home support which seem to parallel our fortunes.[117] Administration rhetoric to the contrary, Americans have not been able to see a "crusade," especially in Vietnam. The slow and sometimes ridiculous incongruity of our technology in the undeserving swamps of that far land has even cheated us of our usual pride of "a job well done": Vietnam is the longest and least successful war in our history. Deprived of both moral certitude and success, the twin virtues of the American ethic, it has not been very clear, as it once was (World Wars I and II), as to "Whose Side Is God On?" [118] In this article, which is a review of several well-meaning books on Vietnam, Chaplain Edward R. Lawler points out that much of the same source material is used to arrive at radically different conclusions. This must certainly compound the problem "for the citizen of average intelligence and sincerity." [119] Perhaps if television did not remind us so persistently of the brutality of it all, if the right hand did not have to see and know what the left was up to—but there is no escape from the daily and inner confrontation by the people themselves of the measurelessness of their sacrifice for a measured cause. We are left, then, according to Lawler, with *faith*, i.e., "confidence in the sincerity of [our] leaders." [120] But it is clear that such "confidence" has its limits.

To a measured cause one writer sees a "measured response" as right and urges that a constant willingness to negotiate must today be substituted for "unconditional surrender." [121] In "Vietnam and the Warfare State Complex," a reply to Columnist Kraft's fear of the military push to escalation, it is stressed that "the major point is that this is a carefully directed and controlled war." [122] This does not hide frustration with foreshortened weapons, and a distinction can still be argued between an escalation native to technology itself and the Nazi-planned destruction, i.e., the "deliberate inhumanity, that degraded the individual and whole populations in a manner impossible for long-range bombardment." So argues the historian for the Strategic Air Command (SAC), Dr. Alfred Goldberg, in summarizing "Escalation: A Historical Perspective." He goes on to warn that the time interval between phases of escalation has all but vanished with the advent of nuclear weapons:

For the first time in history it may be possible to attain with tactical weapons the most extreme national strategic objective—destruction of an enemy nation—completely and almost immediately.[123]

This is instant Armageddon, and in its blinding light the current restraint, controls, and caution of the major powers is increasingly seen as right. Nuclear warfare at any level had best be avoided, though not at any cost. These are the ominous "lessons" of a study of escalation applied to nuclear realities. Unfortunately, they do not include a definition of "reasonable, acceptable cost."

Second Thoughts on Survival

Can there, indeed, be a reasonable, acceptable cost in nuclear war? For the most part the question is carefully avoided.

Some forms of moral arithmetic are indulged in, such as the exchange of forces and counterforces and hostage cities, but the horrendous possibilities seem to blunt the imagination, and men pull back from the abyss. But would they in actual war? Has the Vietnam conflict, with its graduated pressures and increasing destructiveness which reach the point of no return on the investment and no turn from attrition, become the model of the nuclear war to come? Ought we not to require, with Paul Ramsey,[124] that our power actually be effective in securing the end sought with the least possible destructive side effects, and when that appears improbable or impossible, to condemn the means as threatening to overwhelm the end? The pride and blindness that have historically prevented the military from acknowledging mistakes, especially when the "victors," cannot be afforded in the nuclear age. President Kennedy, in admitting the Bay of Pigs fiasco, was in instant rapport with the age. "I would have been impeached," Nixon is reported to have said, not disclosing whether he could have acknowledged the mistake. Nixon is a different man. And so also was President Johnson.

In all the services only the Air Force chaplains appear to have faced in any rational and moral manner the haunting question, "Is Survival Enough?"[125] The answer they give is "No": as a nation we are against a system (Communism) only because we are *for* certain values such as humanity, freedom, and morality. Victory alone as an answer betokens a childish display of willfulness. Survival alone does not guarantee our superiority or our right simply to exist as decimated and scattered primitives in a world shattered by H-bombs. This attitude is as irrational and meaningless as that of the man who got even by deliberately driving his car into the bright lights of another car—to the death of both drivers.[126]

America is worth living for, fighting for and dying for if need be. And we fully intend to go on doing just that! But in the process, we are not going to toss morality out the window and revert to barbarism! We do not intend to replace reason with blind emotion. We do not intend to allow terror to head us down the slope of violence that leads to universal destruction. This problem *can* be worked out by means other than a nuclear holocaust. If that be the only solution then perhaps we have lost our right to existence! [127]

Between the "Clobber them before they clobber us" school and "There's nothing we can do" people, a "middle ground —a realm of reason" can be found.

It must be recognized that nuclear war is here to stay, at least until it be supplanted by some other weapon. . . . There *can* be limited war even if it be a nuclear war. But even a limited war involving these terrible weapons is not to be entered into lightly. Certain conditions should be present.[128]

These conditions are reduced to two of the usual "just war" requirements, "an obvious and grave injustice" and "war should be considered the last resort." [129] But the deeper concern is the "retention of moral principles" expressed directly in "America's long-term objectives" of constitutional government, equality of opportunity, the basic freedoms of worship, speech, press, assembly, and private property.

What would be the gain if America were to lose her own spiritual integrity while in the process of gaining military victory? Survival then would reduce men to the level of animal existence.[130]

In other words, "America's long-term objectives," clear and moral, must themselves survive a holocaust if we are justly to enter into it. "Victory" alone as "mere survival" is not enough.

So far as it goes this is an impassioned and well-reasoned plea to keep the means fitted snugly to the end, and shows awareness of the very real and tragic possibility of nuclear means overwhelming the end in some final and inhuman manner. But it much too readily accepts without criticism the opinion of "those charged with our national security" that nuclear war can be limited. The dynamics of power as being, and certainly the inherence of escalation in military power, acknowledged elsewhere, is ignored altogether. Moreover, the "just war" arguments are surely naïve and indefinable in this context today. What constitutes "an obvious and grave injustice" and "the last resort" for nations whose very existence is nurtured in pride? Was " 'obliteration bombing' by which an entire population might be brought to surrender" [131] a just act of retaliation or a just tactic for the realization of "America's long-range objectives" in World War II? The fact of such bombing is listed simply as a historical incident in "Man's Progress in Weapons," but no parallel or caution is drawn in moral judgment and the assertion itself is inaccurate, for no population has ever been brought to surrender by such means alone. The assertion reflects the context of a blind commitment to a one-weapon system which engulfs even the chaplains of the Air Force at times.

"The Fable of Nick and Sam" [132] demonstrates again the difficulty of our coming to know ourselves—let alone the enemy—with consequent, and deadly, effect upon our decisions in crises. The setting is the Old West and a quarrel over water rights. Nick plans to shoot Sam in the back with a .45 caliber revolver and "bury him." Sam, however, trains as a quick-draw artist on his .38 caliber revolver so as only to wound (!) Nick who thereupon, with his family, will receive Sam's full Good Samaritan treatment including hospital and living expenses! The small truth that may be here is swallowed up in the sin of *hubris,* the suffocating pride which is tragically blind to the dynamic and ironic ambiguities of our own power,[133] especially military power. Again it is dishearteningly illustrative of the pressures of the military context that such naïve and self-righteous material should find a place in the chaplains' program.

The value that remains in these writings is substantial—the clear and incisive call to consider what lies "beyond survival," the appeal to think and to plan beyond war itself to our own common and human life of the future, the rational and moral demand to keep weaponry in its place as a means only to a lofty and spiritual end. But the appeal seems lost upon "the powers that be," represented by the Secretary of Air Force Office of Information, who requested that the pointed and meaningful title "Is Survival Enough?" be changed to the more immediate and pragmatic concern, "Are You Prepared for Modern War?" [134] In this requested change lies the crux of the problem of military power today—the pathetically shortsighted, if not blind, refusal to look beyond the technology of weaponry and war to the utterly crucial problem of what values can survive their development and use. It is perhaps significant that in the Biblical view man alone of all creation may be exempted from the specific evaluation that "God saw that it was good" which he pronounced upon every other day's work (Gen., chs. 1; 2). Yet into man's hands has the dominion of all nature, including his own, been given, for this is unfinished business and the final determination of good or ill depends upon the subfashioning of man and his world by man himself.

Military power, then, is always in a strait between the rocky structure of Scylla and the treacherous tides of Charybdis. The tides, as raw power, tend to maximize the overreach of abstraction and the overkill of destruction. In an age of surplus power and academic sophistication, the results can mean instant Armageddon, a sobering concern especially for the older services, a challenge to superior technological expertise and control for the younger establishment. Common to both, because common to man, in the rocky enclaves of power, lurks the sin of *hubris*, the fallen angel who constantly stirs the waters of the whirlpool of doom for men and nations.

PART THREE

TOWARD
SOLUTION

Chapter 9

The Illusion
of
Omnipotence

I. WAR NOT AN ACT OF GOD

In his Introduction to *The Makers of Modern Strategy*, Edward Mead Earle justifies the title and study by simply stating that however profound, pervasive, and seemingly inevitable war is, still *"war is not an act of God. It grows directly out of things which individuals, statesmen, and nations do or fail to do."* [1] It is, therefore, our business as men and women who make war to unmake it: it is as simple as that—and as difficult. As Clausewitz once remarked, "Everything is very simple in War, but the simplest thing is difficult." [2]

To say that it is up to us to "unmake" war, that "it is as simple as that," is not to yield to simplistic solutions for its containment or eradication. One such solution, offered to me with great sincerity by a returning veteran, is the abolition of the draft as the first step in the creation of a volunteer military establishment. This would "automatically reduce our Armed Forces to one tenth of its present size, which would still be quite large enough to handle any plausible threats we face today." With many others today this student rightly has lost faith in the steady drumbeat of the cold war calling

Americans to arms against a monolithic Communist conspiracy forever poised to overwhelm the West and all its values. Still, in flying from one myth we must not fall into the arms of another. To reject the notion that Russian Communism is absolutely evil does not necessarily mean that the Russians can then be trusted not to take advantage of us.

The naïveté of the "New Liberals" is sometimes as striking as that of the older liberals whom they often affect to despise. Some are converts who have known the pangs of a new birth through the harsh ministrations of Vietnam's inhumanity to man. With many others today, especially the youth, they lift the latest banners of idealism and modern utopianism skyward and, as it were, storm the very gates of heaven itself to make it their own. The heavenly vision of a warless world, radically secularized in Marxism, is stripped even of this earthly ideology and summoned to appear forthwith like a genie from the bottle to solve at once all of our problems. The "Instant Generation," understandably impatient to accept all men as brothers, sometimes plunges onward to recognize no one as enemy, and to attribute to nations as well as to individuals a principled goodness to match their own. In a curiously pervasive, but often unrecognized Marxian sense, it is the machinery (the draft, the military, the establishment, etc.) which has gone wrong and must be destroyed. It is the Machine, and not men, that is evil. Human nature, "born free," and uninhibited, offers the "last, best hope" for the survival of man.

II. THE VISION OF PEACE

The vision of peace, drained of the forms of faith whether religious or secular, in isolated communes and pathetic dropouts, sometimes remains aloft like a balloon on a string, almost detached from the world. This is the tragedy of despair with the world, of sidetracked and wasted intelligence and good-

THE ILLUSION OF OMNIPOTENCE

ness. At other times and in different people, the vision acts like a vacuum that indiscriminately sucks into itself any and every means "to get the job done." Jesus warned of this latter danger long ago in the parable of the man delivered from one unclean spirit only to become the unwitting host of seven more spirits "worse than the first" (Matt. 12:43–45). The tragic discrepancy between high ideals and deep moral compulsions on the one hand, and their often sudden and bewildering exploitation by the claim of ethical freedom on the other, can be seen in a rising number of commune and drug-culture instances. Whatever may be said for the necessity at times for violent revolution, the proliferation of violent means in the hands of those supposedly devoted to "peace" is more than ironic. It is demonic. In confusing, frustrating, and surprising ways the tragic ambiguities which beset and betray the noblest intentions of men are revealed. The bizarre story of the Manson "family," knowing only "love" and its exercise, becomes pathetically sad and obscene in its revelation of venomous depths of violent hatreds in Charlie and his girls, which were probably unknown and surprising even to themselves. In a different context and manner, Sergeant Michael Bernhardt, who did not fire at My Lai, found to his agonized surprise that it did not take "a real nut, a real maniac, a real psycho" to shoot up women and children: "I found out that an act like, you know, murder for no reason could be done by just about anybody." [3]

On the other hand, there are the "squares," often the cynics who have accepted at face and lasting value the harsh, unfeeling rule of power in human life as "the way it is and let's make the most of it." Here the forms of faith are intact, even rigid. God is a God of power and even Mary and Jesus become rule makers and binders, sheer miracle workers and judges in the end, threatening violence and finally using it in the inevitable, and glorious, final showdown with evil. If we erase the face of Christ and substitute the face of Marx,

or Lenin, or perhaps even Stalin, the picture may not change
much, for the final arbiter can still be arbitrary, ultimate
Force.

The fountainhead of much Western utopianism cast in
martial terms is Augustine. His doctrine of the Two Cities—
the City of God and the City of Man—follows hard upon his
often grim view of human nature. The essential dualism of
the West, recognizing a basic and eternal distinction between
the Creator and his creation, is rigidified in Augustine and the
two kinds of nature actually opposed to each other. The
Greek "natural virtues" (wisdom, courage, temperance, justice, etc.), which are later made stepping-stones to the "super-
natural virtues" (faith, hope, love) in Aquinas, are in Augustine
the feeders of *hubris*, i.e., pride and self-righteousness, and
hence are at war with the divine Will. Man has no goodness of
himself, but only as the "gift of God," i.e., *grace* (freely given).
The drama of man is this, that he is at war with God who
wills to save some and assigns the rest to perdition, in his own
time, at the end of history. History (Augustine is the first philosopher of history in the West) is the story of the City of
Man, of man's prolonged but futile struggle with the power
of God. Therefore, earthly governments are "great robberies,"
intent upon self-love, expressed in *cupiditas*, the desire for
earthly things. Nevertheless, governments exist by God's con-
cession, for a time, and as forms of order perform the necessary
function of constraint upon the seething, rebellious nature
of men. Christians, belonging also to the City of God, which
hovers over and informs the City of Man like the eternal forms
of Plato, know in the midst of daily strife the inner peace of
caritas, of love for God and neighbor for God's sake.[4]

III. THE SWORD OF GOD

The dichotomy is real but the vision lingers and impels to
faith and action. Faith requires patience in the long-term will

of God, which has often led to the too easy acceptance of the *status quo* and the postponement of the Kingdom to another world. But man is also impatient. Openly at times, but more often subtly and almost unconsciously, he has sought to translate the vision and to bring in the Kingdom on his own. Marxism is but the latest and most determinedly efficient of such attempts. From Constantine onward it was increasingly easy for the governing class to identify itself with the will of God as enjoined by Paul and developed by Augustine, to create the close, hierarchical collaboration between church and state in the Middle Ages. The development of the doctrine of the "divine right of kings" followed naturally, to hold almost undisputed sway until the American and French Revolutions. Even their success hardly lessened the authority of the state or its source as transcendental. "Let every person be subject to the governing authorities. For there is no authority except from God" (Rom. 13:1), Paul had said. The state became the sword of God. "If you do wrong, be afraid, for he does not bear the sword in vain; he is the servant of God to execute his wrath on the wrongdoer" (v. 4). The doctrine of the just war became the logical extension of the divine right of the true state to enforce the rule of God upon other groups or states. The compulsion to unity from both the model of the Empire and the dream of the church encouraged many internal conflicts where the participants actively sought identification with the imagined one will of the Lord. Warfare outside the Christian family of rising nations, against the enemies of the Empire, especially the Crusades against the Muslims, was less confusing and ambiguous because the identification was assumed to be automatic, since no status was given to heathen faiths. The arbitrary and unconditional nature of such "crusades" reminds one of the Old Testament conquest of Canaan and its Baals. They prefigure the modern religious wars of the post-Reformation period, and the ideological wars of our own times against the Nazi and Communist faiths and tyrannies.

The problem of pluralism, of allowing "rival" faiths, has been a particularly thorny issue in the West since Constantine and the confirmation of Christianity as the religion of the state. No longer could the gods be on both sides as they were at Troy. The Pantheon, where the astute Romans carefully placed the images of foreign gods in equal notches on a level with the domestic variety, was swept clean to promote the worship of the one true God. This meant also the one true culture, an arrogant conviction that troubles us as lately as Vietnam and My Lai and concerning which the late Scott Buchanan suggested that our attitude may disqualify us at the start from empire-building.[5] The Romans, on the other hand,

very early learned to recognize and honor the "languages, institutions and laws" of the peoples that for one reason or another came under their aegis. They neither assimilated these heterogeneous legalities, nor did they ex-communicate and ghetto-ize them. They undertook to enforce the living law of the group, even though this often raised serious threats to the integrities and viabilities of both the larger and the smaller communities.[6]

IV. THE TWO REALMS

It is profoundly interesting that Luther, an Augustinian, collapses the ancient hierarchical hold of the church upon the state while reinforcing the dichotomy between the "Two Realms" of the sacred and the secular. The religious life becomes autonomous, and the secular is left to its own devices. Into this latter vacuum Machiavelli and Hobbes bring the amoral means of power. For power is still the key: to the nature of God whom we must obey because he *commands,* and to the relation of man to the state which now becomes simply *subject.* As Alasdair MacIntyre observes, for the first time "the State becomes distinct from society."[7] The web of social relations which once bound superiors and inferiors "in all sorts of ways" is swept away to reveal the autonomous individual who makes contracts with the state instead of finding function and status in caste levels and guild associations. In the privileged sanctuary of his conscience the individual confronts his God and *believes* in an appropriating way that his mercy and forgiveness erase all distinction between sinner and saint. So *Faith,* i.e., *right belief,* becomes the basis and guarantor of morality, of right action. The scene of that action, however, is the world, which is the province of the state. "For the first time," writes J. N. Figgis of the post-Reformation period, "the Absolute Individual confronts the Absolute State." [8]

In the next century, René Descartes provided seemingly irrefutable proof of the priority, insularity, and private judgment of individual self-consciousness. By that time, too, Thomas Hobbes had secularized and made political the Augustinian-Reformational view of the timeless bestiality of man's nature, a "condition which is called war; . . . of every man against every man." [9] The solution to such deadly anarchy of sovereign individuals is the sovereign state whose only function is to keep the peace. "This is . . . that great LEVIATHAN, . . . that *mortal god*" [10] which looks to nothing beyond itself for its validity, and whose sole function is to control the incipient violence of men. The ancient natural law of the Stoics, given a beneficent though still omnipotent face in Aquinas' God, is reduced to "the law of self-preservation," and justice becomes the mere keeping of the social contract by which the absolute sovereign was first created. With vivid and brutal frankness Hobbes describes the "state of nature" among societies which together lack as yet a sovereign will:

In all times, kings, and persons of sovereign authority, because of their independence, are in continual jealousies, and in the state and posture of gladiators, having their weapons pointing, and their eyes fixed on one another; that is, their forts, garrisons, and guns upon the frontiers of their kingdoms; and continual spies upon their neighbors; which is a posture of war. . . .

To this war of every man against every man, this also is consequent; that nothing can be unjust. . . . Where there is no common power, there is no law, no injustice.[11]

Even the ambiguous and ineffectual "just war" concept of Augustine and the church is cut off at its source. The criteria for human behavior arise from within the individual conscience and private judgment, and is concerned only with survival. It is Machiavelli, the first political scientist of modern times, who teaches the Prince (whether that be a person or a people, i.e., the Sovereign) how to grow as well as how to survive—by the many routes of expediency.

Such is twentieth-century man, in the West at least: atomized, insulated, and reduced to units of power which, save for the intervening state, operate pretty much as laws unto themselves. With the so-called "death of God" it is the nation-state that commands and compels allegiance. As autonomous subjects, individuals are far more easily compelled by the absolute state—hence the rise of mass armies, Hobbes's power units organized into the living Machine and run on pure expediency. The church has ceased as the middleman for conscience. It can try, in concerned leaders and as bodies that pass resolutions, to support the lonely conscientious objector, and by criticism it can hope to modify the position of the state. But it is evident that the church at best is not very effectual. Rather, it is generally supportive of "the powers that be," for its own teaching is that "they are of God." Perhaps "the powers" are not accepted quite as readily today as they may have been in periods of the past. Nonetheless, they represent the rule of law, which for most people is always preferable to chaos. And although law may no longer have the face of God as in the medieval synthesis, still it argues for a certain continuity and security in the affairs of men. Curiously, for all the ferment Machiavelli and Hobbes reflected and even set in motion, they treated human nature itself as timeless and unchanging, the inevitable and ceaseless selfish warring of the human animal. This means that the individual, unconstrained by any social bonds to fraternity and goodness, was determined in his very nature to assert and to secure for himself by any means his own sovereignty and survival. The transience of political orders only highlights the essential antisocial nature of man.

Both the observation of the flux of man's political arrangements and the conviction of his natural decadence are secularized half-truths from the Bible. The wars of modern times and the fearful prospect of Armageddon itself only confirm for many Christians the truth as they have always known it. Did not God himself lead his people into the Promised Land and command them in many instances to spare not even the women and children of the enemy in battle? Did not Jesus foresee to the end of time "wars and rumors of wars"? The millennium indeed cannot come until Christ has met and defeated the vast armies of Gog and Magog (Russia: the "people from the north"?)[12] on the plains of Megiddo. Thus, in bizarre but nonetheless effective ways the Judeo-Christian heritage is all too readily misused in unthinking and emotionally aggressive ways to support the unhampered power of the state in situations of "enemy" confrontation. The support is not limited to the literalistic beliefs of so-called "fundamentalist" Christian groups. As pointed out earlier, quite sophisticated but more politically oriented segments of the Christian community join with the self-styled "evangelicals" to give moral grounding and emotional fervor to a martial spirit which is at home in the Armed Forces. But not only in the Armed Forces—in the hometowns from which servicemen come and to which they may return, the nurturing of a martial faith makes it easy to identify soldiering with salvation. The "God and country" preaching of the Carl McIntires—and there are many of them—is illustrative of much grass roots understanding of the gospel, so that many would be hard put to distinguish it from "Americanism." When one's politics and culture are made sacred, as happens in today's jungle competition of fang and claw, extreme self-righteousness, if not fanaticism, must result.

V. THE IDOLATRY OF AMERICANISM

How far we have traveled this road may be suggested by two facts. The first is that apparently only in communist countries is the equivalent of the Committee on Un-American Activities to be found. It even sounds silly to suggest a Committee on Un-English, or Un-French, or Un-Italian Activities! It is silly for us, too, but seriously silly. So far has the private domain of the individual conscience, believing before God, accepted the golden calf of the state as the easier and immensely more real and comfortable image of the faith. The second fact is the worship we accord the flag. Recently a cover story in *Time* was devoted to the phenomenon,[13] and one case of desecration of the flag was ruled upon by the Supreme Court.[14] Don MacLean, writing in the *Berkeley Daily Gazette,* is alarmed "that the American flag has become a religion which divides rather than unites the people—into those of us who worship the flag, and those of us who don't." Recalling his own military service with the Marines, he makes it clear that he was proud to fight for his country, its principles, and its way of life. But "I certainly wasn't defending the flag. As a symbol of America, the flag is fine, but that's all it is." [15] But that's not all it is for many Americans—many of whom have never been near the military, or not for a long time. *Time* says:

The flag has always occupied a much stronger place in American life and mythology than have flags in other countries. . . . In "one nation under God," the idea implies divinity. For many Americans, the flag is literally a sacred object.[16]

The article then quotes Arthur Stivaletta, an organizer of the April, 1970, "Wake Up America" rally in Boston: "I see the flag as I see God: a supreme being." Rev. Billy Graham doesn't go quite so far, but far enough, in comparing the flag to the Queen of England and to what the black man means by "soul." [17]

This is idolatry, and the depth of the divisiveness which it is bringing into American life in these bitter and confusing times may be seen in the recently revealed gap in understanding of the Christian faith—and America—which has developed between the Carl McIntires, father and son. The senior McIntire is an internationally known right-wing hard-liner who recently tried every possible stratagem to get Vice-President Ky from Saigon to address a war rally in Washington and failed only because the project was deemed patently explosive. He has repeatedly called for unilateral victory and has blessed without caution the American sword: "The sword that preserves order and executes judgment and wins the wars against the aggressors must be a good sword." [18]

The "good [American] sword," obviously, is God's sword. The image here is from Paul, as quoted earlier: "If you do wrong, be afraid, for he does not bear the sword in vain; he is the servant of God to execute his wrath on the wrongdoer" (Rom. 13:4). But how do we know that we are the "servant of God" and have the right to bear his sword? Who gave us the right to judge others and name the "wrongdoers" in the family of nations and who are thus worthy of his wrath to be executed through us? Who are we to lift a specific relation which Paul says obtains between ruler and ruled and try to make it fit the imposition of one state's will upon others? Why? Because through our whole history runs the conviction that God has called us like Abraham "out from among them," from an old and evil world to be the New Israel in a New Promised Land. And the proof of the pudding lies in the fantastic success we have made of the venture. John Calvin helped us to fashion a work ethic that won't quit. He taught us that despite the total depravity of man and the mystery of who shall be saved, yet "by their fruits ye shall know them." Success became the oblique but powerfully confirming indicator that "God is at work in you, both to will and to work for his good pleasure" (Phil. 2:13, RSV). Even with the dilution of this spiritual conviction under the massive impact of modern secularism, still "nothing succeeds like success" and it has told its own story in all the earth. Americans are obviously "with it," working with the grain of things, with God. By belief-full history and daily confirmation it is easy to assume that we are the chosen few to enlighten the earth and bring it, even if not always willingly, into a "century of peace," as well as plenty. This is a dream of which President Nixon himself has spoken fervently.[19]

It is when this dream, this way of life, this "Americanism," has been threatened or blocked in its God-given expansionism, as we have understood it, that we have gone to war. Consciously we do not go to war for "cheap" ends, for land and plunder, or even glory, but always for principles, for morality: "to make the world safe for democracy," for "the right of self-determination," for "freedom from aggression." Paul R. Schratz, a retired Navy captain quoted before, has noted this, and made an interesting observation. In the American experience, he says, "morality forbade the use of power to coerce except for total ends, that is, for moral or ideological ends." [20] Then he suggests the key to our difficulties in Southeast Asia: This is a war of limited objectives and Americans historically, fighting as they have believed for the highest of principles, have supported only *total* wars which were popular because they were "crusades." Such was the Spanish-American War of 1898, and both world wars, but not the limited wars of 1812, the Mexican War, Korea, and now Vietnam.

Enter now the younger McIntire, also a minister, who sees the gravest of dangers here. The "American way of life," he says, has become "a spiritually totalitarian force" which is an alien rival to the Christian faith. It has adapted forms of faith and created expectations of ultimate concern which subtly but unequivocally compel allegiance of all who would call themselves, not Christians, but Americans.

The American faith . . . operates from its own confession of Creator —the sovereign people; of Redeemer—the American dream; of sin

—the malevolence of un-Americans; and centrally, of a spiritual peoplehood—all Americans of reason and goodwill who accept the American ideal.[21]

The shocking degree of identification of "Americanism" as a faith with the Christian gospel is revealed in the bitter words of Rev. Michael Lord, who organized a rally for Lieutenant "Rusty" Calley on the day his sentence was handed down:

There was a crucifixion 2000 years ago. . . . I don't think we need another crucifixion of another man named "Rusty" Calley. Jesus Christ was crucified because he did his Father's work. Calley did what he was told to do.[22]

The bumper sticker leaves no room for doubt or shared loyalties: "America! Love it or leave it." Another sticker provides aggressive content for the loving we should bear America: "Stand up for America!" The next act is *marching,* and that demand has been upon us continuously now for a generation.

VI. "NUCLEARISM" AS A FALSE GOD

The idolatry here is deep, pervasive, and subtle. "War," Edward Earle has said, "is not an act of God." But he was not quoting Paul, nor the elder McIntire, nor perhaps even Freud, who toyed with the idea of a natural urge to destruction in man. Still, for all the hand of God or nature which may or may not be revealed in the violent outbursts in human relations we call war, the disrupted relations *are* human, and the sword and its uses are ours. War is not an act of God, but we have made it the act of *gods,* of nation-states and peoples, and even persons, trying to prove our mastery of Olympus. For it is not that the gods have moved away, as Trygaeus complained in the fratricidal Greece of the Peloponnesian War, but rather that men have stormed Olympus itself and taken over the heavenly arsenal of Hephaestus. Like the discovery of fire, the fission and fusion of the atom have made gods of men and opened up hitherto unimaginable possibilities for good or ill. Only now, in the age of the atom, the claim to power is at last made total. Prometheus breaks his chains and dethrones Zeus: "God is dead." The attempt to match limitless power to limitless ends is surely presumptive of divinity. The modern military as the focus of such power—and war as its issue—stand always on the threshold of blasphemy, for they bid fair to destroy not only man's works, but God's work which is man himself.

Robert Jay Lifton, a psychiatrist at Harvard, calls this "nuclearism," which is "the passionate embrace of nuclear weapons as the solution of our anxieties," not simply as the only possible defense against the enemy, but as "a means of restoring a lost sense of immortality" shattered by Hiroshima. Ironically we embrace the death-bringer (as we desperately hope) to save us from death. We "turn to the weapons, and to their power. . . . Nuclearism, then, is a secular religion, a total ideology in which grace, the mastery of death, is achieved by means of a new technological deity." [23] This is that "false God," as Lifton suggests, which arises in different forms in every age and culture to challenge and to corrupt life at its center. The center in today's world is the ultimacy of power itself and its managers, and here Satan will take his seat if he can. The process is aided immeasurably by the very nature of the military which, as we have seen, pushes readily and almost irresistibly to the utmost limits.

The military is a most singular and peculiar institution. No other institution known among men presumes to fuse and to control the ultimates of human existence and behavior. The elements of military power—the rational, the decisive, the concrete, the dynamic—each has its particular expression and followers in every society, and each to some extent involves the other elements in the total process of its existence. Thus we may say that academia emphasizes the rational, that government stresses decision-making, that the economic is concerned with the concrete (livelihood), and perhaps the arts more especially express the dynamic. Yet government must be rational, and business and academia are involved in decision-making. The military, however, seeks a fusion of the elements in pristine purity and in almost equal proportions in a manner to create a unique species of power in the human community. Let us, for example, compare the academic understanding and use of power to that of the military. Man is a rational animal and academia is both the expression of and the training establishment for the exercise and development of that vital dimension of man's being. But there is no *necessity* to do other than explore and explain the rational in the academic sector. The ease and persistence with which educators tend to dwell in the abstract is proverbial. But the military is rationally involved for the purpose of controlling violence, the raw force of being, and whatever its indulgence in the abstract it can never remain there long, but must descend to the concrete and physical.

The will, too, is involved in the daily choice and pursuit of truth on a college campus. Especially at the administrative levels the "capacity to make decisions" becomes important, perhaps even decisive for that institution and its impact upon society. But such decision-making hardly involves the ultimate in terms of the "life or death" of persons and societies. At such a point, the military in one form or another is called in (as at Kent State, etc.), to "do the dirty work." It is not simply that professors, students, and citizens lack the aptitude, skill, or means to kill or to spare, but that only the military (or police) are professionally trained and legally endowed to make and *to execute* such decisions of ultimacy. Again, speaking of the means, academicians may and do resort to many different kinds of sanctions to persuasively enforce certain expectations of behavior, i.e., grades, degrees, restrictions, even expulsion. But they are not designated actually to use the brute force, which is always assumed to lie back of the rational and emotional appeals of normal persuasion. Such "raw force" is the hard currency, usually unseen but always *there,* which gives ultimate validity to the free flow of the paper money of the usual constraints upon human behavior. It is the military, in some form or other, and it alone as an institution, which on given occasions is called upon as the last resort to point the actual gun and perhaps to pull the trigger. Government, the courts, business, the church—the *civil* institutions of man are the *raison d'être* of the military, and for this reason the military is sometimes said to be parasitic. It creates nothing of itself; it can only ensure that other institutions can; its business is *order.* It is the last resort, protecting the institutions it is called to serve, but not protected in turn. It is the last resort, and it exercises jurisdiction beyond which no one else may venture, for that is the void.

Finally, the dynamism of military power is almost unimaginably enhanced by the tension of the opposites which it must hold in balance. To cap and uncap the volcano at will—but by a rational will—asks more in risks and sanity than most men are capable of, perhaps than any men are fully capable of today when the power given them is socially ultimate. There is no firm place upon which to stand in order to manipulate the fulcrum by which to move the world. Structure for containing and directing military power is an utter necessity, but structure must not become an end in itself to cancel out the flexible use of military power when the need suddenly arises. Moreover the ultimacy of its power is such that no "canceling out" structures could possibly succeed for long. All man's institutions run risks of brittleness and collapse when the attempt is made to preserve them intact. The military, directly related to unshaped power and never knowing when it may be called upon to use it, must constantly review and adjust its pressure gauges. The military does not simply elect to live with the rumbling of the volcano or the tremors of an impending earthquake. It encamps on the fault, over the fissure and pit itself, and even presumes to control and to use the seething and uncertain power for its own purposes. It is hardly to be wondered at that such "managers of violence," and sometimes the peoples they represent, succumb to the illusion of omnipotence and elect to "play God." Long ago Xerxes the Great, undoubted master of an empire and an army which appeared as numerous and inexhaustible as the sands of the seashore, could not abide the contrariness of a single storm that destroyed his bridge across the Hellespont. He spared neither gold nor zeal for that upon which his fancy lighted. On the way to the stubborn and ignorant Greeks, he adorned a great tree which he liked with golden chains and posted guards about it.[24] The utter confidence with which we have thrown our giant resources into tiny Vietnam, and the progressive surprise and frustration which have been ours, despite gold and power, at least suggest that confidence in our might allowed little or no place for careful and conscientious assurance of our right to be there. The easy adoption of the "military solution" is militarism, a form in which the "False God" has often appeared, and is arising today.

The concept of "False God," to which Lifton has called attention, is one of the oldest of human symbols. A reading of the sacred literature of many peoples shows how the adversarial struggle between good and evil assumes cosmic and personal dimensions. In Western sacred literature Satan (or the devil) emerges as anti-God, "the spirit of this world" (as base and intractable), who becomes personified in or represented by tyrants who seek total power and thus oppose God himself. The implementation of tyrannical power generally has had to do with the building and unleashing of armies. But one of the revered titles of God in the Old Testament is "Lord of Sabaoth," or "Lord of hosts," a claim that includes war-making powers by God. Yet, although Jehovah was often reduced to simply a martial role, his claim in this title alone is much larger. For the Semites comprehended all forces and beings of heaven and earth in martial terms as "hosts," or armies, and the Hebrews understood these all to be under the command of the one Lord. So the Greeks translated the title "Sabaoth" as *Pantokrator*, the "Almighty." "The designation pictures the universe, in its spiritual and material aspects, as forming a vast army, in numerous divisions, of various kinds of troops, in orderly array under the command of Jehovah." [25] Thus, to limit the omnipotence of the Lord by reducing his authority to only a division of life, or to allow any part to assume autonomy or independence from his command, was spiritual (and even social) treason. It was idolatry, the worship of a false god, and a capital offense. "Shall the ax boast itself against him that heweth therewith?" (Isa. 10:15), asks Isaiah. Mighty Nebuchadnezzar learned the hard way, according to Daniel, that the earth was not gained by "the might of my power . . . and majesty," but "the Most High ruleth in the kingdom of men, and giveth it to whomsoever he will" (Dan. 5:30–37). Perhaps the gravest horror in the entire Hebrew experience concerned "the abomination of desolation." This was the flagrantly blasphemous erection of an image and an altar to Zeus in the Holy of Holies of the Temple by soldiers of the hated Antiochus IV who called himself Epiphanes ("Manifestation of God"). A century later Herod the Great abandoned his attempt to display the Roman eagles atop the newly refurbished Temple only after a bloody massacre. [26]

It was not unnatural, then, for the early Christians, suffering persecution, to identify Roman emperor worship as a false God worship and to scorn as well as to fear Nero, Caligula, and others as prototypes of that anti-Messiah, or Antichrist, who must arise at the end of time to confront and be defeated by the Risen Lord. The power of this idea to capture the imagination and give insight into the mysterious and dark abyss of human nature is found as well in the bizarre misuse to which its truth has sometimes been put. Jesus warned of others calling themselves Christ, who would call and men would answer, overwhelmed by their miracles. He was tempted to become such a wonder-worker himself. Significantly, the temptation took place in a wilderness after a period of physical and mental exhaustion when the need for bread and people and power was most urgent (Matt. 4:1–11). Bread for his hungry body, the attention of people to support his faltering ego, and power to organize the totality of his existence—these are legitimate needs of man. When they become ends in themselves and comprise the whole of existence, they are idolatrous, for "man does not live by bread alone." He does not because he cannot—he is built for the spirit and eternity, which are the gifts of God. This is that fundamental aspect of the illimitable, the transcendent, the final end to which man aspires but cannot simply create. The wonder-working element in the three temptations is the illusion of man convinced of the limitlessness of his own powers. To be enamored of his prowess is characteristic of modern man, for he has done miraculously well in accumulating material wealth (if not in distributing it equitably), in analyzing his psychic needs (if not in harnessing them well), and he stands now on the threshold of world (and reaching for universal) order. The exhilaration of such undreamed of leaps in human progress and potential for the future is dampened only by the multiplicity of the problems that they have created. The complexity and pressure of the problems have kept pace with the geometric progression of power in the modern world so that the future itself may appear to be approaching like a juggernaut of doom: "future shock."

It is here that Jesus' last temptation[27]—to order and accomplish everything by resort to the military—is so pertinent today. How can we pursue with any degree of freedom at all the goods of life without order, and who is better equipped—who else *is* equipped—to handle the confusing traffic which threatens complete breakdown in this age of technological and population explosion? Add to these considerations the ultimacy of the power which must somehow be held in check, and the military at once becomes central to human life and its future on this planet in ways without parallel in the past. In 1861 an American novelist wrote on the domination of war as like

a great tempest which blows upon us all, mingles with the church organ, whistles through the streets, steals into our firesides, clinks glasses in barrooms, lifts grey hairs of statesmen, invades the class-rooms of our colleges, rustles the thumbed pages of our scholars. It offers inescapable tests.[28]

The imagery suggests the titanic and irreversible power of the tempest of the Civil War which has been poignantly and unforgettably recorded in Margaret Mitchell's *Gone with the Wind*—the sudden eclipse of a whole way of life. That war, the first truly modern holocaust, occurred more than a century ago, and we know that however dominating it was for its own and successive generations, it has been dwarfed by the wars of this century. The holocausts through which we have passed are as nothing compared to the leap in imagination we must make to picture general war of the future. War has become civil war for mankind in our time. The societies of men have become one pool, and a single ripple carries to the farthest shore. Today the wind is always there, brewing the mightiest storm in history.

It could be the end of history. Only this time it would not be by water, concerning which it is said that God himself repented (Gen. 8:21–22), but by fire storm—"The Fire Next Time," as one social activist has already announced, prophesy-ing perhaps more than he knew.[29] It is the fire storm which we have already encapsulated and delivered with precision, as though bottling the jagged edges of the sun and in our rising temerity commanding the orb itself to stand still. We are like the rain dancers of ancient tribes for whom the occasional coincidence of ceremonies with the coming of the rain was proof natural of their cosmic powers. Or, in our own image of ourselves, we are the Brahmans of ancient India whose very sophistication in contrast to the crudity of their lusty Vedic forebears led them to view the sacrificial ritual as coercing even the gods to appear.[30] The temptation to "play God," to be or to follow Antichrist, to express the demonic, is the temptation of every age and of every man. It is most especially the temptation of this age and of American man for the very simple but profound reason that the claim to omnipotence appears so realizable—if we can stave off destruction.

It is precisely at the point of threatened destruction that the claim to omnipotence becomes illusory. The ultimate power we have achieved in splitting the atom turns out to be the power literally to destroy ourselves. We have achieved omnipotence of a sort—the omnipotence to DESTROY. Surely this is the terrible warning signal that the claiming of total power, and the presumption of using it, are actually illusory and a delusion. It is fantasy and the ultimate "sin against the Holy Spirit," for which there is no forgiveness because it mocks reality and comes to believe its own mockery. One sees and recoils in awe before the crazed passions of Xerxes the Great, a Tamerlane, or a Hitler. But what of the deep wave of resentment that swept our own country in protest of the conviction of Lieutenant Calley and the call for exoneration of his deeds as fully to be expected in war? Just like Jesus Christ, "he did what he was told to do. . . . We train them to kill."

VII. THE CALLEY CASE

Is that all? Do we train our soldiers like machines to kill, and expect nothing else from them? Are there no reasons, no purposes which make sense, no moral ends to justify the killing? Lieutenant Calley claims none were given him other than that as communist, the enemy was inherently, irreversibly evil and (whatever their age) should be "wasted" with no further thought. When this total attitude is expressed in gunning down unarmed and defenseless women, children, and old men, it is among other things a betrayal of the ancient code of professional fighting men. The Army, in its "white paper" defense of the Calley trial and conviction, went behind The Hague and Geneva conventions to the "long . . . unwritten law" of humane treatment of prisoners and stressed that

the United States has historically led the way in adopting humane rules, which recognize that an enemy, who has laid down his arms, and his wife, children and elders are human beings, entitled to humanitarian concern and mercy while taking no active part in hostilities.[31]

The restrained, chivalric image of men in uniform as "honorable" may be dismissed as an anachronistic holdover from medieval times, but not without regret, and more moderate and rational voices began to say so, after the initial pro-Calley outburst.[32] In the general furor over the conviction of Lieutenant Calley it was almost completely overlooked that some men in his company refused to shoot the defenseless, and one was reported to have shot himself in the foot in order to be evacuated out of the mess.[33] Second (and third) thoughts began to raise the question that if the Calleys who obey no restraints are made martyrs and heroes, what are we to do with the nameless others who strive against incredible odds, including other Calleys, to maintain some sense of decency and humanity in the midst of the hell of war? For it could not even be said that Charley Company had suffered unduly in comparison with other units. Actually, the deepening frustration of not being able to claim the glory of contact with the enemy was part of the mental and emotional preparation for the sweep through supposedly enemy-infested My Lai. Met by unarmed civilians, the focus of resentment and hatred turned indiscriminately upon those left behind as "the Enemy" to be "wasted."

Partly, at least, such unacceptable deeds are the aberrant expression of the crusader attitude which Americans have applied to all their wars: "bound by a cosmology that contrasts absolute American purity with absolute Communist depravity." [34] It is clear that such an attitude has strong theological and cultural roots in our understanding of Biblical justice (an "eye for an eye," and guilt which may apply to the family and race).[35] To some extent such conceptions are at war with the soldierly ideal. Even General Eisenhower wrote that World War II was far too personal to allow him to entertain a captured German officer in accordance with traditional soldierly etiquette: "Because only by the utter destruction of the Axis was a decent world possible, the war became for me a crusade." [36] The insistence upon "unconditional surrender" is, of course, further illustration of the same totally aggressive spirit. The tension and ambiguities of the soldierly and crusader ideals have been evident as well in the Calley and subsequent trials of American servicemen in Vietnam. In the Calley case, the jury, composed of combat officers who (save for one) had served longer and more hazardous tours of duty in Vietnam than Lieutenant Calley, gave him "every benefit of a doubt" and found him guilty of premeditated murder. Harassed and defamed by many after the verdict, the jurors must have felt the bitter irony that their own restraint in many a potential My Lai could so easily be shouted down while Lieutenant Calley, at the very least lacking in self-control and convicted of senseless killing, was being made a folk hero and "a great American" worthy of addressing a joint session of Congress! [37] This is not to deny compassion to this tragic figure who was also a victim, nor does it exonerate others who stand in the shadows and may never be brought to trial. It is simply to say that justice, never perfect, never entire among finite and faulty men, must begin somewhere, and crowds are poor indicators of either truth or justice. If allusion must be made to the "crucifixion that happened 2000 years ago," it would be well to remember that it was Barabbas, a murderer, whom the crowd set free.

VIII. WHEN MEANS ENGULF THE END

The difficulties and the tragedy are that the tensions and ambiguities of the conflicting ideals extend from the command centers to the battlefield, and on to the American society itself. The fluid nature of guerrilla warfare does not fit well with the soldierly ideal of recognized and accepted restraints and rules. Compounded in Vietnam by the generally held belief that "the Oriental mind" is something opaquely mysterious —an attitude that is certainly racist in many—[38] and unable to achieve the anticipated quick victory by more conventional means, the temptation to drop to lowercase morality has been exceedingly strong. Given the myths of "never having lost a war" and the unquestioned finality of American technology, it should not be surprising that official U.S. policy has progressively led to obliteration tactics for the enemy wherever he may be found.[39] Edward M. Opton, Jr., and his colleagues at the Wright Institute, in testimony before the Congressional Conference on War and National Responsibility which was convened in Washington early in 1970, claimed that not only whole villages, but "whole districts and virtually whole provinces" have been subjected to "free fire" and "kill" zoning. At first an attempt was made to relocate unarmed villagers but "the pressure of the vast number of refugees thus created— at least one quarter of the entire rural population of South Vietnam—" has led to policies essentially genocidal in that no warnings are now given and "anything that moves is fired upon." [40] Added to this, they said, is the "perfectly routine" business of "prepping an area" in which individual pilots feel free to shoot at will into any homes or villages in so-called Viet Cong territory. Comprehensive destruction of rice stores, of course, threatens starvation for women and children long before the soldiers themselves begin to suffer. The sporadic but much heralded "winning the hearts and minds" of the Vietnamese people seems a drop in the bucket compared to the insistent daily practice of treating *all* Vietnamese as "dinks," "gooks," and "slopes," and the admitted prevalence of torture, dropping suspects from helicopters, "plinking" at scared and running natives from passing air and land vehicles, etc.[41] Returning veterans, slow to relive their experiences, nevertheless have confirmed beyond doubt the routinization of "ruleless" behavior, in the lower grades especially, which gags the imagination and logically matches the total methods applied more abstractly by the high command. Many of the men rightly have found it hypocritical at best to distinguish between a high-level order to obliterate an area indiscriminately by artillery or gunships and shooting the same civilians at point-blank range.

How is it, the foot soldier must wonder, that "to kill women and children at less than 500 paces is an atrocity; at more than 500 paces, it's an act of heroism"? [42]

If we "train them to kill," and only that, there is no difference, of course. Then the most efficient, massive, and total means possible are quite in order. The ambiguity and hypocrisy lie in the desperate attempt to retain "honor and decency" while progressively utilizing the power to kill for its own sake. We have come to that; we have proved our power to destroy on a scale that dwarfs previous wars. But we are not satisfied. For many, the dissatisfaction has amounted to a growing nausea for the killing which has come to outweigh the easy and early justifications for our involvement and which, in continuance, has seemed to lack any end beyond our clearly demonstrated ability to "waste" more lives than the other side. The means, literally, have engulfed the end. We are pulling out of Vietnam because it seems endless, inexhaustible, without victory. The power to kill has failed to accomplish anything else. There are those, many in fact, who believe that total power has not been employed, or at least not soon enough, that "we have fought with one hand tied behind our backs." But a growing number of veterans both overseas and at home have become increasingly appalled at the comprehensiveness of our devastation. One of these, Representative Paul N. McCloskey (Rep., Calif.), a decorated Marine Corps hero, early in 1971 challenged the President himself for leadership of the nation in order to hurry our exit from Vietnam. The proud omnipotence with which we almost carefreely rushed into this far and weak (?) little nation to solve its problems has evaporated as illusory.

There is a question whether we can take it or not. Has the military been pressing behind the scenes for a nuclear solution to the problems of Southeast Asia, as Hans Morgenthau has feared? [43] He has understood the mood of some military leaders to be that "the indefinite continuation of the war [may] destroy the Armed Forces as an effective instrument of national policy." The tensions have been severe and deepening between the received ideals and the daily compromises of this war, reflected not only in the growing alienation of Americans of all persuasions from continuing the effort, but ominously in drug escapism, mutinies, and emerging and serious hostilities between men and their officers. Hence, above all, the Armed Forces have wanted a quick end to the war. Naturally, an "Algerian solution," i.e., a pullout without victory, in other words (for many) *defeat,* has been resisted at the highest levels. No army is voluntarily going to opt for defeat if it can possibly manage a "victory." Moreover, the tactical employment of a few nuclear bombs clearly could create the surety of victory at the local level. The political implications of widening the war belong, in the view of these tacticians, with the civilian high command, not the military. But, as we have seen, the "politics of manhood," which unimaginatively, and sadly, equate the nation's integrity and maturity with the raw coerciveness of force, operates at that level—not only so, but significantly through much of the nation, as the Calley rallies have shown.

It seems odd, and ominous, that the conscientious and painstaking willingness of Army professionals to keep their own house in order—which is what the trials after My Lai surely mean—should so easily and categorically become the object of unreasoning vituperation by citizens high and low. For once, the generation (and even culture) gap was bridged, bringing George Wallace and the Veterans of Foreign Wars into harmonious clamor with thousands of students and middle-class "straights" across the nation. The object of this sudden contempt and hatred was the professional volunteer Army they say they want. Or is such an army to be simply an extensive enlargement of the "Dirty Dozen" concept,[44] prejudged to begin with? Then the rest of us could really wash our hands of the "dirty business." This would complete and confirm the subliminal and periodically overt rejection of the military which has characterized America's relations to its Armed Forces from the beginning.

It would also reassure us that evil is located in persons or peoples or events outside ourselves. Then the difficult and embarrassing moral distinctions and decisions which we are now called upon to make in applying means to ends would no longer confront us in tortured conscience. This has been our problem with Vietnam, that it has refused to let us alone, though we tried to leave it with the military. As the first truly "world war," Vietnam has daily obtruded itself into our living rooms where we tried to sit at ease, and it has forced us in a meager, but perhaps decisive, way to look at the horrible instrument of war. Like a ghastly surgery, if it could have been gotten over with quickly, we could have absorbed its brutality. But it's not surgery—it's a disease, like an inoperable cancer in the body of mankind for which amputation or medieval bloodletting only hastens the death of the patient.

IX. WHEN ILLUSIONS BREAK

The truth is, that Americans do not understand the nature of power although they are the world's supreme example of power. Americans have discovered and used and benefited from power in fantastically successful ways. We have been fascinated by power, which means that we have been both attracted and repelled at the same time. But what has repelled us—the harsh extremes and side effects of applied force—we have created myths to hide in order to preserve in pristine purity the illusion that power in American hands is *ipso facto* good. When that illusion is broken as in Vietnam, and now especially in the trials for alleged war crimes by our *own* "managers of violence," we are surprised, hurt, disillusioned, and in the mood to strike out in blind frustration against the truth about ourselves. It is the Army that has "crucified" Calley, the System that has made a few "scapegoats" for the highly placed leaders who "deserve to go to jail if anyone does"; it is the "dirty Communists" who have seduced us to play dirty ourselves and ruined our virtue; it is "the supreme crime of war" that cannot be bound by any rules whatsoever. Almost anyone but ourselves is responsible for the "way things are." We sense that the indictment of Calley is an indictment of ourselves as a people, and we feel tricked and confused that we now stand at the bar for crimes of death when we thought we were using blanks in a well-understood game. By definition Americans do not commit war crimes—we have been the nemesis of those who do. There have been "incidents," of course, explainable and hence excusable. But that atrocities have actually happened in Vietnam (until the Calley conviction they were not anchored down in history, not really real) now forces the unacceptable truth upon us of our guilt along with the Germans, the Japanese, the North Vietnamese —*the Enemy*. It is unbearable to discover the enemy in ourselves.

There is no detectable repentance because there is no real (which means particular, personal) assumption of guilt. Both the Vice-President and Chief of Staff General Westmoreland have made that absolutely clear. "I feel no guilt," says the

General, "not in the least." [45] And the Vice-President has asserted that as Americans it is time we quit kicking ourselves around.[46] When the Machine breaks down, who can blame the Machine? It is amoral. The parallel to the average German's reaction to the denazification attempt to acquaint him with the Nazi war crimes is depressing:

> The effort was a failure. Our propagandists found that it is almost impossible to induce people to think about what they prefer to forget. With few exceptions, Germans interviewed . . . stood at a far emotional distance from the Nazi crimes, feeling personally and morally uninvolved and unconcerned, or they denied the facts, or they projected the guilt on others, they rationalized and justified the atrocities, or they simultaneously engaged in several or all of these mental maneuvers, little inhibited by logical consistency.[47]

X. WHERE THERE IS PAIN—THERE IS HOPE

This is not, fortunately, the whole truth for us. There are those who search for wisdom and seek to profit from the bitter experiences of others and from the sometimes novel experiences given a people. Novel experiences abound for us today in "the way things are." The huge military establishment, literally the standing army so much feared by our Founding Fathers, has been a reality for a generation. Added to this fact is the undreamed-of power of the atom which we have conquered and a technology which has created the illusion of limitless expansion. Like Germany and Japan, we are undergoing a painful awakening from a dream of measureless greatness. But unlike those once powerful enemies, in large measure we still have control over our own destiny. Shakespeare reminds us that in times of great peril there is choice to be made at high tide:

> There is a tide in the affairs of men,
> Which, taken at the flood, leads on to fortune;

Omitted, all the voyage of their life
Is bound in shallows and in miseries.[48]

We are at the "flood" stage, but the "victory" can now be
only of the spirit. Illusions are not easily parted with—
especially when they become *delusions* for our having tried so
hard to make them real. The withdrawal symptoms from the
delusions of grandeur, of omnipotence, of purity, are bound
to be depressing, frightening, even disintegrating. We are at
such a stage now, but there is hope in our pain, for we are
closer to the truth and nearer to greatness than when we—for
so long—felt nothing at all. To rediscover ourselves and our
future as a people determined to be human in the highest
and best sense is to require humaneness at the center of the
modern experience of power, i.e., the military. It is surely
significant that the military is not least, nor last, in requiring
such a goal, in pursuing such a hope.

Here the experiences of others can be helpful. The President
has publicly expressed fear that America could not well survive the shock of admitting a mistake in Vietnam, and there
is considerable question that he will allow our guilt to stand
at My Lai. Nation-states simply do not do that sort of thing,
lest the credibility of their sovereignty (which is really an assertion of omnipotence as the "mortal god") is called into
question and the wolves begin to gather for the kill. Yet our
Fathers forced Britain to acknowledge defeat, and Britain did
not find the world had come to an end with the loss of its
colonies. Rather, it went on to build and to hold for more
than a century a world of its own, perhaps the most humane of
empires. Just possibly the British learned a degree of humility
in that "incident" which modified the inevitable illusions of
grandeur that plagued its rise to world power. France, losing
both Asia and Africa, and Germany and Japan crushed, have
nevertheless rebounded to greater, if less pretentious, strength
and affluence.

Germany in particular is instructive, and the Nuremberg trials and the Pacific trials in which General Tomoyuki Yamashita was convicted and hanged, although not ordering and probably unable to restrain his troops, are at the least compelling.[49] Although it took some initial prodding by alert newsmen to bring the My Lai situation to light, the Army moving ponderously nevertheless moved, and against its own. "The significant point," Representative Jerome Waldie (Dem., Calif.) has said, is that "this is the first time in history that a country which has not lost a war has admitted to having been involved in an atrocity." [50] In the white paper which the Army released in defense of the Calley trial and conviction, the Army contended that morally and legally it could not do otherwise.

Throughout the Vietnam war the Geneva conventions have had far more importance and weight than mere guides of conduct or courtesy on the battlefield. . . .

The conventions have been ratified by the United States and, as formal treaties, they are binding on both American civilians and their armed forces. Under the constitution, these treaties constitute part of the "supreme law of the land." Hence, in effect, the conventions are equal to the force of laws enacted by the Congress.

Accordingly, such conventions, which we have ratified,

cannot be abandoned and adopted again at will by U.S. armed forces, depending upon the character of the conflict or the non-observance of the conventions by the enemy.[51]

The Army has continued investigation of alleged misconduct by American soldiers. Whether this will be to the fullest in view of fear expressed at the highest of civilian levels of "tarnishing" the military image remains to be seen. Beyond this lies a much more difficult terrain which needs to be negotiated: Can the military and civilian leadership take the hard additional and decisive step of denouncing the more abstract and impersonal policy decisions involving starvation, defoliation, "free fire," and massive "sweep and kill" operations which likewise make no pretense of distinguishing combatant from noncombatant? Here officers and civilian leaders to the highest levels of the nation may need to feel and accept particular degrees of guilt, for the Machine is a living Machine which responds to the decisive, and sometimes irrational, will. The consequences of some high-level decisions, though not directly intended, must come under moral judgment as unacceptable "side effects":[52] in this case not far removed from genocide, once an ugly word identified solely with the inhuman enemy.

XI. NEEDED: RULES IN WARFARE

It is clear that I am suggesting the need of rules in warfare. This is far from evident to many today, both to the cynical who find all rules matters of expediency, and to the utopians who so passionately believe that war conducted in any manner at all is a crime. Yet, it must be admitted that there is a certain "honor even among thieves," if they are to be successful, i.e., there must be certain "behaviors" which can be counted upon, the expectation of obedience to certain rules of relationship and action. Indicting war as a crime does not ban it. The difficulty is that the nature of man and the nature of power are such as to require in every society, and especially in today's highly complex groupings of men, *a power to coerce,* the agency of last resort to force conformity to necessary rules of behavior. Without rules man could not even survive, let alone progress and find fulfillment and happiness. Absolute freedom is part of the illusion of omnipotence, the claimed ability to "do anything we want to do." But of course we can't. We are finite and bound by laws both physical and spiritual. Rational maturity for persons or for states is the coming to recognize and to accept the rules of order which serve to integrate and to identify us to ourselves and to others. It means also the appreciation of and the cooperation with other such complex and deciding units of power. In this mood and toward this end, we now turn—the *possibility* and the *necessity* of humanizing the military if we are to make and to keep man himself and his societies humane.

Chapter 10

The Humanizing
of
the Military

In this book I have suggested that power is the expression of being, and hence cannot be avoided. Anything that exists at all is an expression of "the power to be," and to the extent that it compels attention to and acceptance of this fact it uses or exerts power to persuade, and perhaps, as in willful beings, to force in cruder ways. But persons, being rational as well as volitional, can project and organize power in things and even other selves in ways to multiply unbelievably the total thrust and threat of power. In our time, man has done this to a near ultimate degree by splitting the atom and at once releasing and controlling the energy of suns. The sum total of power is now so great, matched by the participation of so many under the twin pressures of technological expansion and population explosion, that the need for managers has become acute. It is not unreasonable, given the urgency of the problems facing us today in the distribution and use of power, that the military are looked to increasingly. As historically the "managers of violence," the military have noted and are attempting to change with "the changing nature of power" [1] and the developing needs of their respective societies.

I. THE ARRIVAL OF THE MILITARY MANAGER

For instance, the change in the military structure from the singular and spectacular hero leaders whose charisma and exploits won decisive victories in battle, to the less colorful, even staid, "military managers" who, computer assisted, move power blocs and units about like chessmen on the great board of the world, is profound, and bespeaks a radically new era. Alasdair MacIntyre speaks of such a change in ancient Greece. The insular, closed in, unitary Homeric society, when the gods were close and everyone (nearly) was of one mind and knew what was right and wrong and good and bad, was an age of individual and heroic exploits. But in the age of Greece's greatness, when its sailors traded and fought in the seas and markets of the world, and the gods had abandoned them to fratricidal wars, people were less sure of the good and the right (except those who put Socrates to death). In such a time

the Homeric chieftain's personal values, the values of the courageous, cunning and aggressive king, [were] now, if exercised by the individual in the City-State, anti-social. Self-aggrandizement, the use of the state as something to be preyed upon, these are the only courses open to the individual who wants in the fifth century to behave like a Homeric hero. The social order in which his qualities were an essential part of a stable society has given way to one in which the same qualities are necessarily disruptive.[2]

In a world that cries for oneness and will not be denied, the nation-states with their focuses of powerful and highly competitive military machines are unquestionably anachronistic and disruptive, and there are some military men who are beginning to suspect this. Deeper than the sometimes successful "goodwill ambassadorship" of many of our uniformed personnel abroad is the traditional professionalism of a vocation which is committed to order and the values of service and sacrifice which induce respect and even a certain camaraderie across national boundaries. Harvey Wheeler, in answering a question as to whether America can "restrain itself from further adventures," replies:

No, unless of course, we are able to see how uneconomic it is to maintain the nation-state system and take the lead toward some kind of world order. If we continue to insist on paying the price of maintaining a nation-state system we are going to get into a series of confrontations that can't help but be disastrous.[3]

Wheeler's alternative to the nation-state system is not a homogenized world but something closer to the ancient city-state culture on a universal scale: the deliberate encouragement of cultural pluralism.

That means we are going to have new kinds of communities, smaller ones, more mansize.

You may well find different communities purposely adopting a style and a character marking them off as their own.[4]

What kind of people will it take to accomplish the transition to a real world community? Surprisingly, Wheeler answers: Eisenhower, the military manager par excellence. And exactly for the reason that Ike was scorned while President and still has not achieved a place on the top shelf of American Presidents—his famed "do nothing" attitude! "Eisenhower regarded the presidency as something that should not be strong, shouldn't be a bastion of power and manipulation." Staff work diffused the heroic executive image, and he applied the same technique to the military. Crises had a way of disappearing because he simply refused to make much of them. Wheeler says crises are "artifacts of the modern world," [5] very much the product of men's imagined worlds. With the possibility of collisions between private worlds so vastly enhanced today, there is much to be said for diffusing the

power centers on every possible occasion. Despite Ike's crusader attitude which prevented him from entertaining a German general at the war's end, he was able to overcome this
self-imposed barrier and become the inspiration of the "people to people" ideal. Ike has been called an "Artist in Iron," [6]
but the real iron with which he worked was in men's souls,
bringing together into "one team" such naturally assertive and antagonistic warriors as Montgomery, Patton, and
Churchill himself. The quiet of the "Eisenhower era," which
followed the crisis years of Truman, is so singular in this
generation as to seem "unreal" to some critics. Perhaps, in
such a fermenting and violent period as ours, reality lies in
"creative inaction" as the Taoists teach us:

> Tao invariably does nothing,
> And yet there is nothing that is not done.[7]

Richard Rhodes in his portrait of and tribute to "Ike: An
Artist in Iron," says that in giving all of his adult life to
his country, Ike subdued "an immense inner violence to his
goal of peace." [8] That is the clue. The volcano must be
capped, controlled, used. "We train them to kill" but for
what purpose, and when, and how? Shortly after the My Lai
trial Eric Sevareid reviewed the case and the traditional restraints which professional military men have put upon themselves and which have become the object of attack by those
who insist that war has no rules. "If," he says, "we step
beyond the rules, beyond the Monday-morning quarterback
criticism (of our failures), *we step into the void.*" [9] If, as I
have contended, power and its use are unavoidable, and the
focus of power in every society rests finally in those willing
to assume an "unlimited liability" for the life or death of
their society, then there is always need for the "managers of
violence," those who are willing but not anxious to form the
police and military institutions of the state. The uniqueness

of military power, I have suggested, lies in its fusion of ultimates, its bridging of opposites, the subduing of "an immense inner violence to . . . peace," the creation of a state of "creative inaction."

People who can do this, who can actually manage violence without increasing violence—perhaps even reduce it—and not for the honor of an individual, or a squad, or a division, or even a nation, but for the good of man—such people are not easily come by. Such expectation is a far cry from the simplistic and crude "train them to kill" expectation in the minds of many today. Literally, the military needs the best and most humane men and women it can get in any age, and especially today—people who will not panic at the center of the maelstrom or forget that all men, even the enemy, are human. They must not be the types who gloat in the use of power, who want power for its own sake.

II. WHY *NOT* A VOLUNTEER ARMY?

There are good reasons against a volunteer army: the likelihood of getting the authoritarian and aggressive types (the Pattons who might overwhelm the Eisenhowers and the Bradleys),[10] and in the lower ranks probably a disproportion of the poor and racially deprived groups. Reduction of the American military to an attempted fusion of aggressive and alienated persons would rapidly confirm the separation of the modern military from the parent society and encourage it to be antithetic to the best interests of the nation. It could become a much more powerful, because coherent and arbitrary, bloc than it is now. But above all, it would provide an easy escape for the rest of us from daily confronting the issues of power and conscience, and from our actually sharing in responsibility for the humanness of the nation. Alfred B. Fitt, former Assistant Defense Secretary and now adviser to the president of Yale, although not certain of some of the above arguments, still finds that "the price is too high" for a volunteer army because he has "a felt sense that the burden of military service should somehow be distributed across all classes of American society, even if imperfectly." [11] Mr. Fitt seems to be implying principles of individual obligation to society and equality in its administration with which I fully agree. Deeper than this, however, I am concerned with maintaining our sanity and with what Hans Morgenthau has called "the real source of [our] strength: the moral example [America] has presented to the rest of the world." [12] Our military power, and its tragic consequences from Hiroshima to My Lai, can no longer be ignored, rationalized, or made the responsibility of anyone (or institution) but of ourselves as the people.

Nor ought we to trust its containment and necessary use to others than ourselves. Painful as it is and will be, we need the reminder in every home in the land and at every age level of the real costs of power. The illusion of omnipotence is as appealing to the hardhat and Joe Blow as to the President who cannot lose a war. It also is a symptom of insanity and long before that it rationalizes our inhumanity. The draft with all its imperfections does keep the costs before us. Without it we probably would never have heard of My Lai. And beyond keeping the cost before us, the constant infusion of civilians into the Armed Forces continually encourages its humanization.

III. CAN THE MILITARY BE HUMANIZED?

Without question, the modern military needs humanization. The question is whether it can be done in any sustained and effective way. A curious alliance of "realists" and idealists join forces in denying the effort. Both seem to agree that war, and those involved with it, are inimical to concerns other than the most efficient accomplishment of their jobs, i.e., killing. Yet our study of the elements of military power, the testimony of the vast majority of military thinkers, and the trials of Lieutenant Calley and others, all agree that difficult as it is, it can be done and is being done. So concerned and successful is the effort, in fact, in the view of many from the perspective of lifetime careers, that there is constant danger of the military's own version of self-righteousness: its determined sense of virtues and values superior to the civilian world. "I would prefer that decent people fight the wars, rather than . . . immoral people," says Brigadier General Sidney B. Berry, whom many regard as destined to be a Chief of Staff.[13] And he means it. His attitude finds no place for the morals of a Calley, although at a more abstract level he might find little difficulty in designating a free fire zone, or even, perhaps, triggering tactical nuclear weapons. But it would be according to rules calmly and deliberately, if coldly, fashioned in the service of ideals larger than self, as large as the nation, and capable of expansion to man. Who can question but that this was accomplished in genuinely human ways in Washington, Marshall, Nimitz, Eisenhower, Bradley?

The thoughtful writings of American military men today indicate that just such humanization of the ultimate power they hold is of increasing concern to them. It is of particular importance that this has been coming about among the "innovative elite" and the younger men coming into the services in recent years. The Academies, as we have noted, increasingly are stressing the humanities. Despite continuing problems, the Armed Forces have been ahead of the nation in integrating blacks and whites, and beyond the required "Vietnamization" policies they have undertaken many worthwhile and effective humane endeavors.[14] The My Lai exposé and trials, despite the feared tarnishing of the Army image, are clearly on target, even against the mood of much of the nation. Indeed, there seems more serious and profoundly open thinking going on among a rising number of military opinion makers than may be found among many of their counterparts in government, business, and academia respecting the "changing nature of power." The liberalized policies for the living styles of the troops, the "mod" look which is coming to each of the services in its own way, are at the least an honest attempt to continue exploration in democratizing military power and in giving each man some sense of acceptance as representative of rationality and cultural diversity. Input, even to the modification of policies, as well as output, is being generated. It may not succeed, and there are always risks with shared power. But the alternative in the age of ultimate power is vastly worse, and the idea of democracy as we have attempted to work it out in practice accepts both horns of the dilemma, the enduring tension between negative and positive understandings of the nature of man and the power he uses. The long experience of the military in attempting to fuse dynamic opposites may better prepare its members for the judicious, restrained but creative use of power than "straight" civilians in today's world. Certainly the experience of this century is that we have more to fear from civilian leaders who become fascinated with military gamesmanship and the role of commander in chief (the Kaiser, Hitler, Kennedy, Johnson, Nixon) than the armies they created and commanded, or generals turned President. For reasons I have tried to indicate, military power is that focus of fused power in any society which as ultimate power simply *is* fascinating. In the atomic age a little knowledge of such power can be a dangerous, even disastrous, thing. Japan is perhaps the best modern example of the military strongly influencing—perhaps even commanding—governmental policy. But in the West it is not wise to forget that generally the military has dragged its feet initially on adventures and that our military Presidents have been even slower to engage the enemy. The contrast between Eisenhower and his successors is only the latest in such examples. As *rational* controllers of violence, military people are first of all committed to *order* rather than adventure for its own sake.

IV. THE UNFINISHED BUSINESS
OF THE FATHERS

What is needed is a true partnership between the military institution and the parent society that will preserve the historic subordination of the military to civil control but will also encourage intermingling and the shared sense of responsibilities in every sort of way. It may seem that this is exactly what we now have with the effective marriage of the military to industry and government. But the dichotomy between the military *as such* wherever found, and its civilian world, has remained. It has been a marriage of convenience, of necessity, and the enduring sense of alienation, of difference, of suspicion, has driven each partner to ensure his own ego strength, to build his own empire. The military, always subconsciously fearful of being sent back to its own little cage in the zoo for wild animals, puts no responsible limit on its continued growth. The civilian masters, affecting to despise military crudity, use it at arm's length (or country's length) for their own separate and often differing "needs." We have not really faced up to the permanence of a standing army. The Founding Fathers tried to cut the Gordian knot by rejecting the idea altogether and were not, over the long haul, successful, although their attitude acted in positive ways of restraint. But the restraint could not hold in the face of the twin pressures of nuclear threat and runaway technology, and the future offers little hope of significant lessening of outward pressures. *Therefore, the unfinished business of the Fathers, i.e., the redefinition of power, especially as it is focused in the institution of the military today, to make it acceptable and creatively human rather than hypocritically rejected or cynically allowed to do its worst—this is our task. And there isn't much time.*

In the last analysis, as Adam Yarmolinski, former aide to Defense Secretary McNamara, says, "The American people get the kind of military establishment they deserve." [15] Judging from the furor raised by the Calley conviction, we may deserve "The Dirty Dozen" enlarged to international scope and paid as mercenaries. Left to itself, the military as an organization required as a means to perform an ultimate function for society, cannot and will not develop an adequate ethic. Even its traditional insistence upon humane rules in warfare looks with a keen eye to greater ease of operations where people are not antagonized unnecessarily.[16] The military as a means needs the constant informing of the ends for which it exists, and this can come only from the society it is called to serve. The military, then, needs constant interaction with the civil family of which it is a true member (not an illegitimate son); it needs periodic infusion of new blood, ideas, and the highest ideals ventured by its family to keep it relevant to the deepest purposes of the nation. In a world that has become a family of nations (with all the opportunities and tendencies for quarreling in a family), the larger sense of the family of man must inform the ideals and purposes of nations which are made concrete in the actions and nonactions of our Armed Forces. If we can seriously look at ourselves as a people, *one* of the peoples of the earth, accept our limitations as human and redefine our goals in less than arbitrary and ultimate terms, we have the best chance history has yet afforded a nation to command its awesome power for human good.

It will not be easy. The British may seem to provide an encouraging if partial model of a society which came to terms with its military institution in ways that generally did both credit. But the British, like the Byzantines before them, did not achieve their (at best) partial success in the Nuclear Age in which the demonic depths of being have been revealed to possess all too easily its would-be "managers." Moreover, our religious rather than rational (mis-)understanding of power which compels us to redeem its every use in a crusade, blinds us to those same demonic depths that betray our best intentions. This is the lesson of the Pentagon Papers: that responsible men, obedient to the illusions of power, could so readily lead the nation into the depths while earnestly believing their actions to be just and right. The tragedy is laced with irony, for as a people we deceived ourselves, and the inevitable and bitter decisions that we now must make are so much of our own choosing. The tragedy, of course, must remain as a fact of history that will continue to generate its own effects. But the irony may dissolve as we become aware of and assume responsibility for our own complicity in the irrational demonic.[17]

This is the first stage in our "coming to ourselves." Like the prodigal son, it is taking a while, literally the exhaustion of our vanities and pretensions to absolute power, which, as the late Reinhold Niebuhr reminded us, "means contrition." [18] After that there is still the long journey home. The easiest thing in the world would be to fake it (and the contrition). Our incurable optimism and abiding faith in progress, our constant claim on the future (despite its capacity for "shock"), and our belief in ourselves as the spiritual as well as lineal descendants of daring pioneer stock, will compel us to accept as challenges the salvaging of our misguided adventure in Vietnam and the refashioning of the military in "mod" style to match the mood of the times. "If anyone can do it, we can," and it must be done. We shall probably recall the motto of the fabled Seabees of World War II written quite concretely across half a world: "The difficult we do daily; the impossible takes a little longer."

It is the impossible indeed that has now become necessary in the Nuclear Age: the forswearing of power for destruction, the deliberate redefinition of power for creative human good, and the sustained insight into our propensity for confusing the two. It will not be enough to attempt "salvaging" and "face-saving," or even the "face-lifting" of "the new look" of the modern military. New wine, Jesus once warned, will break the old containers (Matt. 9:17). Not naïve, but certainly bold, thinking must be done respecting the rising necessity of a "moral equivalent for war" to which William James called attention long ago. Karl Jaspers and others have suggested with the utmost seriousness that man may well be approaching a possible new breakthrough, *beyond war,* which will separate him as "postmodern" or "spiritual" man from modern and aggressive man as clearly as "axial" man is now distinguished from ancient and primitive man.[19] A modern French writer, retracing the steps of de Tocqueville in America, concludes that the truly twentieth century revolution is already happening in the United States, "the first revolution in history in which disagreement on values and goals is more pronounced than disagreement on the means of existence." [20] In a far cry from the "merchants of death" thesis of a generation ago, segments of the business community, as well as many of our youth, are coming to the conclusion that war is simply obsolete.[21] If that kind of alliance can be sustained, if the economic bases of war begin to yield seriously to the moral challenge of the young, and we find only peace is profitable, we may indeed be set upon a path for the redefinition of military power. This is not visionary or naïve in the old sense of unilateral disarmament. It is simply (but with the utmost difficulty, since we belong so much to the past) keeping ourselves open to the future and the possibility, at least, that men can, sometimes radically, reorder their existence and relations in more human ways. It is to recognize the "role of expectancy" as "self-fulfilling prophecy" which may work as surely for peace as for war.[22] As "utopic . . . it has nothing in its favor, except that it is absolutely necessary if mankind is to survive." [23]

This may not be push enough, but nothing less will sustain the rethinking about power and the military's power which must be done. The military is not about to vote itself out of existence (what institution ever does?), even though General Eisenhower may have asserted that this is the military's eventual objective.[24] Such an objective is so easily relegated to the future as to dissolve all responsibility for living men. But now arises the paradox: Survival itself in the Nuclear Age may well depend upon the "utopian" abolition of war. Not in some never-never time of the future, which is meaningless, but in ours—at least in initiating serious beginnings. A senior naval officer unerringly strikes to the heart of the agonizing question for a small but growing number in military service today when he says that "the antinomian character of much of the military's rationalization seems to suggest that the military can be humanized only as its own existence is threatened." [25]

In all sorts of fumbling ways, less driven than some by selfish interests and the subtle push of the demonic, many in the military today do grope to make the constructive thrust central to their power. Such sensitive thinkers and leaders must be supported in various ways which can only appear as "short steps," but are nonetheless necessary, on the long road toward solution of the problems of human power. For if the abyss which has opened before us (and within us as the irrational demonic) can in any sense become the threshold of a more human future, it will be well to remember that such crossings in the past have taken centuries rather than years. They have involved not one institution but many, if not all. Revel, for instance, claims that the new twentieth-century revolution can only succeed in America because only here can be found the confluence of five different revolutions at once: political, social, cultural, international, interracial. These revolutions must occur simultaneously or not at all.[26] But even then the crossing will be uneven; not everybody will follow, not everybody will cross. History, which is to say man, moves with the vanguard. The thesis of this book is simply that in the age of power the gravest temptations for its misuse lie precisely with those who are called to manage its most ultimate expressions, but this does not exempt the rest of us who are as inevitably, if in lesser ways, involved in its meaning and use. Unquestionably, the military in our time needs radical curtailing, but even its eradication would not solve the basic problem of human power which would surely surface in other and perhaps even more demonic forms. Our hope lies in the widening and deepening insights of a vanguard in all our institutions who sense when they cannot always see the egoism and aggressiveness of human nature itself which so easily descends to violence. It is a matter of some hope that there are glimmerings of such insight and a core of concern and even readiness for change beyond simple restraint in the military itself. The vanguards now must join if the crossing is to be made. They can do so in "short steps" which to begin with will be faltering and unsure.

V. DEFINING NATIONAL GOALS

Probably the most important such step we could make as a people today would be an intensive effort to define our national goals. Our country is deeply divided and we are vastly unclear as to where we are, or should be, going. The resulting insecurity makes us defensive, and easily set on edge against one another both at home and abroad. Thus the problem of goals is deeply intertwined with the problem of attitudes: it is doubtful if we can do much about defining our goals unless we move at the same time to modify our attitudes.

We are beginning to do this. The sign carried by a young Ohio girl in the 1968 Presidential election, "Please bring us together," struck a responsive chord in the nation.[27] Despite polarization—indeed because of it—there are deep undercurrents of desire and hope, reservoirs of positive willingness to declare a moratorium on aggressive actions, to encourage deliberately an *etiquette of civility* both at home and abroad. In an ancient, but similar, "warring states" period Confucius initiated a "deliberate tradition" [28] of manners and grace that defined in five great relationships the ways in which men (and nations) ought to act toward one another. The process is slow by which men *act,* and then come to *believe in their acts* and a general climate of expectation gives substance to the habits of a whole society. It is time to turn around our acts in which we have come to believe so tenaciously and with such mounting disappointment and even fear—the aggressiveness of our daily confrontations with one another and the world. The possibilities of confrontation leading to conflict on every level of our society are multiplying with such speed and force today that we need the caution of a new habit (and then conviction) that "a soft answer turneth away wrath" (Prov. 15:1). Somehow we must begin to dilute the basically selfish and increasingly dangerous attitude of competition. If the protests of many of our youth today, many of them from the affluent levels of this nation, have any meaning at all, it is clearly the conviction that widely shared goals—as wide as mankind—are not only morally right but humanly necessary.

We could begin at home, at the grass roots. Alvin Toffler, in *Future Shock,* asks us to

imagine the historic drama, the power and evolutionary impact, if each of the high-technology nations literally set aside the next five years as a period of intense national self-appraisal; if at the end of five years it were to come forward with its own tentative agenda for the future, a program embracing not merely economic targets but, equally important, broad sets of social goals—if each nation, in effect, stated to the world what it wished to accomplish for its people and mankind in general during the remaining quarter century of the millennium.[29]

We could begin that process with the creation of what Toffler calls "social future assemblies," *ad hoc* committees made up of representatives of the social units of the nation—business, labor, government, church, schools, art, women, ethnic groups—gathered together in every community, possibly paralleling or modeled upon the existing political party organizations. The power of a concern to generate a "people's response" is evident in numerous consumer, environmental, and sensitivity groups which have been springing up around the nation. They suggest that similar rather spontaneous groups concerned with redefining national priorities and goals could arise with a little prodding and leadership.[30] This could be an exciting exercise in "participatory democracy" at a time when so many are "turned off" from the Machine of Big Government, in which they feel they have no voice at all. Such "brainstorming" committees could possibly become standing committees for constant review of national social goals, and the possible input of fresh ideas and faces to the national bureaucracy, which at best is in a highly creaking condition today, could be vastly important.

On the international level, the United Nations already provides a world forum for such a world discussion of the national aims of states. In reaching down to the grass roots, in inviting participation at community levels respecting the goals of the nation in the world community, we could begin to develop the idea of "a kind of world order that doesn't deny the nation-state necessarily, but simply supplements and overrides it in certain areas." [31] The effort should encourage clarification of aims of sovereign states, bring national purposes under some degree of international scrutiny and judgment, and thereby assist in tempering both national aspirations and suspicions of those aspirations.[32] It would be a bold stroke if America would take the initiative in some such delineation of, and accommodation to, the "manifest destiny" syndrome of nations and men. If such a project appears naïve, it can hardly match the naïveté of assuming that we can go on as we have been doing, or that humaneness will be achieved by imposition from above.

At the very least the military establishment needs to know that the nation is fully aware of where it is going before it commits its young men to the battlefield, that it has rationally defined its goals which make sense among men, that in achieving its purposes it has consciously rejected the illusion of omnipotence and is prepared to limit itself in significant ways in order to remain human and indeed promote the human community. This is simply asking what more and more people are demanding: that we develop a set of priorities that we can live with, that we can devote ourselves to, and that we can accomplish with moral pride. But it would be done in the light of the day, the world's day. It would be a spiritual counterpart (but not without political significance) to our highly successful invitation to the world to accompany us in man's first landing on the moon. *This* "giant step for mankind" could be of infinitely greater consequence to the future of man.

VI. OPTIONAL SERVICE

A further suggestion conceivably could be as meaningful. Retaining the concept of Reserve-expansible military forces, such forces could well be encouraged to participate in useful social service beyond the fragmentary efforts of some units today. This could be done in two ways: (1) by broadening the concerns and activities of inactive Reservists (committed to monthly training but not on active duty) to include badly needed community work, such as in hospitals, schools, perhaps assistance to community police forces, etc.; and (2) by actively cooperating with the already established "alternative service" possibilities which now exist or might additionally be created, such as ACTION (now including VISTA, the Peace Corps, etc.), the long-established and admirable Friends Service Committee and other religious and humanitarian efforts in this country and abroad.

With regard to broadening Reserve training and use beyond the techniques of bearing weapons and drilling (which are rather quickly mastered), to positive community involvement, the immediate result would be the dissipation of the almost unbelievable boredom that exists among many trainees today. The sense of positive accomplishment in humane endeavor would do much to make the training and "stand by" duty acceptable as being useful and meaningful. This is especially important in the lower ranks where there is little or no interest in promotion to command positions. It would also serve as appreciated outlets for the concerned idealism of many youth today who are already strongly motivated to "do something about the environment," or the schools, or the hospitals, and who at the very least see the military as "wasting their time." It *is* wasting their time in altogether too many instances. Reserve training is often negative education which further distorts the image of the military and the wisdom of the society. With cities dying for lack of attention to roads, to ghettos, to garbage, it does seem that without threat to the labor market Reservists in periodic training could lend a hand to the benefit of all concerned.

Adam Yarmolinsky, in his important Twentieth Century Fund Study, *The Military Establishment*, lifts up the same appalling social needs in reminding us that the military alone has no manpower shortage, even in times of peace. The time has now come, he says, when the military must make "the transition from primacy to competition among equals" in the allocation of the nation's manpower and other resources. In the nature of the case this will not be easy:

It will be as difficult for this generation of the American military as for the first-born who has to learn that while his parents still care for him, he is not an only child anymore. But the transition has to be made; one way—among others—to encourage it would be to make the opportunity to draw on a national service pool available to other priority claimants on public spending, or to make voluntary service with such other claimants grounds for exemption from military service.[33]

The point is, of course, that the nation has needs which are deeper and lie beyond the needs of defense, that is, we are beginning to ask with the utmost seriousness, *Defense of what?* and *Is survival enough?* The deterioration within is so serious that its claims must now be given priority equal to, or perhaps even surpassing, the needs of defense. The nation has never assumed such responsibility for shortages in medical and social needs at home, but

if . . . the principle of mandatory service were not only accepted but also applied beyond the military to other forms of national service, equally urgent and important for the country, the military would have the benefits of a public policy declaration in favor of a priority allocation of manpower as befits a critical public function, but it would not be identified as the sole repository of the responsibility for safeguarding the nation's security and its most sacred values. Other activities—the education of disadvantaged children, the delivery of health services to groups whose health needs are badly neglected, the organization of communities to achieve genuine participation in American society, the preservation of domestic public order with justice—all these and more could then be recognized, as they are not now, as essential in the same sense that the military function is regarded as essential.[34]

Doubtless this will conjure up for some the specter of the monolithic state further encroaching upon the freedom of its citizens. This is part of the rationale for protesting the military draft. Still, that right of the state seems firmly and morally established—the right to preserve itself as part of the larger good of man and the responsibility of its citizens to assist it in doing so. But man owes more than mere security to the state. In deeply personal ways he owes his very humanness to the constraints and requirements (laws) of society, as well as to the opportunities for certain freedom and growth which being in community provides for man. Socrates long ago suggested this in describing "the laws" as his parents, to whom he owed both his life and its well-being.[35] Modern psychology has confirmed that we can hardly be human without interaction with others, with all that this entails in assuming responsibilities which both limit and open up freedom for men. It would seem, then, that some limited form of universal service, carefully safeguarded and made optional in the type of service to be rendered, is both morally sound and socially necessary today.

There is here the opportunity to push beyond the nation-state concept to recognition of the needs of man. Universal military service rightly has never been bought in this country. The chances of bureaucratization and waste of time and money, and, most important, the lives of impressionable young people, are too great. The negative education of the Reserve training units is bad enough. But formally and actively to provide and promote different options of service, all meaningful, all acceptable, and international as well as national, would be to tap the energies of the intelligent, resourceful, and exceptionally dedicated youth of today for the world's work which so desperately needs doing. It would provide a positive cause *to be for*, rather than the inequitable draft to be against. It would win sympathy or at least grudging respect for the Establishment as showing some capacity for personal interest in those whose services it must require, and beyond them to the increasingly desperate social needs of the nation and world. Perhaps most important, such optional service could bring the polarized groups of our youth (and elders) together in some kind of *working*, if not always fully understood and appreciated, consensus. The education as to the needs and claims of the human society, both civil and military, would be an ongoing thing as well as a constant reminder that as a people we also belong to the family of man.[36]

I have no doubt but that given other options, many would still choose the military because of temperament, particular skills and interests, and perhaps encouraged by a balancing agent of shorter time or promotional and career benefits. Considering the "unlimited liability" under which military persons are called to live and die, some adjustments in their favor would doubtless be just. In this connection, it would be wise to allow for shorter military careers, perhaps only ten years for retirement, perhaps two- to five-year "hitches" with significant terminal benefits in education, career training, low interest rates for business loans, etc. The ROTC should be encouraged to have a respected place on many campuses on the simple basis of need for the best and most humanly educated persons to serve in the Armed Forces. With the prospect increasing that most people will have more than one career in the future, indeed that retraining once or more in a lifetime will be required in the national interest, the attractiveness and feasibility of one of those careers being willingly and usefully spent in some branch of the service, seems reasonable. Together these options could bring about a volunteer military force, or nearly so, but the pool from which selection, or rather acceptance, would be made, would be vastly greater. The parallelism of service, the equality of so-called civil or military duty, would help to mitigate the jealousies and hostilities which now pit even the best-intentioned people against one another.

At the national level, some kind of Council or Review and Policy Board, made up of a broad spectrum of military and civic leaders, including, doubtless, governmental representatives, but more importantly representatives of the Peace Corps, VISTA, the Friends Service Committee, science, education, and business could materially assist in creating the necessary team-work for the definition and control of military power in this country. John Kenneth Galbraith suggests that business, for instance, is already disenchanted with its marriage to the military and is ready to settle for some restraint on the growth of the liaison. He calls for a "special body of highly qualified scientists and citizens to be called, perhaps, the Military Audit Commission" whose function as "an independent arm of the Congress" would be to advise authoritatively on proposed weapons systems, their effect on international tensions, profits, etc.[37] Yarmolinsky proposes something similar: "a joint congressional committee on the military constructed to make it a watchdog over the Pentagon rather than a poodle for it." [38]

These suggestions illustrate to some degree the principle of what Alvin Toffler calls "adhocracy," the bypassing of hierarchy already established in favor of groups of specialists called in to "brainstorm" solutions.[39] Such a group, but broader based and made permanent, perhaps by statute, might constitute a strong advisory board to the Congress and/or the President. As a permanent working group it could possibly grow out of the earlier suggested "grass roots" exercise in exploring national goals. Discovered leaders might be selected upward, or appointed, to help define the national goals at the highest levels. But they could go farther: they might give particular attention to the *means,* i.e., to the manpower and resources, for achieving such goals. They should in their separate and several capacities of representing and promoting distinct and necessary branches of service in the country, *both* civil and military, come to appreciate and accept one another as performing necessary and important service beyond the nation to the world. It would be enlightening, as well as fascinating, to see the hard-core military officer and the soft-core pacifist, the humanitarian and the profit-wise industrialist, learning from one another in the common pursuit of national and human goals. Something of this mutual and growing appreciation would surely trickle down to "the troops" and help set the mood and the conditions for the uniting of men and nations.

VII. AMERICA FIRST—
IN THINGS OF THE SPIRIT

Years ago, before My Lai, when there was hardly a cloud the size of a man's hand on the horizon of America's conscience, G. Ashton Oldham penned words that seemed like a clarion call to social conscience but today have the curiously hollow ring of half-truth, the most subtle and dangerous of all truths. Like imperial England, which proudly bore "the white man's burden," America then saw only the generosity of its strength, and was almost blithely certain that it could be

> first, not only in things material,
> But in things of the spirit.
> Not merely in science, invention, motors, skyscrapers,
> But also in ideals, principles, character.
> Not merely in the calm assertion of rights,
> But in the glad assumption of duties.
>
> Not flouting her strength as a giant,
> But bending in helpfulness over a sick and wounded world like
>   a Good Samaritan.
> Not in splendid isolation,
> But in courageous cooperation.
>
> Not in pride, arrogance, and disdain of other races and peoples,
> But in sympathy, love, and understanding.
> Not in treading again the old, worn, bloody pathway which ends
>   inevitably in chaos and disaster,
> But blazing a new trail along which, please God, other nations
>   will follow into the new Jerusalem where wars shall be no
>   more.[40]

It is obvious that these words are from the age of our innocence, blandly assertive of America's dreamlike superiority, which we felt then, instead of the rough and tempered hope of its greatness, which can be the only basis of our claim today, now that a sword prevents our reentering the garden of innocence. For a moment, under the youthful Kennedy, the nation again caught its breath in renewed expectancy of the Dream. But on a crushing, bitter November day, and in the wintry days that followed, Camelot died and we awoke to find the Round Table really broken and the knights all scattered and dead. Like Sir Galahad, whose strength was "as the strength of ten" because his heart was pure, we found the Grail—only to tarnish it. Which is to say that to come to ourselves is to awaken to the real world where the only gardens are *made* and not given, and the serpent is party to our every intention and effort.

Still the Dream lingers—the Promise of a new earth and the One City of Man. As worldly-wise and pragmatic a theoretician of the politics of power as Hans Morgenthau finds that America's strength actually resides in its uncomfortably high moral compulsion that "the American Revolution was not made for America alone but for mankind." [41] Morgenthau goes on to say:

It is exactly because the United States has been fascinated with military power—with the number and efficiency and the destructive capability of nuclear warheads—that it has neglected the real source of its strength: the moral example it has presented to the rest of the world. [42]

If Revel is right, that the revolution of the twentieth century is one of values and is already beginning in the United States, then the Dream itself is valid. But it can be claimed only in ways that are fully and humbly human, and not as Camelot.

A Bibliographical Note

The reservoir of writings which lies back of this book seems oceanic in range and diversity. Yet wider seas break upon the horizon almost daily. The Pentagon Papers, prematurely released, only suggest the almost limitless resources for the study of war and the military which, it is hoped, will be more available in the future than they have been in the past. This study makes no claim to either classified secrets or exotic materials. I have used those sources which lie close at hand, readily available to everyone: books well worn by the generations, and military journals, with some civilian periodicals. The system of rather full notes is designed to assist the serious student who may desire greater detail and additional references. For intensive study, however, it may be helpful briefly to indicate certain general sources as well as the specific core of contemporary writings used in this work.

GENERAL SOURCES

The foundations, it is evident, are laid in the classics, from the Great Greeks to our own Founding Fathers, and include

Augustine, Luther, and Calvin quite as much as Hobbes, Descartes, and Locke. In our own time, which is also theological as well as political, Reinhold Niebuhr, Paul Tillich, Arnold Toynbee, Dietrich Bonhoeffer, Alfred Whitehead, Martin Buber, and Karl Jaspers have been the most seminal for me; but a plethora of other thinkers to whom I have been exposed attests to the richness and depth of contemporary thinking about man and his future: Walter Lippmann, John Bennett, Paul Ramsey, Hans Morgenthau, Max Lerner, Scott Buchanan, John Hutchison, John Cobb, Harvey Seifert. More specifically, studies bearing directly upon war, the military institution, and militarism range as widely and include Xenophon, Clausewitz, C. W. Oman, Quincy Wright, Walter Millis, Glenn Gray, Morris Janowitz, Samuel Huntington, and Alfred Vagts. A host of others, from Thucydides, Caesar, Machiavelli, Grotius, Vatell, Maurice de Saxe, Baron de Jomini, and Napoleon to Liddell Hart, J. F. C. Fuller, Russell Weigley, James Flexner, Lynn Montross, and Herman Kahn, have recorded campaigns, left memoirs, described armies, and outlined tactics and principles. Lastly, to the provocative interest of Freud and James in the psychology of war must be added today's gathering insights into the nature of violence as a whole spectrum of attitudes and actions. Erich Fromm, John Masland, Rollo May, and others representing the deepening interest of government (see the National Commission on the Causes and Prevention of Violence, etc.) have contributed greatly to understanding the phenomenon especially as it has been expressed in our own history as a people.

SPECIFIC SOURCES

These are of two kinds: (1) Unclassified military directives and studies that include *The Armed Forces Officer; Principles and Problems of Naval Leadership;* histories of military units and the chaplains corps; studies by the President's Committee on Religion and Welfare in the Armed Forces; and the *Moral Leadership Program* materials which have varied considerably in content and acceptance in the several branches of the American Armed Forces. These latter materials include the Duty-Honor-Country series of the Army; the *Because of You, This Is My Life, Our Moral and Spiritual Growth: Here and Now,* as well as the more recent Vietnam-inspired *Personal Response Project* materials of the Navy; and the attractive, but loosely titled, packets of Air Force materials. (2) But the core of the work is found in contemporary military journals, with some assistance from a number of civilian periodicals. Altogether these publications cover roughly the post-World War II period but concentrate on the years 1955–1971. The military journals, given in order of importance to this study by service branch are:

ARMY: *Military Review; Army; Military Affairs; Armor.*

NAVY (and MARINE CORPS): *United States Naval Institute Proceedings; Naval War College Review; Marine Corps Gazette.*

AIR FORCE: *Air University Review; Air Power Historian; Air Force and Space Digest; Airman.*

GENERAL: *Journal of the Armed Forces; The Chaplain.*

Civilian publications which have been of particular interest, aside from news magazines and newspapers, include *The Center Magazine* with its "Occasional Papers," *Vital Speeches, Saturday Review, Congressional Quarterly Weekly Review, Atlantic, The Progressive, The Wall Street Journal, The New Republic, Foreign Affairs, The Bulletin of Atomic Scientists, The Christian Century, Harvard Business Review, America, The Nation, Annals of the American Academy of Political Science, The American Political Science Review, Christianity and Crisis.*

Notes

PREFACE

1. Quincy Wright, *A Study of War*, 2 vols. (The University of Chicago Press, 1942; abridged by Louise L. Wright, 1 vol., 1964); Walter Millis, *Arms and Men: A Study of American Military History* (Mentor Book, The New American Library, 1956); Alfred Vagts, *A History of Militarism: Civilian and Military*, rev. ed. (Meridian Books, Inc., 1959); Lynn Montross, *War Through the Ages*, rev. and enlarged 3d ed. (Harper & Brothers, 1960).

2. Morris Janowitz, *The Professional Soldier: A Social and Political Portrait* (The Fress Press of Glencoe, 1960); Samuel P. Huntington, *The Soldier and the State: The Theory and Politics of Civil-Military Relations* (The Belknap Press of Harvard University Press, 1964).

3. Leon Bramson and George W. Goethals (eds.), *War: Studies from Psychology, Sociology, Anthropology* (Basic Books, Publishers, Inc., 1964).

4. See Aristophanes, *Peace*, newly translated from the Greek by Robert Henning Webb (The University Press of Virginia, 1964).

5. Ward Just, *Military Men* (Alfred A. Knopf, Inc., 1970); first published under the title "Soldiers" in *Atlantic*, Oct. and Nov., 1970.

6. *Ibid.*, pp. 5 f. (*Atlantic*, Oct., 1970, p. 60).

7. See the cover story in *Time*, "The Military Goes Mod," Dec. 21, 1970.

8. Ward Just, in his excellent study which is almost altogether based upon interviews, too quickly and unjustly, I believe, brushes aside written sources (*Military Men*, pp. 5 f.).

Chapter 1. THE MILITARY AND THE CRISIS OF CONFIDENCE

1. Fletcher Knebel and Charles W. Bailey, *Seven Days in May* (Harper & Row, Publishers, Inc., 1962); movie version in 1964.

2. Hans Morgenthau, "What Price Victory?" *The New Republic,* Feb. 20, 1971, p. 23.

3. Flora Lewis, "U.S. 'Manhood' at Issue," *Los Angeles Times,* May 14, 1970, Editorial, Part II, p. 7.

4. Hugh Davis Graham and Ted Robert Gurr, *Violence in America: Historical and Comparative Perspectives,* A Report to the National Commission on the Causes and Prevention of Violence, June, 1969 (Signet Book, The New American Library, 1969), p. 3.

5. A definition of the military function adopted by Samuel P. Huntington, *The Soldier and the State,* pp. 11 ff., from Harold Lasswell. See Harold D. Lasswell, *The Analysis of Political Behaviour: An Empirical Approach* (Archon Books, The Shoe String Press, Inc., 1966), especially Ch. II: "The Garrison State and Specialists in Violence."

6. Daniel Berrigan, *They Call Us Dead Men* (The Macmillan Company, 1966), pp. 172–173.

7. See especially General David M. Shoup, U.S. Marine Corps (Ret.), "The New American Militarism," *Atlantic,* April, 1969; and Colonel James A. Donovan, U.S. Marine Corps (Ret.), *Militarism, U.S.A.* (Charles Scribner's Sons, 1970).

8. Henry Steele Commager, "America's Heritage of Bigness," *Saturday Review,* July 4, 1970, pp. 10–12.

9. *Ibid.*

10. *Ibid.,* p. 12.

11. Shoup, "New Militarism," p. 52.

12. Harvey Wheeler, *Democracy in a Revolutionary Era* (An Occasional Paper by The Center for the Study of Democratic Institutions, 1970), pp. 9–11.

13. *Ibid.,* p. 11.

14. See Henry Steele Commager, "The Americanization of History," *Saturday Review,* Nov. 1, 1969, pp. 24–25, 54.

15. Lieutenant General Sir John Winthrop Hackett, British Army, in the Lees Knowles Lectures (1962, n.p.), cited by Colonel Harold R. Aaron, U.S. Army, "The Good Guys and the Bad Guys," *Army,* Feb., 1967, p. 66.

16. Shoup, "New Militarism," p. 52.

17. Huntington, *The Soldier and the State,* pp. 465–466.

18. Rudyard Kipling, "Tommy," *Departmental Ditties and Ballads and Barrack Room Ballads* (Doubleday, Page and Co., 1915), p. 149.

Chapter 2. THE EVOLUTION OF THE MILITARY AS AN AMERICAN PROBLEM

1. See Bernard Bailyn, *The Ideological Origins of the American Revolution* (The Belknap Press of Harvard University Press, 1967), p. 62, n. 7, which lists a surprising number of "other examples of the almost excessive concern of the colonists for standing armies."

2. As political journalists John Trenchard and Thomas Gordon popularized Locke and radical Whig ideas on both sides of the Atlantic in *The Independent Whig* and *Cato's Letters: Essays on Liberty, Civil and Religious,* roughly spanning the years 1719–1723. Clinton Rossiter probably deserves credit for renewed interest in these writers, and David L. Jacobson in *The English Libertarian Heritage* (American Heritage Series, The Bobbs-Merrill Company, Inc., 1965), has made a "judicious abridgment" of the material for the first time since 1755. All page numbers cited are from Jacobson.

3. *Cato's Letters,* No. 25, Sat., April 15, 1721, p. 71.

4. Jacobson, *Heritage,* p. xlvii. See also Bailyn, *Ideological Origins,* pp. 63–66 especially, for a vivid description of the political climate.

5. *Cato's Letters,* No. 73, Sat., April 21, 1722, pp. 195–196.

6. The story of the Huguenots and their influence upon the creation of the new republic is a fascinating one and not well enough known. Three Presidents of the Continental Congress, including Elias Boudinot who signed the Treaty of Peace with Great Britain; John Jay, one of the authors of *The Federalist* papers and first Chief Justice of the State of New York and of the United States; General Francis Marion, the "Swamp Fox" of the Carolinas; and other colonial leaders were of Huguenot descent and represented "almost universal adoption of the patriot side in the War." See Samuel Dubose and Frederick A. Porcher (eds.), *A Contribution to the History of the Huguenots of South Carolina,* republished for private circulation by T. Gaillard Thomas (The Knickerbocker Press, 1887), as a pamphlet entitled "Commemoration of the Bi-Centenary of the Revocation of Nantes," Oct. 22, 1885, at New York (Huguenot Society of America, 1886), containing a "historical oration on The Edict of Nantes and its Recall," pp. 39, 53–54, especially.

7. By the Treaty of Ripon (Oct. 26, 1640) "Charles agreed to pay the Scotch army £850 a day until a permanent settlement could be

made" (William L. Langer, *An Encyclopedia of World History* [Houghton Mifflin Company, rev. ed., 1948], p. 376).

8. *Ibid.*, p. 425.

9. *Infra*, pp. 41–43.

10. Montross, *War Through the Ages*, pp. 364 f.; Langer, *World History*, p. 446.

11. Broader, surely, than simply the pay of soldiers: the larger contest was the struggle for the prizes of empire and the industrial revolution which, relative to the military, would come to full force in the twentieth century; cf. *infra*, pp. 37 ff.

12. Montross, *War Through the Ages*, pp. 375 f., 384 f.

13. *Cato's Letters*, No. 25, p. 71.

14. Bailyn, *Ideological Origins*, p. 65. The treatise was Molesworth's *An Account of Denmark* (1694). A succession of disastrous wars with Sweden led to the absolute monarchy of Frederick III in 1665, and eventually, in order to pay for the wars, to the infamous *stavnsbaand*, which bound all Danish farmers' sons from 14 to 36 years of age to the estates on which they were born. Cf. Sven Henningsen, *Encyclopædia Britannica*, 14th ed. (Encyclopædia Britannica, Inc., William Benton, Publisher, 1958), Vol. VII, p. 208.

15. *Cato's Letters*, pp. 71–72 (emphasis and spelling in original).

16. Jacobson, *Heritage*, p. xlvii.

17. Also of the struggle with Charles I, reflected in Parliament's Petition of Right (1628), which prohibited the billeting of soldiers in private homes. See Langer, *World History*, p. 375.

18. Bailyn, *Ideological Origins*, pp. 115–116.

19. *Ibid.*, pp. 124, 119–122.

20. Cited by Bailyn, *Ideological Origins*, p. 117, n. 24, from Josiah Quincy, *Memoir of the Life of Josiah Quincy Jun . . .* (Boston, 1825), p. 67; John Adams, *Diary and Autobiography*, Vol. II, pp. 74, 79 [cf. Lyman H. Butterfield, *et al.* (eds.), *Diary and Autobiography of John Adams*, 4 vols. (The Belknap Press of Harvard University Press, 1961)]; Lawrence H. Gipson, *The British Empire Before the American Revolution*, 12 vols. in process (Alfred A. Knopf, Inc., 1936–   ), Vol. XI, p. 281.

21. Bailyn, *ibid.*, p. 62, citing Trenchard, *An Argument*.

22. John C. Fitzpatrick (ed.), *Writings of George Washington from the Original Manuscript Sources, 1745–1799*, 39 vols. (1931–1944), Vol. VI, p. 155.

23. James Thomas Flexner, *George Washington in the American Revolution (1775–1783)* (Little, Brown and Company, 1967), p. 508.

24. *Writings of Washington*, Vol. XXVI, pp. 222–229; Flexner, *George Washington*, pp. 506–507.

25. *Writings of Washington,* pp. 374–398: "Sentiments on a Peace Establishment," enclosed in a letter to Hamilton, as Chairman of the Committee of Congress on the Peace Establishment. See Edmund Cody Burnett, *The Continental Congress* (The Macmillan Company, 1941), Chs. XXVIII, XXIX, on Congress' fear of the Army, etc.

26. Worthington C. Ford, *et al.* (eds.), *Journals of the Continental Congress 1774–1789,* 34 vols. (Government Printing Office, 1904–1937), Vol. XXVII, pp. 518, 524.

27. Dudley W. Knox, *A History of the United States Navy* (G. P. Putnam's Sons, 1936), p. 44.

28. Clinton Rossiter (ed.), *The Federalist Papers* (Mentor Book, The New American Library, 1964), Nos. 3, 4, especially pp. 42, 47 f.

29. *Ibid.,* No. 26, pp. 170 f.; Nos. 24–25, pp. 157–167. Hamilton had a glaring and humiliating example in Shays' Rebellion in 1786 which proved a fiasco for both the national and state governments, and galvanized action toward a stronger central government. Cf. Russell F. Weigley, *History of the United States Army* (The Macmillan Company, 1967), pp. 84 f.

30. Rossiter (ed.), *The Federalist Papers,* No. 41, p. 257.

31. *Ibid.,* No. 8, pp. 66–71; No. 41, pp. 260 f.

32. *Ibid.,* No. 41, pp. 257–260; and on Hamilton, see No. 26, pp. 173 ff.

33. *Ibid.,* No. 41, p. 258.

34. Weigley, *History,* pp. 90–92.

35. *Ibid.,* pp. 99–104.

36. James Ripley Jacobs, *The Beginning of the U.S. Army, 1783–1812* (Princeton University Press, 1947), pp. 244–246.

37. *Ibid.,* pp. 245, 280 ff.

38. See Russell F. Weigley, *Towards an American Army: Military Thought from Washington to Marshall* (Columbia University Press, 1962), pp. 21–28; and *History of the United States Army,* for a more detailed discussion of the slow and hesitant growth of the American Army.

39. Milton B. Herr and S. L. A. Marshall, "United States of America: VIII. Defense, Army," *Encyclopaedia Britannica,* Vol. XXII, pp. 760 f.

40. Weigley, *History,* pp. 175 f.

41. *Ibid.,* pp. 187–188.

42. *Ibid.,* pp. 232 ff.

43. *Ibid.,* pp. 208–211.

44. *Ibid.,* pp. 211–212.

45. *Ibid.,* pp. 256–264.

46. *Ibid.,* p. 262.

47. Knox, *History of the United States Navy,* pp. 317–319.

48. Weigley, *History,* the title of Ch. XII.

49. *Encyclopædia Britannica,* Vol. XXII, p. 760.

50. Weigley, *History,* pp. 353, 420 f.

51. Bert Cochran, *The War System: An Analysis of the Necessity for Political Reason* (The Macmillan Company, 1965), p. 135.

52. Using the full 780-man force as compared with our present 3,456,000 standing force (1970–1971) means a ratio somewhat less than 100. However, if we add the National Guard and Reserves, Coast Guard, and the huge contingent of civilians involved with the military establishment (see *infra,* pp. 53 f.), the ratio is about 300!

53. In the fluid situation of the last few years, during which Secretary McNamara was attempting closure of some bases while the Vietnam conflict was expanding, and especially since President Nixon has embarked upon his cutbacks, the exact number and strength of bases has been difficult to keep up to date. See *The Statistical Abstract of the United States, 1970* (Department of Commerce, Washington, D.C., 1970); *U.S. News & World Report,* April 21, 1969, p. 60; Donovan, *Militarism, U.S.A.,* pp. 52–54.

54. Rhode Island, Delaware, Connecticut, New Jersey, Massachusetts, Maryland, and New Hampshire, plus Vermont (admitted 1791).

55. *Statistical Abstract, 1970,* p. 249; *Report of the Defense Advisory Commission on Professional and Technical Compensation,* commonly called after the name of its Chairman, Dr. Ralph J. Cordiner (U.S. Government Printing Office, 1957), Vol. II, p. 1.

56. *The Wall Street Journal,* May 28, 1969, p. 1.

57. *Statistical Abstract, 1970,* p. 249.

58. *U.S. News & World Report,* Oct. 5, 1970, p. 41.

59. *The Wall Street Journal.*

60. *Ibid.*

61. *U.S. News & World Report,* Oct., 1970, pp. 40–41: government workers, 16 percent (from 1,348,000 in July, 1969, to an estimated 1,360,000 in mid-1971); Armed Forces, 18 percent (3,547,000 in June, 1968, to a planned 2,908,000 in June, 1971); and private defense jobs, 33 percent (from 3,524,000 in 1968 to an estimated 2,400,000 in 1971).

62. *Ibid.,* April 21, 1969, p. 60.

63. A. E. Lieberman, "Updating Impressions of the Military-Industrial Complex," *California Management Review,* Summer, 1969, p. 59.

64. *U.S. News & World Report,* Oct. 5, 1970, p. 40.

65. *Ibid.,* p. 60.

66. *Ibid.,* Feb. 2, 1970, p. 30.

67. Fred C. Cook, *The Warfare State* (The Macmillan Company, 1962), p. 21, put the cost at "77 cents of every dollar." Cochran, *The War System,* pp. 138–139, estimates that under Eisenhower it was "about four fifths" and larger if subsidies to clients are included; under Kennedy this went up another notch.

68. Senator J. William Fulbright, "Militarism and American Democracy: The Complex," *Vital Speeches of the Day,* May 15, 1969, p. 456.

69. *Congressional Quarterly Weekly Review, Special Report: The Military-Industrial Complex,* May 24, 1968, p. 1156.

70. *Ibid.,* p. 1157.

71. *Ibid.,* pp. 1157–1158.

72. "Representative Rivers Brought Jobs to His District," *Los Angeles Times,* Jan. 3, 1971, Sec. I, p. 6.

73. *Ibid.*

74. *Congressional Quarterly Weekly Review,* p. 1155.

75. *Ibid.,* p. 1157.

76. Kenneth Clark, *Civilization: A Personal View* (Harper & Row, Publishers, Inc., 1970), Ch. 13.

77. Fulbright, "Militarism and American Democracy," p. 456.

78. *Harvard Business Review,* May–June, 1968, p. 58. See also Senator William Proxmire, "The Pentagon vs. Free Enterprise" (*Saturday Review,* Jan. 31, 1970, p. 15), who finds "entrenched" positions reflected in 84 of the top 100 companies, and 18 of the top 25 companies, in the successive years 1967–1968.

79. *Hearings Before the Committee on Banking and Currency,* House of Representatives, Ninetieth Congress, Second Session on H.R. 15683, April 10 and 11, 1968 (U.S. Government Printing Office, 1968), pp. 68, 65–66.

80. *Ibid.,* pp. 66–67; cf. *The Wall Street Journal,* June 6, 1969, p. 27, where Grumman Aircraft Corporation defends the practice.

81. *Hearings,* pp. 70–83. In one case GAO accused a company of 150 percent profit! See *The New York Times,* April 3, 1965, p. 12.

82. Ralph E. Lapp, *The Weapons Culture* (W. W. Norton & Company, Inc., 1968), pp. 186–187.

83. Lieberman, "Updating Impressions," Summer, 1969, p. 53.

84. *Hearings,* p. 63.

85. *Ibid.,* p. 68.

86. "The Power of the Pentagon," *The Progressive,* June, 1969, p. 5.

87. The introductory essay, "The People Versus the Pentagon," was prepared especially for *The Progressive* by ten senators and representatives who initiated the Congressional Conference on the Military Budget and National Priorities, held March 28–29, 1969, on Capitol Hill.

88. *Ibid.,* p. 6.

89. *Ibid.* See also George E. Berkly, "The Myth of War Profiteering," *The New Republic,* Dec. 20, 1969, pp. 15 f. Lieberman's study ("Updating Impressions"), as well as other statements by leading economists of late, appears to support this view.

90. *The Progressive,* June, 1969, p. 6.

91. Cited by Donald McDonald in "Militarism in America," *The Center Magazine,* Jan., 1970, p. 15.

92. A recent study of the University of California at San Diego, by its own select committee, raises some doubt as to the validity of this contention, although the study itself seems ambiguous. See *Los Angeles Times,* Feb. 15, 1971, Part I, pp. 3:1–2, 24:1.

93. Fulbright, "Militarism and American Democracy," p. 457.

94. Walter Adams and Adrian Jaffe, *Government, The Universities and International Affairs: A Crisis in Identity,* Special Report Prepared for the U.S. Advisory Commission on International Educational Cultural Affairs, Ninetieth Congress, First Session, House Doc. No. 120 (U.S. Government Printing Office, 1967), pp. 10 f.

95. McDonald, "Militarism in America," p. 15. Dr. John Esterline, a colleague and a former Director, Office of East Asian Programs, Bureau of Educational and Cultural Affairs, Department of State, points out that the Department of State spends upward of $35 million annually on educational exchange programs with foreign nations "much of which is social science research."

96. *Ibid.,* p. 16. The State Department, long unhappy with the disproportionate amount of funds available to the Department of Defense, has, following the Camelot debacle (see *infra,* pp. 63 ff.), become "reluctant" to get involved in basic social science research of the sort the Pentagon is doing. "Article 203" by Congress now specifically limits Defense projects to those directly related to its mission. See *Los Angeles Times,* Jan. 25, 1970, Editorial, Sec. F, p. 2: "Research Hurt by Defense Fund Limit."

97. *Ibid.* See Irving Louis Horowitz, "The Life and Death of Project Camelot," *Trans-action,* Nov.–Dec., 1965, for a full account and evaluation of the project.

98. *Los Angeles Times,* Feb. 22, 1970, "Opinion," Sec. G, p. 1.

99. Cited in McDonald, "Militarism in America."

100. Senator J. William Fulbright, "The Governance of the Pentagon," *Saturday Review,* Nov. 7, 1970, p. 24.

101. *Ibid.,* p. 23. Senator Frank Church and others have been incensed at Defense's refusal to supply the Senate Foreign Relations Committee with a copy of "the secret military agreement with Thailand." See *San Francisco Chronicle,* Aug. 15, 1969, p. 19.

102. The Honorable Angier Biddle Duke, "Military Power and Foreign Policy: A Time to Review," *Vital Speeches,* Aug. 1, 1969, pp. 630–631.

103. McDonald, "Militarism in America," p. 16, citation from Senator McCarthy.

104. Roger Hilsman, *To Move a Nation* (Doubleday & Company, Inc., 1967), pp. 61–88, especially p. 85.

105. *San Francisco Chronicle,* Aug. 11, 1969, p. 12. Miles Copeland's book is entitled *Game of Nations* (Simon and Schuster, Inc., 1970).

106. Hilsman, *To Move a Nation,* pp. 86–87.

107. *Los Angeles Times,* Jan. 6, 1971, Part I, p. 10:1.

108. *Ibid.,* March 3, 1971, Part I, p. 1:5–6.

109. Arthur R. Miller, "The Surveillance Society: Just How Far Can It Go?" *Los Angeles Times,* Sept. 6, 1970, "Opinion," Sec. C, pp. 1–2.

110. "The New Militarism," *The New York Times,* April 6, 1969, Editorial, Sec. 4, p. 10E:2.

111. Senator William Proxmire, "Blank Check for the Military," *Vital Speeches,* April 15, 1969, pp. 401–404.

112. *Ibid.* "Buying in" is the practice of grossly underestimating the cost of a project in order to procure the contract and then relying upon the established technique of "overruns" to stay in business and even make a sizable profit.

113. *Ibid.* Example: of eleven major weapons systems begun in the 1960's, only two performed up to standards electronically.

114. Richard Stubbings, "Improving the Acquisition Process for High Risk Electronics Systems," cited by Senator Proxmire, "Blank Check," p. 402.

115. *Time,* June 1, 1970, p. E6; "The Pentagon vs. Free Enterprise," *Saturday Review,* Jan. 31, 1970, p. 16.

116. In specific response to "Pentagon Says It Can't List Foreign Arms Aid," *Los Angeles Times,* Jan. 7, 1971, Part I, p. 5.

117. See *Reports to Congress on Audits of Defense Contracts,*

Hearings Before a Subcommittee on Government Operations, House of Representatives, Eighty-ninth Congress, First Session (U.S. Government Printing Office, 1965).

118. McDonald, "Militarism in America," p. 24.

119. *The Progressive,* June, 1969, p. 54.

120. *Ibid.*

121. In all the confusion as to who should take credit or blame for the raid and the various stages of its planning and execution, it is at least clear that various concerned persons and agencies, including General Abrams, had little or no knowledge of the project. See "POW 'Rescue' Issue Remaining," *Los Angeles Times,* Dec. 4, 1970, Part II, p. 8; also, Dec. 5, 1970, Editorial, Part I, p. 12:1.

122. Fulbright, "Governance of the Pentagon," p. 24.

123. Herman Kahn, "If Negotiations Fail," *Foreign Affairs,* July, 1968, p. 630.

124. Donovan, *Militarism, U.S.A.,* Chs. VIII, IX, pp. 152–190, especially pp. 170–171.

125. Fulbright, "Governance of the Pentagon," p. 24. The controversial CBS documentary, *The Selling of the Pentagon,* released in early 1971, focused national attention upon military public relations activities.

126. *San Francisco Chronicle,* June 24, 1970, Editorial, p. 44.

127. Fulbright, "Governance of the Pentagon," p. 24.

128. Cited by McDonald, "Militarism in America," p. 17.

129. *Los Angeles Times,* Jan. 25, 1970, "Opinion," Sec. F, pp. 1–2.

130. Senator Fulbright's estimate after hearing the Comptroller General, *Los Angeles Times,* Jan. 5, 1971, Part I, p. 4.

131. *Ibid.,* Jan. 25, 1970.

132. *Ibid.,* Jan. 5, 1971, p. 4.

133. " 'Poor Man's' Arms Race Peril," *San Francisco Chronicle,* Aug. 20, 1969, p. 12.

134. Lieutenant General Robert H. Warren, U.S. Air Force, "Military Assistance Program: Foreign Military Sales," *Vital Speeches,* July 15, 1969, pp. 602 f.

135. Cited by Senator Joseph S. Clark, "America's Foreign Aid Policy: Reappraising Its Relevancy," *Vital Speeches,* March 1, 1967, p. 302.

136. *The New York Times,* Nov. 20, 1969, p. 2.

137. Lee Foster (ed.), *The New York Times Encyclopedia Almanac, 1971* (The New York Times Book and Educational Division, 1970), p. 713.

138. *The New York Times,* Nov. 20, 1969. Of $173.4 billion

estimated world military expenditures in 1968, the U.S. spent $79.3 and the U.S.S.R. $39.8 billion (figures are adjusted to real buying power).

139. *Ibid.*, pp. 25–26. Senator Fulbright puts our destructive capacity even higher ("Militarism and American Democracy," p. 456); Robert S. McNamara, "U.S. Nuclear Strategy: Missile Defense," *Vital Speeches,* Oct. 1, 1967, p. 739.

140. *The New York Times,* Dec. 16, 1969, p. 1.

141. *Ibid.*, March 9, 1969, Sec. IV, p. 7.

142. Cited by Senator Fulbright, "Militarism and American Democracy," p. 456.

143. See Ralph E. Lapp, "Correcting Our Posture," *The New Republic,* March 28, 1970, p. 15.

144. McNamara, "U.S. Nuclear Strategy," p. 743.

145. John Wicklein, "Attack Carriers—An Outflanked Maginot Line; Navy Backs Interventions to Justify Floating Airfields," *Los Angeles Times,* Feb. 22, 1970, "Opinion," Sec. G, p. 1.

146. The Congressional Hébert Committee listed in 1960 more than 1,400 retired officers of the rank of major and above, employed by 100 companies manufacturing 80 percent of American armaments. See Cochran, *The War System,* pp. 143–145.

147. Proxmire, "The Pentagon vs. Free Enterprise," p. 15. "More than 2,100 retired officers of the rank of colonel or higher. . . . The ten companies employing the largest number . . . had 1,065 . . . an average of 106, three times the average number employed in 1959."

148. *Ibid.*

149. *The New York Times Encyclopedia Almanac, 1971,* p. 706.

150. Cited by Cochran, *The War System,* p. 164.

151. Richard J. Barnet, *The Economy of Death* (Atheneum Publishers, 1970), as reviewed by Marjorie Driscoll, *The New York Times Calendar,* April 5, 1970, p. 46.

Chapter 3. THE AMBIVALENCE OF CIVILIAN-MILITARY RELATIONS

1. Marcus Cunliffe, *Soldiers and Civilians: The Martial Spirit in America, 1775–1865* (Little, Brown and Company, 1968).

2. The explicit thesis is set forth by Russell F. Weigley, *History of the United States Army,* p. xi. In this chapter I am especially indebted to Professor Weigley, and to Samuel F. Huntington, *The Soldier and the State.*

3. Compare *Writings of Washington,* Vol. XXXVII, pp. 47–48,

and "Sentiments on a Peace Establishment," Vol. XXVI, pp. 222–229, with *The Works of Alexander Hamilton*, ed. by Henry Cabot Lodge, 12 vols., Federal Edition (The Knickerbocker Press, G. P. Putnam's Sons, 1904), Vol. VII, pp. 25, 56–57.

4. Weigley, *Towards an American Army*, p. 27; Saul K. Padover, *Jefferson*, abridged by the author (Mentor Book, The New American Library, 1952), pp. 124–125.

5. Huntington, *The Soldier and the State*, p. 196.

6. *Ibid.*, pp. 203 f.

7. *Ibid.*

8. John M. Swomley, Jr., *The Military Establishment* (Beacon Press, Inc., 1964), p. 3.

9. The Navy was exempted: there was no Anglo-Saxon tradition of naval usurpation of power, and potential enemies would have to cross the ocean; hence a permanent navy seemed essential and safe.

10. *The Constitution of the United States of America*, Article II (Second Amendment). See Thomas James Norton, *The Constitution of the United States: Its Sources and Its Application* (special ed. rev.; distributed exclusively by the Committee for Constitutional Government, Inc., 1943), pp. 194–206.

11. Witness the MacArthur-Truman, McNamara–military chiefs feuds, for example, as well as the continuing President-Senate battles on the Vietnam and Cambodia engagements.

12. Huntington, *The Soldier and the State*, p. 164.

13. *Ibid.*, pp. 143–144.

14. *Ibid.*, pp. 144–145.

15. Pendleton Herring, *The Impact of War: Our American Democracy Under Arms* (Farrar & Rinehart, Inc., 1941), p. 31; Samuel Enoch Stumpf, *A Democratic Manifesto* (Vanderbilt University Press, 1954), pp. 116 f.

16. Reinhold Niebuhr, *The Irony of American History* (Charles Scribner's Sons, 1952), pp. 24 f.

17. Huntington, *The Soldier and the State*, p. 145.

18. *Ibid.*

19. *Ibid.*, p. 147.

20. *Ibid.*, p. 148.

21. Theodore Roosevelt, Henry Cabot Lodge, Elihu Root, Albert J. Beveridge, A. T. Mahan, Herbert Croly, Leonard Wood, Henry Adams, and Brooks Adams. See *ibid.*, pp. 270 ff.

22. Huntington, *The Soldier and the State*, p. 153.

23. The terms "extirpation" and "transmutation" have been borrowed from Huntington, *ibid.*, pp. 155 f.

24. Alfred B. Fitt, "National Guard: A New Mission Needed," *Los Angeles Times*, Sept. 13, 1970, "Opinion," Sec. D, p. 1.

25. *Official Proceedings of the National Guard Association*, 66th Annual Convention, 1944, pp. 28–29, 44; 1948, pp. 111, 242–244, 254–255; 1949, pp. 202–210.

26. "National Guard," *Encyclopædia Britannica*, Vol. XVI, p. 146. Approximately 165,000 of the 396,000 troops raised for Washington were states' militia.

27. As the National Guard of the United States it can be ordered to active service by the President after Congress declares an emergency. See *ibid.*, p. 147.

28. Jack Raymond, *Power at the Pentagon* (Harper & Row, Publishers, Inc., 1964), pp. 300–301; Fitt, "National Guard."

29. Huntington, *The Soldier and the State*, p. 177.

30. *Ibid.*, p. 178. See pp. 485–486, n. 14, for bibliography dealing with this problem.

31. *Ibid.*, p. 191.

32. *The Papers of Thomas Jefferson*, ed. by Julian P. Boyd (Princeton University Press, 1950–   ), Vol. VII, p. 106.

33. Huntington, *The Soldier and the State*, p. 198.

34. *Ibid.*, p. 199.

35. On May 1, 1966, the Navy forsook its 124-year tradition of bureau service and created six "systems commands" under the Chief of Naval Materiel. See Thomas W. Ray, "The Bureaus Go On Forever," *United States Naval Institute Proceedings* (hereinafter cited as *NIP*), Jan., 1968.

36. Herbert Spencer, *Principles of Sociology (1877–1896)*, pitted the industrial vs. the military society. See his "The Military and the Industrial Society," in Bramson and Goethals (eds.), *War: Studies*, pp. 291–308.

37. Huntington, *The Soldier and the State*, p. 225; Bramson and Goethals (eds.), *War: Studies*.

38. Huntington, *ibid.*, pp. 225–226.

39. *Ibid.*, p. 229. Weigley speaks of the period as "Twilight of the Old Army: 1865–1898" (*History*, Ch. XII).

40. Clark R. Mollenhoff, *The Pentagon: Politics, Profits and Plunder* (G. P. Putnam's Sons, 1967), pp. 36–40.

41. "Summit Failure a Market Tonic," *The New York Times*, May 22, 1960, Sec. 3F:8.

42. Alexis de Tocqueville, *Democracy in America*, specially edited and abridged for the modern reader by Richard D. Heffner (Mentor Book, The New American Library, 1956), Book II, pp. 189 f.

43. Huntington, *The Soldier and the State,* p. 205.

44. *Ibid.,* p. 206. From 1802 to 1861, of 37 generals, not one was a West Pointer, 23 had practically no military experience, and 11 others entered the service with the grade of captain or higher. Regular officers actually quit the service in order to reenter from civilian life at a higher grade!

45. "Every officer in the Revolutionary Army . . . was also a politician" (Huntington, *The Soldier and the State,* p. 207). As we have seen, Hamilton tried to politicize the Army during the Adams Administration (*supra,* p. 47).

46. An office created by Congress in 1821 but which led to such friction that it was finally abolished in favor of the general staff principle. See Weigley, *Towards an American Army,* pp. 162–176.

47. General Winfield Scott, best known of the early Commanding Generals of the Army, from 1841 to 1861, was nominated for President by the Whigs in 1852.

48. Weigley, *Towards an American Army,* p. 27.

49. "I will not accept if nominated and will not serve if elected." See Huntington, *The Soldier and the State,* pp. 231 ff., for discussion of this "political neutrality."

50. *Ibid.,* p. 261; cf. Millis, *Arms and Men,* pp. 55–56 f., for the roots of this obedient service as early as Jefferson to "explore the new domain" of the Louisiana Purchase.

51. Huntington, *The Soldier and the State,* p. 262.

52. *Ibid.*

53. Hans J. Morgenthau, *Politics Among Nations* (Alfred A. Knopf, Inc., 1954). Others who have recently treated of "power" are Adolf A. Berle, *Power* (Harcourt, Brace and World, Inc., 1969); H. D. Lasswell and A. Kaplan, *Power and Society* (Yale University Press, 1950); Bertrand de Jouvenel, *On Power, Its Nature and the History of Its Growth,* tr. by J. F. Huntington (The Viking Press, Inc., 1949). See review of Berle by Carl J. Friedrich, *Saturday Review,* April 11, 1970, pp. 26–28.

54. Huntington, *The Soldier and the State,* pp. 458–459.

55. *Ibid.,* pp. 461–463.

56. S. L. A. Marshall, "Armed Services Suffer from a Poor 'Image' on Television," *Los Angeles Times,* May 17, 1964, Editorial Section.

57. James Bassett, "World War II—Last of the Noble Causes," *Los Angeles Times,* April 4, 1965, Calendar Section, pp. 3, 5.

58. Marjorie Driscoll, "Adm. Hardtack Harry and Two Wars to Fight," *Los Angeles Times,* Nov. 19, 1967, Calendar Section, p. 35.

59. Even General Westmoreland was singularly exempt until quite

recently, with angry voices in (and out of) Congress directed toward his bosses, the President and the Pentagon. Likewise, his successor, General Abrams, has occasioned little overt hostility. Westmoreland fell into disfavor in some circles when he appeared to assume the role of apologist for the policies that put him and his men into Vietnam.

60. Charles C. Moskos, Jr., "Civilian Society to Blame: Anti-Militarism—Intellectuals' New Anti-Semitism," *Los Angeles Times*, Sept. 6, 1970, "Opinion," Sec. C, p. 1:5.

61. Translated from the French by Lily Emmet (Harper & Row, Publishers, Inc., 1970).

62. Raymond, *Power at the Pentagon*, p. 330, reflecting an address by General Maxwell D. Taylor, then Chairman of the Joint Chiefs of Staff, to the graduating class at West Point, June 5, 1963.

63. At least one lonely voice has risen to challenge this generally accepted thesis: Marcus Cunliffe in *The Martial Spirit in America*, Ch. X.

64. Huntington, *The Soldier and the State*, p. 217.

65. From a Civil War peak of over $1 billion the Army was reduced to $35 million in 1871. Naval expenditures averaged $20 million annually until 1890—about *one fifth* the cost of a modern conventional carrier today!

66. Huntington, *The Soldier and the State*, p. 228. Yet this can be overdrawn, as Janowitz points out. Often enough, as military instructors at universities, serving in arsenals and depots, and especially those involved in the social whirl of the South and West, where most of the posts were located, they developed civilian friends (Janowitz, *Professional Soldier*, p. 176).

67. Barton C. Hacker, "The United States Army as a National Police Force: The Federal Policing of Labor Disputes, 1878–1898," *Military Affairs*, April, 1969, p. 261.

68. Sidney Forman, *West Point: A History of the United States Military Academy* (Columbia University Press, 1950), pp. 216–217.

69. Huntington, *The Soldier and the State*, p. 229.

70. *Ibid.*, p. 230.

71. *Ibid.*, p. 232.

72. James S. Pettit, "How Far Does Democracy Affect the Organization and Discipline of Our Armies, and How Can Its Influence Be Most Effectually Utilized?" *Journal of the United States Military Service Institution*, Vol. XXXVIII (1906), pp. 2, 38.

73. Weigley, *Towards an American Army*, p. 169.

74. Huntington, *The Soldier and the State*, pp. 251–252.

75. *Ibid.*, p. 254.
76. *Ibid.*, p. 8.
77. *Ibid.*, p. 257.
78. *Ibid.*, p. 259.
79. *Ibid.*, p. 268.
80. *Ibid.*, p. 288.
81. *Ibid.*

Chapter 4. THE PRIORITY OF REASON

1. Paul Tillich, *Love, Power, and Justice: Ontological Analyses and Ethical Applications* (London: Geoffrey Cumberlege, Oxford University Press, 1954), pp. 37, 47.

2. *Ibid.*

3. *Ibid.*

4. *Ibid.*

5. Harvey Seifert and Howard J. Clinebell, Jr., *Personal Growth and Social Change: A Guide for Ministers and Laymen as Change Agents* (The Westminster Press, 1969), p. 193.

6. John Bennett, *Foreign Policy in Christian Perspective* (Charles Scribner's Sons, 1966), p. 66.

7. Bertrand Russell, *Power: A New Social Analysis* (W. W. Norton & Company, Inc., 1938), p. 35.

8. Morgenthau, *Politics Among Nations*, p. 8.

9. Walter Millis, *A World Without War* (Washington Square Press, 1961), p. 122.

10. Bennett, *Foreign Policy*, p. 66.

11. Henry E. Eccles, *Military Concepts and Philosophy* (Rutgers University Press, 1965), p. 29.

12. Walter Millis, *War and Revolution Today* (An Occasional Paper by The Center for the Study of Democratic Institutions, 1965), p. 11.

13. Huntington, *The Soldier and the State*, p. 11.

14. Millis, *War and Revolution Today*, p. 11.

15. *Ibid.*

16. Lieutenant General Sir John Winthrop Hackett, British Army, "The Profession of Arms," Part I: "Wellsprings in History," *Military Review* (hereinafter cited as *MR*), Oct., 1963, p. 35.

17. Cited by Colonel Harold R. Aaron, U.S. Army, "The Good Guys and the Bad Guys," *Army*, Feb., 1967, p. 66 (italics added).

18. Aristophanes, *Peace*, pp. 13–14.

19. Bramson and Goethals (eds.), *War: Studies*, pp. 71–77.

20. Arnold J. Toynbee, *War and Civilization* (Oxford University Press, 1950). The whole volume is to this point.

21. William James, *The Moral Equivalent of War* (American Association for International Conciliation, Feb., 1910), No. 27, p. 4.

22. Bramson and Goethals (eds.), *War: Studies*, p. 14.

23. *Ibid.*, pp. 66–67.

24. *Ibid.*, pp. 133–145.

25. *Ibid.*, pp. 177–193.

26. Wright, *A Study of War*, Vol. I, pp. 62–74.

27. R. A. Preston, Sydney E. Wise, and H. O. Werner, *Men in Arms: A History of Warfare and Its Interrelations with Western Society*, rev. ed. (Frederick A. Praeger, Inc., Publishers, 1962), pp. 9–13.

28. Walter Bagehot, *Physics and Politics* (Alfred A. Knopf, Inc., 1948), p. 55.

29. Montross, *War Through the Ages*, p. 76.

30. F. E. Adcock, *The Greek and Macedonian Art of War* (University of California Press, 1957), p. 65.

31. Preston, *et al.*, *Men in Arms*, p. 18.

32. Montross, *War Through the Ages*, pp. 7–14.

33. *Ibid.*, pp. 16–17.

34. Adcock, *Art of War*, p. 72.

35. Toynbee, *War and Civilization*, pp. 38–39.

36. Montross, *War Through the Ages*, pp. 18–22.

37. Preston, *et al.*, *Men in Arms*, p. 29.

38. As securing the Mediterranean coast to wither the Persian fleet.

39. Montross, *War Through the Ages*, p. 24. See Xenophon, *Hellenica*, Books VI and VII; *Anabasis*, Books I–III (Vol. I), IV–VII (Vol. II), tr. by Carleton L. Brownson (Harvard University Press, 1961).

40. Cited in Preston, *et al.*, *Men in Arms*, p. 3.

41. Fearing military dictatorship, Rome early divided generalship on alternate days of battle.

42. Against Pompey's lieutenants. The "army without a general" after Pompey left it, fled and were repeatedly trapped and spared by Caesar until they simply gave up. Cf. Montross, *War Through the Ages*, pp. 79–80.

43. One of the longest-lived empires, with one fourth of Rome's manpower. *Ibid.*, p. 105.

44. *Ibid.*, pp. 104–105, 125.

45. Preston, *et al.*, *Men in Arms*, pp. 56–57; C. W. Oman, *The*

Art of War in the Middle Ages, A.D. 378–1515, rev. and ed. by J. H. Beeler (Great Seal Books, Cornell University Press, 1953), pp. 33–55.

46. *Ibid.,* p. 94.

47. Cavalry had dominated since the battle of Adrianople, A.D. 378, when the Roman emperor Valens and 40,000 of his tightly packed infantry were annihilated by heavy Gothic horse.

48. Montross, *War Through the Ages,* p. 173.

49. Oman, *Middle Ages,* p. 114.

50. Preston, *et al., Men in Arms,* p. 96. See Niccolò Machiavelli, *The Art of War,* rev. ed. of the Ellis Farneworth translation, with an introduction by Neal Wood (The Bobbs-Merrill Company, Inc., 1965).

51. Herman Kahn, *On Escalation: Metaphors and Scenarios* (Frederick A. Praeger, Inc., Publishers, 1965), pp. 57–58.

52. Hugo Grotius (1583–1645), Dutch theorist, *De jure belli et pacis;* Emmerich von Vattel (1714–1767), Swiss jurist, *Law of Nations,* are both mentioned frequently in studies of the period. Cf. Montross, *War Through the Ages,* pp. 329, 319.

53. Maurice de Saxe, 1696–1750, Marshal of France, *Mes Reveries sur l'Art Guerre* (Paris, 1756); cf. Montross, *ibid.,* pp. 378–384, and David H. Zook, Jr., and Robin Higham, *A Short History of Warfare* (Twayne Publishers, Inc., 1965), pp. 106–107.

54. Montross, *War Through the Ages,* pp. 321 ff.

55. Brigadier General William A. Mitchell, U.S. Army, *Outlines of the World's Military History* (Harrisburg, Pa.: Military Service Publishing Company, 1940), pp. 323–326.

56. Baron de Jomini, *Summary of the Art of War,* tr. by Major O. F. Winship, U.S. Army, and Lieutenant E. E. McLean, U.S. Army (G. P. Putnam and Co., 1854).

57. From *Napoléon en Exil, ou l'echo de Sainte-Hélène* (1822), by B. E. O'Meara, Vol. II, p. 248, quoted by Major General J. F. C. Fuller, British Army (Ret.), *The Conduct of War, 1789–1961* (Rutgers University Press, 1961), p. 45.

58. *The Mind of Napoleon,* a selection from his written and spoken words ed. and tr. by J. Christopher Herold (Columbia University Press, 1955), pp. 221–222 (letter, 1806; conversation, 1800's).

59. Cited by Colonel Vachee in *Napoleon at Work* (English tr., 1914), p. 7, quoted in Fuller, *The Conduct of War,* p. 48.

60. Montross, *War Through the Ages,* p. 510.

61. Vagts, *Militarism,* pp. 75–76.

62. General Karl von Clausewitz, *Vom Kriege;* English translation, *On War,* by Colonel J. J. Graham, new rev. ed., with intro-

duction and notes by Colonel F. M. Maude, C.B. (Late R.E.), 3 vols. (Barnes & Noble, Inc., 1966), Vol. I, p. 26.

63. According to Colonel Graham (*ibid.*, Vol. I, p. xxxvii), Clausewitz was a pupil of Kiesewitter, who indoctrinated him in the philosophy of Kant (cited in Fuller, *The Conduct of War*, p. 60).

64. Clausewitz, *ibid.*, Vol. I, p. 304.

65. *Ibid.*, pp. 129, 21.

66. *Ibid.*, p. 25.

67. Montross, *War Through the Ages*, p. 585.

68. Weigley, *Towards an American Army*, p. 41.

69. *Ibid.*, pp. 43 ff., especially Ch. V, "Henry W. Halleck and George B. McClellan, The Disciples of Dennis Mahan."

70. Concerning Marxian skeptical relativism, cf. Melvin Rader, *The Enduring Questions* (Holt, Rinehart and Winston, Inc., 1956), p. 526.

71. Bramson and Goethals (eds.), *War: Studies*, p. 225.

72. Weigley, *Towards an American Army*, pp. 80–81, 88.

73. Adam Badeau, *Military History of U. S. Grant*, 3 vols. (Appleton, 1882), pp. 642–644; cited in Weigley, *ibid.*, p. 93.

74. A. D. Wales, "Grant: His 'Mystery' and Genius," *Journal of the United States Military Service Institution*, Vol. XXXIX (1906), pp. 5–6; cited in Weigley, *ibid.*

75. Ulysses S. Grant, *Memoirs*, 2 vols. (Charles L. Webster, 1886), Vol. II, p. 365.

76. Weigley, *Towards an American Army*, pp. 160–176. The office of Commanding General later yielded to the general staff recommendations of Schofield.

77. Forrest C. Pogue, *George C. Marshall: Education of a General* (The Viking Press, Inc., 1963), adapted by John S. Spore, "F. C. Pogue," *Army*, Nov., 1963, pp. 22–28, 30–36.

78. General S. L. A. Marshall, U.S. Army (Ret.), *The Officer as Leader* (Harrisburg, Pa.: Stackpole Books, 1966), pp. 17–18.

79. Major General J. F. C. Fuller, *The Reformation of War* (London: Hutchinson, 1923), Preface.

80. Eccles, *Military Concepts*, p. 288. See also Commander Bruce Keener, III, U.S. Navy, "The Principles of War: A Thesis for Change," *NIP*, Nov., 1967.

81. Tristram Coffin, *The Passion of the Hawks* (The Macmillan Company, 1964), p. 264; paperback ed., *The Armed Society: Militarism in Modern America* (Penguin Books, Inc., 1964).

82. *Army Green Book: A Status Report on the U.S. Army* (Nov., 1964), several articles, especially Major General H. H. Caughey,

U.S. Army, "The Army's Schools of Battle"; R. McClintic, "Services Study Education Report," *Journal of the Armed Forces*, Oct. 29, 1966; "Sailors Ride Crest of Scholarly Wave," *Los Angeles Times*, San Gabriel Valley Eastern Edition, March 12, 1967; Lieutenant Colonel W. M. Hartness, U.S. Army (Ret.), "Social and Behavioral Sciences Counter Insurgency," *MR*, Jan., 1966; Rear Admiral Robert W. McNitt, U.S. Navy, "The Naval Postgraduate School: Sixty Years Young," *NIP*, June, 1970; Lieutenant Commander Charles W. Cullen, U.S. Navy, "From the Kriegsacademie to the Naval War College: The Military Planning Process," *Naval War College Review* (hereinafter cited as *NWCR*), Jan., 1970.

83. H. O. Werner, "Breakthrough at the U.S. Naval Academy," *NIP*, Oct., 1963; Cullen, "From the Kriegsacademie"; Just, in *Military Men*, confirms the pain, the "uphill battle" for the "soft science" teachers but finds "most of the action at the Point is now in the social sciences" (pp. 33–40).

84. Janowitz, *The Professional Soldier*, pp. 131–135.

85. Major General William C. Westmoreland, U.S. Army, "West Point Today," *Army*, April, 1963; Master Sergeant Kenneth Allen, "Torch of Rhodes," *Airman*, July, 1970, brings us up-to-date: so far the Air Force Academy has made the list thirteen times and was the only service academy to be represented in 1970, with *two* selectees!

86. Commander B. I. Edelson, U.S. Navy, "The Ph.D. in Uniform," *NIP*, Nov., 1966.

87. Major C. M. Guelzo, U.S. Army, "Soldiers Who Are Scholars," *Army*, July, 1963; "Encourage the Thinkers!" *Army*, "Letters," Nov., 1962; Lieutenant Colonel K. M. Hatch, U.S. Army, "Creative Thinking in the Military Profession," *MR*, Aug., 1966; Colonel Robert B. Rigg, U.S. Army, "Thinking About Military Thinking," *Army*, Feb., 1966; Major J. L. Hillard, British Army (Ret.), "Military Innovation and Creative Thinking," *MR*, Nov., 1968.

88. Colonel J. E. Mrazek, U.S. Army, "Rembrandts of the Military Art," *Army*, July, 1965.

89. James D. Atkinson, reviewing *The Liddell Hart Memoirs*, 2 vols. (London: Cassell, 1965; New York: G. P. Putnam's Sons, 1966), in "Liddell Hart and Warfare of the Future," *Military Affairs*, Winter, 1965–1966, p. 162.

90. Albert William Sherower, "Bonaparte at Headquarters," *MR*, Oct., 1968, p. 72.

91. Colonel Mark M. Boatner, III, U.S. Army, "The Principles of War and the Renaissance of Generalship," *Army*, Sept., 1967.

92. Major William F. Muhlenfeld, U.S. Army, "Our Embattled ROTC," *Army*, Feb., 1969.

93. From 4 percent high school graduates in World War I to 73 percent in 1962; from 14 percent possessing "something above" high school in 1952 to almost 20 percent becoming college graduates in 1962; cf. Colonel Harry A. Buckley, U.S. Army, "The Class of '68— from Campus to KP," *Army*, Jan., 1969, pp. 24–25.

94. Lieutenant Colonel Zeb B. Bradford, Jr., U.S. Army, and Major James R. Murphy, U.S. Army, "A New Look at the Military Profession," *Army*, Feb., 1969.

95. Major General John H. Hay, U.S. Army, "A Profession Comes of Age," *Army*, April, 1969; see also "Wave of the Future," a report on a debate between Dr. Russell F. Weigley, Dr. Roger W. Little, and General Bruce C. Clarke, U.S. Army (Ret.), *Army*, April, 1969.

96. Just, *Military Men*, pp. 33–40.

97. Department of the Army, Pamphlet 16–11, *Character Guidance Discussion Topics*, Duty-Honor-Country, Series II, Sept., 1963, Ch. I: "Courage" and Ch. IV: "Practical Wisdom."

98. Commander M. W. Cagle, U.S. Navy, "A Philosophy for Naval Atomic Warfare," 1957 Prize Essay, *NIP*, March, 1957; Lieutenant Colonel C. M. Ferguson, Jr., U.S. Army, "A New U.S. Military Philosophy," *NIP*, Jan., 1961, quoting p. 44.

99. Commander S. T. Delamater, U.S. Navy, "Ideological Responsibility," *NIP*, June, 1962.

100. George D. Patterson, III, "Should Politics Be Taboo?" *NIP*, Sept., 1962, p. 40; Captain G. M. Hageman, U.S. Navy, "The Navy's Politico-Military Program—Where Pen Meets Sword," *NIP*, Nov., 1963, p. 44.

101. Commander M. J. Travers, U.S. Navy, "The Restless Mind," *NIP*, Aug., 1964.

102. Commander J. T. Strong, U.S. Navy, "Professionalism—a Wardroom Debate," *NIP*, May, 1966; R. J. Stillman, "The Pentagon's Whiz Kids," *NIP*, April, 1966; Edelson, "The Ph.D. in Uniform."

103. Raymond G. O'Connor, "Current Concepts and Philosophy of Warfare," *NWCR*, Jan., 1968.

104. Joseph C. Wylie, *Military Strategy* (Rutgers University Press, 1967).

105. Vice Admiral Lynn D. McCormack, U.S. Navy, "Naval War College Opening Address," *NWCR*, Nov., 1954.

106. Eccles, *Military Concepts*, pp. 41, 128.

107. Major Craig B. Gartrell, U.S. Marine Corps, "ITV in the

Marine Corps," *Marine Corps Gazette* (hereinafter cited as *MCG*), March, 1969.

108. *The Journal of the Armed Forces,* June 1, 1968, pp. 7–8.

109. *Los Angeles Times,* Nov. 13, 1970, Part I, p. 4.

110. United States Navy and United States Marine Corps, *Moral Leadership: The Protection of Moral Standards and Character Education Program, NavPers No. 15890* (1957) (hereinafter cited as *NavPers 15890*), p. 18.

111. Colonel W. H. Bowers, U.S. Air Force, "Qualitative Educational Requirements for Professional Military Education," *Air University Quarterly Review,* Summer, 1961; Major W. M. Henderson, U.S. Air Force, "The Analysis Mystique," *Air University Quarterly Review,* Jan.–Feb., 1967. (*Air University Quarterly Review* was succeeded by *Air University Review* with the Sept.–Oct., 1963, issue; these periodicals are hereinafter cited as *AUQR* and *AUR*.)

112. General J. P. McConnell, U.S. Air Force, "Strategy and Analysis," *AUR,* Jan.–Feb., 1966; Major J. W. Chapman, U.S. Air Force, "American Strategic Thinking," *AUR,* Jan.–Feb., 1967.

113. Lieutenant Colonel W. E. Simons, U.S. Air Force, "The Liberal Challenge in the Military Profession," *Air Force Magazine,* Feb., 1967. Cf. Harold Brown, then Air Force Secretary, "The Military Professional," *Aero-Space Historian,* Winter, 1966, on the "military mind."

114. Lieutenant Colonel G. K. Fleischman, U.S. Air Force, "Myth of the Military Mind," *MR,* Nov., 1964, p. 8; Major General K. P. Barquist, U.S. Air Force, "A Military Career: Public Understanding," *Vital Speeches,* July 1, 1964.

115. General James Ferguson, U.S. Air Force, "Wanted: New Ideas," *AUR,* Jan.–Feb., 1969, p. 4.

116. *Ibid.,* p. 5.

117. Dr. William J. Price, "Some Aspects of Air Force–University Relations," *AUR,* Jan.–Feb., 1970, pp. 58–59.

118. T. R. Sturm, "Where the Student Is the Bullseye," *The Airman,* April, 1969, pp. 20–21.

119. See n. 85, p. 358, *supra.*

120. Bill Madsen, "How to Succeed by Really Trying," *The Airman,* Sept., 1970; General John D. Ryan, U.S. Air Force, "Professional Military Education," *The Airman, ibid.*

121. Janowitz, *Professional Soldier,* Ch. 5, "Social Origins."

122. United States Air Force Chaplain Board, *Our Moral Defenses: Research Material for USAF Moral Leadership Program* (hereinafter cited as *USAF MLP*), July–Aug.–Sept., 1965.

123. "Air Force Education and Training: By the Power of His Knowledge," *The Airman*, 20th Anniversary Issue, Sept., 1967, pp. 6–8.

124. Martin Blumenson, "Some Thoughts on Professionalism," *MR*, Sept., 1964.

125. See "Hail to the Chief!" *Army*, Jan., 1964, a tribute and evaluation of the President's understanding of the role of the military by his Military Aide, Major General C. V. (Ted) Clifton, U.S. Army.

126. Just, *Military Men*, p. 42.

127. Colonel F. X. Kane, U.S. Air Force, "Trends in Military Thought," *AUR*, Sept.–Oct., 1966.

128. See further, Hartness, "Social and Behavioral Sciences"; T. W. Adams, "The Social Scientist and the Soldier," *Army*, March, 1964.

129. Such as flood control, bridge-building, harbor construction, rescue operations, and even actual governing of disaster areas such as resulted from the great San Francisco fire.

130. J. P. Leacacos, "The Search for and Development of Soldier-Statesmen," *Army*, April, 1963; Colonel David M. Ramsey, Jr., U.S. Army, "People Diplomacy and World Understanding," *MR*, Jan., 1966.

131. Westmoreland, "West Point Today."

132. Major General W. B. Rosson, U.S. Army, "Understanding Civic Action," *Army*, July, 1963, p. 46, in lead article.

133. Adams, "The Social Scientist and the Soldier," pp. 50–52.

134. The Honorable Stephen Ailes, "Prepared to Deter, to Fight, to Build," *Army Green Book*, Nov., 1964, lead article, pp. 36–40.

135. Lieutenant Colonel John J. Saalberg, U.S. Army, "Army Nationbuilders," *MR*, Aug., 1967, p. 50.

136. General Harold K. Johnson, Chief of Staff, U.S. Army, "Land Power Missions Unlimited," *MR*, pp. 41–42.

137. Lieutenant Colonel Josiah A. Wallace, Jr., U.S. Army, "The Principles of War in Counter Insurgency," *MR*, Dec., 1966.

138. Lieutenant Colonel Irvin M. Kent, U.S. Army, "The Commander and Civil-Military Relations," *MR*, April, 1967, p. 13. See also R. J. Bower, "Military Objectives in the Nuclear Age," *MR*, May, 1966; Major D. R. Hughes, U.S. Army, "The Wolfhounds Understand," *Army*, Nov., 1962 (The "Wolfhounds" is the adopted name of the 27th Infantry, U.S. Army, stationed at this writing in Thailand and engaged largely in civic action).

139. Hughes, "The Wolfhounds Understand," pp. 20–24.

140. *Ibid.* (from the Honorable Robert S. McNamara, "The Paradox of the Soldier," quoting a letter received by President Kennedy from Major General W. F. Train concerning his son Lieutenant W. F. Train, II), pp. 28–29.

141. Sir Stephen King-Hall, "Power Politics in the Nuclear Age," *Newsletter,* No. 1235, March 16, 1961, pp. 1930–1932, cited by Eccles in *Military Concepts,* p. 31.

142. Captain Carl H. Amme, U.S. Navy (Ret.), "The Changing Nature of Power," *NIP,* March, 1963.

143. *Ibid.,* p. 28.

144. James A. Field, "Origins of Maritime Strategy and the Development of Sea Power," *NWCR,* March, 1955.

145. *Ibid.,* p. 16: "The important hydrographic work of Matthew Maury and of the various exploring expeditions— . . . to discover the source of the Amazon; . . . the first charting of the River Jordan and the Dead Sea; the Byrd expeditions, etc."

146. Rear Admiral John D. Chase, U.S. Navy, "The Function of the Navy," *NIP,* Oct., 1969, p. 31.

147. Field, "Origins of Maritime Strategy," p. 22.

148. George E. Lowe, "Vietnams and Munichs," *NIP,* Oct., 1966, p. 71.

149. Lieutenant Commander Thomas M. Bader, "Swords and Plowshares," *NWCR,* Oct., 1969, pp. 21–22.

150. *Ibid.*

151. Delamater, "Ideological Responsibility." A remarkably objective and sympathetic treatment of our ranking enemy in Vietnam may be found in "General Vo-nguyen-Giap: Insurgent Threat or Leader of a People?" by Arthur D. Jackson, Supply Corps, U.S. Navy, *NWCR,* Nov., 1967; also, Captain José M. Amaral, Brazilian Navy, "Meeting the Threat of Communism in the Western Hemisphere," *NWCR,* Sept., 1968; and a series of lectures to the Naval War College by Prof. Lyman B. Kirkpatrick on "Cold War Operations: The Politics of Communist Confrontation," appearing in *NWCR,* Nov. and Dec., 1967; Jan., 1968.

152. *Personal Response Project Resource Materials: Vietnam Supplement,* frontispiece letter by Rear Admiral James W. Kelly, Chief of Chaplains, U.S. Navy, dated Dec., 1966, covering rough materials unpublished.

153. Major J. R. Lewis, U.S. Marine Corps, "One Response to Personal Response," *MCG,* March, 1968.

154. Captain K. J. Snyder, U.S. Marine Corps, "Friendship: A Principle of War," *MCG,* March, 1968.

155. Major General Janos M. Platt, U.S. Marine Corps, "Military Civic Action," *NWCR*, April, 1970, pp. 29 f.

156. *Personal Response Project*, p. P-5 of Preface.

157. *Ibid.*, letter.

158. *Ibid.*, Preface, P-2; letter.

159. General Curtis E. LeMay, U.S. Air Force, "Civic Action by the Air Force—The Air Commandos," *Vital Speeches*, Dec. 15, 1963.

160. Senator Barry Goldwater, "McNamara in for Dayan?—!!!" *Los Angeles Times*, June 25, 1967, "Opinion."

161. Major General R. H. Anthis, U.S. Air Force, "Twentieth Century Centurions," *AUR*, Canadian Confederation Centennial, 1867–1967, issue Jan.–Feb., 1967.

162. *Ibid.*, p. 22.

163. Major Laun C. Smith, Jr., U.S. Air Force, "Civic Action—a Weapon for Peace," AUR, July–Aug., 1968, Section "Books and Ideas," reviewing Edward B. Glick, *Peaceful Conflict, the Non-Military Use of the Military* (Harrisburg, Pa., Stackpole Books, 1967), and Hugh Manning, *The Peaceful Uses of Military Forces* (Frederick A. Praeger, Inc., Publishers, 1967).

164. *Ibid.*, p. 98.

165. Major Margaret B. Layne, U.S. Air Force Reserve, "Operation Haylift," *The Air Reservist*, Feb., 1968.

166. Lieutenant Colonel Malcolm S. Bounds, U.S. Air Force, "Military Civic Action," *AUR*, May–June, 1969, pp. 69, 71.

167. *Ibid.*, p. 75.

168. Ted R. Sturm, "Domestic Action—What It Is and How It Works," *The Airman*, July, 1970, p. 4.

169. Captain Robert P. Everett, U.S. Air Force, "The Airman's General," *The Airman*, Aug., 1969, p. 9.

170. Ed Blair, "Time to Get Involved," *The Airman*, July, 1970, pp. 9 f.

171. Everett, "The Airman's General."

172. Major Daniel B. Jorgenson, Chaplain, U.S. Air Force, *Air Force Chaplains 1947–1960*, 2 vols. (U.S. Government Printing Office, 1961), Vol. II, pp. 330 f.

173. See "My Responsibilities in Democracy," Moral Leadership Program, U.S. Air Force, Jan.–Feb.–March, 1964, pp. 34 f.

Chapter 5. THE RISK OF THE IRRATIONAL

1. Clausewitz, *On War*, Vol. I, p. 26.

2. Paul Tillich, *Systematic Theology*, 3 vols. (The University of Chicago Press, 1951, 1957, 1963), Vol. I, pp. 72–73, 93–94.

3. Clausewitz, *On War*, Vol. I, p. 26.

4. *Ibid.*

5. Tillich, *Systematic Theology*, Vol. I, pp. 152–153, 184–185.

6. Clausewitz, *On War*, Vol. I, p. 21.

7. *Ibid.*, pp. 47, 49.

8. Hackett, "The Profession of Arms," Part II: "Today and To-morrow," *MR*, Nov., 1963, p. 57.

9. Eccles, in *Military Concepts*, says that "the aweome responsibility of life and death is the single most important military element" (p. 70), and he would like to substitute "risk" for "security" in the language (p. 62).

10. E. M. Walker, "Xenophon," *Encyclopædia Britannica*, Vol. XXIII, pp. 836–837. Cf. Xenophon, *Anabasis*, p. 100.

11. Montross, *War Through the Ages*, pp. 55–68.

12. *Ibid.*, p. 77.

13. William J. Fulbright, "The American Character—We Must Revise and Strengthen It," *Vital Speeches*, Jan. 1, 1964; cf. Tillich, *Systematic Theology*, Vol. I, pp. 93 f.

14. See Scott Buchanan, *Rediscovering Natural Law* (An Occasional Paper by The Center for the Study of Democratic Institutions, 1962), pp. 6–13, for an interesting exposition of this failure of the Greeks.

15. Toynbee, *War and Civilization*, pp. 92 f.

16. The symbol of the "demonic" suggests more than antidivine forces in individual and social life. It "shows religious traits" and participates "in a distorted way in the power and holiness of the divine." It is "distorted self-transcendence" to which the military, dealing with and claiming ultimates, is particularly subject. See Tillich, *Systematic Theology*, Vol. III, pp. 102–103.

17. *Réimpression de l'Ancien Moniteur depuis la Réunion des États Généraux jusqu'au Consulat, Aug. 25, 1793* (Paris, 1840–1845), Vol. XVII, p. 478 (cited in Fuller, *Conduct of War*, p. 32).

18. Arnold J. Toynbee, *A Study of History*, 10 vols., 2d ed. (London: Oxford University Press, 1956), Vol. IV, p. 151, n. 2.

19. Colonel F. N. Maude, "Conscription," *Encyclopædia Britannica*, 11th ed., Vol. VI, p. 972.

20. Machiavelli, *The Art of War*, pp. xii–xv. Machiavelli largely drafted the famous military ordinance of Dec. 6, 1506, which conscripted 10,000 rural residents of the Florentine republic into a standing militia against Pisa and the emperor.

21. Fuller, *Conduct of War*, p. 28.

22. *Ibid.*, p. 33. For fuller treatment of this theme, see S. B. Mc-

Kinley, *Democracy and Military Power*, with an introduction by Charles A. Beard, new and enlarged ed. (The Vanguard Press, 1941).

23. Fuller, *Conduct of War*, p. 33.

24. Montross, *War Through the Ages*, p. 121.

25. Fuller, *Conduct of War*, pp. 37–41, quoting Toynbee, *A Study of History*, Vol. IV, pp. 156–157, with reference to Henri Bergson's *Les Deux Sources de la Morale et de la Religion*.

26. Fuller, *Conduct of War*, p. 42, quoting from *Oeuvres de Guibert* (1803), Vol. IV, p. 74.

27. Thomas Carlyle, *On Heroes, Hero-Worship and the Heroic in History* (Thomas Y. Crowell & Co., n.d.), p. 317.

28. Vagts, *Militarism*, pp. 164–165.

29. Montross, *War Through the Ages*, p. 683.

30. Vagts, *Militarism*, pp. 220–222; Zook and Higham, *A Short History*, p. 239.

31. Clausewitz, *On War*, Vol. I, pp. 2, 27–33.

32. Major General Sir George Aston, KCB, *The Biography of the Late Marshal Foch* (The Macmillan Company, 1929), pp. 81, 85, quoting in part from the Marshal's own lectures.

33. Émile Marie Louis Madilin, "Ferdinand Foch," *Encyclopædia Britannica*, Vol. IX, p. 433.

34. Vagts, *Militarism*, p. 350.

35. Montross, *War Through the Ages*, p. 686.

36. "*Mon centre cede, ma droite recule, situation excellente. J'attaque!*" (Aston, *Foch*, pp. 154 f.)

37. Montross, *War Through the Ages*, p. 730, citing B. H. Liddell Hart, *The Real War, 1914–1918* (Little, Brown and Company, 1964).

38. General Robert Lee Bullard, U.S. Army, *Personalities and Reminiscences of the War* (Doubleday, Page & Co., 1925), p. 77.

39. Vagts, *Militarism*, p. 258.

40. H. G. Nicholas, "Churchill," *Encyclopædia Britannica*, Vol. V, p. 787.

41. See Samuel E. Morison, *History of United States Naval Operations in World War II*, 15 vols. (Little, Brown and Company, 1947–1962), Vol. IV, pp. 116–121.

42. Major General Ottavio di Casola, Italian Army, *MR*, Jan., 1964, p. 43.

43. Lieutenant Colonel F. K. Kleinman and Robert S. Horowitz, *MR*, April, 1964. Cf. Irwin Shaw, *The Young Lions* (Random House, Inc., 1948).

44. Kleinman and Horowitz, *MR*, April 1964, p. 80.

45. Anthony Harrigan, "War and Morality," *MR*, June, 1964.

46. Major General Edmund S. Sebree, U.S. Army (Ret.), "Learning to Lead," *MR*, May, 1966, p. 60.

47. Lieutenant Colonel W. I. Gordon, "What Do We Mean By 'Win'?" *MR*, June, 1966, p. 3.

48. Atkinson on *The Liddell Hart Memoirs*, "Liddell Hart and the Warfare of the Future," *Military Affairs*, Winter, 1965–1966. Captain B. H. Liddell Hart, British Army, was knighted Jan. 1, 1966.

49. *Ibid.*, p. 163, quoting from *Memoirs*, Vol. I, p. 139.

50. *Ibid.*

51. Colonel Robert B. Rigg, U.S. Army, "Limitation, Escalation and Sanctuaries in War," *Army*, Nov., 1963, p. 66.

52. Rear Admiral C. G. Coggins, U.S. Navy, "Weapons of Mass Destruction," *MR*, June, 1963. Admiral Coggins was formerly Chief of Atomic, Biological, and Chemical Warfare, U.S. Navy; at the time of this article he was Chief of the Medical and Health Division, California State Disaster Office, Sacramento, California.

53. These interviews were made on Aug. 8–9, 1966. From numerous conversations since then, especially with Navy chaplains and other officers, I am convinced that this broad spectrum of concern and conviction is representative. The general doubt has deepened if anything in the intervening years, especially respecting Vietnam, although strong holdouts such as the Senior Chaplain mentioned above are still to be found.

54. Harrigan, "War and Morality," pp. 81–82.

55. *Ibid.*, p. 84.

56. Lieutenant Colonel Kenneth E. Kay, U.S. Army, "The Teton Men," *Army*, Jan., 1964.

57. Colonel Anthony P. Wermuth, U.S. Army, "The Relevancy of Ethics," *Army*, June, 1962; see also Charles A. Lofgren, "How New Is Limited War?" *MR*, July, 1967.

58. Colonel Anthony L. Wermuth, U.S. Army, "The Media of Earth's Armed Forces," Part I: "Hiding Military Light"; Part II: "One Legacy from Douhet," *MR*, Jan.–Feb., 1963; two of three articles from a book-length manuscript, "One More Generation." General Guilio Douhet, Italian prophet of the air offensive, elaborated unilateral theories of air supremacy, independence, and its unlimited use in *The Command of the Air*, first published in Italy (1921, 1927), English translation by Dino Ferrari (Coward-McCann, Inc., 1942).

59. "It is magnificent, but it is not war!" *Ibid.*, Part II, p. 47.

60. Colonel Robert W. Seldon, U.S. Army, "Rational Victory," *NIP*, Feb., 1968.

61. Captain S. O. Tiomain, Irish Army, "Clausewitz: A Reappraisal," *MR*, May, 1963, p. 78.

62. Colonel D. A. Alberti, U.S. Army, "The Tactical Nuclear Battlefield: Business as Usual?" *MR*, Aug., 1963; Major A. R. Wheelock, U.S. Army, "Keeping Limited War Limited," *MR*, Dec., 1963; Lieutenant Commander Charles W. Koburger, Jr., U.S. Coast Guard, "Lower Spectrum War," *MR*, July, 1968; Lieutenant Colonel John R. Byers, U.S. Army, "Win, Terminate, or What?" *Army*, Oct., 1968.

63. Captain Carl H. Amme, Jr., U.S. Navy (Ret.), "The Soldier and the Bomb," *Army*, Sept., 1967.

64. Major General Ottavio de Casola, Italian Army, "The Nature of Future Wars: An Italian View," *MR*, Jan., 1964, p. 43.

65. Colonel Daniel F. Riva, U.S. Air Force, "Disarmament: Hope or Hoax?" *MR*, Aug., 1964, p. 28.

66. Brigadier General Henry C. Huglin, U.S. Air Force (Ret.), "Perspective on Nuclear Weapons," *MR*, Aug., 1968.

67. Dr. Carl A. Larson, "Biological Warfare: Model 1967," *MR*, May, 1966.

68. Robert J. Bower, "Military Objectives in the Nuclear Age," *MR*, May, 1966.

69. Gordon, "What Do We Mean By 'Win'?" pp. 3 f. The subject was tackled again in 1966 and in the following years by the graduating classes with essentially the same results: cf. Byers, "Win, Terminate, or What?", p. 30.

70. Colonel Joseph F. H. Cutrons, U.S. Army, "Peace in Vietnam: An Acceptable Solution," *Army*, Nov., 1966.

71. Lieutenant General James Gavin, U.S. Army (Ret.), "Military Power: The Limits of Persuasion," *Saturday Review*, July 30, 1966, p. 18.

72. *Ibid.*, p. 19.

73. Brian Bond, "The Indecisiveness of Modern War," *MR*, Dec., 1967, p. 51.

74. Cited in Koburger, "Lower Spectrum War," p. 6.

75. Byers, "Win, Terminate, or What?"

76. Major General W. G. F. Jackson, British Army, "Nuclear Proliferation and the Great Powers," *MR*, June, 1967, p. 72.

77. Lieutenant James Binder, U.S. Army, "The Must Case for the ABM—Truly, a Weapon for All Seasons," *Army*, May, 1969.

78. Eugene Hinterhoff, "The Delicate Balance," *MR*, Dec., 1968, p. 79.

79. Lieutenant General Harbakhsh Singh, Indian Army, "The Victorious Will," *MR*, Aug., 1967.

80. Colonel Robert B. Rigg, U.S. Army, "Orwellian World: Computerized Statistics Sitting in Judgment on Command Personnel," *Army*, March, 1967.

81. William A. Reitzel, "The Cause of War," *NWCR*, April, 1955, p. 35.

82. Brigadier General Dale O. Smith, U.S. Air Force, *NIP*, Oct., 1956. Here a guest writer reflects an attitude more typical of the Navy than of his own service, but of his own more than of the Army, i.e., for both Navy and Air Force, nature as a potential and uncertain enemy is very real.

83. James D. Atkinson, "Must We Have World War III?" *NIP*, July, 1956.

84. Captain George L. Raring, U.S. Navy, "The Atom, the Navy, and Limited War," *NIP*, Feb., 1962.

85. William H. Hessler, "Patience: Bedrock Strategy in the 1960's," *NIP*, Feb., 1965.

86. William H. Hessler, "War: Always an Art," *NIP*, April, 1958.

87. Amme, "Changing Nature of Power"; *supra*, p. 135.

88. George E. Lowe, "Balanced Forces or Counter Forces: Does It Make a Difference?" *NIP*, April, 1962.

89. Captain Harold E. Shear, U.S. Navy, review of *Design for Survival*, by General Thomas S. Powers, U.S. Air Force (Ret.), with Albert S. Arnhym (Coward-McCann, Inc., 1965), *NIP*, Jan., 1966; and Rear Admiral James Calvert, U.S. Navy, review of *An End to Arms*, by Walter Millis (Atheneum Publishers, 1965), *ibid.*

90. Amme, "Changing Nature of Power."

91. Stefan T. Possony, "Battle: No Longer the Payoff?" *NIP*, Aug., 1970, p. 37.

92. Lieutenant Charles L. Parnell, U.S. Navy, "Victory in Limited War," *NIP*, June, 1969, p. 30.

93. See "1974" by Rear Admiral Worth H. Bagley, U.S. Navy, *NIP*, Feb., 1970, wherein is projected a situation of war with the U.S.S.R. for which we are unprepared, largely because of the ambiguity of Soviet intentions. In "Hostile Coexistence," Lieutenant Colonel George B. Fink, U.S. Army, *NIP*, April, 1967, writes an imaginary letter from a Chinese Communist official setting forth the "doctrine of protracted struggle."

94. Robert McClintock, "An American Oceanic Doctrine," *NIP*, Feb., 1970; Commander James McNulty, U.S. Navy, "Soviet Sea Power: Ripple or Tidal Wave?" *NIP*, July, 1970; Frederick J. Cox,

"The Russian Presence in Egypt," *NWCR*, Feb., 1970; Bagley, "1974."

95. Harold W. Rood, "Distance Rampart," 1967 Prize Essay, *NIP*, March, 1967; Colonel H. A. Crosby, U.S. Army (Ret.), "The Case for Anti-Ballistic Missiles," *NIP*, July, 1967; Lieutenant Douglas M. Johnston, Jr., U.S. Navy, "ABM: The High Cost of Living," *NIP*, Oct., 1967; Joseph I. Coffey, "Stability and the Strategic Balance," *NIP*, June, 1967; Captain Paul R. Schratz, U.S. Navy, "The Caesars, the Sieges and the ABM," 1968 Prize Essay, *NIP*, March, 1968.

96. Colonel R. D. Heinl, Jr., U.S. Marine Corps, "The Right to Fight," *NIP*, Sept., 1962. This was a phrase often heard during the periodic "battles" of the Corps to survive as an organization, but accurately reflects the intense self-consciousness of the Marines' conception of their mission, as reiterated by General Krulak recently.

97. Lieutenant General Victor H. Krulak, U.S. Marine Corps (Ret.), "The Cost of Freedom," *NIP*, July, 1970, pp. 71–72.

98. Captain Robert J. Hanks, U.S. Navy, "Against All Enemies," 1970 Prize Essay, *NIP*, March, 1970, pp. 26, 24, citing in part "dissinct disservice" by *The National Observer*.

99. Captain K. W. Simmons, U.S. Navy, "Morality and the Communist Menace," *NIP*, Jan., 1962, p. 83.

100. Samuel P. Huntington, "To Choose Peace or War: Is There a Place for Preventive War in American Policy?" *NIP*, April, 1957.

101. Maurice Matloff, "The American Quest for National Security," *NIP*, May, 1963, p. 87.

102. Robert B. Asprey, "The King of Kill," *MCG*, May, 1967.

103. Colonel R. S. N. Mans, OBE (Officer of the British Empire), "The New Conflict," *MCG*, Oct., 1968; Major R. M. Cooke, U.S. Marine Corps, "Political Restraints," *MCG*, June, 1967; Lieutenant Colonel Jack L. Miles, U.S. Marine Corps, "The Fusion of Military and Political Considerations," *MCG*, Aug. and Sept., 1968 (General C. B. Gates Award).

104. Cf. 1st Lieutenant Ord Elliott, U.S. Marine Corps, "Why We Are in Vietnam," *MCG*, Oct., 1968; 1st Lieutenant T. Zalewski, U.S. Marine Corps, "God, Country and Corps," "Opinion," *MCG*, Nov., 1968; Jerry D. Owen, "The Uniform and Responsibility," *MCG*, Dec., 1968.

105. Commander Bruce Keener, U.S. Navy, "The Principles of War: A Thesis for Change," *NIP*, Nov., 1967, p. 36.

106. Lieutenant Commander Thomas E. McGovern, Jr., U.S. Naval Reserve, "An Analysis of War," *NWCR*, May, 1968, pp. 37–39.

107. Captain John D. Chase, U.S. Navy, "South of Thirty," 1967 Prize Essay, *NIP*, April, 1967.

108. The Honorable Robert A. Frosch, Assistant Secretary of the Navy for Research and Development, "Navy Research and Development," *NWCR*, Dec., 1968, pp. 7–11.

109. Captain William O. Miller, U.S. Navy, "Belligerency and Limited War," *NWCR*, Jan., 1969, p. 23.

110. See George C. Wilson, "Tide with the Navy in Reshaping of Military: Expected to Dominate in 10 Years," *Los Angeles Times*, Jan. 24, 1971, Sec. A, pp. 1, 20. Shrinkage of overseas bases, desire to draw enemy fire away from the land, and the increasing presence of the Soviet Navy have combined to focus attention upon the merits of the sea for successful defense.

111. Joseph M. Salmon, "Thesis on Decline," *Air Power Historian*, Oct., 1959, p. 236.

112. Brigadier General R. C. Richardson, III, U.S. Air Force, "The Fallacy of Minimum Deterrence," *AUQR*, Spring, 1960.

113. Colonel A. P. Sights, Jr., U.S. Air Force, "Limited War for Unlimited Goals," *AUQR*, Spring, 1962.

114. Captain Thomas C. Pinckney, U.S. Air Force, "Overkill and Underthought," *AUR*, July–Aug., 1964.

115. Dr. Thomas F. Statton, "The Battle for Men's Minds," *Air Power Historian*, July, 1960, p. 146.

116. *Los Angeles Times*, Sept. 13, 1966, Editorial, Part II-5.

117. Colonel Paul S. Deems, U.S. Air Force, "Woodcraft and Warfare," *AUR*, Summer, 1963.

118. *Ibid.*

119. V. J. Gregory, "Cain to Zeus," *Air Power Historian*, April, 1965.

120. Colonel A. P. Sights, Jr., U.S. Air Force, "We Can Win a Nuclear War," *AUR*, Sept.–Oct., 1963.

121. *Ibid.*, p. 45.

122. Major General Dale O. Smith, U.S. Air Force (Ret.), "In My Opinion," *AUR*, Jan.–Feb., 1965.

123. Rodney C. Loehr, "American Security and the Balance of Power in the Nuclear Age," *AUR*, Jan.–Feb., 1966.

124. David A. Robinson, "Learning to Live with the Nuclear Spread," *Air Force and Space Digest*, Aug., 1966.

125. Maurice Matloff, review of *The Decision to Drop the Bomb*, by Len Giovannitti and Fred Freed, and "The Irreversible Decision, 1939–1950," by Robert C. Batchelder, *AUR*, Sept.–Oct., 1966.

126. Arnold J. Toynbee, "Democratic Control in a Totalitarian Age," *Moral Leadership*, April–May–June, 1963.

127. Colonel G. O. Ashley, U.S. Air Force, "In My Opinion," *AUQR*, Summer, 1962.

128. Loehr, review in *AUR*, Jan.–Feb., 1966, p .85.

129. Lieutenant Colonel T. C. Pinkney, "Thoughts on the Limitations of War," *AUR*, Jan.–Feb., 1969, especially p. 80.

130. Herman S. Wolk, "The New American Military," *Air Force Magazine*, April, 1966.

131. Herman S. Wolk, "Vietnam and the Warfare State Complex," *Air Force and Space Digest*, April, 1967, p. 43.

132. Major John W. Chapman, U.S. Air Force Reserve, "American Strategic Thinking," *AUR*, Jan.–Feb., 1967.

133. Amoretta M. Hoeber, "Strategic Defense," *AUR*, July–Aug., 1968, p. 71.

134. Major General Cecil E. Combs, U.S. Air Force, "On the Profession of Arms," *AUR*, May–June, 1964.

135. Lieutenant Colonel Arnold J. Celick, U.S. Air Force, "Humane Warfare for International Peacekeeping," "In My Opinion," *AUR*, Sept.–Oct., 1968.

136. Lieutenant Colonel Ray L. Bowers, U.S. Air Force, "The Twentieth Century Penchant for the Offensive," *NIP*, Sept., 1967, p. 60.

137. Wolk, "The New American Military"; Wesley Posvar, "The Political Environment for Military Planning," *Air Force and Space Digest*, Dec., 1966.

138. Clausewitz, *On War*, Vol. I, p. 19; cited by Robert D. Miewald, "On Clausewitz and the Application of Force," *AUR*, July–Aug., 1968, p. 76.

139. *Ibid.*, pp. 76–77, citing *On War*, Vol. I, p. 100 (italics in the original). The dictionary defines *coup d'oeil* as "a brief survey, as at one glance."

Chapter 6. THE FASCINATION FOR THE CONCRETE

1. Walter Millis, "The Peace Game," *Saturday Review*, Sept. 24, 1960, pp. 38–39.

2. Eccles, *Military Concepts*, p. 35.

3. So Engels to Marx, commenting on *On War*: "Fighting is to war what cash payment is to trade, for however rarely it may be necessary for it actually to occur, everything is directed towards it, and eventually it must take place . . . and must be decisive" (Karl Marx and Frederick Engels, *Selected Correspondence 1846–1895*, with explanatory notes, tr. by Donna Torr [International Publishers Co., Inc., 1942], p. 100).

4. Clausewitz, *On War,* Vol. I, pp. 3–4.

5. *Ibid.,* p. 241.

6. See n. 3 *supra.*

7. Montross, *War Through the Ages,* p. 148.

8. This is not to underestimate the humaneness both brought to the war-making of the day, but the overformalized tactics would be all too easily swept away in an age to come, and "martinet" would take its place as a word of contempt. Cf. *Ibid.,* pp. 318 f., 335 f., 340.

9. Toynbee, *War and Civilization,* p. 132.

10. Adcock, *Art of War,* pp. 5, 16. "Peltasts" were so named after the small, light shield or *pelta* they carried, which, together with a short sword and light armor, made for mobility and encouraged tactical scouting and skirmishing.

11. Montross, *War Through the Ages,* p. 45.

12. Oman, *Middle Ages,* p. xiv.

13. "Greek fire" appeared to be different from earlier flame-throwing compounds and devices and its secret is not yet fully known; quicklime probably was a distinguishing ingredient—it is actually ignited by water and thus understandably confused the Arabs. See Montross, *War Through the Ages,* pp. 123–124.

14. *Ibid.,* p. 157.

15. *Ibid.,* pp. 165–169; Oman, *Middle Ages,* pp. 116 ff.

16. Preston, *et al., Men in Arms,* pp. 121–123.

17. Fuller, *Conduct of War,* p. 33.

18. Colonel E. M. Lloyd in his *History of Infantry* (Longmans Green & Co., 1908) remarks that "the state of the unmounted arm is an index to conditions in any age"; cited in Montross, *War Through the Ages,* p. 158.

19. Fuller, *Conduct of War,* p. 313.

20. Preston, *et al., Men in Arms,* pp. 56 f.

21. "In retrospect, Napoleon's failure to follow through on his orders for the supplying of his army must remain as the principal cause for its ultimate collapse" (Major Eugene W. Massengale, U.S. Army, "The Inner Soldier," *MR,* June, 1967, p. 94). See also Air Marshal Sir Robert Saundby, Royal Air Force (Ret.), "The Ethics of Bombing," *MR,* Feb., 1968.

22. Fuller, *Conduct of War,* p. 85.

23. According to Sigmund Neumann, both Engels and Marx were fully aware "that modern warfare is of a fourfold nature—diplomatic, economic, psychological, and only as a last resort military"; cited in Earle (ed.), *Makers of Modern Strategy,* p. 156.

24. Glenn Gray, *The Warriors: Reflections on Men in Battle*

(Harcourt, Brace and Company, 1959; Torchbook, Harper & Row, Publishers, Inc., introduction by Hannah Arendt, 1967), pp. 28–39.

25. *Ibid.*, p. 33.

26. *Ibid.*

27. Quoted in Colonel Suire, French Army, "Fear and Courage," *MR*, Aug., 1964, p. 80; thus something of the universality of the emotion is attested to, a German quote by a French author in an American military magazine! See also Moskos, "Anti-Militarism— Intellectuals' New Anti-Semitism."

28. Major General Louis Kaufman, U.S. Army Reserve, President of Los Angeles City College, has called my attention to the similarity of football to military gamesmanship.

29. Gray, *The Warriors,* pp. 35–36.

30. *Ibid.*, p. 51.

31. *Ibid.*

32. World War I; Juenger kept a diary, which is quoted without source by Gray, *ibid.,* p. 52.

33. *Ibid.*

34. *Ibid.*, pp. 52–53.

35. John B. Noss, *Man's Religions,* 2d ed. (The Macmillan Company, 1956), pp. 281–284.

36. Gray, *The Warriors,* pp. 55–56.

37. James M. Merrill, *Uncommon Valor: The Exciting Story of the Army* (Rand McNally & Company, 1964), p. 40.

38. Montross, *War Through the Ages,* p. 769, quotes from Hitler, dated Sept. 19, 1933, and April 14, 1934.

39. Vagts, *Militarism,* pp. 250–251.

40. Bramson and Goethals, *War: Studies,* pp. 102–103.

41. Gray, *The Warriors,* pp. 12, 14–15. A recent editorialist, Charles C. Moskos, Jr., also calls attention to this literal swing of opposites "in an actual fire-fight with the enemy" in Vietnam: "The scene is generally one of utmost chaos and confusion. Deadening fear intermingles with acts of bravery and bestiality and, strangely enough, even moments of exhilaration" ("Anti-Militarism—Intellectuals' New Anti-Semitism").

42. "Violence in America," *Time* Essay, July 28, 1967.

43. Richard Matheson, *The Beardless Warriors* (Little, Brown and Company, 1960); except "Dec. 14, 1944," in F. Van Wyck Mason (ed.), *American Men at Arms* (Pocket Books, Inc., 1964), p. 393.

44. "Air Raids Simulated for Museum Exhibit," *Los Angeles Times,* March 28, 1968, p. 24; "Spectacles: Shoot-'Em-Up in Chicago," *Time,* March 29, 1968, p. 65.

45. Cited by Lieutenant General James M. Gavin, U.S. Army (Ret.), *War and Peace in the Space Age* (Harper & Brothers, 1958), pp. 204–205.

46. So Archbishop William Temple is reputed to have said of Christianity, adding "and for that very reason, will doubtless outlast them all." He emphasized the doctrine of the resurrection of the body. Cf. *Nature, Man and God* (London: Macmillan & Co., Ltd., 1934).

47. Cf. "Violence in America," p. 19.

48. Cf. Jules Loh, "Idolatry of Guns: Being a Treatise on Their Mystique," *Los Angeles Times,* Nov. 12, 1967, "Opinion."

49. Raymond, *Power at the Pentagon,* p. 331.

50. *Ibid.,* quoting General Maxwell Taylor.

51. Cadet Edward L. Constantine, Jr., U.S. Army, in "Cerebrations," *Army,* March, 1968, p. 78.

52. Lieutenant Colonel Bernard Dautremer, French Army, "Modern Army," *MR,* June, 1966; Larson, "Biological Warfare."

53. Lieutenant Colonel Martin Blumenson, U.S. Army, "The Bayonet: To Toy or to Terrorize?" *Army,* Oct., 1968, p. 49, quoting comments of officers.

54. Lieutenant Colonel Richard A. McMahon, U.S. Army, and Captain John A. Hottell, III, U.S. Army, in "Cerebrations," *Army,* July, 1968, p. 76.

55. Similar strategic impasses have been reached before and have always led to innovations in tactics. Cf. the Greek phalanx and the innovation of the peltasts, gunpowder, and the development of bloodless maneuvers by Vauban, etc. The great danger at this stage is, of course, the development of *tactical* nuclear weapons which may break the stalemate by escalation to the employment of total force. See Herman S. Wolk, "Are Nuclear Weapons Obsolete?" *MR,* Jan., 1967, p. 69. See also: Brigadier General G. S. Heathcote, British Army (Ret.), "Service Life in 1976," *MR,* July, 1967; Colonel Richard S. Ware, Jr., U.S. Army, "Forecast, A.D. 2000," *MR,* June, 1967; and Brigadier General H. C. Huglin, U.S. Air Force (Ret.), "Perspective on Nuclear Weapons," *MR,* Aug., 1968.

56. Liddell Hart, *Memoirs,* Vol. I, p. 382, cited in Atkinson, "Liddell Hart and the Warfare of the Future," p. 162.

57. Lieutenant Colonel V. Bokariev, Soviet Army, "Cybernetics," *MR,* Nov., 1964; Robert D. Miewald, "Military Managers," *MR,* July, 1967.

58. Lieutenant Colonel Rolfe L. Hillman, Jr., U.S. Army, "The Processes of Military Communication," *Army,* March, 1963; Lieutenant Colonel John C. Bennett, U.S. Army, "Hyperfaceopus," *Army,*

March, 1966; "Hyperfaceopus" is a coined word for paper prolifera-tion in bureaucracy.

59. Wermouth, "Relevancy of Ethics."

60. The weakness of the machine and our slavery to it are illus-trated in the frustrating, even pitiful, failure of such marvels as the Sheridan, the "Rolls-Royce of tanks," but much "too rich" for the jungles and swamps of Vietnam, and in the widely publicized electronic personnel sensors which, however, have nothing to show when the Viet Cong refuse to light campfires! The abortive Son Tay POW raid, it is clear, was put together and followed through almost mechanically with actually little hope of success in terms of freeing prisoners (this question was hardly asked), because our intelligence gathering is too sophisticated to make sense out of the simple and nearly "timeless" movements of the Vietnamese. See Just, *Military Men,* pp. 151 ff.; and Stuart M. Loory, "Story Behind Raid on Son Tay Prison: The Problem of Intelligence," *Los Angeles Times,* Feb. 2, 1971, Part I, pp. 1, 10.

61. General William C. Westmoreland, U.S. Army, "The Man at the End of the Line: The Combat Infantryman," *Army,* Nov., 1968, p. 30.

62. Donald O'Connell, "Economic Factors Affecting Strategy," *NWCR,* Jan., 1955; Wassily Leontief, "National Economic Prob-lems," *ibid.*

63. Stephen E. Ambrose, "Seapower in World Wars I and II," *NWCR,* March, 1970, pp. 42–43.

64. J. Carlton Ward, Jr., "United States Science and Technology," *NWCR,* May, 1968, pp. 5–15 especially.

65. Lieutenant Commander James Strong, U.S. Navy, "The Paper War—*Quo Vadis?*" *NIP,* May, 1962.

66. Eccles, *Military Concepts,* p. 8, quoting a letter from a senior officer on duty in the Pentagon, June 21, 1960.

67. To borrow a phrase from Alvin Toffler, *Future Shock* (Random House, Inc., 1970).

68. John G. Stoessinger, "Power and Elements of National Power," *NWCR,* March, 1968, p. 26.

69. Commander J. A. Meacham, U.S. Navy, "The Mine as a Tool of Limited War," *NIP,* Feb., 1967.

70. *Ibid.,* p. 53.

71. Cf. Robert A. Frosh, "Navy Research and Development," *NWCR,* Dec., 1968, pp. 7 ff.

72. Colonel William O. Davis, U.S. Air Force Reserve, "The Ordering of Technological Warfare," *AUQR,* Spring, 1960.

73. Witness the growing gap between industrialized and semi- or

non-industrialized nations, to which Barbara Ward, *The Rich Nations and the Poor Nations* (W. W. Norton & Company, Inc., 1962), early called attention.

74. Brigadier General R. C. Richardson, III, "Stalemate in Concepts," *AUQR,* Summer, 1960, pp. 5–8.

75. Major General Orvil A. Anderson, U.S. Air Force (Ret.), "Militarism or Anti-Militarism: The Real Threat to American Security," *Air Power Historian,* July, 1961.

76. Major Joseph P. Martino, U.S. Air Force, "Forecasting the Progress of Technology," *AUR,* March–April, 1969, p. 20.

77. Colonel Archie J. Knight, U.S. Air Force, and Colonel Glen F. Herzberg, U.S. Air Force, "The Question of National Defense Organization," *AUQR,* Summer, 1960.

78. Miewald, "On Clausewitz," pp. 76–78, quoting from *On War,* Vol. I, p. 78.

79. Clausewitz, *ibid.,* p. 77.

80. *Los Angeles Times,* Feb. 2, 1971, Part I, p. 10.

81. Bowers, "The Twentieth Century Penchant for the Offensive."

82. Celick, "Humane Warfare for International Peacekeeping."

83. Miewald, "On Clausewitz," pp. 76 f.

84. So Luke pictures it (ch. 4:3–8). Matthew, however, interposes the temptation of bidding for attention to a miracle from the pinnacle of the Temple, and climaxes with the appeal to martial glory (ch. 4:3–9).

Chapter 7. THE TENDENCY TO STRUCTURE

1. Otto Heilbrunn, *Partisan Warfare* (Frederick A. Praeger, Inc., Publishers, 1962), pp. 21 f.

2. Cited in Preston, *et al., Men in Arms,* p. 33.

3. Montross, *War Through the Ages,* p. 113.

4. Oman, *Middle Ages,* pp. 75–77.

5. Raymond, *Power at the Pentagon,* pp. 72–73, 80–81, 287–288; Janowitz, *Professional Soldier,* pp. 153 ff.

6. Vagts, *Militarism,* p. 480, quoting de Gaulle in Paul Reynaud, *In the Thick of the Fight 1930–1945* (Simon and Schuster, Inc., 1955), p. 286.

7. McKinley, *Democracy and Military Power,* pp. 90 f.

8. Montross, *War Through the Ages,* p. 86.

9. Vagts, *Militarism,* pp. 67, 69.

10. *Ibid.,* p. 120, quoting Napoleon, in Gourgand, *Journal im-*

médiat, Vol. II, pp. 43 f. Montluc, a former Marshal of France (1502–1577), was equally candid: "Let us own that we soldiers would be nothing without kings. If we obey them, that is obeying . . . God" (*Commentaries,* Vol. III, pp. 504 f.).

11. Vagts, *Militarism,* pp. 107, 147.

12. Preston, *et al., Men in Arms,* pp. 70–73.

13. Vagts, *Militarism,* p. 147.

14. *Ibid.,* p. 156.

15. Alexis de Tocqueville, *Democracy in America,* tr. by Henry Reeve, 2 vols., rev. ed. (The Colonial Press, 1900), Vol. II, pp. 250 f. This enterprising and perceptive young French nobleman traveled widely in America between May, 1831, and May, 1832.

16. Vagts, *Militarism,* p. 156; see also Janowitz, *Professional Soldier,* p. 23. Cunliffe, *The Martial Spirit in America,* disputes this generally held position.

17. Weigley, *Towards an American Army,* p. 78.

18. Hacker, "The United States Army as a National Police Force," p. 262.

19. Janowitz, *Professional Soldier,* p. 24.

20. Vagts, *Militarism,* p. 36.

21. Janowitz, *Professional Soldier,* p. 25.

22. Cf. Montross, *War Through the Ages,* pp. 764–766; Fuller, *Conduct of War,* pp. 175–177.

23. Vagts, *Militarism,* p. 371.

24. My last ship was a single-engine screw, yet, uniformly, the plural "engines half power," "engines full speed ahead," etc., was called when under way.

25. Vagts, *Militarism,* pp. 29–30.

26. *Ibid.,* p. 30.

27. *Ibid.*

28. Weigley, *Towards an American Army,* p. 2.

29. *Ibid.,* p. 4.

30. *Ibid.,* p. 81.

31. The final destruction of the armies of Antichrist, supposedly near the ancient city of Megiddo in northern Palestine, and accepted literally by many Christians (Ezek., ch. 38; Rev., ch. 13; etc.). See *infra,* pp. 293–295.

32. Janowitz, *Professional Soldier,* Ch. 5, "Social Origins," pp. 79–101; quote, reflecting Janowitz, from Coffin, *Passion of the Hawks,* p. 69.

33. Janowitz, *Professional Soldier,* p. 236.

34. Vagts, *Militarism,* pp. 311–312.

35. *Ibid.*, p. 99.

36. I refer here especially to the well-known close church-state relationship which Episcopalians, springing from the Anglican Church of Great Britain, have historically maintained in this country. The abundant martial imagery in pietistic and especially fundamentalist churches is vividly expressed in hymns ("Onward, Christian Soldiers," "The Son of God Goes Forth to War," etc.), dress (Salvation Army, the uniforms of orders, etc.), doctrine (warfare of Good and Evil, the "blood of Christ" who yet shall be "victorious," with his "armies of the saints," Paul's soldier moralizing).

37. Janowitz, *Professional Soldier*, p. 98.

38. See Daniel Bell (ed.), *The Radical Right* (Doubleday & Company, Inc., 1963), pp. 285–289.

39. Vagts, *Militarism*, p. 412.

40. See *Facts on File News Year, 1960–1961*, ed. by Lester A. Sobel, *et al.* (Facts on File, Inc. 1962), pp. 365–366. General Walker was reprimanded, and, resigning his commission, was for some time involved prominently in political movements of the Right.

41. "The remnant" is a frequently used symbol in both the Old and New Testaments, and is closely bound up with the ideas of being chosen by God for his work and Kingdom, and hence in possession of the "truth": never the many, but the "few faithful ones," are given the task of saving the age.

42. General James M. Gavin, U.S. Army (Ret.), has been one of the most outspoken critics of contemporary military strategy, especially in Vietnam.

43. Janowitz, *Professional Soldier*, pp. 90 f. The innovators are such in methodology and "leadership styles" (heroic or managerial), rather than in the substance of the military ethic and way of life: they are "not representative men, but rather exaggerations of . . . conflicting themes in the military profession." Cf. *ibid.*, p. 154, and the whole of Ch. 8, "The Elite Nucleus."

44. Pennsylvania Military College (now part of PMC Colleges), Chester, Pa., as cited in "Wave of the Future," *Army*, April, 1969.

45. Morris Janowitz and Roger W. Little, *Sociology of the Military Establishment*, rev. ed (Russell Sage Foundation, 1965).

46. "Wave of the Future," p. 66. This is now a reality on some bases! See also: Colonel H. E. Nelson, U.S. Marine Corps, "Inspection: The Key to Command," *MCG*, April, 1968.

47. Huntington, *The Soldier and the State*, pp. 465–466; cf. *supra*, pp. 32–33.

48. "Wave of the Future," p. 65.

49. Brigadier General Lynn D. Smith, U.S. Army, "Maybe We Need a New Medal," *Army*, Jan., 1969. The Chief of Staff was General Matthew Ridgway.

50. Just, *Military Men*, pp. 107 f.

51. *Ibid.*, cited in footnote, p. 108.

52. *Time*, Dec. 21, 1970, pp. 20–22; *Life*, Feb. 5, 1971.

53. Buckley, "The Class of '68: From Campus to KP," p. 28.

54. "The Dangerous Words Captain Eisenhower Wrote in 'Infantry Journal' and Earned the Displeasure of the Chief of Infantry," *Army*, June, 1967.

55. Just, *Military Men*, Ch. 6, "Machines."

56. Thomas S. An, "Mao Tse-Tung Purges Military Professionalism," *MR*, Aug., 1968; Colonel Irving Heymont, U.S. Army (Ret.), "The Israeli Career Officer Corps," *MR*, Oct., 1968.

57. Abbott W. Sherower, "Creative Command: Bonaparte at Headquarters," *MR*, Oct., 1968, p. 72; Major Reginald Hargreaves, British Army (Ret.), *MR*, Feb., 1968.

58. Just, *Military Men*, p. 24.

59. Colonel Gordon A. Moon, II, U.S. Army, "Creativity," *Army*, May, 1967, p. 43.

60. *Supra.* p. 90.

61. James E. Hawes, Jr., "Management vs. Bureaus," *MCG*, Feb., 1967, p. 40.

62. Lieutenant Commander Byron A. Wylie, U.S. Navy, "Equal Opportunity: Challenge to Navy's Management," *NIP*, Sept., 1970, p. 35.

63. Samuel L. Gravely, Jr.; cf. *Los Angeles Times*, June 3, 1971, Part I, p. 3:4–6.

64. *Ibid.*, pp. 37, 34–35.

65. But problems persist. See two opposing points of view by two black lieutenants: "A Black Officer's Story, Farewell to the Navy," *San Francisco Chronicle*, July 4, 1970, p. 4:4–7, and "Black Officer Says Navy Is Not Racist," *San Francisco Chronicle*, Aug. 24, 1970, p. 14:4–5.

66. Vice Admiral James Calvert, U.S. Navy, "The Fine Line at the Naval Academy," *NIP*, Oct., 1970, p. 63.

67. Wylie, "Equal Opportunity," p. 36.

68. Major Reginald Hargreaves, "The Uncertain Image," *NIP*, Feb., 1967, pp. 78–79.

69. Note the specific words invariably used to distinguish the two types of service: "enlisted *rates*," but "officer *ranks*." Confirmation of the endurance of this attitude is found in the recent decision of the

U.S. Court of Military Appeals to uphold the conviction of a young Navy lieutenant (j.g.) for fraternizing with an enlisted man: See "Officers and Troops Must Not Fraternize," *Los Angeles Times,* June 30, 1971, Part I, pp. 5, 6–8.

70. Calvert, "The Fine Line," p. 67.

71. See *supra,* pp. 126 ff.

72. See Ray, "The Bureaus Go On Forever," p. 50.

73. Lieutenant Commander K. M. Duff, U.S. Navy, "Two Birds in the Hand," *NIP,* Sept., 1969, p. 61.

74. Ambrose, "Seapower in World Wars I and II," especially pp. 29 f.; *supra,* pp. 188–189.

75. Commander R. H. Smith, U.S. Navy, "Not Enough Good Men," *NIP,* May, 1967, p. 90.

76. Lieutenant Commander Steven H. Edwards, U.S. Navy, "Image of Command," *NIP,* Feb., 1970, p. 38. The Sargasso Sea, near the West Indies, is so full of seaweed that it posed a distinct threat to early sailing vessels, including Columbus' expeditions.

77. Rear Admiral E. B. Strauss, U.S. Navy (Ret.), "Stars, Stripes and Gresham's Law," *NIP,* March, 1968. Sir Thomas Gresham, English financier, observed that of two coins of equal debt-paying value but unequal intrinsic value, the coin of greater intrinsic value tended to be hoarded, leaving the cheaper coin to circulate.

78. Clifford E. Smith, "The Implications of 'New View' for Motivating Officer Behavior," *AUR,* March–April, 1969. "Slipping the surly bonds" is from "High Flight" by John Gillespie Magee, Jr., a pilot killed in World War II; it is a favorite among airmen.

79. Morris Janowitz, *The New Military: Changing Patterns of Organization* (Russell Sage Foundation, 1964).

80. Lieutenant Colonel W. E. Simons, U.S. Air Force, "Military Professionals as Policy Advisers," *AUR,* March–April, 1969.

81. Lieutenant Colonel Robert H. Drumm, U.S. Air Force, "The Air Force Man and the Cultural Value Gap," *AUR,* May–June, 1968.

82. Colonel Thomas A. Fleek, U.S. Air Force, "An Examination of the 'Military Mind,' " *AUR,* Nov.–Dec., 1969, p. 96.

83. Major Donald Sandler, U.S. Air Force, "Discipline and Officer Training, Conflicting Interests," *AUR,* March–April, 1969, pp. 90–91.

84. *Ibid.,* p. 90.

85. Miewald, "On Clausewitz," p. 77, citing Clausewitz, *On War,* Vol. I, p. 79.

86. *Ibid.*

87. Lieutenant Colonel E. M. Abramson, U.S. Air Force, "Security

and the Decision-Making Function," in "In My Opinion," *AUR*, Sept.–Oct., 1967, p. 73.

88. Lieutenant Colonel Lewis M. Jamison, U.S. Air Force, "The Information Explosion—Can the Air Force Handle It?" *AUR*, March–April, 1969; Lieutenant Colonel Robert H. Drumm, "Mega-management for the Space Age," *AUR*, July–Aug., 1970.

89. Jamison, "The Information Explosion."

90. Fleek, "An Examination of the 'Military Mind,' " p. 96.

91. Ferguson, "Wanted: New Ideas," p. 5.

92. Henry S. Kariel, "The Ideological Vacuum," *The Nation*, April 18, 1966; Walter Lippmann, *The Good Society* (Little, Brown and Co., 1937), and *Essays in the Public Philosophy* (Little, Brown and Company, 1955).

93. Dependence upon natural law is rather prominent in the Moral Leadership Training materials of all the services.

94. See Janowitz, *The Professional Soldier*, p. 80. My personal impressions of a career in military service support Janowitz.

95. See also "A Center Symposium: Has America Become a Militarized Society?" *The Center Magazine*, Jan., 1970, pp. 34–37.

96. Janowitz, *The Professional Soldier*, p. 492.

97. Clausewitz, *On War*, Vol. I, p. 79.

98. The dictionary defines a machine as "a device consisting of two or more resistant, relatively constrained parts, which, by a certain predetermined interaction, may serve to transmit and modify force and motion so as to produce some given effect, or do some desired kind of work." It is like a chain "with one link fixed."

99. James H. Breasted, *Ancient Times, A History of the Early World* (The Atheneum Press, 1916), p. 198.

100. In 612 B.C., at the hands of the Medo-Persian alliance. The world's relief is reflected in the Hebrew prophet Nahum's exultant shout (cf. Nahum 2:8, 13; and ch. 3 entire). Nineveh became forever a vast heap of rubbish, a vague tradition.

101. Jacob Abbott, *History of Xerxes the Great* (Harper and Brothers, 1850), p. 96. Ancient figures tend to exaggeration, but at least for that day the army of Xerxes was huge.

102. Breasted, *Ancient Times*, pp. 500–502.

103. Vagts, *Militarism*, pp. 86–88; Zook and Higham, *A Short History*, pp. 54–56.

104. Reify: "To make real or concrete; materialize: to *reify* an idea. . . . From the Latin *res, rei,* thing" (Funk & Wagnalls *Standard College Dictionary*, Text ed. [Harcourt, Brace and World, Inc., 1966]), p. 1134.

105. Martin Buber, *I and Thou* (Charles Scribner's Sons, 1937); Tillich, *Systematic Theology*, Vol. I, pp. 90 f., 168 ff.

106. Gray, *The Warriors*, p. 10.

107. *Ibid.*, p. 8.

108. *Ibid.*, p. 83. Cf. Matheson in Mason (ed.), *American Men at Arms*, pp. 389 ff.

109. Gray, *The Warriors*, p. 143.

110. Hacker, "The United States Army," p. 260.

111. *Ibid.*, citing Lieutenant William Wallace, U.S. Army, "The Army and the Civil Power," *Journal of the Military Service Institution of the United States*, Vol. XVII (1895), p. 254.

112. William D. Franklin, "Douhet Revisited," *MR*, Nov., 1967, pp. 65, 68.

113. Lieutenant Colonel Stanley D. Fair, U.S. Army, "The Ghost of Ypres," *Army*, Feb., 1967, p. 55. Germany initiated gas warfare at the Second Battle of Ypres, France, on April 22, 1915, and achieved complete tactical surprise over the Allies, but did not press its advantage.

114. Franklin, "Douhet Revisited," pp. 68, 67.

115. Marshall Erwin Rommel, Hitler's "Desert Fox," excited this kind of professional respect and even personal liking among those who opposed him in the struggle for Africa. Vietnam has generated extremely little of this attitude, which always has rough going in guerrilla-type warfare because the enemy refuses to play according to "civilized rules," (i.e., ours).

116. Gray, *The Warriors*, pp. 143–145 (italics added).

117. *Ibid.*, p. 150.

118. *Ibid.*, p. 148.

119. *Ibid.*, p. 179.

120. *Ibid.*, pp. 26–27.

121. Tocqueville, *Democracy in America*, Vol. II, pp. 318–319.

122. Richard Nisbet, *The Quest for Community* (Oxford University Press, 1953), pp. 3–7.

123. As Marx long ago observed. See "Speech at the Anniversary of the People's Paper," April, 1856, reprinted in Rader, *The Enduring Questions*, pp. 521–522.

124. Nisbet, *The Quest*, pp. 11–12, 109, citing F. W. Maitland.

125. See René Descartes, *The Meditations* in *The Philosophical Works of Descartes*, tr. by E. S. Haldane and G. T. Ross (Cambridge: The University Press, 1931).

126. Title of a Beatles' lyric which reflects separation and alienation.

127. Richard G. Hubler, "Books: Polish War Novel Captures Horror of '39," a review of *The 1000 Hour Day*, by W. S. Kuniczak (Signet Book, The New American Library, 1968), *Los Angeles Times*, May 28, 1967, "Calendar Section" p. 28.

128. Eugene M. Emme, "Technical Change and Western Thought, 1914–1945," *Military Affairs*, Spring, 1960, pp. 6 f.

129. Jerry Green, "Civilian on Horseback," *Army*, July, 1963, p. 31.

130. "John Fitzgerald Kennedy," *Army*, Jan., 1964, p. 23.

131. Lieutenant General Garrison H. Davidson, U.S. Army, "Tomorrow's Leaders," *Army*, Oct., 1964, p. 21.

132. Colonel Adolph Reiniche, West German Army, "Technology's Challenge to Leadership," *MR*, March, 1963.

133. Durand Echiverra and O. T. Murphy, "The American Army: A French Estimate in 1777," *Military Affairs*, Spring, 1963, p. 5.

134. See *supra*, pp. 224–226.

135. Lieutenant Colonel Charles M. Ferguson, U.S. Army, "Strategic Thinking and Studies," *MR*, April, 1964.

136. Suire, "Fear and Courage," p. 81.

137. Dautremer, "Modern Army," p. 30.

138. William C. House, Jr., "Attitudes Toward People," *MR*, Dec., 1966, pp. 55–56.

139. Lieutenant Colonel Martin Blumenson, U.S. Army Reserve, "Four Eventful Years: General Harold K. Johnson, 'Most Remarkable Man,' " *Army*, Aug., 1968, p. 23.

140. General William C. Westmoreland, U.S. Army, "The Man at the End of the Line: The Combat Infantryman," *Army*, Nov., 1968.

141. Just, *Military Men*, p. 103.

142. "Bill Mauldin's Willie and Joe Look at THE NEW ARMY," *Life*, cover story, Feb. 5, 1971, pp. 20 ff.

143. Title of the article by Captain Carl H. Amme, U.S. Navy (Ret.), in *NIP*, March, 1963.

144. Commander Stephen T. De LaMater, U.S. Navy, "The Navy Image," *NIP*, April, 1963, p. 28.

145. Major Carl M. Guelzo, U.S. Army, "Chore or Challenge: A Professional Ethic for the Nuclear Age," *NIP*, May, 1964, p. 29.

146. Captain G. H. Lathop, Jr., U.S. Naval Reserve, "Crisis in Leadership," *NIP*, July, 1964; Captain Paul R. Schratz, U.S. Navy, "The Ivy-Clad Man on Horseback," *NIP*, March, 1965; Captain Arnett B. Taylor, U.S. Navy, "Treat Sailors Like Spare Parts?" *NIP*, Oct., 1966.

147. Eccles, *Military Concepts*, p. 6.

148. *Ibid.*, pp. 85, 154.

149. Francis J. McHugh, "Eighty Years of War Gaming," *NWCR*, March, 1969; Colonel William F. Long, Jr., U.S. Army, "Urban Insurgency War Game," *NWCR*, May, 1969.

150. Commander Albert J. Ashurst, U.S. Navy, "Decision-Making and the School of Naval Command Staff," *NWCR*, Oct., 1967; Vincent Davis, "American Military Policy: Decision-Making in the Executive Branch," *NWCR*, May, 1970.

151. Lieutenant Commander Jan S. Prokop, U.S. Navy, "The Next Step," *NIP*, July, 1967.

152. J. Carlton Ward, "United States Science and Technology," *NWCR*, May, 1968, p. 20.

153. The Honorable Robert A. Frosh, "Navy Research and Development," *NWCR*, Dec., 1968, p. 13.

154. J. H. Huizinga, "Vietnam: A European View," in "Scrapbook," *MCG*, Jan., 1968, p. 9.

155. Captain J. C. Longino, U.S. Navy, "The Study Business," *NIP*, June, 1967, p. 63.

156. Eccles, *Military Concepts*, p. 6.

157. *NavPers 15890*, Chapter XIII.

158. *Ibid.*, p. 1.

159. Wolk, "The New American Military."

160. Fleek, "An Examination of the 'Military Mind,' " p. 95.

161. Chapman, "American Strategic Thinking," *AUR*, Jan.–Feb., 1967; see especially comments on Bernard Brodie, pp. 30–31.

162. W. E. Simons, "Liberal Challenge," p. 44.

163. Drumm, "The Air Force Man and the Cultural Value Gap."

164. Matloff, review, in *AUR*, Sept.–Oct., 1966.

165. See "The Appeals of Democracy," *USAF MLP*, April–May–June, 1963, especially Toynbee's article: "Democratic Control in a Totalitarian Age," pp. 42–49.

166. Colonel Garland O. Ashley, U.S. Air Force, "Off We Go . . . Where?" *AUR*, Summer, 1963.

167. Ned Calmer, *The Strange Land* (Charles Scribner's Sons, 1950); excerpt "Corporal Albert Selig" in Mason (ed.), *American Men at Arms*, p. 388.

Chapter 8. THE TENDENCY TO EXCESS

1. Max Lerner, *The Age of Overkill: A Preface to World Politics* (Simon and Schuster, Inc., 1962), p. 107.

2. Tillich, *Systematic Theology*, Vol. III, pp. 93 f. and elsewhere.

3. Lerner, *The Age of Overkill*, p. 109.

4. Clausewitz, *On War*, Vol. I, pp. 3–4.

5. *Ibid.*, pp. 6–7.

6. Vagts, *Militarism*, p. 182.

7. Toynbee, *War and Civilization*, pp. 37–38, quoting in part from Xenophon, *Respublica Lacedaemoniorum*, Ch. IX, and Herodotus.

8. Gray, *The Warriors*, pp. 132–138.

9. Eric Larrabee, "The Pursuit of Peace," *Atlantic*, Nov., 1965, p. 63.

10. See Herman Kahn, *On Thermonuclear War* (Princeton University Press, 1960), and *Thinking the Unthinkable* (Horizon Press, Inc., 1962).

11. Chapman, "American Strategic Thinking"; W. E. Simons, "Military Professionals as Policy Advisers"; McConnell, "Some Reflections on a Tour of Duty," *AUR*, Sept.–Oct., 1969.

12. Tristram Coffin, *The Passion of the Hawks*, p. 22, says frankly: "War is not of the soldier's making. He frequently knows too well its consequences, and may listen with alarm to the cries of the hawks in the Senate."

13. Cf. Bramson and Goethals (eds.), *War: Studies*, pp. 177–193.

14. James, *The Moral Equivalent of War*, p. 4.

15. Fuller, *Conduct of War*, pp. 67–68.

16. Cf. Montross, *War Through the Ages*, pp. 496–497.

17. Coffin, *The Passion of the Hawks*, p. 246.

18. *Ibid.*, p. 175.

19. Herold (ed.), *The Mind of Napoleon*, p. 205.

20. This quote has appeared several times recently. See Just, *Military Men*, p. 28.

21. Clausewitz, *On War*, Vol. I, pp. 36–37, 241.

22. Montross, *War Through the Ages*, p. 585.

23. Fuller, *Conduct of War*, p. 35.

24. Quoted in Hoffman Nickerson, *The Armed Horde 1793–1939* (G. P. Putnam's Sons, 1940), p. 91.

25. Clausewitz, *On War*, Vol. II, pp. 159–160.

26. John Dryden, *Cymon and Iphigenia*, line 400, in John Bartlett, *Familiar Quotations*, 11th ed., rev. and enlarged, ed. by Christopher Morley (Little, Brown and Company, 1939), p. 177.

27. Robert D. Heinl (ed.), *Dictionary of Military and Naval Quotations* (United States Naval Institute, 1966), p. 300.

28. Vagts, *Militarism*, p. 125; Montross, *War Through the Ages*, p. 730.

29. Cf. Preston, *et al.*, *Men in Arms*, pp. 255 f. Bloch published

in St. Petersburg in 1897–1898 a six-volume study of war, published in 1899 in German, the last volume only published in English (Ginn and Company, 1902) under the title: *The Future of War in its Technical, Economic & Political Relations.* The study influenced the calling of The Hague Conferences (1899, 1907) but little else.

30. Preston, *et al., ibid.,* pp. 289, 296, 320.

31. Millis, *A World Without War,* p. viii.

32. Fulbright, "The American Character," pp. 164–166.

33. "Is Violence Un-American?" editorial in *The Nation,* Sept. 6, 1965.

34. "Violence in America," *Time* Essay, July 28, 1967.

35. *Ibid.*

36. Larrabee, "The Pursuit of Peace," p. 62, quoting Dr. Brock Chisholm, onetime Deputy Minister of Health in Canada.

37. *Ibid.*

38. *Ibid.*

39. *Ibid.,* p. 63.

40. W. H. Ferry, "What Price Peace?" *Bulletin of Atomic Science,* Sept., 1963, p. 19.

41. *Ibid.,* p. 20.

42. *Ibid.*

43. Coffin, *The Passion of the Hawks,* p. 104.

44. Rigg, "Limitation, Escalation," p. 66.

45. William H. Willson, "Nuclear War Odds Reach High Point," *Los Angeles Times,* March 10, 1968, "Opinion," Sec. G.

46. Fuller, *Conduct of War,* p. 13.

47. *Ibid.*

48. *Ibid.,* p. 217, quoting Guglielmo Ferraro, *Peace and War,* tr. by B. Prichard (Books for Libraries, Inc., 1933), p. 148.

49. Fuller, *Conduct of War,* p. 13.

50. Sir Winston Churchill, *The Second World War, Vol. I: The Gathering Storm* (Houghton Mifflin Company, 1948), pp. 17, iv–v.

51. Fuller, *Conduct of War,* pp. 308, 312–313.

52. *Ibid.,* p. 314. Yet, in the preface to *The Reformation of War,* a younger and more optimistic Fuller could confidently assert: "In war there is nothing mysterious, for it is the most common sense of all the sciences"; *supra,* p. 125.

53. Rigg, "Limitation, Escalation," pp. 62 f.

54. *Ibid.,* p. 70.

55. *Ibid.,* p. 68 (see charts).

56. Wolk, "Are Nuclear Weapons Obsolete?" p. 69.

57. Edward Teller, "Planning for Peace," *MR,* May, 1967.

58. Wolk, "Are Nuclear Weapons Obsolete?" p. 70.

59. Hinterhoff, "The Delicate Balance"; Nevelle Brown, "The Balance Between the Superpowers: Into Strategic Deadlock," *MR*, March, 1967.

60. *Supra*, p. 253.

61. Lofgren, "How New Is Limited War?"; William D. Franklin, "Clausewitz on Limited War," *MR*, June, 1967.

62. Charles B. McDonald, "Official History and the War in Vietnam," *Military Affairs*, Spring, 1968, p. 3.

63. See Byers, "Win, Terminate, or What?"; George Lictheim, "1975," *Army*, Jan., 1968; Wing Commander K. Tongue, Royal Australian Air Force, *MR*, Oct., 1967.

64. "John Fitzgerald Kennedy," *Army*, Jan., 1964.

65. Clark C. Abt, "Tactical Nuclear Operations in Limited Local Wars: To Use or Not to Use," *Army*, Oct., 1964, pp. 39–44.

66. Lieutenant Colonel Walter H. Root, U.S. Army, "Tactical Nuclear Weapons in Limited War," *MR*, Oct., 1967, p. 12.

67. Amme, "The Soldier and the Bomb."

68. Colonel Walter Beinke, U.S. Army, "Flexible Response in Perspective," *MR*, Nov., 1968; Lieutenant Colonel Louis H. Hollier, U.S. Marine Corps, "Nuclear Policy and Military Strategy," *MR*, Dec., 1968.

69. Beinke, "Flexible Response," p. 52; Lieutenant Commander Charles W. Koburger, Jr., "Lower Spectrum War."

70. Colonel A. R. Richstein, U.S. Army, "Power and Purpose," *MR*, Sept., 1968.

71. Colonel Thomas W. Bowen, U.S. Army, "But They're So Different," *Armor*, May–June, 1969, pp. 30–31.

72. Bond, "The Indecisiveness of Modern War," p. 52.

73. Louis Stockwell, "Civilian Control," *Journal Critique, The Journal of the Armed Forces*, Nov. 18, 1967, quoting General Ridgway, *The Korean War* (Doubleday & Company, Inc., 1967). See also Martin Blumenson, "Thought of a Leader," on *The Korean War*, by General Matthew Ridgway, "Book Reviews," *Army*, Jan., 1968, p. 75.

74. Cagle, "A Philosophy for Naval Atomic Warfare," p. 249.

75. *Ibid.*, p. 253.

76. *Ibid.*, p. 254.

77. *Ibid.*

78. Colonel H. Ashton Crosby, U.S. Army (Ret.), "The Case for Anti-Ballistic Missiles," *NIP*, July, 1967.

79. Lieutenant Douglas M. Johnston, U.S. Navy, "ABM: The High Cost of Living."

80. Captain Carl H. Amme, Jr., U.S. Navy (Ret.), "NATO Strategy and Flexible Response," *NIP*, May, 1967.

81. Lieutenant Charles L. Parnell, U.S. Navy, "Victory in Limited War," 1969 Prize Essay, *NIP*, June, 1969, p. 30.

82. Harold W. Rood, "Distant Rampart," 1967 Prize Essay, *NIP*, March, 1967.

83. Captain Robert J. Hanks, U.S. Navy, "Against All Enemies," 1970 Prize Essay, *NIP*, March, 1970, p. 27.

84. Shoup, "The New American Militarism," *Atlantic*, April, 1969. See also: Captain Gordon S. Hodgson, U.S. Navy, "Of Hawks and Doves," 1967 Prize Essay, *NIP*, May, 1967.

85. Cited in Cagle, "A Philosophy for Naval Atomic Warfare," pp. 257–258.

86. Schratz, "The Caesars, the Sieges, and the ABM," p. 32.

87. Captain Paul R. Schratz, U.S. Navy, "Red Star Over the Southern Sea," 1970 Prize Essay, *NIP*, June, 1970, p. 31.

88. Captain Ralph E. Williams, U.S. Navy (Ret.), "After Vietnam," 1970 Prize Essay, *NIP*, April, 1970.

89. John G. Stoessinger, "Power and Elements of Natural Power," *NWCR*, March, 1968, p. 27.

90. Hans J. Morgenthau, "Organization of a Power System: Unilateralism and the Balance of Power," *NWCR*, Feb., 1968.

91. Brigadier General Edwin F. Black, U.S. Army, "The Quest for Common Ground," *NIP*, Jan., 1968, p. 30.

92. Williams, "After Vietnam," p. 23.

93. Coffey, "Stability and the Strategic Balance," pp. 43, 45.

94. *Ibid.*, p. 47.

95. Williams, "After Vietnam," p. 22.

96. Robert McClintock, *The Meaning of Limited War* (Houghton Mifflin Company, 1967), pp. 239 ff.

97. Commander Roy Beavers, U.S. Navy, "A Doctrine for Limited War," *NIP*, Oct., 1970, p. 30.

98. *Ibid.*

99. *Ibid.*, p. 31.

100. Frederick J. Honigan, "Postwar International Relations: Problems and Conflicts in Asia," *NWCR*, Feb., 1968, p. 34.

101. Henry E. Eccles, "The Russian Maritime Threat; An Approach to the Problem," *NWCR*, June, 1969, p. 14.

102. Beavers, "Limited War," especially pp. 26–27, 34.

103. Possony, "Battle: No Longer the Payoff?" p. 37.

104. Schratz, "Red Star Over the Southern Sea," p. 24.

105. Matloff, "The American Quest for National Security."

106. Captain Paul R. Schratz, U.S. Navy, "Clausewitz, Cuba and Command," *NIP*, Aug., 1964, p. 27.

107. The "minimum morality" adopted from John Courtney Murray, S.J., *Morality and Modern War* (The Church Peace Union, 1959).

108. Schratz, "Clausewitz, Cuba and Command," p. 28.

109. *Ibid.*

110. *Ibid.*, p. 30.

111. W. R. Van Cleave, "The Nuclear Weapons Debate," *NIP*, May, 1966, p. 38.

112. Harold Brown, "Air Power in Limited War," *AUR*, May–June, 1969.

113. Colonel Frederick J. Adelman, U.S. Air Force, "Gradualism—a Flexible Response," "In My Opinion," *AUR*, May–June, 1969, pp. 65–67; Colonel William C. Moore, U.S. Air Force, "History, Vietnam, and the Concept of Deterrence," *AUR*, Sept.–Oct., 1969, pp. 62–63.

114. Lieutenant General Bernard Schriever, U.S. Air Force (Ret.), "Technology and Aerospace Power in the 1970's," *AUR*, Sept.–Oct., 1969, pp. 62–63.

115. Lieutenant Colonel T. C. Pinckney, U.S. Air Force, "Thoughts on the Limitation of War," *AUR*, Jan.–Feb., 1969, p. 82.

116. Major Philip D. Caine, U.S. Air Force, "The United States in Korea and Vietnam: A Study in Public Opinion," *AUR*, Nov.–Dec., 1968, p. 51.

117. *Ibid.*

118. Chaplain (Lieutenant Colonel) Edward R. Lawler, "Whose Side Is God On?" in "Books and Ideas," *AUR*, March–April, 1969.

119. *Ibid.*, p. 101.

120. *Ibid.*, adopted as a rational conclusion and basis for moral certitude from Commander John J. O'Connor, Chaplain, U.S. Navy, *A Chaplain Looks at Vietnam* (The World Publishing Company, 1968).

121. Loehr, "American Security," p. 85.

122. Wolk, "Vietnam and the Warfare State Complex," p. 43.

123. Alfred Goldberg, "Escalation: A Historical Perspective," *NIP*, June, 1966, pp. 66–67.

124. Paul Ramsey, *War and the Christian Conscience: How Shall Modern War Be Conducted Justly?* (Duke University Press, for the Lilly Endowment Research Program in Christianity and Politics, 1961).

125. "Is Survival Enough?" *USAF MLP,* Oct.–Nov.–Dec., 1960.
126. *Ibid.,* "Outline," p. 1.
127. *Ibid.,* pp. 6–7.
128. *Ibid.,* p. 10.
129. *Ibid.*
130. *Ibid.*
131. *Ibid.,* "Attention All Chaplains: The Dynamics of Moral Leadership base newspaper articles," No. IV: "Man's Progress in Weapons."
132. *Ibid.,* No. VI.
133. Cf. Niebuhr, *The Irony of American History.*
134. "Is Survival Enough?", *USAF MLP,* "base newspaper articles."

Chapter 9. THE ILLUSION OF OMNIPOTENCE

1. Edward Meade Earle (ed.), *Makers of Modern Strategy: Military Thought from Machiavelli to Hitler* (Princeton University Press, 1944), p. vii (italics added).
2. Clausewitz, *On War,* Vol. I, p. 77.
3. Erwin Knoll and Judith Nies McFadden (eds.), *War Crimes and the American Conscience* (Holt, Rinehart and Winston, Inc., 1970), p. 110.
4. See Augustine, *The City of God,* tr. by Marcus Dodds (Modern Library, Inc., 1950), especially Chs. XII–XIX; J. N. Figgis, *The Political Aspects of St. Augustine's "City of God."* (Peter Smith, 1963).
5. Scott Buchanan, *Rediscovering Natural Law* (The Center for the Study of Democratic Institutions, 1962), pp. 14–22.
6. *Ibid.,* p. 19.
7. Alasdair MacIntyre, *A Short History of Ethics* (The Macmillan Company, 1966), p. 124.
8. *Ibid.,* citing J. N. Figgis, *Political Thought from Gerson to Grotius* (Cambridge University Press, 1916).
9. Thomas Hobbes, *Leviathan,* Parts I and II, with introduction by Herbert W. Schneider (The Liberal Arts Press, The Bobbs-Merrill Company, Inc., 1958), p. 106.
10. *Ibid.,* Part II, p. 142.
11. *Ibid.,* Part I, p. 108.
12. Cf. Ezek., ch. 38, especially v. 15, and ch. 39; and Rev. 20:7–9 which describe a usurper king who symbolizes the heathen hordes who in the final Day will assault the Israel of God. The references telling that these hordes are from "the uttermost parts of the

north" have many times in my youthful hearing been applied to Russia and "the hordes of Communism."

13. *Time*, July 6, 1970, pp. 8–15.

14. *Los Angeles Times*, March 25, 1971, Part I, p. 4:2–3.

15. Don McLean, Editorial, *Berkeley Daily Gazette*, July 1, 1970, p. 8.

16. *Time*, July 6, 1970, p. 15.

17. *Ibid.*

18. *Los Angeles Times*, Jan. 30, 1971, Part I, p. 19:1–6.

19. At the time of this writing, the latest reference was an Address to the Nation on April 7, 1971.

20. Schratz, "Red Star Over the Southern Sea," p. 24.

21. "McIntire's Son Calls Patriotism False Faith," *Los Angeles Times*, Jan. 30, 1971, Part I, p. 19:1–3.

22. *CBS Evening News*, March 31, 1971.

23. Robert Jay Lifton, "False God," *Atlantic*, Oct., 1970, p. 106.

24. Abbott, *History of Xerxes the Great*, p. 98.

25. *The New Westminster Dictionary of the Bible*, edited by Henry S. Gehman, rev. ed. (The Westminster Press, 1970), p. 410.

26. See Harry M. Buck, *People of the Lord* (The Macmillan Company, 1966), pp. 507–517, especially.

27. According to Matthew (ch. 4:1–11). Luke makes it the middle temptation (ch. 4:1–13).

28. As described in Earle (ed.), *Makers of Modern Strategy*, p. vii.

29. James Baldwin, *The Fire Next Time* (The Dial Press, Inc., 1963).

30. William Theodore de Bary (Gen. Ed.), *Sources of Indian Tradition* (Columbia University Press, 1958), Vol. I, pp. 3–4, 13–14.

31. *Los Angeles Times*, April 7, 1971, Part II, p. 8:5.

32. D. J. R. Bruckner, "Reform in the Military: A Long, Long Road Awinding Back to Moral Sanity," *ibid.*, p. 8:3–4; Editorial: "Law, Justice and the Lieutenant," *ibid.*, p. 8:1–2; William F. Buckley, Jr., "Calley Is No Scapegoat," *ibid.*, April 8, 1971, Part II, p. 7:5–6; James J. Kilpatrick, "Justice Requires Calley Penalty," *ibid.*, April 9, 1971, Part II, p. 7:5–6; as well as a growing number of Congressmen and other national figures.

33. Knoll and McFadden (eds.), *War Crimes*, p. 122.

34. *Ibid.*, p. 107.

35. An early and strong strain in Old Testament justice: Ex. 21:23–25; Joshua, ch. 7.

36. Gray, *The Warriors*, p. 147.

37. *Los Angeles Times*, April 1, 1971, Part I, p. 25:1.

38. The charge against Calley specified "Oriental human beings," and the almost universal use of terms such as "gooks," "slopes," etc., is indicative enough. President Nixon spoke of the "anguish" which roused him from sleep brooding over the conviction of Lieutenant Calley. What of the families of the deceased at My Lai? The altogether too easy preference for "American lives" to be saved over those of our South Vietnamese allies, much less the worth of enemy lives, is also racist.

39. I have been surprised at the ease with which some members of a sincere, mature and concerned Christian adult class, following the conviction of Lieutenant Calley, felt that in war "win is the name of the game," and that *faced with defeat, anything might be acceptable* to achieve victory. Self-preservation still seems the strongest of motives even among Christians who have had 2000 years to reflect upon the willing sacrifice of their Master!

40. Knoll and McFadden (eds), *War Crimes,* pp. 113–118.

41. Illustrated in the case of the first general officer charged with atrocities in the Vietnam war: *Los Angeles Times,* June 3, 1971, Part I, pp. 2–3.

42. Knoll and McFadden (eds.), *War Crimes,* p. 115.

43. Morgenthau, "What Price Victory?" p. 23.

44. *The Dirty Dozen,* the title of a recent movie, the plot of which involves an offer of pardon to a bunch of hardened criminals if they will undertake a dangerous mission.

45. *Los Angeles Times,* April 3, 1971, Part I, pp. 1:6, 8:1.

46. *Ibid.*

47. Knoll and McFadden (eds.), *War Crimes,* p. 120.

48. Shakespeare, *Julius Caesar,* Act IV, line 217.

49. The question of General Westmoreland and higher officials comes sharply into focus with this parallel. See *Time,* April 12, 1971, pp. 19 f.

50. *Los Angeles Times,* April 3, 1971, Part III, p. 14:1–5. However, see *Progress-Bulletin,* June 2, 1971, p. 1:6–7, recalling that Brigadier General Jacob H. Smith was convicted of ordering atrocities in the Philippines and was forcibly retired from the Army by President Theodore Roosevelt in 1902.

51. *Los Angeles Times,* April 7, 1971, Part II, p. 8:6.

52. As twelve Roman Catholic bishops of New England stated unequivocally in a joint pastoral letter: *Los Angeles Times,* June 1, 1971, *Pomona Progress-Bulletin,* May 29, 1971.

Chapter 10. The Humanizing of the Military

1. *Supra,* pp. 134–135.

2. MacIntyre, *A Short History of Ethics,* p. 11.

3. Wheeler, *Democracy in a Revolutionary Era,* p. 19.

4. *Ibid.,* p. 28.

5. *Ibid.,* p. 19.

6. Richard Rhodes, "Ike: An Artist in Iron," *Harper's Magazine,* July, 1970.

7. William Theodore de Bary (Gen. Ed.), *Sources of Chinese Tradition* (Columbia University Press, 1960), Vol. I, p. 58.

8. Rhodes, "Ike," p. 70.

9. *CBS Evening News,* April 2, 1971.

10. See the interview with General Bradley and his whimsical but pointed dissociation of himself from Patton with respect to the wearing of medals, *Los Angeles Times,* March 21, 1971, Sec. C, pp. 1:3–4; 10:1–8.

11. *Los Angeles Times,* Jan. 31, 1971, "Opinion," Sec. F, p. 2.

12. Hans Morgenthau, "The Present Tragedy of America," *World View,* Sept., 1969, p. 15.

13. Lewis H. Lapham, "Case Study of an Army Star," *Life,* Sept. 25, 1970, p. 68.

14. *Supra,* pp. 131 ff.

15. Adam Yarmolinsky, *The Military Establishment: Its Impacts on American Society* (A Twentieth Century Fund Study, Harper & Row, Publishers, Inc., 1971), p. 419.

16. See the Army "white paper," reviewed in part in *Los Angeles Times,* April 7, 1971, Part I, p. 8:5.

17. Reinhold Niebuhr, *The Irony of American History,* pp. vii–viii, distinguishes *pathos* (suffering caused by natural evil), *tragedy* (conscious choice of evil for the sake of good), and *irony,* which involves an unconscious weakness that leads to evil.

18. *Ibid.,* p. viii.

19. Karl Jaspers, *The Origin and Goal of History* (London: Routledge & Kegan Paul, Ltd., 1953); John B. Cobb, Jr., *The Structure of Christian Existence* (The Westminster Press, 1967).

20. Jean-François Revel, "Without Marx or Jesus," *Saturday Review,* July 24, 1971, p. 15.

21. John Kenneth Galbraith, *How to Control the Military* (A Signet Broadside, The New American Library, 1969), pp. 61–65.

22. See Karl Jaspers, *Man in the Modern Age,* tr. by Eden and Cedar Paul (London: Routledge & Kegan Paul, Ltd., 1959), who

asserts that a meaningful "forecast of the future" must be an "active" one which having been made "becomes one of the determinants of the future" (p. 205).

23. Revel, "Without Marx," p. 15.

24. I have not been able to document this, although the statement has been attributed to him in military circles, and similar sentiments have been voiced in justification of the military in the present age.

25. Captain Roland Faulk, CHC, U.S. Navy (Ret.), letter dated Tuesday, July 27, 1971.

26. Revel, "Without Marx," p. 15.

27. See Leon E. Panetta and Peter Gall, *Bring Us Together: The Nixon Team and the Civil Rights Retreat* (J. B. Lippincott Company, 1971), p. 4.

28. See Huston Smith, *The Religions of Man* (Mentor Book, The New American Library, 1958), pp. 162–182, for a captivating discussion of the Confucian methodology.

29. Toffler, *Future Shock*, p. 423.

30. John Gardner's *Common Cause* is very suggestive at this point.

31. Wheeler, *Democracy in a Revolutionary Era*, p. 18. The national myth, he says, would begin to be subordinated to the building of a "transcendent myth."

32. It is believed by many that had we been more specific in including South Korea in our sphere of critical interest, the North Koreans would never have launched the war.

33. Yarmolinsky, *The Military Establishment*, p. 415.

34. *Ibid.*, pp. 415–416.

35. Plato, *The Crito*, cited in Rader, *The Enduring Questions,* pp. 37–46.

36. See *Los Angeles Times*, June 1, 1971, Part II, p. 6: The Papal Commission on Justice and Peace has called for an international statute to assure the rights of conscientious objectors and to encourage optional service in civilian areas of need.

37. Galbraith, *How to Control the Military*, p. 82.

38. As reflected by Eric F. Goldman in "A Sober Judgment on the Pentagon," in a book review on Yarmolinsky, *The Military Establishment,* in *Life*, Feb. 5, 1971, p. 8.

39. Toffler, *Future Shock*, Ch. 7.

40. *Masterpieces of Religious Verse*, edited by James Dalton Morrison (Harper & Brothers, 1948), p. 517.

41. Thomas Paine, cited by Morgenthau in "The Present Tragedy of America," p. 14.

42. *Ibid.*

Index